The World of William Glackens

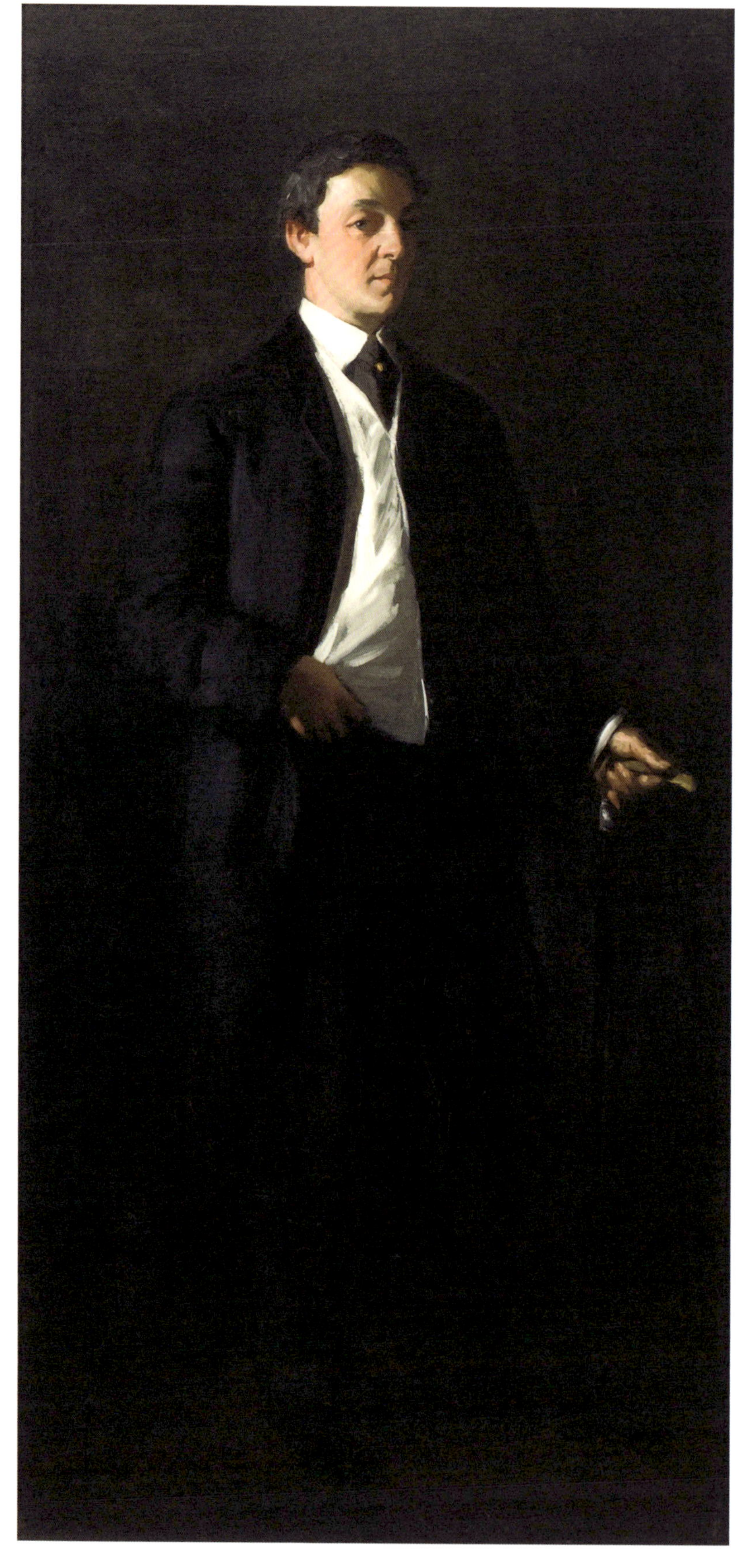

THE WORLD OF

William Glackens

The C. Richard Hilker Art Lectures

Essays by

Colin B. Bailey

Avis Berman

Carol Troyen

Richard J. Wattenmaker

H. Barbara Weinberg

Sansom Foundation, Inc.

This publication was organized by
Doris Palca with the help of:

Deborah Lyons: *Editor*
Valerie Leeds, Emily Russell:
Editorial Consultants
Jennie Goldstein: *Picture Researcher*
Thea Hetzner: *Proofreader*
Nancy Wolff: *Indexer*

Michael Russem, Kat Ran Press
Design & Typesetting

Printed by Capital Offset Company, Inc.
Concord, New Hampshire

Stock: 100 lb. Mohawk Superfine

Distributed by:
D.A.P./Distributed Art Publishers, Inc.
155 Sixth Avenue, 2nd floor
New York, New York 10013

ISBN: 978-0-615-41981-7

FRONTISPIECE
Robert Henri
William Glackens, 1904
Oil on canvas
78 × 38 in. (198.1 × 96.5 cm)
Sheldon Museum of Art,
University of Nebraska, Lincoln;
NAA—Thomas C. Woods Memorial

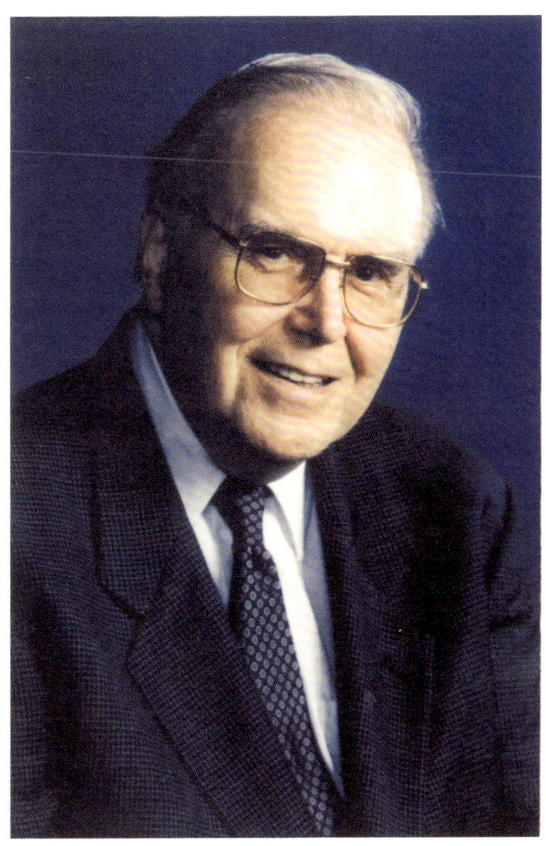

This book is dedicated to C. Richard Hilker,
President of the Sansom Foundation 1991–2001

Contents

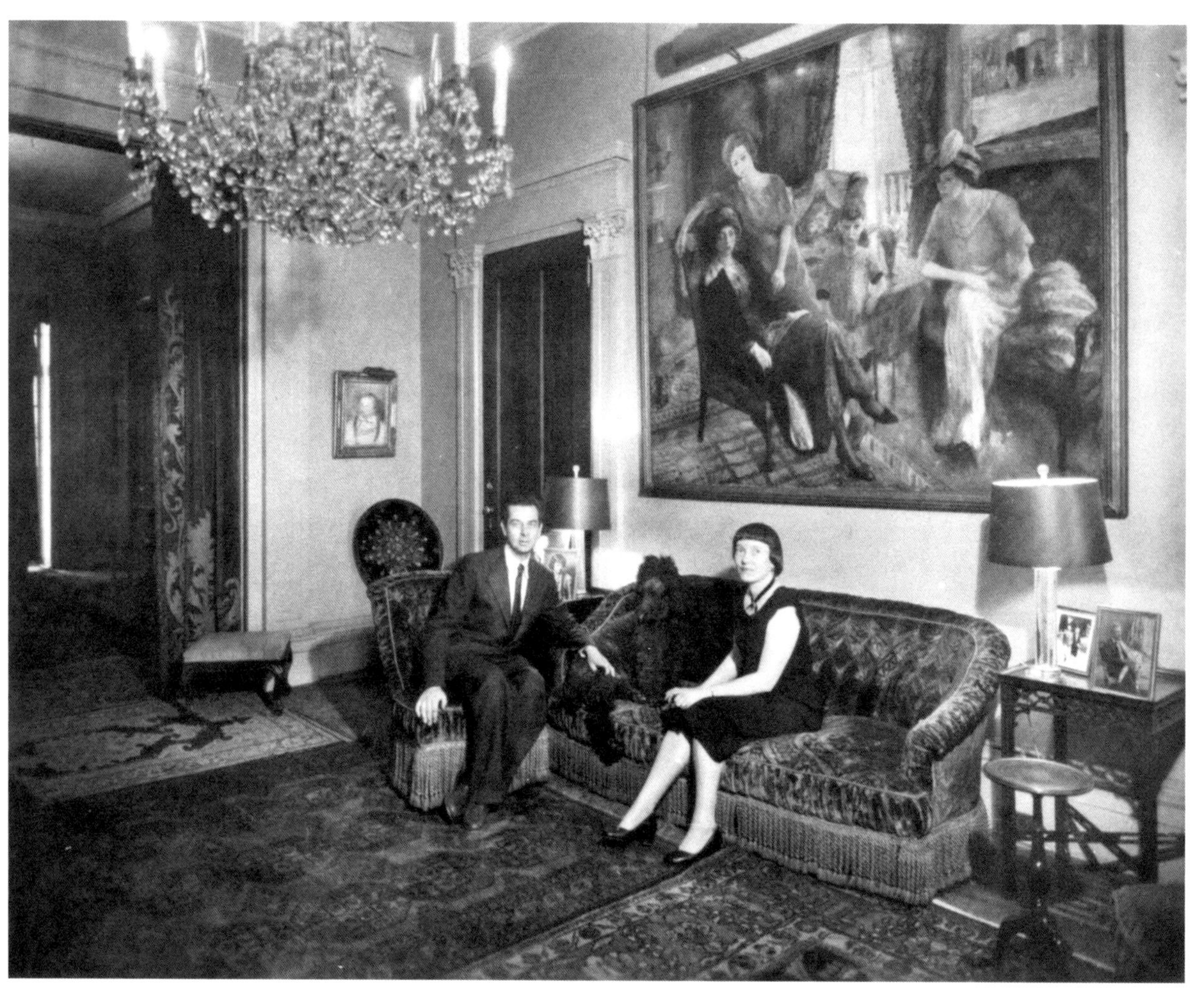

Ira and Nancy Glackens with dog,
Lucifer, seated beneath William
Glackens's *Family Group*, n.d.
Photograph by Peter A. Juley & Son
Museum of Art, Fort Lauderdale,
Nova Southeastern University, Florida;
Bequest of Ira Glackens

Preface

The Sansom Foundation takes great pleasure in the publication of the first series of lectures delivered in the C. Richard Hilker Art Lecture Series.

The lecture series, and this volume, would not have been possible but for the generosity of Ira Glackens and his wife, Nancy, who began the Sansom Foundation in 1956, naming it after the street in Philadelphia where Ira's father, the renowned American painter William J. Glackens, was born in 1870. Since its inception, the Foundation has supported a number of charitable organizations with proceeds from the estate of this important and prolific artist.

Following the deaths of Ira and Nancy Glackens in 1990, C. Richard Hilker, Indiana native, decorated World War II veteran, and a close friend and financial advisor to the Glackens family, was elected President of the Sansom Foundation. During Mr. Hilker's tenure as President, the Sansom Foundation continued to support a number of causes as the scope and philosophy of its philanthropic focus began to broaden, and its contribution to the arts began to increase.

In particular, the Museum of Art/Fort Lauderdale (now the Museum of Art/Fort Lauderdale, Nova Southeastern University), which, through Richard Hilker's efforts, had received Ira Glackens's bequest of his extensive private art collection, opened its Glackens Wing in 2001, funded in large measure by the Sansom Foundation and dedicated to the permanent display of William Glackens's work, as well as that of his contemporaries. The Museum, and its continuing endeavors to keep William Glackens before the public eye, remains one of the Foundation's primary beneficiaries.

After C. Richard Hilker's death in January 2001, the Board of Directors of the Sansom Foundation decided to commemorate his leadership by underwriting a series of scholarly lectures focusing on representational American art from the late nineteenth century to the early twentieth century. Those lectures have now been collected and published in this volume.

The first lecture in the series was delivered on December 9, 2003, at the Hirshhorn Museum and Sculpture Garden of the Smithsonian Institution, Washington, D.C., by Richard J. Wattenmaker, former director of the Smithsonian Institution's Archives of American Art. His presentation of "The Sketchbook Studies of William Glackens" explores the integral relationship between Glackens as draftsman and keen observer, as demonstrated by his sketchbooks, and Glackens as painter, in the composition of his finished canvases.

Colin B. Bailey, Deputy Director and Peter Jay Sharp Chief Curator of the Frick Collection, delivered the May 24, 2006, lecture at the National Academy Museum and School of Fine Arts in New York City. "The Origins of the Barnes Collection, 1912–15" focuses on the crucial years during which Dr. Albert C. Barnes began to acquire his impressive (and much publicized) collection, and on the primary role his friend William Glackens played in its formation.

The May 23, 2007, lecture, "A Need for Portraits: John Sloan, Robert Henri, and John Butler Yeats," also given at the National Academy Museum, was presented by noted art critic and scholar Avis Berman, who explores the intense artistic and personal relationships among Sloan, Henri, and Yeats, and the impact these friendships had on the art of the time.

This was followed on December 4, 2008, with "How the American Impressionists and Realists Kept the Wolf from the Door," by H. Barbara Weinberg, the Alice Pratt Brown Curator of American Paintings and Sculpture in the American Wing of The Metropolitan Museum of Art in New York. Given at the New-York Historical Society, this lecture profiles the careers of a number of New York-based American Impressionists and Realists, revealing their need to multitask in order to continue their artistic endeavors in financial circumstances that were often less than secure.

The final lecture presented in this volume was given on December 3, 2009, at the New-York Historical Society by Carol Troyen, Kristin and Roger Servison Curator Emerita of American Paintings at the Museum of Fine Arts, Boston. "Collateral Damage: George Bellows and the Great War" treats with Bellows and his artistic response to World War I, particularly to the atrocities committed by the German army during the 1914 invasion of Belgium.

As the roster of lecturers and their topics demonstrate, it is one of the Sansom Foundation's primary goals to encourage original research that results in significant contributions to the scholarship of American art. Each of the distinguished lecturers whose work appears in this volume has indeed made such a contribution. We extend the Sansom Foundation's sincere thanks to these scholars for furthering that goal.

We also wish to express the gratitude of the Sansom Foundation's Board of Directors to our fellow director Jorge H. Santis, Curator of the Glackens Collection at the Museum of Art/Fort Lauderdale, Nova Southeastern University, who, in his capacity as the Sansom Foundation's Director of Education, has spearheaded this project, and has dedicated tireless effort to make each lecture a memorable event.

As we celebrate this first volume of the C. Richard Hilker Art Lectures, we also look forward to inaugurating the second installment of lectures in the series in 2011, and the eventual publication of a companion volume of those lectures.

Frank Buscaglia
PRESIDENT
SANSOM FOUNDATION, INC.
SEPTEMBER 2011

The Sketchbook Studies of William Glackens

RICHARD J. WATTENMAKER

Lecture given on December 9, 2003

Hirshhorn Museum and Sculpture Garden

Washington, D.C.

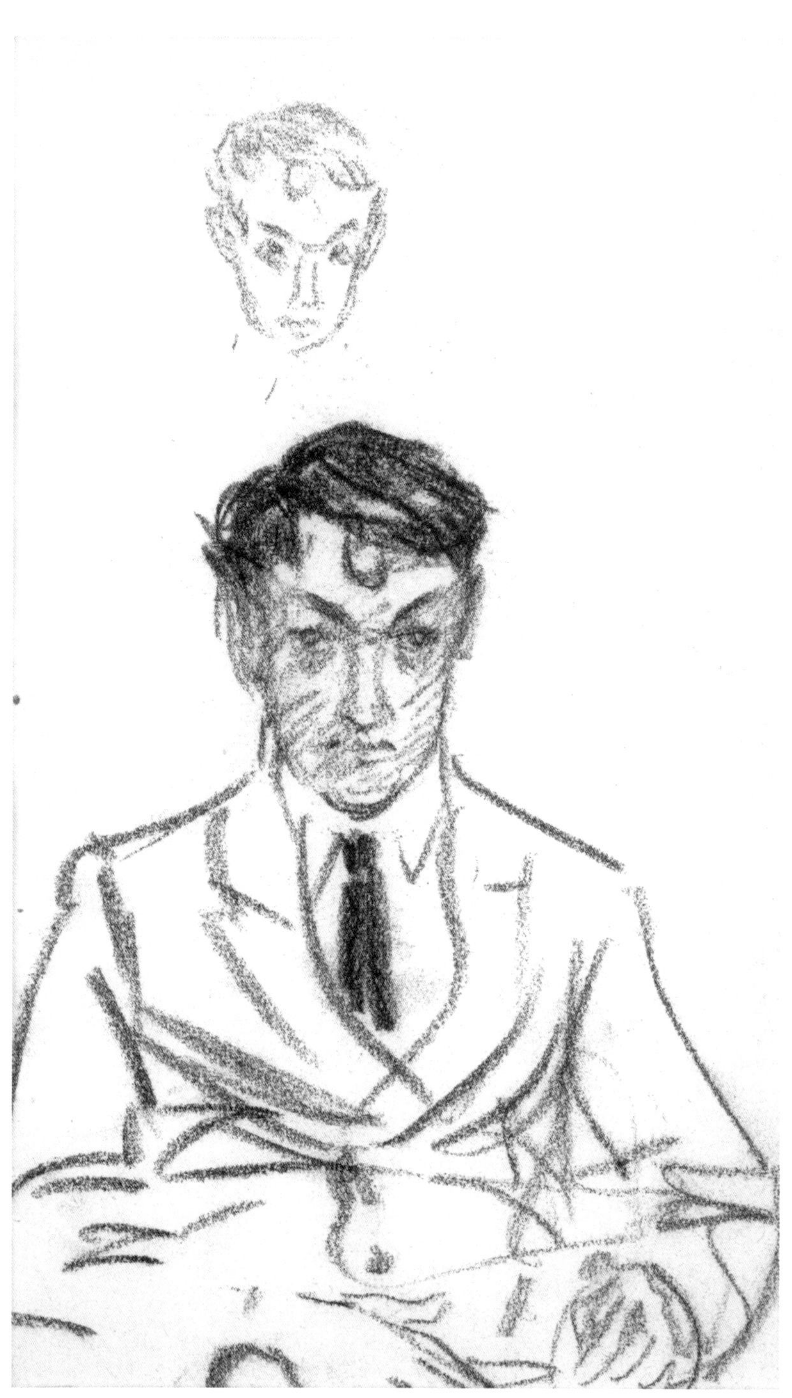

The Sketchbook Studies of William Glackens

RICHARD J. WATTENMAKER

> We should look back to the magazines of fifteen years ago and more and see how the swift, expressive draftsmanship that marks a Glackens painting today is the direct continuation of the quality that informed those remarkable drawings that date from the artist's days as an illustrator. . . . In his painting, which embodies more perfectly perhaps than any other in this country the great discoveries that the Impressionists made in the realm of color, the artist is still keeping close to the interest in the subject before him which underlies the distinguished character of the drawings.
>
> —WALTER PACH, 1922

William J. Glackens (1870–1938) played a leading role in the second generation of American painters who experimented with the colorful picture ideas of the French Impressionists and Post-Impressionists. By creatively transforming their aesthetic explorations, he made an original and personal contribution to the international tradition of Impressionism.

The painter's son, Ira, revealed just how fundamental drawings were in his father's practice: "Father never went out without a sketchbook in his pocket, and a stub of a certain kind of pencil intended for marking laundry packages, which he greatly favored; it had just the right tooth on the paper. These sketchbooks were the artist's most prized possessions, and he mourned when one was lost. They were more valued by him than his paintings, for they contained the material for his many [painted] beach and crowd scenes, and were the records of a lifetime of observing humanity."[1]

Glackens's early career was defined by his draftsmanship. He first made his living working as a newspaper illustrator in Philadelphia beginning in the 1890s. Acclaimed later for his illustrations for leading publishers of large circulation popular magazines—*McClure's*, *Scribner's*, *Saturday Evening Post*, *Harper's Weekly*, *Collier's*, and many others—to which he regularly contributed drawings, including

Fig. 1
William Glackens
Self-Portrait, c. 1910
Charcoal on paper
8½ × 4½ in. (21.6 × 11.4 cm)
Museum of Art, Fort Lauderdale, Nova Southeastern University, Florida: Gift of the Sansom Foundation
92.59A

covers, Glackens worked regularly as a professional illustrator through 1913, and from time to time thereafter.[2] In a retrospective essay summing up their early days, his colleague John Sloan (1871–1951) wrote: "Glackens was certainly the greatest draughtsman who lived this side of the ocean. He could draw anything he wanted to in any way he wanted to. He had the ability to bring back mentally what was an emotional state. His drawings of New York streets, tenements, fire escapes, pushcarts, and people were full of incidents and more alive than life could ever be. He would make a drawing over and over again until he got what he really wanted. He was never satisfied."[3]

During the time Glackens worked for the *Philadelphia Press*, from 1892 to 1894, he attended night classes at the Pennsylvania Academy of the Fine Arts, determined to become a painter. The major motivation was Robert Henri (1865–1929), an artist five years his senior with whom Glackens shared a studio in Philadelphia in these years.[4] Henri, who had traveled abroad from 1888 to 1891, had briefly experimented with Impressionism but made the Dutch and Spanish masters Hals, Rembrandt, and Velázquez his models. Among contemporaries, Henri admired Duveneck, Whistler, Sargent, and, most of all, Manet. Henri considered these painters to be opposed to the academic training then practiced in art schools in France, Germany, and the United States. He therefore appeared as something of a pacesetter in the staid academic atmosphere of the Philadelphia art world. Henri encouraged his young friends—Glackens, Sloan, Everett Shinn, and George Luks, among them—to seek their inspiration for their paintings directly from life, as they were doing in their graphic work. Sloan later recalled, "As for studying the old masters in the original, I was still satisfied technically with the methods Henri

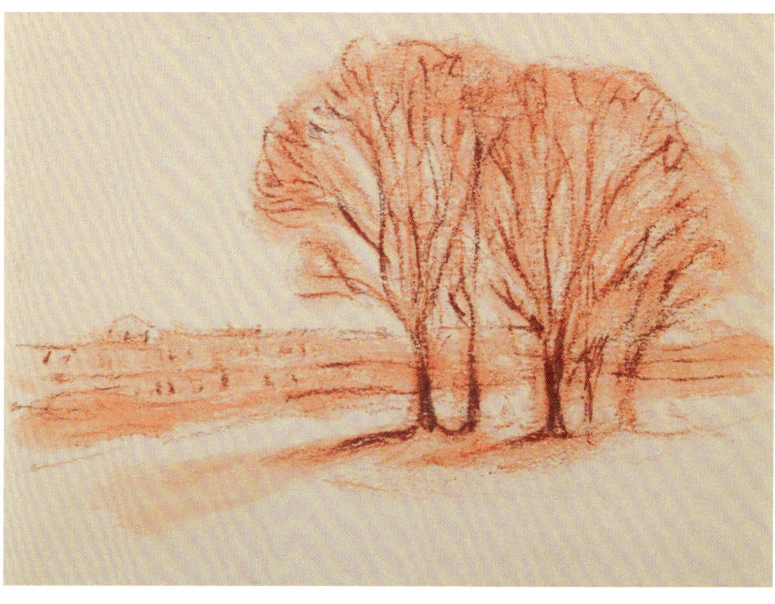

Fig. 2
Study for *Philadelphia Landscape*, c. 1893
Red chalk on paper
6¾ × 9⅜ in. (17 × 24 cm)
Museum of Art, Fort Lauderdale, Nova Southeastern University, Florida: Gift of the Sansom Foundation
92.48

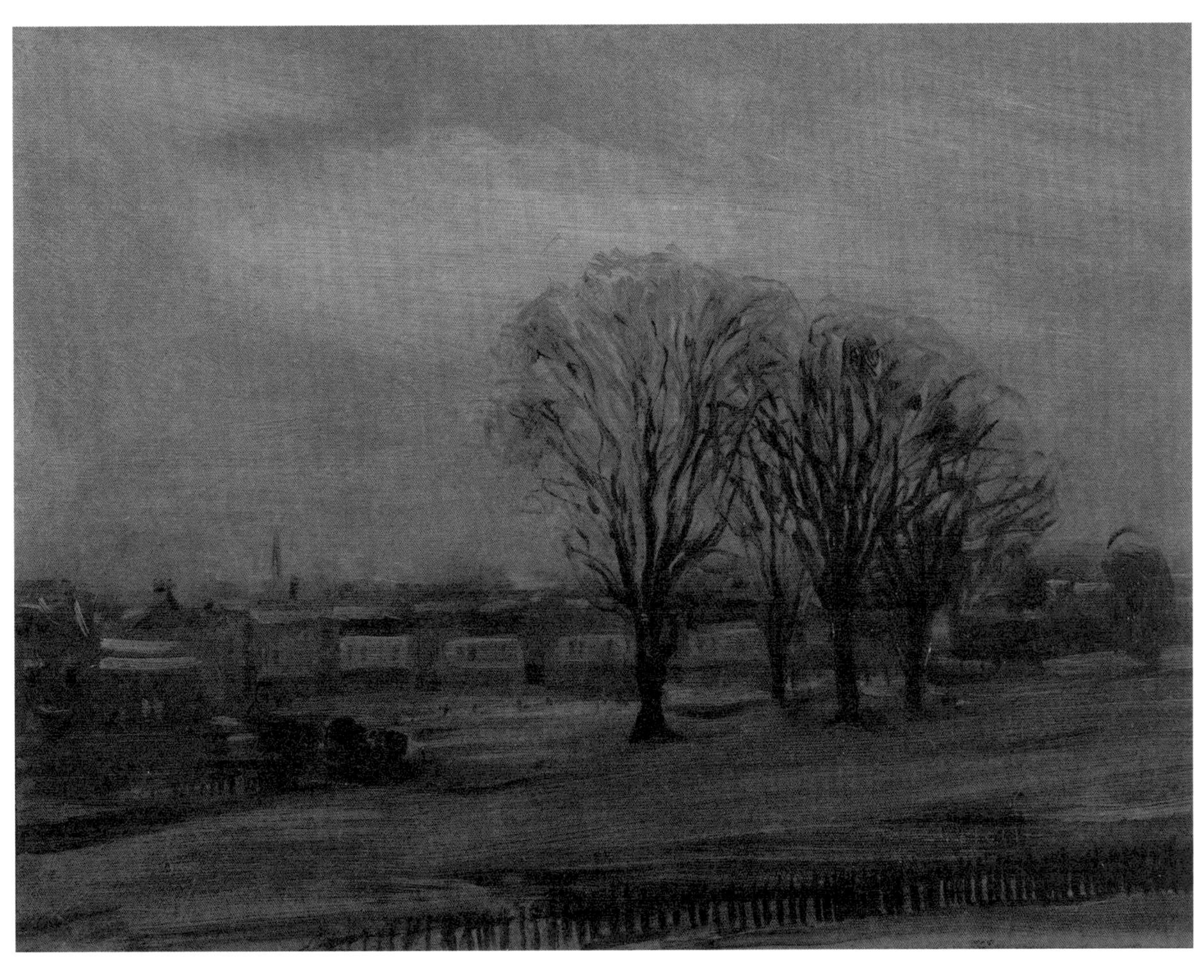

Fig. 3
Philadelphia Landscape, c. 1893
Oil on canvas
17¾ × 24 in. (45.1 × 60 cm)
Museum of Art, Fort Lauderdale,
Nova Southeastern University, Florida:
Gift of the Sansom Foundation
92.41

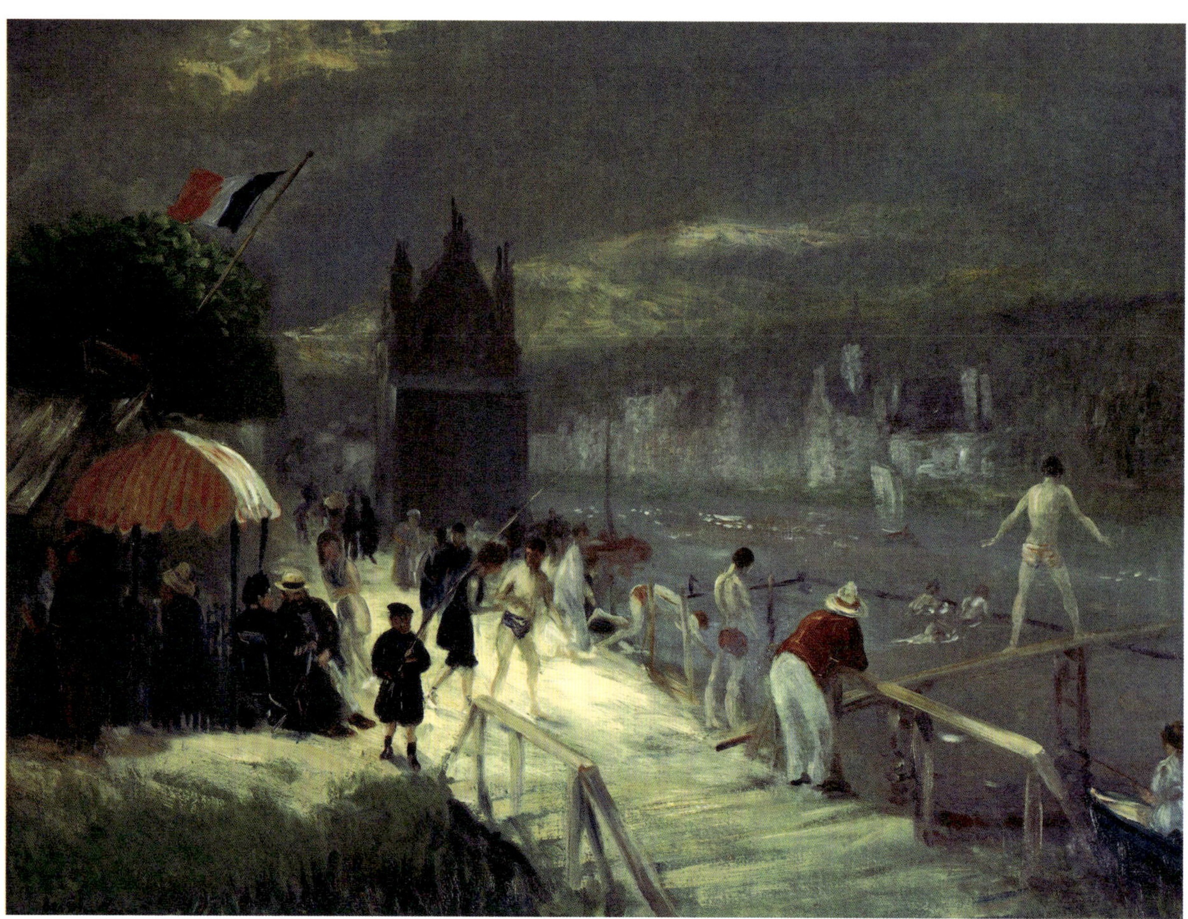

Fig. 4
Château-Thierry, 1906
Oil on canvas
24 × 32 in. (61 × 81.3 cm)
The Huntington Library, Art Collections, and Botanical Gardens, San Marino, California; Gift of the Virginia Steele Scott Foundation 83.8.19

had brought us through his study of Manet, Velásquez, Goya and Frans Hals. The [John G.] Johnson and [Joseph E.] Widener collections were available for study of Rembrandt and other Dutch masters. Our prime interest was painting pictures, of life, of the world around us."[5]

Henri's revolt was of course a very minor one—a belated and tame rebellion compared to the upheaval against academicism which had already been fought successfully in Paris in the 1860s and 1870s. While Glackens was by nature reserved and not inclined to reminisce, Sloan has left us extensive memoirs about the early days of his career in Philadelphia, and of Henri's importance at this time. "[He] had that magic ability as a teacher which inspires and provokes his followers into action," he wrote. "He was a catalyst; he was an emancipator, liberating American art from its youthful academic uniformity, and liberating the individual artist from repressions that held back his natural ability."[6] Henri's broadening tendencies were transforming: "From Whitman to Emerson, Henri carried on the spirit of free-thinking and belief in individual expression, hatred of orthodoxy and suspicion of institutions. In the precious 'fin de siècle' atmosphere of

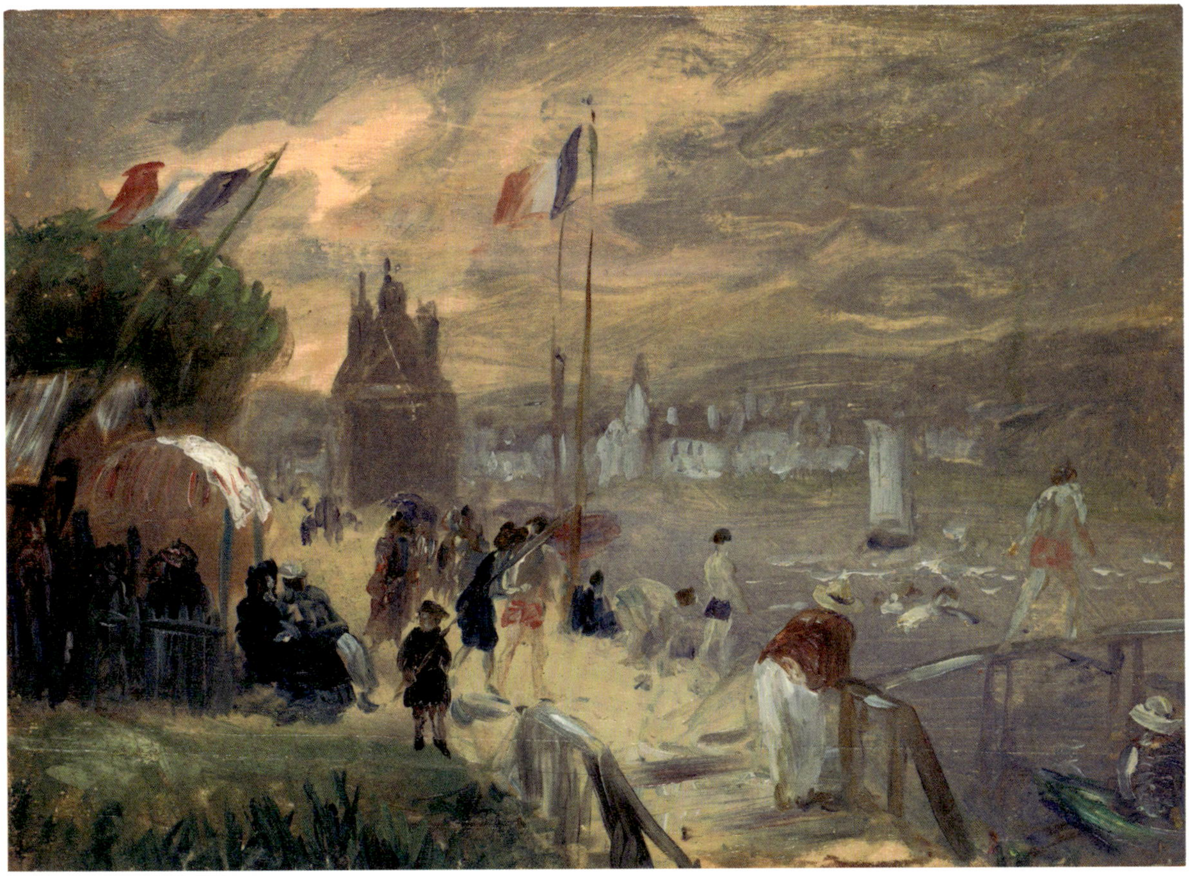

Fig. 5
Study for *Château-Thierry*, 1906
Oil on panel
6¼ × 8¾ in. (15.9 × 22.2 cm)
The Huntington Library, Art Collections, and Botanical Gardens, San Marino, California; Gift of the Virginia Steele Scott Foundation
83.8.20

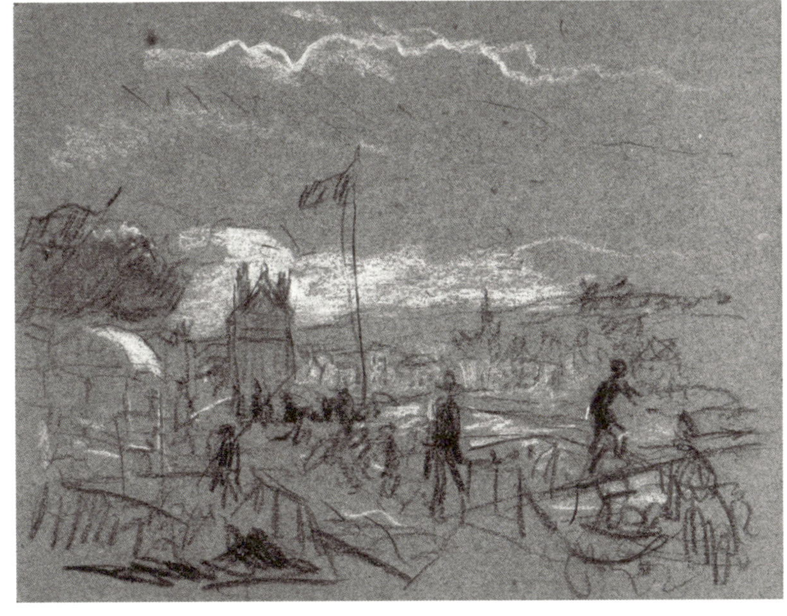

Fig. 6
Study for *Château-Thierry*, 1906
Chalk and pastel on paper
5½ × 7 ¼ in. (13.9 × 18.4 cm)
Museum of Art, Fort Lauderdale, Nova Southeastern University, Florida; Gift of the Sansom Foundation
(Sketchbook 94.93)

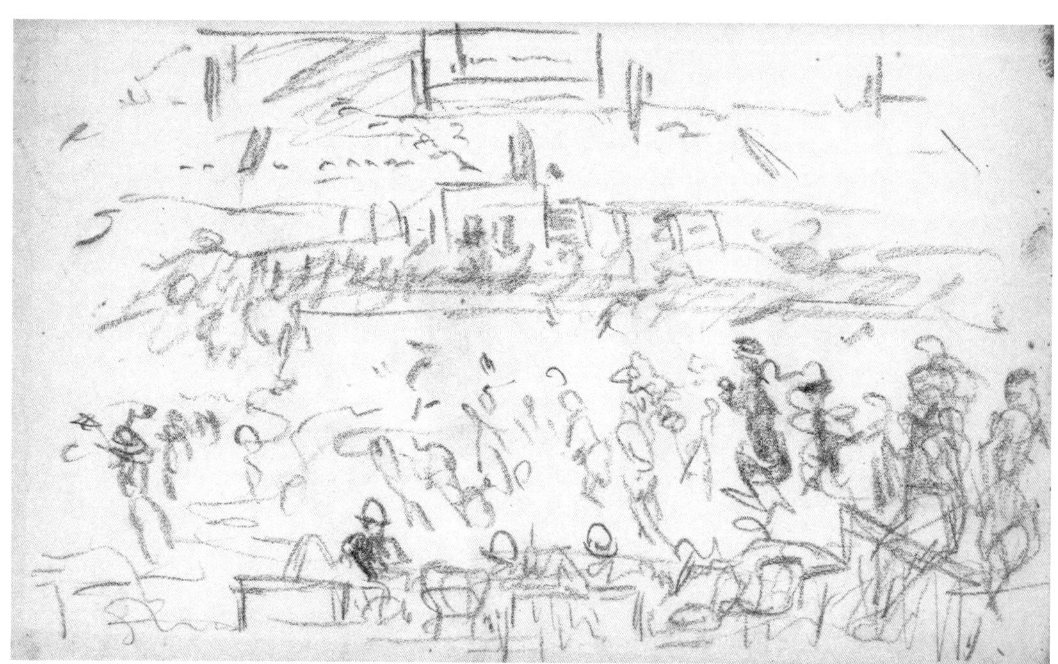

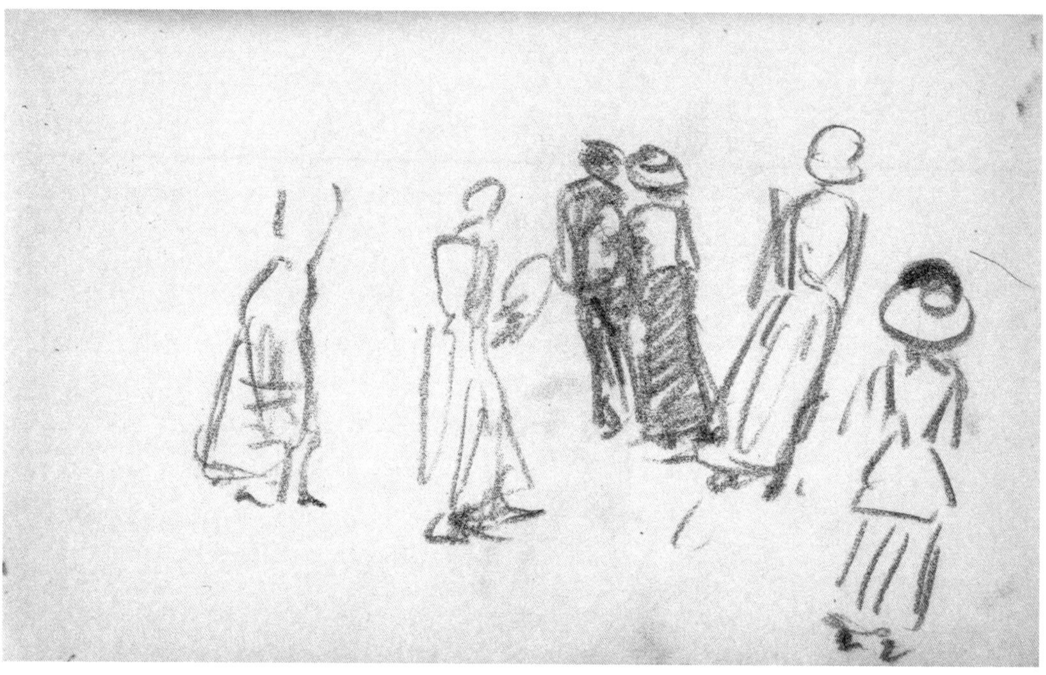

Fig. 7
Study for *Skating Rink, New York City*, 1906
Crayon on paper
5⅛ × 8¼ in. (13 × 21 cm)
Museum of Art, Fort Lauderdale, Nova Southeastern University, Florida; Gift of the Sansom Foundation
(Sketchbook 94.88)

Fig. 8
Study for *Skating Rink, New York City*, 1906
Crayon on paper
5⅛ × 8¼ in. (13 × 21 cm)
Museum of Art, Fort Lauderdale, Nova Southeastern University, Florida; Gift of the Sansom Foundation
(Sketchbook 94.88)

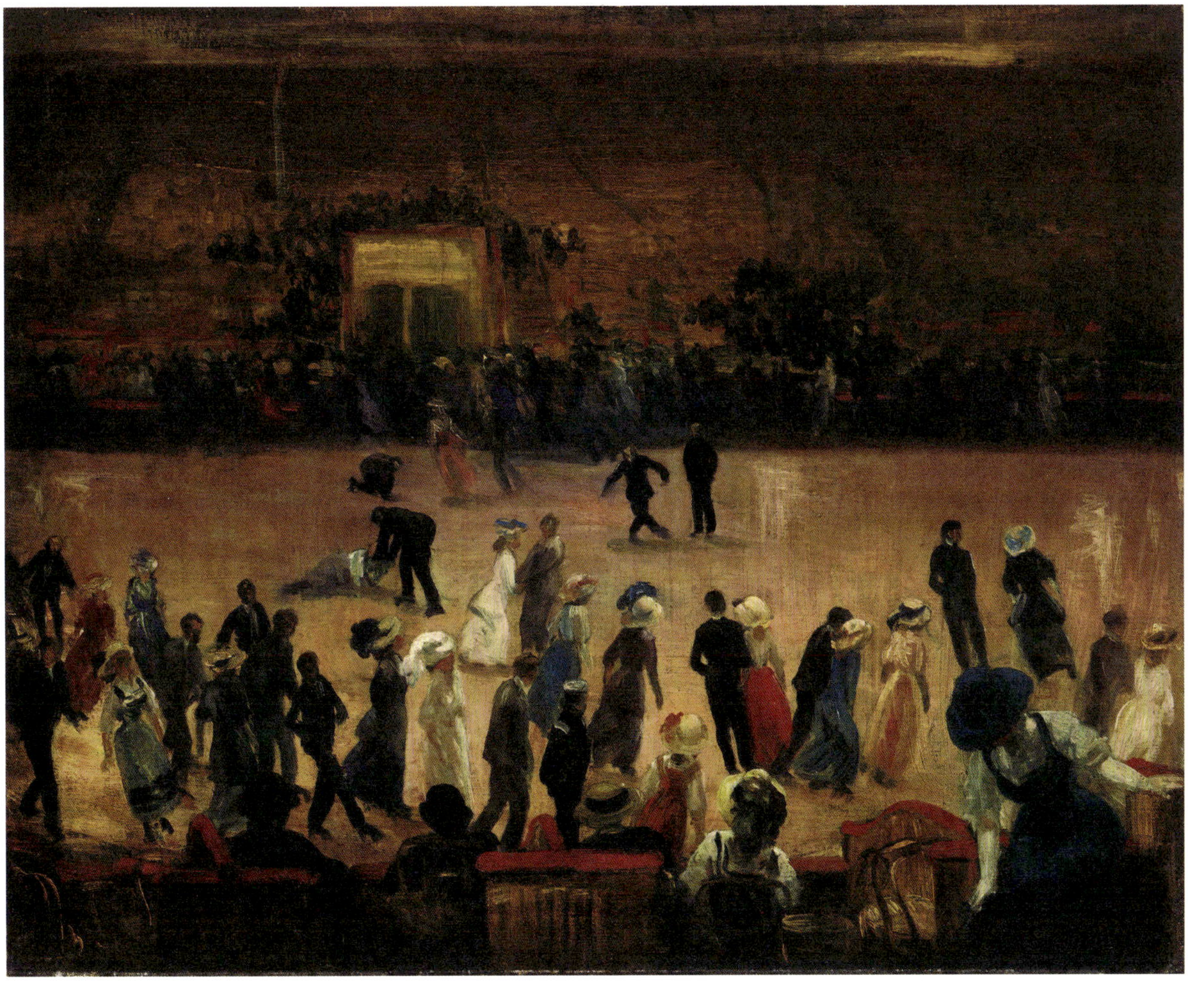

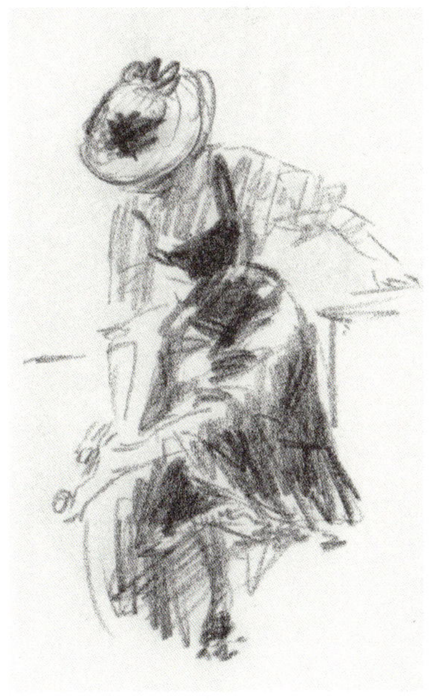

Fig. 9
Skating Rink, New York City, c. 1906
Oil on canvas
26 × 33 in. (66 × 83.8 cm)
Philadelphia Museum of Art;
Gift of Meyer P. Potamkin and
Vivian O. Potamkin, 2000

Fig. 10
Study for *Skating Rink, New York City*, 1906
Crayon on paper
8¼ × 5⅛ in. (21 × 13 cm)
Museum of Art, Fort Lauderdale,
Nova Southeastern University, Florida;
Gift of the Sansom Foundation
(Sketchbook 94.88)

Fig. 11
Study for *Café de la Paix*, 1906
Crayon on paper
5⅛ × 8¼ in. (13 × 21 cm)
Museum of Art, Fort Lauderdale,
Nova Southeastern University, Florida;
Gift of the Sansom Foundation
(Sketchbook 92.52)

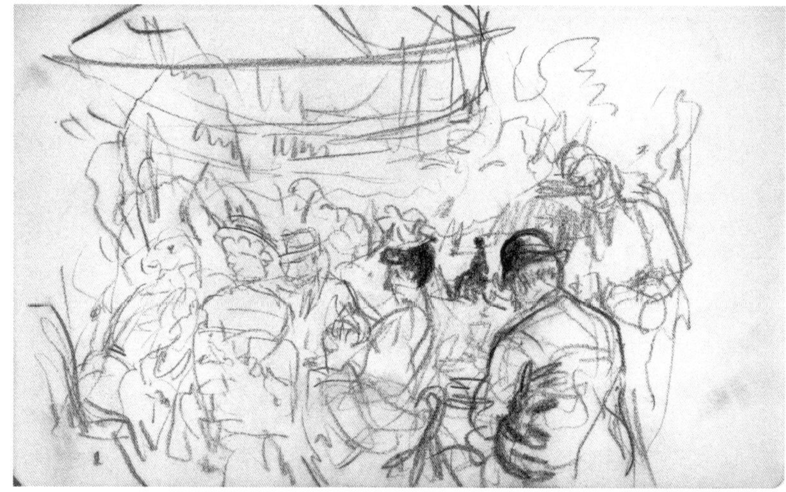

Fig. 12
Study for *Café de la Paix*, 1906
Crayon on paper
5⅛ × 8¼ in. (13 × 21 cm)
Museum of Art, Fort Lauderdale,
Nova Southeastern University, Florida;
Gift of the Sansom Foundation
(Sketchbook 92.52)

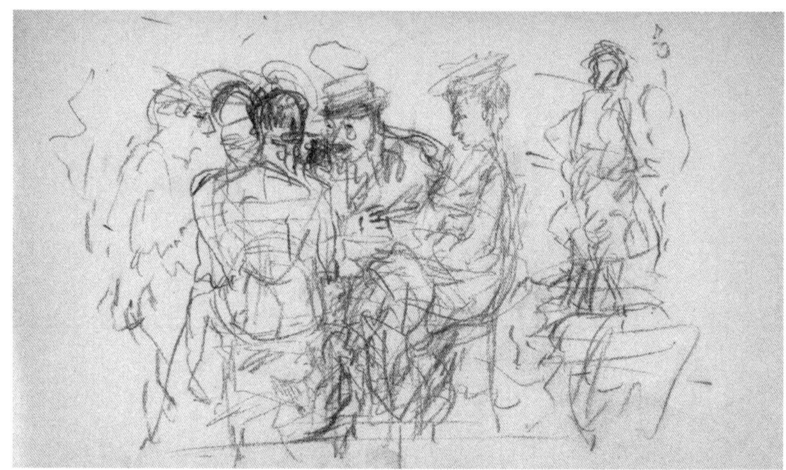

the nineties his bold advocacy of painting *pictures* rather than seeking 'art for art's sake' was heresy. It was revolutionary to say that an interest in life was more important than aesthetics."[7]

In pursuit of his aspirations to be a painter, in June 1895 Glackens went to Paris for a fifteen-month period of concentrated painting and sketching, free from newspaper deadlines and editors' whims. Soon after arriving, he went on to Italy, but we have no record of his travels there; in August, in the company of Henri and Elmer Schofield, he made an extended bicycle trip through northern France to the Lowlands. He wrote to a friend in early September: "Our principal interest was in the galleries of Belgium and Holland. I could dilate to a great length on the wonders of the Dutch Masters, Franz Hals and Rembrandt, their big wholesome and very often clumsy drawing. . . . We saw everything to be seen in the north, and gathered from it fresh convictions."[8] They visited Antwerp, Brussels, Rotterdam, The Hague, Haarlem, and Amsterdam, and revealed in the northern French countryside, the Ardennes, and the Valley of the Marne. A

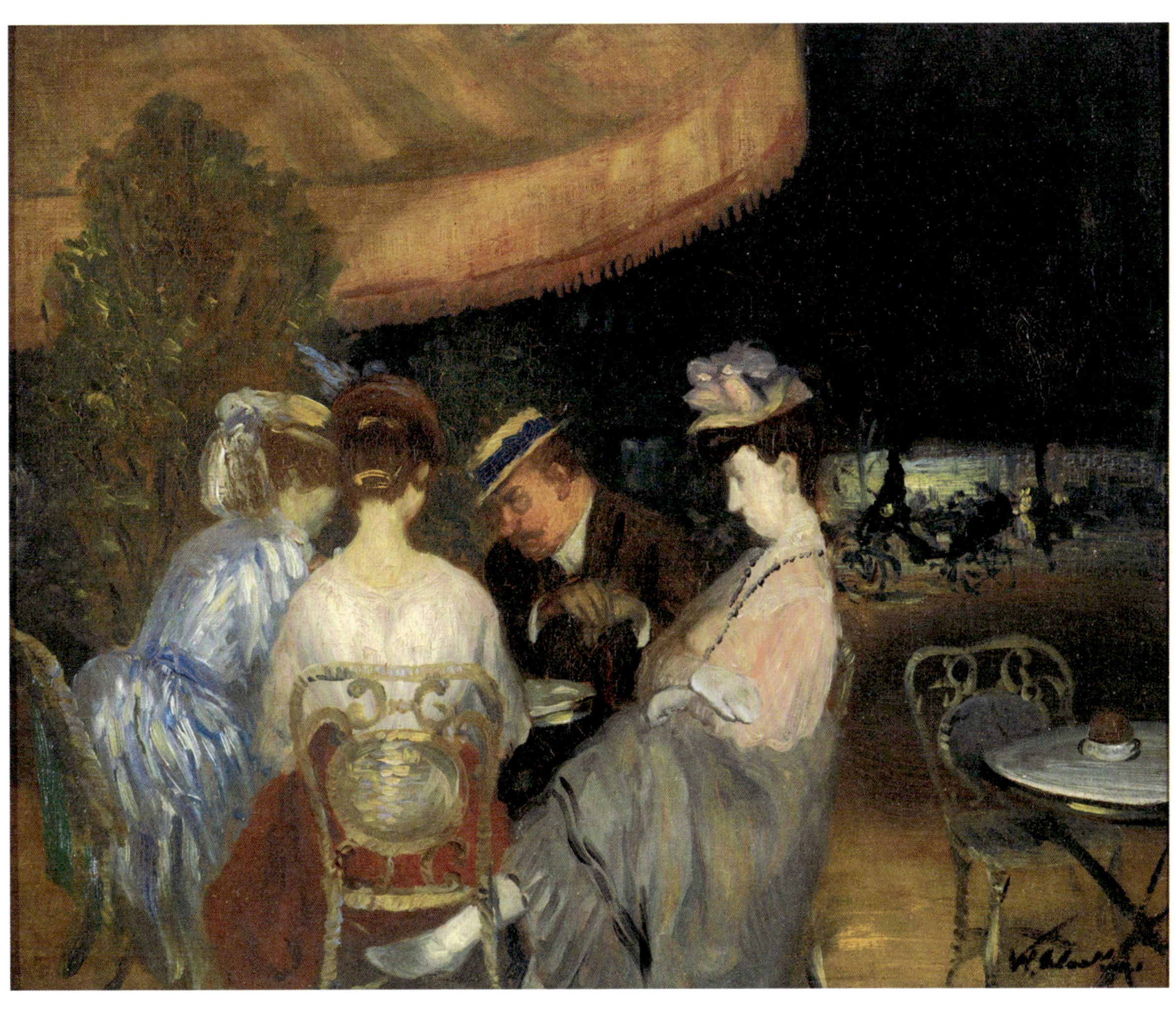

Fig. 13
Café de la Paix, 1906
Oil on canvas
15 × 18¼ in. (38.1 × 46.4 cm)
Museum of Art, Fort Lauderdale,
Nova Southeastern University, Florida;
Bequest of Ira Glackens 91.40.146

lifetime affinity was formed; Glackens remained a Francophile for the rest of his life.

In Paris, Glackens rented a large studio in Montparnasse and painted. The canvases he produced were stimulated by firsthand acquaintance with the art of Manet, whose influence is reflected in their vigorous brushstrokes and intense luster. Glackens had seen work by Manet at the Metropolitan Museum of Art before his trip to Europe, at the latest by 1894:

> This is the second time that I have seen the Manets, and they seem greater to me than they did the first time. I understood them then but I understand them better now, and I hope will keep on doing so every time I look at them. The 'boy with the sword,' belongs I think to the Spanish period of Manet's life, I mean when he was influenced by Velásquez and before he went to Holland. The head of the boy is undoubtedly suggested of the great Spaniard. In fact there is the head of a prince in another room by Velásquez that is quite reminiscent of Manet's boy. These two pictures by Manet and Whistler's *White Girl* [National Gallery of Art, Washington, D.C.] have a family resemblance. The only difference is that Whistler is more aesthetic. The intention of both men is identical, and their theory of drawing the same. We gloated over these three pictures all afternoon [at the Metropolitan], and we came back the next day and gloated over them until it grew dark, and then we went back to Philadelphia.[9]

Glackens had also had an opportunity to see Manet's work in March 1895, when the Durand-Ruel Galleries, which had opened a branch in New York in 1894, presented an exhibition of fifteen of the French artist's major compositions including *A Bar at the Folies Bergère* (The Courtauld Gallery, London), *Music in the Tuileries* (National Gallery, London), *Races at Longchamp* (The Art Institute

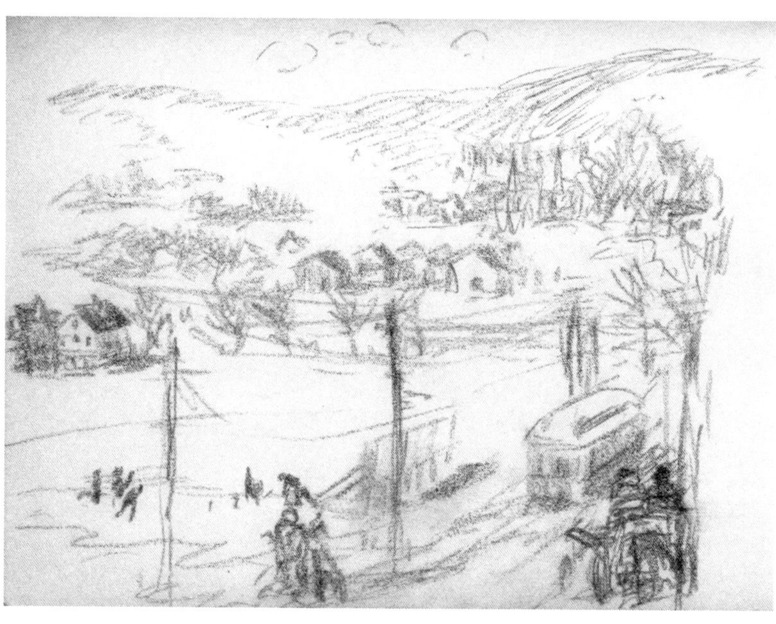

Fig. 14
Study for *View of West Hartford*, 1907
Crayon on paper
5⅛ × 8¼ in. (13 × 21 cm)
Museum of Art, Fort Lauderdale, Nova Southeastern University, Florida; Gift of the Sansom Foundation
(Sketchbook 94.84)

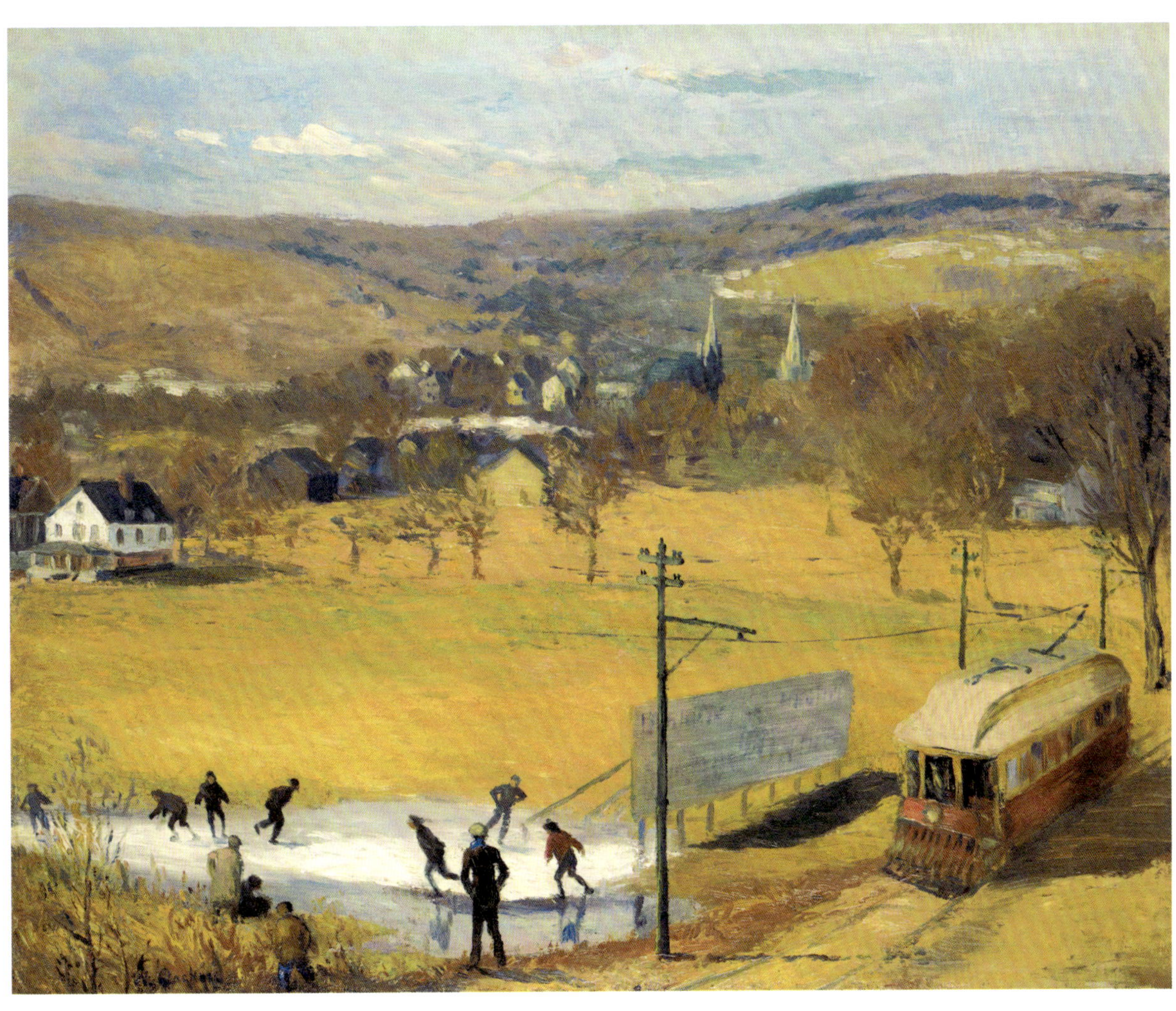

Fig. 15
View of West Hartford, 1907
Oil on canvas
26⅝ × 32¹⁄₁₆ in. (67.6 × 81.4 cm)
Wadsworth Atheneum Museum of Art, Hartford, Connecticut; The Ella Gallup Sumner and Mary Catlin Sumner Collection Fund 1957.243

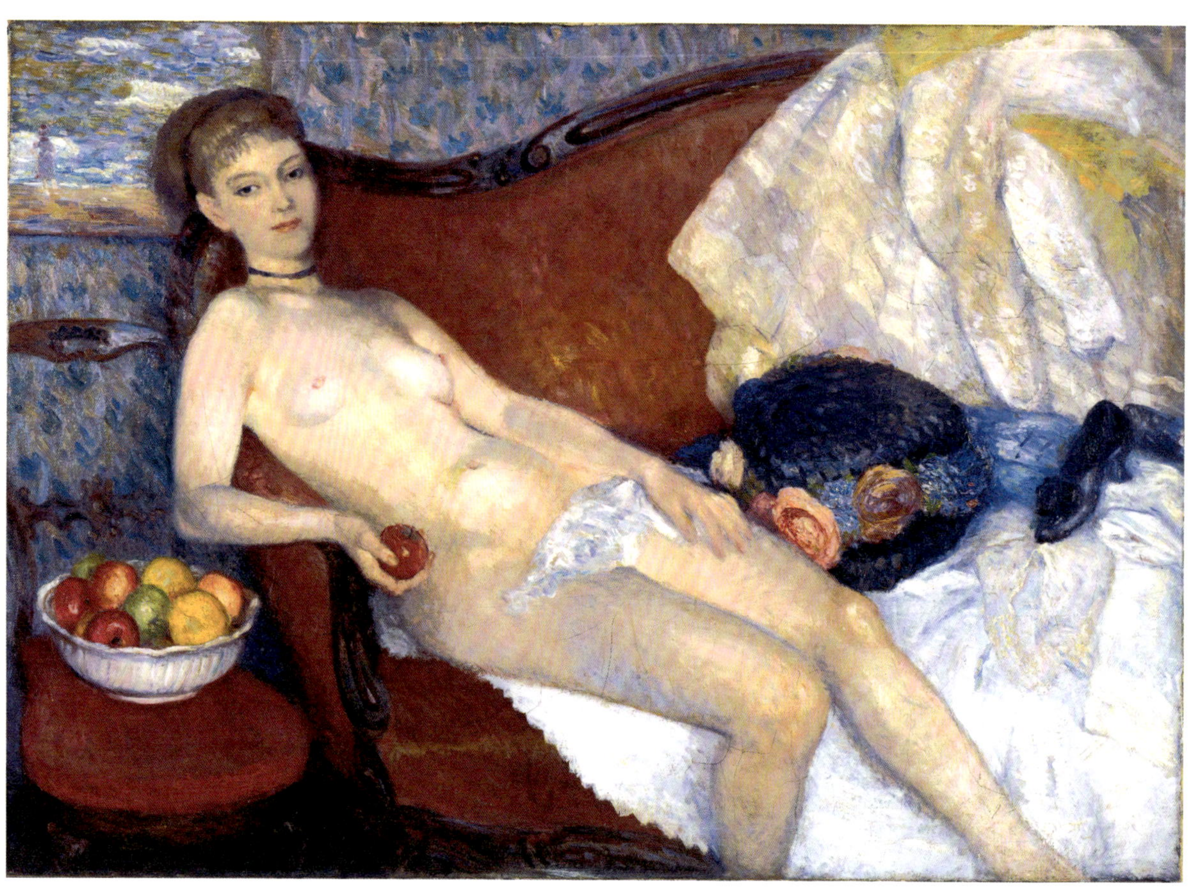

Fig. 16
Nude with Apple, 1909–10
Oil on canvas
40⅝ × 57½ in. (103.2 × 146.1 cm)
Brooklyn Museum; Dick S. Ramsay Fund 56.70

Fig. 17
Édouard Manet
Olympia, 1863
Oil on canvas
51⅛ × 74¼ in. (130 × 189.9 cm)
Musée d'Orsay, Paris

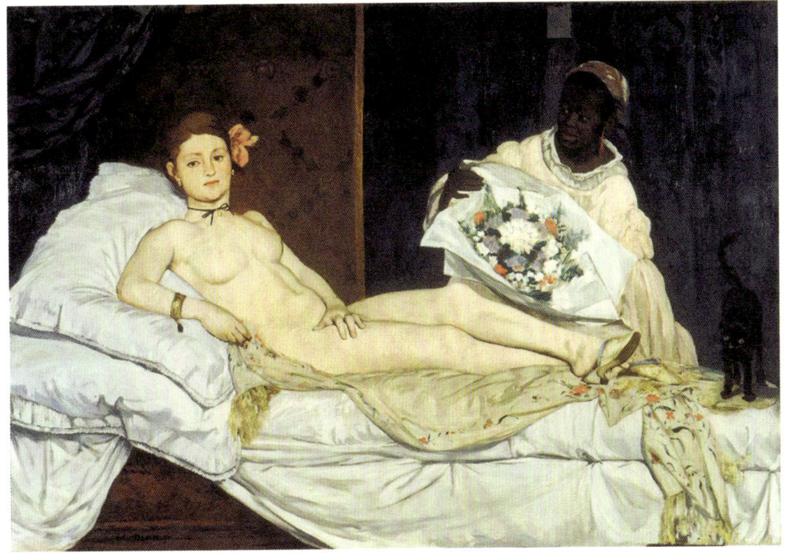

Fig. 18
Study for *Nude with Apple*, 1909
Crayon on paper
5½ × 9¼ in. (14 × 23.5 cm)
Museum of Art, Fort Lauderdale,
Nova Southeastern University, Florida;
Gift of the Sansom Foundation
(Sketchbook 92.59)

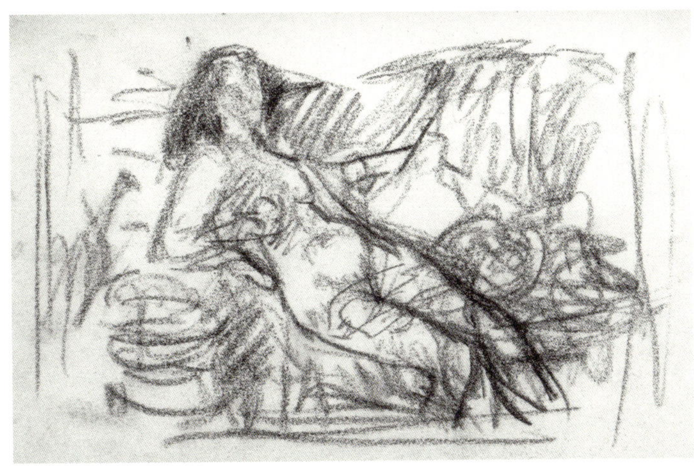

Fig. 19
Study for *Nude with Apple*, 1909
Crayon on paper
9¼ × 5½ in. (23.5 × 14 cm)
Museum of Art, Fort Lauderdale,
Nova Southeastern University, Florida;
Gift of the Sansom Foundation
(Sketchbook 92.59)

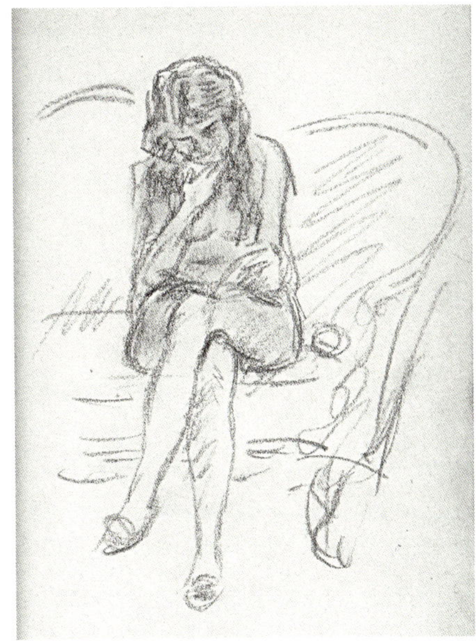

Fig. 20
Study for *Cape Cod Pier*, 1908
Crayon on paper
5⅛ × 8¼ in. (13 × 21 cm)
Museum of Art, Fort Lauderdale, Nova Southeastern University, Florida; Bequest of Ira Glackens
(Sketchbook 94.132)

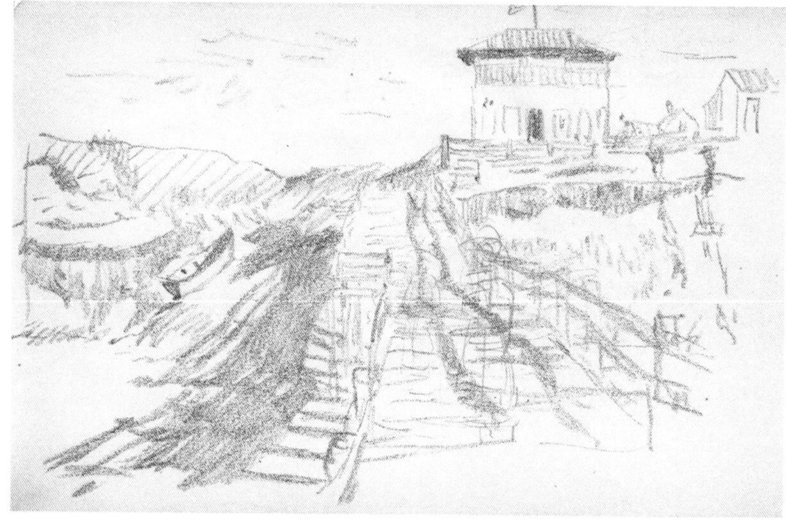

Fig. 21
Study for *Cape Cod Pier*, 1908
Crayon on paper
5⅛ × 8¼ in. (13 × 21 cm)
Museum of Art, Fort Lauderdale, Nova Southeastern University, Florida; Bequest of Ira Glackens
(Sketchbook 94.132)

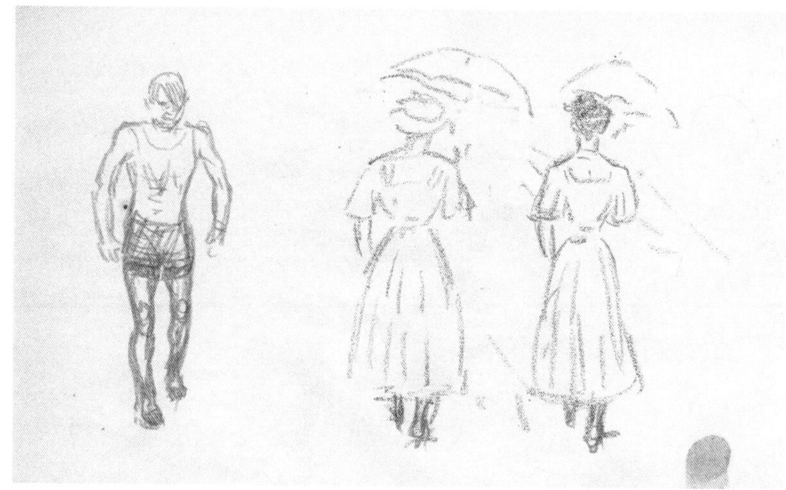

of Chicago), *Masked Ball,* and *The Tragic Actor* (National Gallery of Art, Washington, D.C.), all of which were to have an impact on Glackens's subsequent painting.[10]

"The Louvre is a wonderful gallery," Glackens wrote, "there is no need of any other school."[11] He expanded on his dismissive attitude toward formal instruction in France: "Here in Paris I am buried beneath five hundred sleeping art students. The Paris art student is a delusion, with very very rare exceptions he has mistaken his vocation; he should never have attempted art for he knows nothing, absolutely nothing, about it."[12] Returning to Philadelphia in the fall of 1896 with "stacks of canvases," Glackens moved almost immediately to New York to take up a new position as an illustrator for the *New York Herald.* The young artist no longer enjoyed uninterrupted freedom to paint, and so during the early years of the new century his time was divided between painting and magazine and book illustration, including a trip to Florida and Cuba to cover the Spanish-American

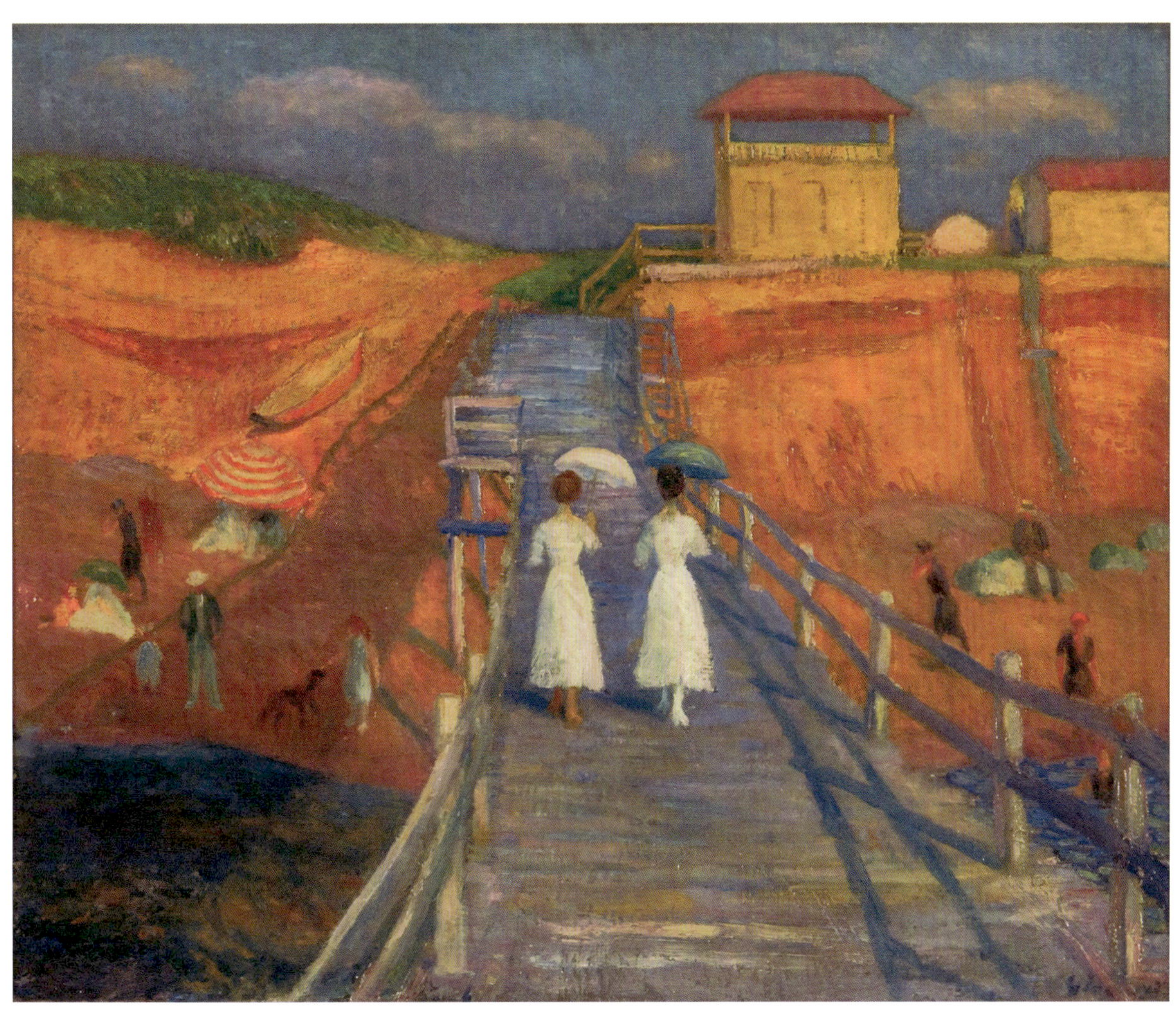

Fig. 22
Cape Cod Pier, 1908
Oil on canvas
26 × 32 in. (66 × 81.3 cm)
Museum of Art, Fort Lauderdale,
Nova Southeastern University, Florida;
Gift of an anonymous donor 85.74

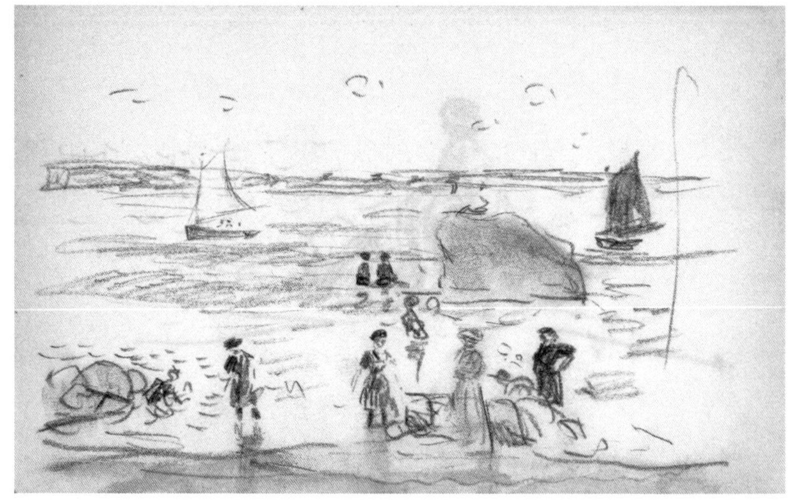

Fig. 23
Study for *Rock in the Bay, Wickford*, 1909
Crayon on paper
5 × 8½ in. (12.7 × 21.1 cm)
Museum of Art, Fort Lauderdale, Nova Southeastern University, Florida; Gift of the Sansom Foundation
(Sketchbook 94.101)

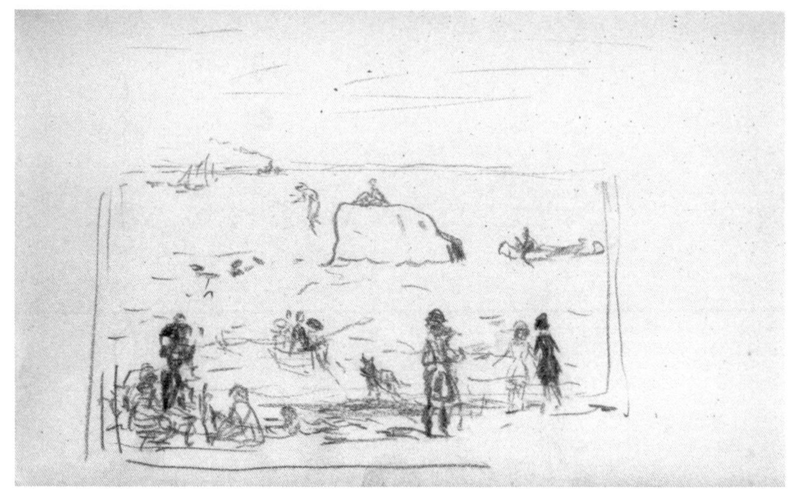

Fig. 24
Study for *Rock in the Bay, Wickford*, 1909
Crayon on paper
5 × 8½ in. (12.7 × 21.1 cm)
Museum of Art, Fort Lauderdale, Nova Southeastern University, Florida; Gift of the Sansom Foundation
(Sketchbook 94.101)

War for *McClure's* magazine. But he persevered, and in 1903 critic Charles FitzGerald wrote: "[William] Glackens is an illustrator who has come to the front, even in the slow eyes of officialdom, by sheer ability and without any of the accidental helps that some have had. . . . He is now engaged in the tedious business of making himself known as a painter."[13]

Despite the direction of Henri's preferences and influence, it would be erroneous to suppose that the young generation was unaware of Impressionism, which all American artists knew, both in the original French form and its American variations. On this subject we have Sloan's own words, albeit negative ones:

> In the nineties, we were opposed to Impressionism, with its blue shadows and orange lights because it seemed "unreal"; we chose our colors from observation of facts and qualities of *the things* we painted, with little reference to phenomena of light effects. . . . Our palette consisted of earth colors with occasional use of blue and green and yellow to

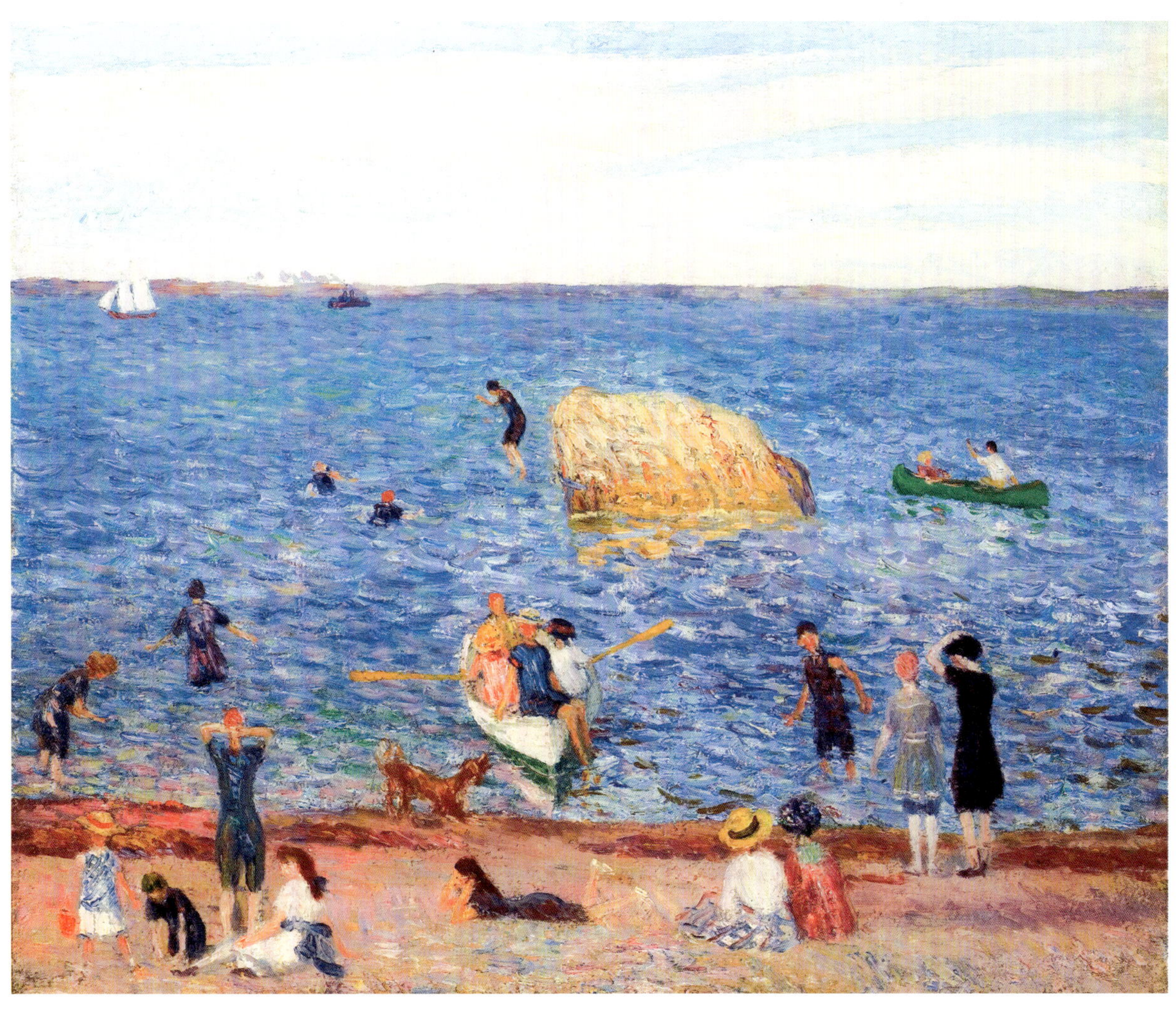

Fig. 25
Rock in the Bay, Wickford, 1909
Oil on canvas
26 × 32 in. (66 × 81.3 cm)
New Jersey State Museum Collection,
Trenton; Museum Purchase FA1985.34

Fig. 26
Study for *Bathing at Bellport, Long Island*, 1912
Crayon on paper
5⅙ × 8⅙ in. (13 × 21 cm)
Museum of Art, Fort Lauderdale, Nova Southeastern University, Florida; Gift of the Sansom Foundation (Sketchbook 92.131).

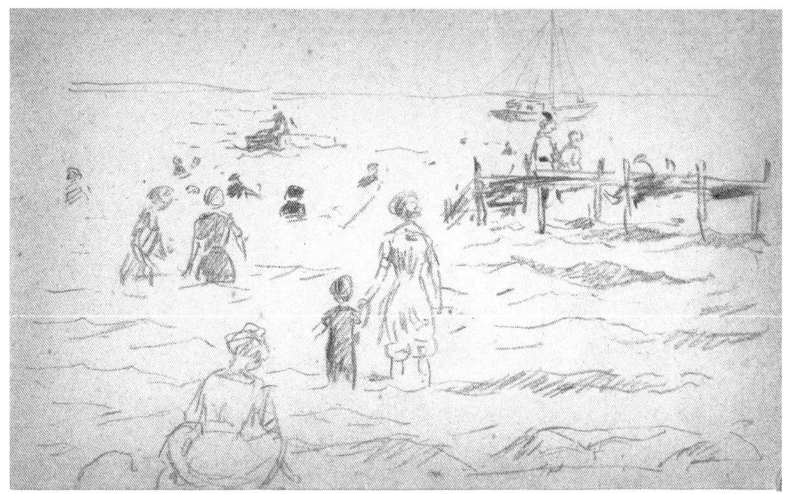

> "kick up" neutral tones. This was a simple palette to control and sufficient for our purposes. Manet and Goya and Hals were our masters, and there can be seen a relationship with Whistler in Glackens' and my early work, which came via Velásquez. Our pictures were "tonal," and when successful, caught the mood of the city streets.[14]

Setting aside Sloan's assertion that he and his colleagues "chose our colors from observation"—in this case a method absorbed by the way in which the Dutch and Spanish masters of the seventeenth century had "observed qualities of things"—it is clear that the young men consciously rejected the Impressionists' bright color and method of paint application. Moreover, on the basis of what Sloan says, we can see that the "realistic" manner in which they elected to paint represented a deliberate choice and was not ultimately due to the limitations imposed by the academic training of the day. The likely explanation of their attitude is that their early adherence to the style of the old masters naturally led them to seek the single most dazzling of the modern innovators as a model, the one who provided a direct link with, and confirmation of, their choice of such painters as Hals and Velázquez—viz., Manet. Rembrandt, Hals, and Velázquez are agelessly contemporary models—depending, of course, on which aspects of their work an artist chooses to stress.

In order to understand why Glackens and his confreres considered themselves progressive, and, indeed, to appreciate the fact that by American standards to some extent they were, it should be kept in mind that Glackens was a "working man" rather than a typical artist rising through the ranks of the art schools. His development therefore evolved apart from the set pace of art school curricula and according to his own interests and timetable. The nineties was a period of flux wherein strong currents of changing styles commingled and competed; Art Nouveau, Pre-Raphaelitism, Impressionism, and the Arts and Crafts movement all stood out against the background

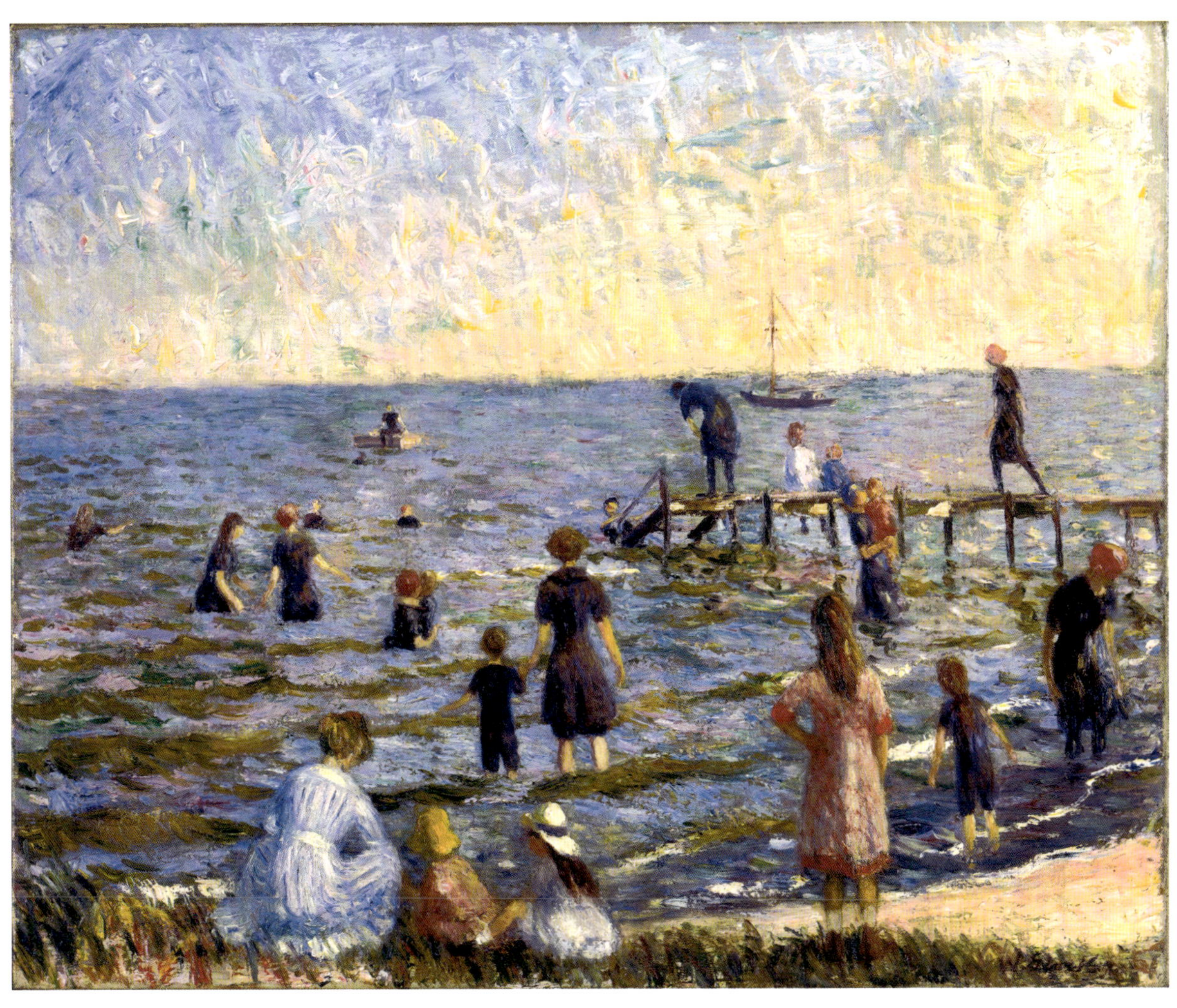

Fig. 27
Bathing at Bellport, Long Island, 1912
Oil on canvas
26 1/16 × 32 in. (66.2 × 81.3 cm)
Brooklyn Museum; Bequest of
Laura L. Barnes 67.24.6

of a dominant French academicism and the established American orthodoxy, both of which stressed illustrative verisimilitude and attention to detail.

Glackens had an ease and command of rendering incident that, coupled with his unerring recall, served him well throughout his career as a painter. His sketches are inextricably linked with his painted compositions, and the artist adhered throughout his entire forty-five-year-long career to a practice of careful planning and preparation. No matter how summary, his sketches provided Glackens with often embryonic compositional formats and working notes for rendering picture motifs. Glackens's notebooks are filled with page after page of single and multiple figure groups, often in compositional settings that were transferred directly to the oils without losing their immediacy as he progressively honed his skills in the complex, fugitive, and difficult medium of oil paint. The picturesque aliveness of everyday things and episodes is caught with an eye and a mind quick to observe and, with as quick, sure, and knowing a hand, transferred onto the paper or canvas by way of those tersely descriptive, gently crisp touches and lines. Gestures rendered in the paintings retain the best qualities of his multi-figure compositions, above all the same liveliness and conviction, captured rapidly within the small dimensions of his sketchbook pages.

In addition to his colleagues, many contemporary critics noted this solid foundation of drawing as one of the fundamental hallmarks of Glackens's paintings. "It would be impossible to exaggerate the importance of Glackens's drawings in the development of his power both as an illustrator and painter," wrote Everett Shinn (1876–1953) in a very thoughtful and detailed memoir. "We cannot separate the influence of his line, developed through his drawing, from the body of his painting. For though he used color to build form, he depended on line to give it structure."[15]

Glackens began, as we have said, and like so many of his colleagues—Henri, Sloan, Luks, and later, George Bellows and Edward Hopper, to cite a few—by paying rapt attention to the paintings of Manet, the effect of whose early work was the dominant influence on Glackens's painting style and color until 1908. He then turned his attention to Manet's Impressionist associates and successors. By the early 1900s, Monet, Renoir, Pissarro, Sisley, and their lesser contemporaries— painters such as Raffaëlli, Steinlen, and Forain—had all played an important role in the formation of Glackens's drawing style; all were well known in America. Pissarro, especially, took up themes of bustling figures on the boulevards, seen from the high vantage points of windows, and rendered figures as simplified, even abstracted, units set off by the buildings and avenues of Paris, as well as crowded markets, bridges, and quais in Rouen, Dieppe, and other French locales. Within this Pissarroesque context of generalized and

Fig. 28
Study for *Girl Roller Skating, Washington Square*, c. 1912–14
Sketchbook 640, *New York City 1914*
Charcoal on paper
8¼ × 5⅜ in. (21 × 13.7 cm)
Pennsylvania Academy of the Fine Arts, Philadelphia; Gift of the Sansom Foundation 2008.11.2

Fig. 29
Study for *Girl Roller Skating, Washington Square*, c. 1912–14
Sketchbook 640, *New York City 1914*
Charcoal on paper
8¼ × 5⅜ in. (21 × 13.7 cm)
Pennsylvania Academy of the Fine Arts, Philadelphia; Gift of the Sansom Foundation 2008.11.2

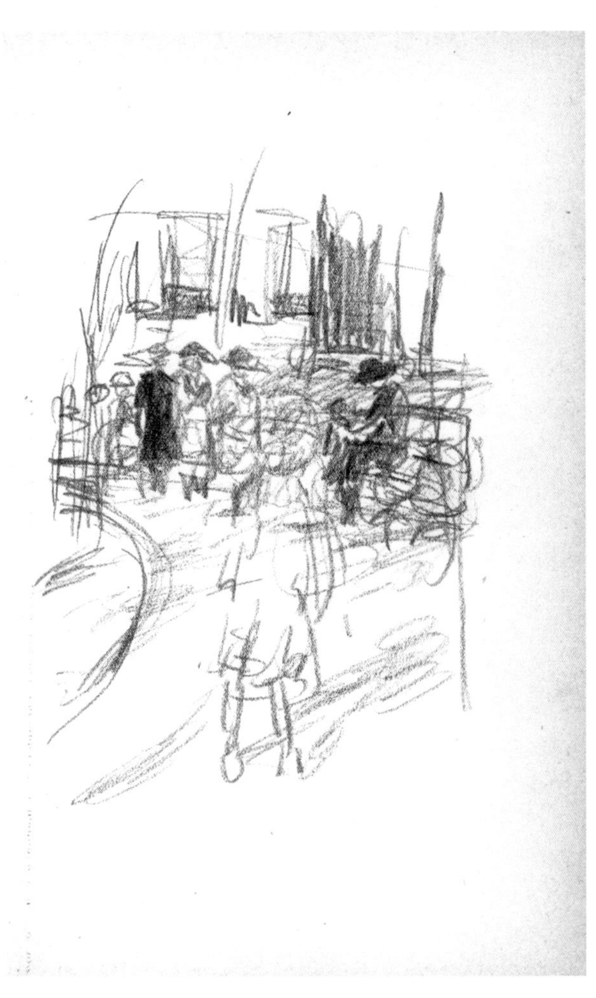

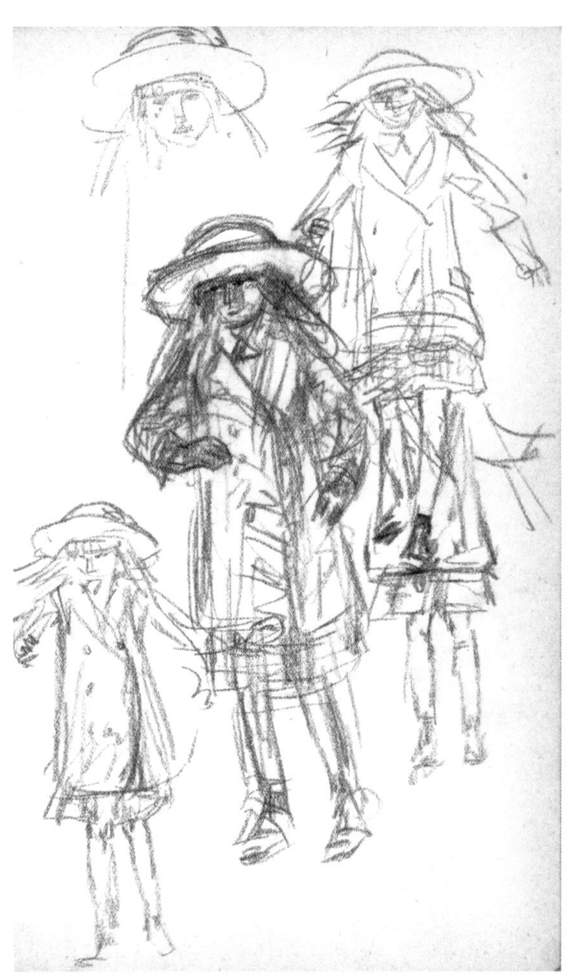

simplified crowds, Glackens introduced groups, figures, and gestures taken from his sketches. Beach scenes are filled with figures that stroll, bend, dive, and swim. His scenes of New York's Central Park and Washington Square—drawings as well as paintings—like the French artist's scenes, are often seen from an elevated vantage point (Glackens's studio on the third floor of a building at 50 Washington Square South looked out on the park) and are peopled with children sledding and skating, jumping rope, roughhousing, riding and falling off their bikes; babysitters wheeling strollers; women alighting from buses, scurrying along, bundled up in the rain, and holding umbrellas; and Italian-American parades celebrating Garibaldi, whose statue in the park is often depicted in Glackens's drawings and paintings.

By 1908 Glackens had completely transformed his style, relinquishing a predominantly dark palette. He paid careful attention to his American contemporaries Ernest Lawson, Maurice Prendergast, Alfred Maurer, and Marsden Hartley, whose work reinforced what ideas he was learning from the French. Guided by their example, he systematically adopted a forthright Impressionist technique. With this deliberate reeducation, Glackens produced his first exclusively Impressionist compositions, adapting to his work the brightness and intensity of color that characterized these new French and American sources. By early 1910 one critic could write that "Mr Glackens, clever man that he is, charming artist when he wants to be, [is now painting] with yet a brand new manner, showing a seashore with bathers and a group of summer visitors. It is fearfully and wonderfully made with splashes of white to indicate boats, with masses of pigment the meaning of which leaves the spectator in great doubt."[16] Two months later, in April 1910, Glackens played an important role in the seminal Exhibition of Independent Artists.

Three years later, the landmark International Exhibition of Modern Art—known as the Armory Show—opened in New York with great fanfare in February 1913. Glackens served as chairman in charge of selections in the American section, and in an interview he gave on American art in the show he remarked with characteristic directness that

> American art is above everything else skillful. American painters and sculptors are technical marvels. . . . Their painting is the kind that wins prizes. But it is not the kind of painting in which one feels that the artist is actually enjoying himself. Indeed, this skill in America is limited, limited by a lack of bravery—a fear of freedom or of honesty. It is a skill enslaved by academies. . . . We have no innovators here. . . . Everything worthwhile in our art is due to the influence of French art. We have not yet arrived at a national art. . . . I am afraid that the American section of this exhibition will seem very tame beside the foreign section. But there is a promise of a renaissance in American art. The signs of it are everywhere. This show coming at the psychological moment is going to do us an enormous amount of good.[17]

Fig. 30
Girl Roller Skating, Washington Square, c. 1912–14
Oil on canvas
24 × 18 in. (60.9 × 45.7 cm)
Brooklyn Museum; Bequest of Laura L. Barnes 67.24.1

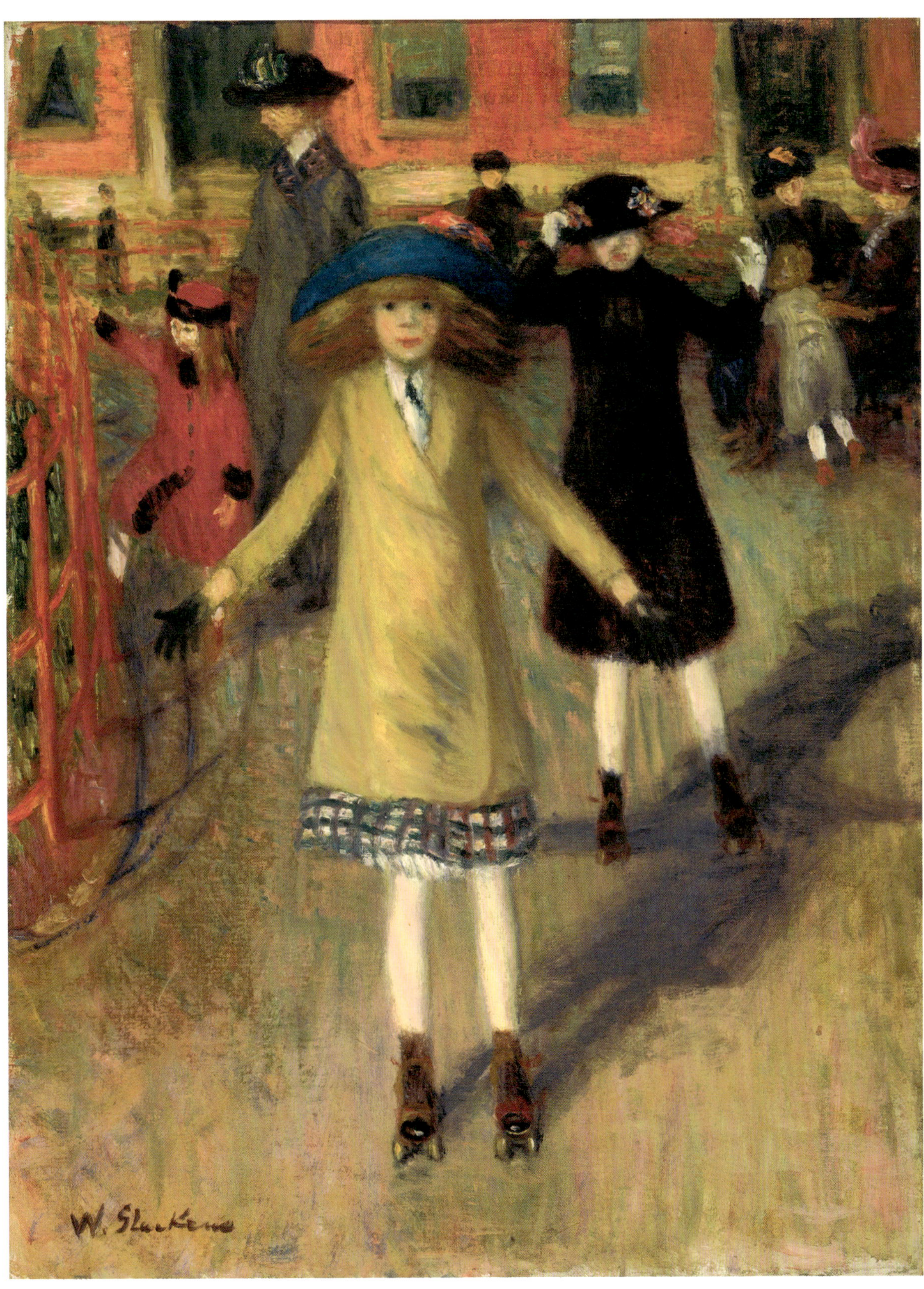
W. Glackens

Fig. 31
Study for *After Bathing: Vacation Home*, 1913
Crayon on paper
8¼ × 5 in. (21 × 12.7 cm)
Museum of Art, Fort Lauderdale, Nova Southeastern University, Florida; Gift of the Sansom Foundation
(Sketchbook 94.99)

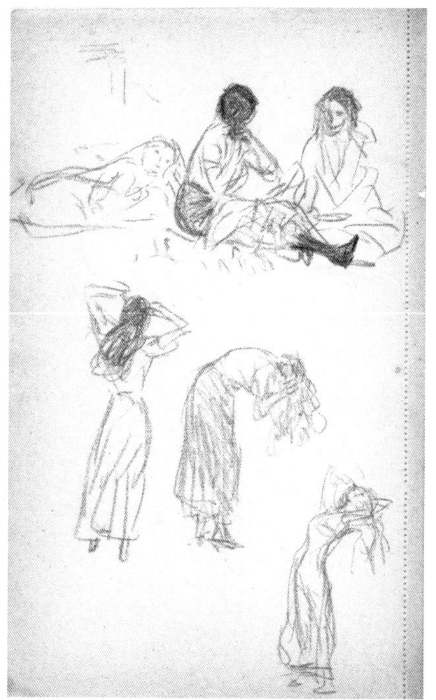

Fig. 32
Study for *After Bathing: Vacation Home*, 1913
Crayon on paper
5 × 8¼ in. (12.7 × 21 cm)
Museum of Art, Fort Lauderdale, Nova Southeastern University, Florida; Gift of the Sansom Foundation
(Sketchbook 94.99)

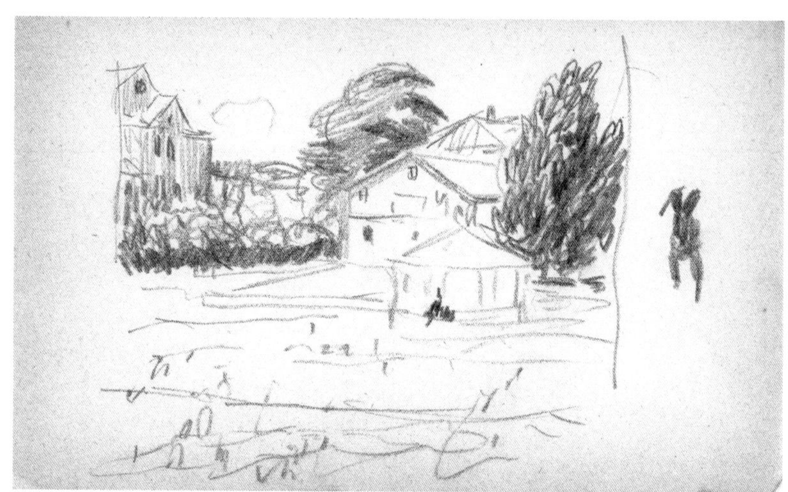

Fig. 33
Study for *After Bathing: Vacation Home*, 1913
Crayon on paper
5 × 8¼ in. (12.7 × 21 cm)
Museum of Art, Fort Lauderdale, Nova Southeastern University, Florida; Gift of the Sansom Foundation
(Sketchbook 94.99)

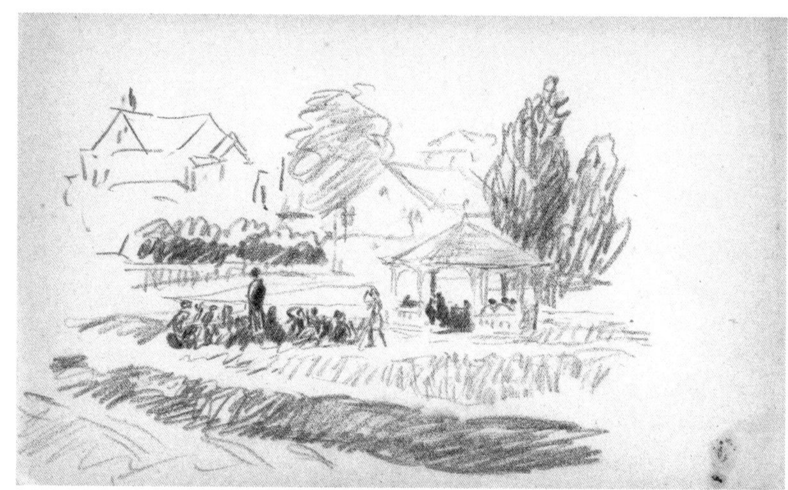

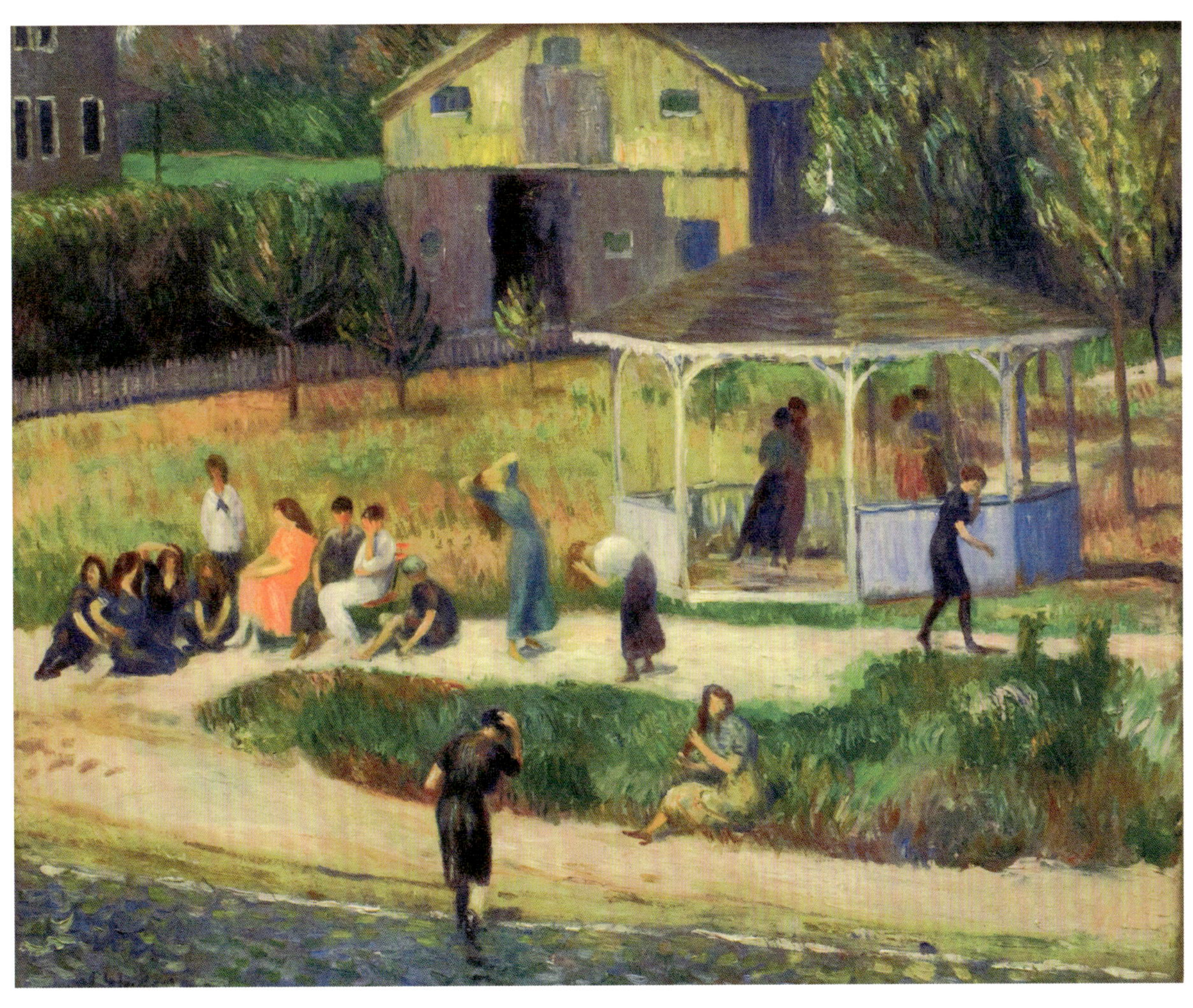

Fig. 34
After Bathing: Vacation Home, 1913
Oil on canvas
26 × 32 in. (66 × 81.3 cm)
The London Collection

Drawings such as *Figure Sketches No. 2* (Fig. 35) typify the kinds of rapid sketches Glackens made on his preferred brown wrapping paper with the black crayon pencil described above by his son and so precisely by his friend Everett Shinn.[18] Glackens frequently placed these sorts of figures of men, women, and children in a horizontal format, striding along in the wind. Others are standing or caught in motion; for example the man in the lower register holding his coat or the girl lower center of the group carrying and balancing on her head a bundle, which serves as a counterpoint to the hats of the other figures. The strokes are crisp shorthand notations that nonetheless bestow a sense of completeness on each individual. At the same time, the arrangement of the drawing's lines as ordered linear elements and the viewpoint from which the various figures are seen give to the twelve ostensibly separate entities an interrelatedness, a compositional unity. This unified design is further enhanced by the artist's control of the intensity and scale of the figures, with their palpable effects of movement back and forth and in and out in space. On either side of the girl, for instance, is a woman, one striding into the distance at her right while the other, on the left, strides purposefully toward us—the emphatic dark units of arms and feet emphasize their motion. Some figures are drawn in heavy black, while others are lightly stroked on the sheet, and our eye moves all over the page, darting from figure to figure without settling definitely anywhere, but responding naturally to the sense of vivid animation that pervades the entire grouping. Compositional linkage among the twelve figures is achieved by this linear patterning, and by the movement up and down by the six figures within each of the two horizontal registers, resulting in a coherent sequence within each register and an overall pictorial unity. All inessential motifs, such as the street, architecture, detailed facial features, and foliage are stripped away; the figures are indicated with the utmost economy, yet we have the unmistakable sense of seeing twelve different characters, caught each on his own, moving along, rather than one figure disposed in different guises. Whatever the sources whose styles he integrated into his own drawings—published illustrations of English graphic artists John Leech, Charles Keene, Phil May, and George du Maurier, work by earlier men such as Goya, Daumier, and engraver Paul Gavarni, known through prints, as well as oriental calligraphy—Glackens's work is always characterized by his own distinctive artistic personality.

One can discern in this selection of drawings from Glackens's sketchbooks a number of features that were fundamental to the artist's working method. Made throughout his career to serve as aide-mémoire while he was working at his easel, these drawings give us a glimpse of how Glackens composed his pictures. For his newspaper and magazine illustrations, Glackens often made multiple versions of drawings until he was satisfied with the final result. In the same way,

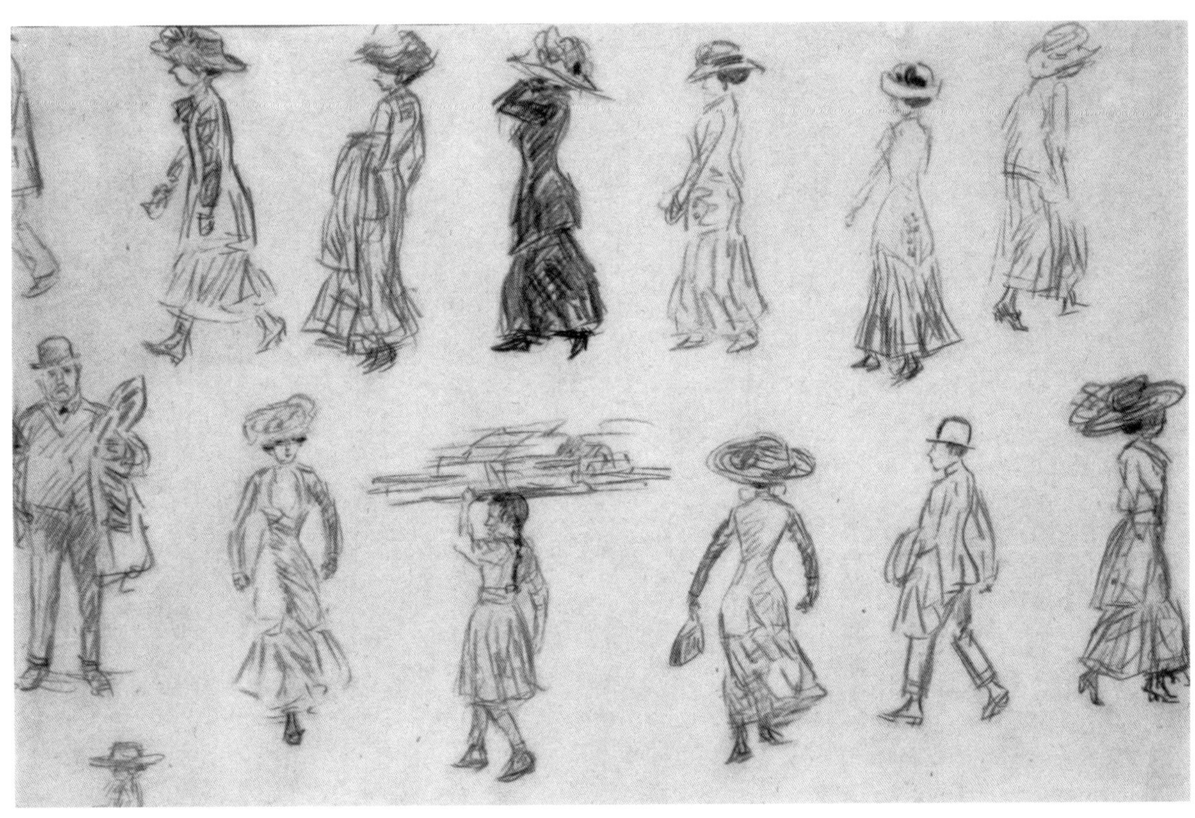

Fig. 35
Figure Sketches No. 2, 1905–10
Crayon on paper
15 × 22¾ in. (38.1 × 57.8 cm)
Smithsonian American Art Museum, Washington, D.C.; Gift of Mr. and Mrs. Ira Glackens 1972.56

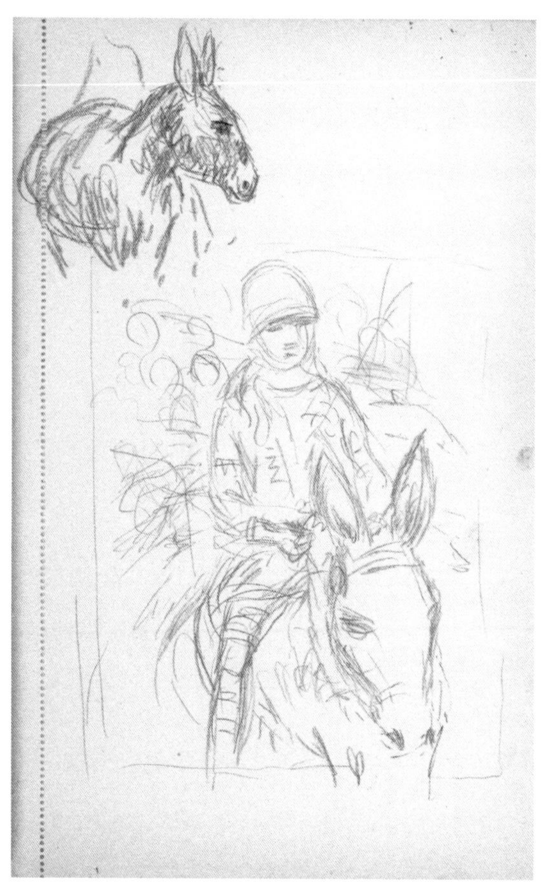

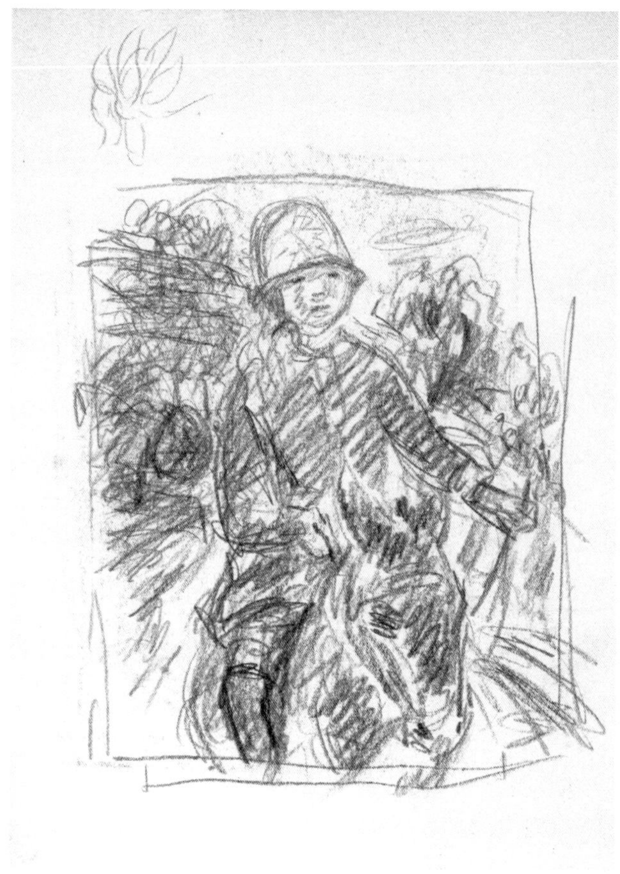

Fig. 36
Study for *The Promenade (Lenna on a Donkey)*, c. 1925
Crayon on paper
9⅛ × 5½ in. (23 × 13.9 cm)
Museum of Art, Fort Lauderdale, Nova Southeastern University, Florida; Gift of the Sansom Foundation (Sketchbook 94.103)

Fig. 37
Study for *The Promenade (Lenna on a Donkey)*, c. 1925
Crayon on paper
9⅛ × 5½ in. (23 × 13.9 cm)
Museum of Art, Fort Lauderdale, Nova Southeastern University, Florida; Gift of the Sansom Foundation (Sketchbook 94.103)

Fig. 38
The Promenade (Lenna on a Donkey), 1927
Oil on canvas
32 × 26 in. (81.3 × 66 cm)
Detroit Institute of Arts; City of Detroit Purchase 30.322

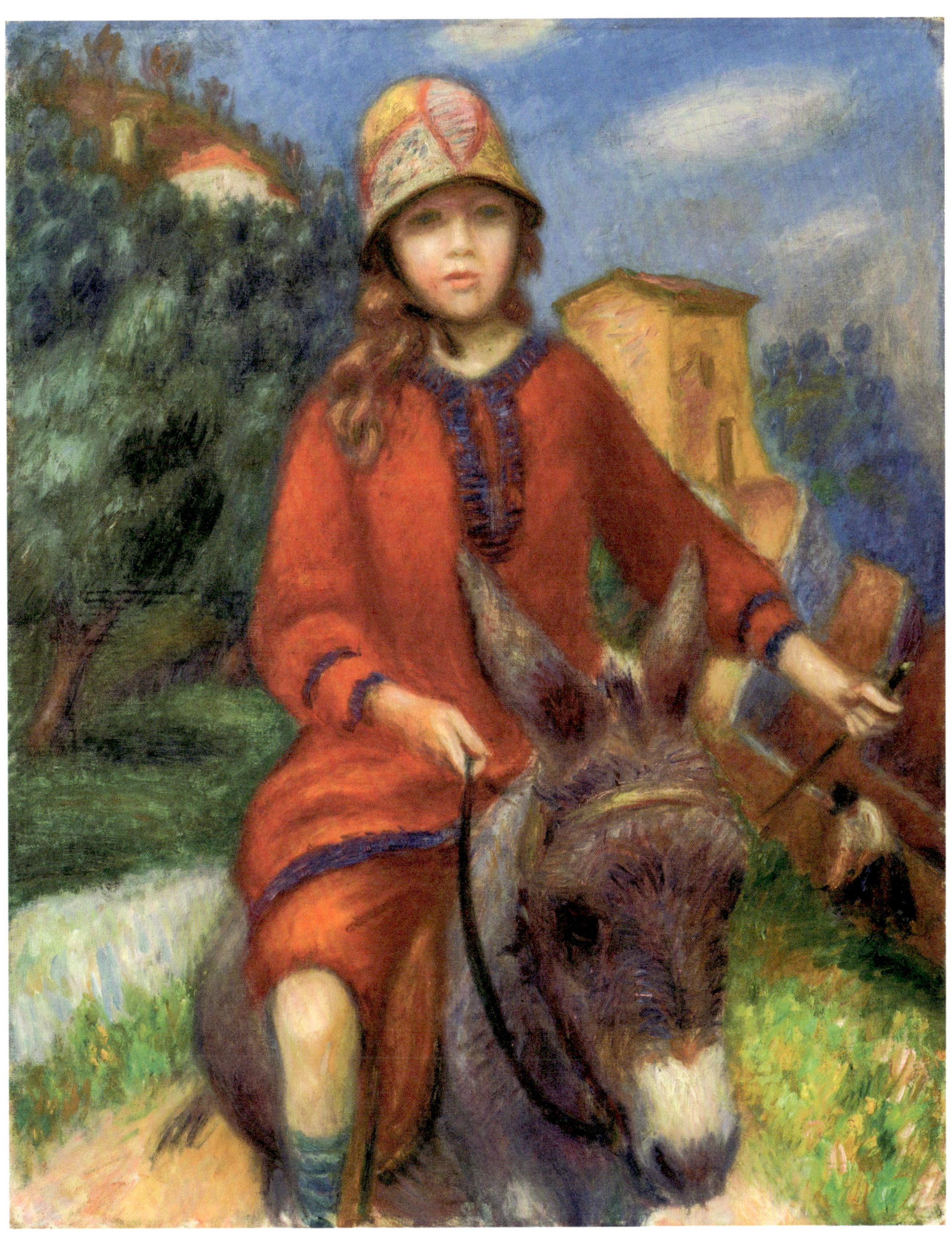

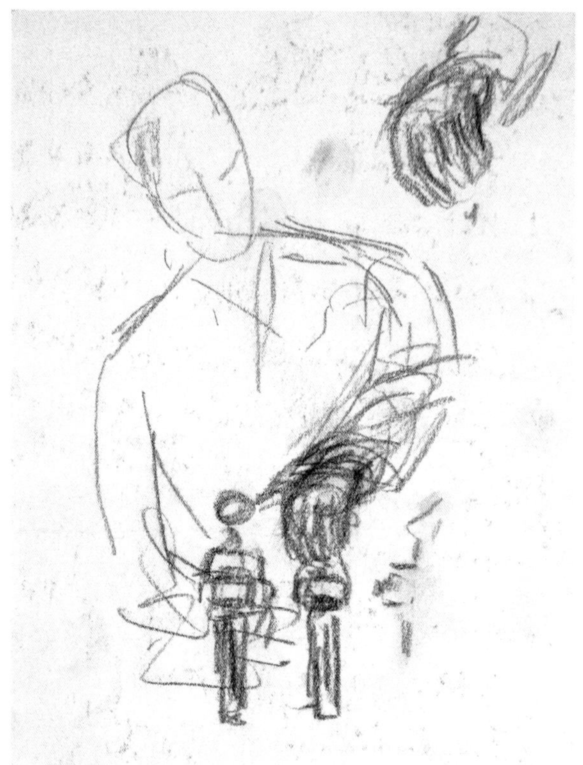

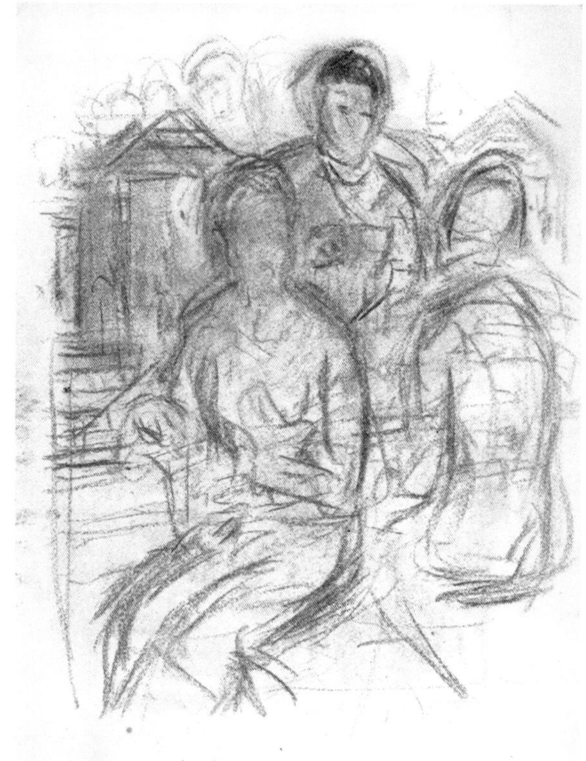

Fig. 39
Study for *The Soda Fountain* (Sketchbook), c. 1933
Carbon pencil on paper
8⅜ × 5⅜ in. (21.3 × 13.7 cm)
Delaware Art Museum, Wilmington; Gift of the Sansom Foundation Inc., 1994

Fig. 40
Study for *The Soda Fountain*, c. 1933
Crayon on paper
9 × 7¼ in. (22.9 × 18.4 cm)
Museum of Art, Fort Lauderdale, Nova Southeastern University, Florida; Gift of the Sansom Foundation (Sketchbook 92.43)

Fig. 41
The Soda Fountain, 1935
Oil on canvas
48 × 36 in. (121.9 × 91.4 cm)
Pennsylvania Academy of the Fine Arts, Philadelphia; Joseph E. Temple and Henry D. Gilpin Funds 1955.3

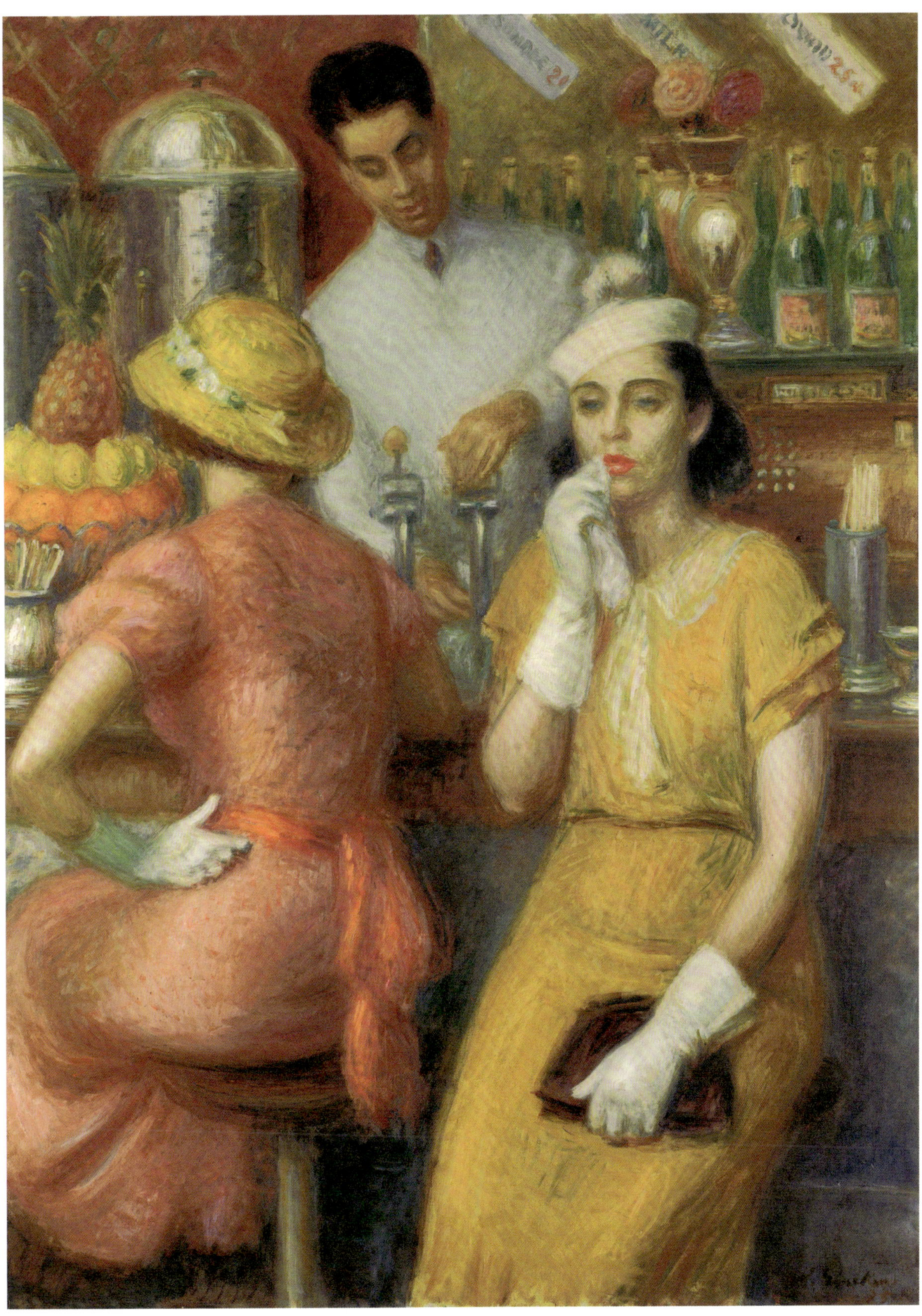
MILK

when the drawings were intended to capture a figure and scene for use in one of his paintings, he would make numerous studies—sometimes as many as twenty—often in different sketchbooks. (He used whichever one he was carrying in his pocket at the time.) Many of the drawings that accompany this essay have figures that are directly transferred, in the medium of color, to the paintings whose first conception they adumbrate.

The sketchbooks document clearly how careful and persistent Glackens was when developing a composition that was to contain many elements. There was nothing casual about his approach to picture making; Glackens was intensely self-critical and applied himself to his objective with tireless industry. In contrast, he made relatively few drawings for his single-figure paintings, preferring to start them by painting directly from his model.

In his oil paintings Glackens's color evinces, by means of its own sparkle and vivacity, the inimitable joy of life that was unmistakably his. There is an intense illumination in his mature work that enlivens the succinct, distilled fact-description of the drawings by means of small, exotic color patches. In the course of his career, Glackens's color ensembles reveal an increasing fluidity of paint handling, the progressive subtlety and spontaneity of his drawing with color, and the harmoniousness of his compositional placement and distribution of colors. William Glackens's sustained growth as an artist constitutes an example of an American painter with a distinctly personal outlook, whose insights were intensified both by direct observation of his surroundings and by the discriminating assimilation of American and European sources. His sketchbook studies are essential to the full understanding of his creative development.

The original publication of "The Sketchbook Studies of William Glackens," in the *Archives of American Art Journal* 44, nos. 1–2 (2004), pp. 1–47, was accompanied by reproductions of twenty paintings and fifty-two drawing studies. Subsequent to that article, the author published *American Paintings and Works on Paper in the Barnes Foundation* (Merion, Pa.: The Barnes Foundation in association with Yale University Press, 2010), in which thirty-four sketchbook studies for fourteen of the seventy-one works by Glackens in the collection of the Barnes Foundation were reproduced.

NOTES

Epigraph: Walter Pach, "William J. Glackens: Master of Color," *Shadowland* 7 (October 1922), p. 76.

1. Ira Glackens, "By Way of Background," in Janet A. Flint, *Drawings by William Glackens, 1870–1938*, exh. cat.(Washington, D.C.: National Collection of Fine Arts, Smithsonian Institution, 1972), unpaginated. See Everett Shinn, "William Glackens as an Illustrator," *American Artist* 9, no. 9 (November 1945), pp. 22–27, 37, for a detailed description of Glackens's technique. "Glackens used a variety of media for his drawing. While engaged in newspaper illustration, he developed a strong line in pen and ink, made more subtle in later years by the substitution of a fine, pointed sable brush for the steel pen. When he began to do magazine illustration [in 1897], the halftone process was available to him. For his tonal work he used wash and tempera, charcoal and carbon pencil, and, sometimes, mixed methods in which all of these appear in one drawing. Red chalk, which he discovered in Paris, was another favorite medium and one he favored for nude studies. Drybrush accounted for some of his finest drawings, especially those made for illustrations. Straight graphite pencil was not a sympathetic medium for him, as he much preferred the rich blacks of the carbon pencil or the elastic range of good charcoal. Watercolor and pastel were used to accent his drawings to give sparkle to some of his illustrations marked for black and white reproduction. The color instinct of the painter was constantly asserting itself.

   "One method used by Glackens, seldom encountered today, is the making of a drawing in blue pencil preliminary to a pen and ink rendering. In many of his pen drawings the presence of this framework in blue may be detected. The blue preliminary provided a basis which was sometimes followed closely in the black ink rendering and, at other times, served merely as a general guide. Blue lines "drop out" in the engraver's negative, leaving the black pen lines sharp and crisp, unsoftened by such erasures as is necessary when graphite is used for preliminary layout.

   "Like most artists, Glackens employed many papers, but he had two favorites. The wrapping paper found in grocery shops in the old days had a beautiful surface for drawing, especially for carbon and chalk. The other was wallpaper sample books. Some of his best drawings in red chalk were done on the backs of these warm-toned papers, that possessed just the right "tooth" for his rapid strokes—No. 2946 Wall, and No. 2947 Border, lie under some of his masterpieces" (pp. 27, 37).

   Shinn is authoritative because he also used the same wallpaper samples for many of his own drawings. What Ira Glackens described as a laundry marking pencil, a DIXON No. 4, corresponds to the carbon pencil described by Shinn.

2. See Nancy E. Allyn, "The Illustrations of William Glackens," in *William Glackens: Illustrator in New York, 1897–1919*, exh. cat. (Wilmington: Delaware Art Museum, 1985), pp. 7–13; and Nancy E. Allyn and Elizabeth H. Hawkes, *William Glackens: A Catalogue of His Book and Magazine Illustrations* (Wilmington: Delaware Art Museum, 1987).
3. "Artists of the Philadelphia Press: George Luks, Everett Shinn, John Sloan," exh. cat., *Philadelphia Museum Bulletin* 41, no. 207 (November 1945), pp. 7–8. In "Life on the Press," his remembrance for the same exhibition catalogue, Everett Shinn recalled: "They carried envelopes, menu cards, scraps of paper, laundry checks and rendered bills or frequently nothing to their work. Glackens, least of all of them, needed pencil and paper. His memory was amazing. . . . One look on an assignment was much the same to him as taking an exhaustive book of that incident from a shelf where at his drawing board he opened it and translated it into pen lines" (p. 9). Contrary to what some commentators have mistakenly claimed, Glackens never used his gift in support of social causes. In 1910 A. E. Gallatin wrote: "His drawings fairly reek with character and his wonderfully expressive line records types in such a truthful and farseeing manner, his penetrating gaze sees so far beneath the surface of things, that we can only marvel at the simple manner in which he attains his ends. The genius for instantly seizing upon the essentials of human make-up . . . with a few rapid strokes of his joyously spontaneous pencil he is able to record unmistakably some type. . . . The subjects which appeal most to Glackens, and the scenes which he is the happiest in depicting, are found in the same slums, mean streets and parks in which Degas finds his inspiration . . . only they are in the proper quarters of New York. . . . But the great difference between Degas and Glackens is that where the former too often seeks for the ugly and repulsive, the painfully sordid, the ultra prosaic, the latter looks only for what gaiety and humor he may discover in the scene. And Glackens is none the less a faithful recorder, an unflinching realist, because his sympathetic pencil is never dipped in gall, as in the case of the brutal brush of the cynic Degas." A. E. Gallatin, "The Art of William J. Glackens: A Note," *The International Studio* 40, no. 159 (May 1910), p. lxviii.
4. The aspiring younger man had his canvases accepted in the annual Academy exhibitions. For example, Glackens entered three canvases in the 64th Annual Exhibition of the Pennsylvania Academy of the Fine Arts: *The Brooklyn Bridge* ($200); *The Cathedral* ($200); and *Portrait* ($250). He listed his address on the entry form as 1717 Chestnut Street, Philadelphia (collection of The Princeton University Art Museum). See Richard J. Wattenmaker, *The Art of William Glackens*, exh. cat. (New Brunswick: University Art Gallery, Rutgers, The State University of New Jersey, 1967), p. 19, cat. no. 87.
5. John Sloan, *Notes*, p. 129. These unpublished notes (1950) for an autobiography are part of the John Sloan Manuscript Collection, Helen Farr Sloan Library and Archives, Delaware Art Museum, Wilmington (hereinafter Sloan, *Notes*).
6. Sloan, *Notes*, p. 50.
7. Sloan, *Notes*, p. 150.
8. Glackens to "Miss Smith" [a friend], September 7, 1895. (This and all subsequent letters from Glackens to Miss Smith, courtesy of Kraushaar Galleries, New York.)
9. Glackens to Miss Smith, November 25 [1894], written from 1717 Chestnut Street, Philadelphia, a studio he shared with Henri. Both Manets were donated in 1889 to the Metropolitan Museum of Art by Erwin Davis. See Charles Sterling and Margaretta Salinger, *French Paintings: A Catalogue of the Collection of The Metropolitan Museum of Art*, vol. 3, *XIX-XX Centuries* (New York: The

Metropolitan Museum of Art, 1967), pp. 30–33, 40–42: *A Boy with a Sword* (1861), inv. 89.21.2, and *Woman with a Parrot* (1866), inv. 89.21.3.

10. See Françoise Cachin and Charles S. Moffett, *Manet: 1832–1883*, exh. cat. (New York: The Metropolitan Museum of Art, 1983), pp. 122–26, 537. See also Walter Pach, "Manet and Modern American Art," *The Craftsman* 17, no. 3 (February 1910), pp. 483–92. "As Edouard Manet saw the life of the Parisian café of his time, or of the French capital, represented in the 'Music in the Tuileries' [National Gallery, London], so William J. Glackens has given us documents of American life in his significant series of pictures, the 'May-Day' [*May Day in Central Park*, c.1905, The Fine Arts Museums of San Francisco], 'At Mouquin's,' 1905 [The Art Institute of Chicago]" (p. 483). This observation is borne out by Glackens's remark in his above-mentioned letter of September 7, 1895, "The Paris Cafes are a never ending source of inspiration to me. The parks at St. Cloud, Suresne and Charenton, all pleasure resorts along the Seine are intensely interesting on Sundays when the French people abandon themselves to the picnic habit."
11. Glackens to Miss Smith, September 7, 1895.
12. Glackens to Miss Smith from Paris, undated but postmarked December 1895. Glackens held firm negative views of all art academies and often expressed these to journalists. See, e.g., his interview with Regina Armstrong, "The New Leaders in American Illustration, IV," *The Bookman* 11 (May 1900), pp. 246–49.
13. Charles FitzGerald, "The Society of American Artists," *New York Evening Sun*, April 3, 1903, p. 6. FitzGerald was subsequently to become a close friend and Glackens's brother-in-law. FitzGerald had been writing perceptively about the artist's work since 1901. See Ira Glackens, *William Glackens and the Ashcan Group: The Emergence of Realism in American Art* (New York: Crown Publishers, 1957), pp. 29–30, 56.
14. Sloan, *Notes*, p. 139.
15. Shinn, "Glackens as Illustrator," pp. 27, 37.
16. Arthur Hoeber, "Art and Artists," *New York Globe and Commercial Advertiser*, February 7, 1910.
17. Guy Pène du Bois, "The American Section, The National Art: An Interview with the Chairman of the Domestic Committee, Wm. J. Glackens," in the special exhibition number of *Arts and Decoration* 3, no. 5 (March 1913), pp. 159–64. Glackens gave the interview to the painter-journalist as part of the publicity campaign for the event.
18. Shinn, "Glackens as Illustrator," p. 37.

The Origins of the Barnes Collection, 1912–15

COLIN B. BAILEY

Lecture given on May 24, 2006

National Academy Museum and School of Fine Arts

New York City

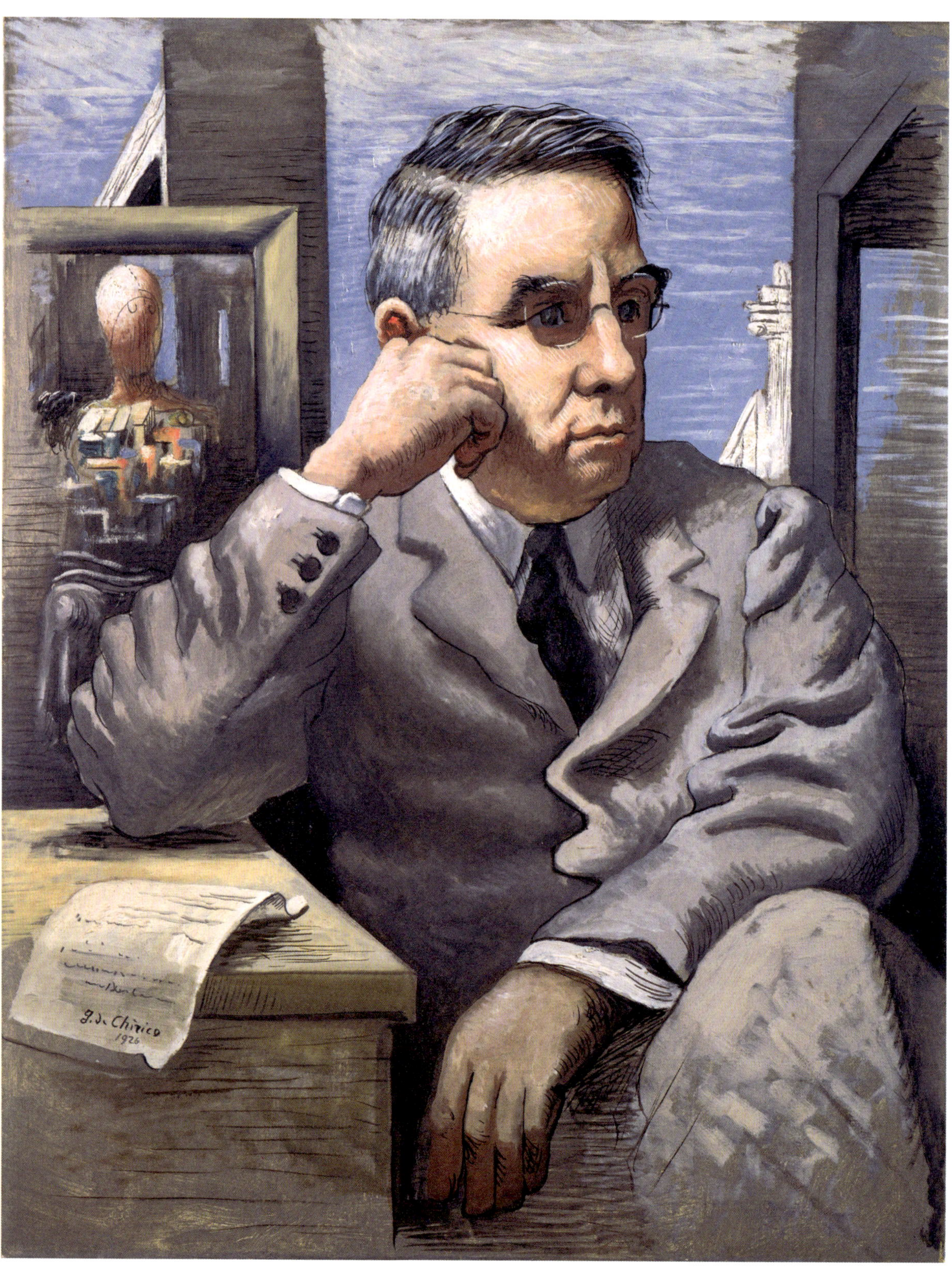
G. d. Chirico
1926

The Origins of the Barnes Collection, 1912–15

COLIN B. BAILEY

Almost since its inception, the Barnes Foundation has been more a subject of controversy than of objective scholarship. This staggering collection of nineteenth- and twentieth-century French painting was best known—not for Cézanne's late *Bathers* (1900–05), Seurat's *Models* (1886–88), or Matisse's *Joy of Life* (1905–06)—but for the eccentric, pugnacious (and at times, repugnant) behavior of its founder, Albert Coombes Barnes (1872–1951). The former restrictions on access to the collection, located some fifteen miles outside Philadelphia in Merion, Pennsylvania, and for a long time open only on weekends, as well as prohibitions not merely of loans, but even of color reproductions, have helped reinforce the isolation of the Barnes Foundation. Who but its former director could have written the article "The Lure and Trap of Color Slides in Art Education: The Time-Released Venom of Their Make Believe"?[1] These restrictions and prohibitions have also allowed the cult of Barnes's personality to become the dominant issue in most accounts of his collection. "The Terrible Tempered Dr. Barnes"; "The Devil and Dr. Barnes"; "Art Held Hostage"; such titles reveal the tenor of most discussions.[2] But it is not the intention here to canonize the founder of this collection or to transform the irascible Medici of Merion into a venerable Saint Albert. Rather, by building on the two fine introductory essays by Richard Wattenmaker and Anne Distel in the catalogue *Great French Paintings from the Barnes Foundation* (1993), and Mary Ann Meyers's excellent recent biography, *Art, Education, and African-American Culture: Albert Barnes and the Science of Philanthropy* (2004), this essay focuses "microscopically" on the years between 1912 and 1915, during which Barnes's taste for modern art was formed. By examining how Barnes went about acquiring his pictures, whom he used as advisors, which writers may have guided his appreciation, and which other collectors offered inspiration, it becomes possible to place the man's truly pioneering activity as a collector in a historical and cultural context. Barnes's achievement during these early years is all the

Fig. 42
Giorgio de Chirico
Dr. Albert C. Barnes, 1926
Oil on canvas
36½ × 29 in. (92.7 × 73.7 cm)
The Barnes Foundation, Merion, Pennsylvania

more impressive when the influences that shaped his aesthetic are given appropriate consideration.

The chronology of Barnes's collecting in the period from 1910 to 1920 has been well documented. After making several unexceptional purchases at auction in New York early in 1912,[3] in February of that year Barnes sent his childhood friend, the Ashcan School painter William Glackens (1870–1938)—or Butts, as he called him—to Paris with $20,000 to buy modern art. Glackens brought back fine paintings by Van Gogh, Renoir, Cézanne, Picasso, Monet, and Sisley, and Barnes was launched.[4] In late May and December of the same year, Barnes himself would go on two more buying trips to Paris.[5] Through his exposure to the Impressionists and Post-Impressionists in dealers' galleries, the sales room, and through conversations with collectors and artists, Barnes developed nothing less than a passion for Renoir—whom he considered the greatest of all painters—and for Cézanne; a strong interest in early Picasso; and an admiration, rather guarded at this point, for Matisse. Back home at Overbrook, Pennsylvania, Barnes remained committed to progressive independents among the Americans—he regularly acquired paintings by Glackens, Alfred Maurer, Ernest Lawson, and Maurice Prendergast—and he immersed himself in the comparatively meager art historical literature and criticism dealing with the modern movement. In an impassioned letter of January 1915 to the aging Philadelphia lawyer and collector John Grover Johnson (1841–1917), Barnes stated: "For over three years I've given more time and effort in trying to find out what is a good painting than I've ever given to any other subject in my life."[6]

From very early on there were certain limitations to Barnes's taste. He wrote that he was attracted above all by "quality in a painting, by pure paint, unmixed with flipness, chicness, or virtuosity of brushing."[7] While we would not be surprised to learn that he showed no interest in conventional or academic painting, he was also suspicious of Impressionism: the visitor to Merion will find very few landscapes by Monet, Sisley, or Pissarro in the Barnes Foundation. Furthermore, and notwithstanding Thomas Hart Benton's recollection that Barnes was "well informed about what was going on in the field of modern experiment,"[8] he was adamantly opposed to the most advanced movements in contemporary art: Cubism, Futurism, and Synchromism. Barnes railed against "the extremists of the modern movement" for compromising the Armory Show of 1913, to which he had refused to lend and which he considered "a promoter's adventure backed by organized capital."[9] In a rather emotional article published in January 1916, Barnes delivered a funeral oration for Cubism, an art form that denied painting its natural vocabulary—the "elements of representation"—and had severed painting's fundamental attachment to the "concrete object."[10] With a philistinism worthy of the most conventional critic, Barnes illustrated Marcel Duchamp's *Nude*

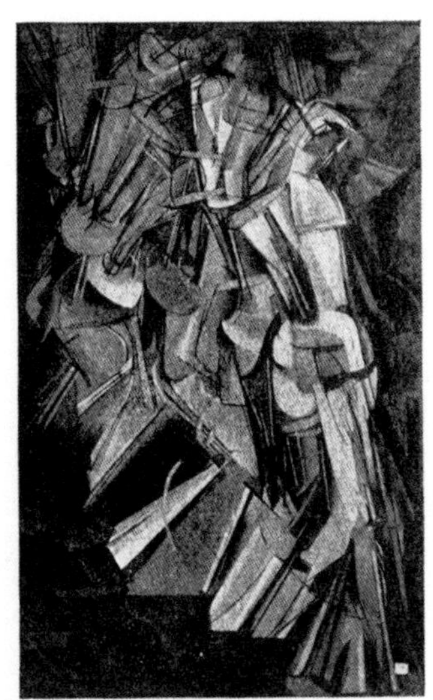

Fig. 43
Illustration of Duchamp's *Nude Descending a Staircase* with Barnes's caption, "Cows Eating Oysters," *Arts and Decoration* (Jan. 1916), p. 123
The Barnes Foundation Archives, Merion, Pennsylvania

Descending a Staircase (1911; Philadelphia Museum of Art) with the title "Cows Eating Oysters" (Fig. 43). He was never able to forgive Picasso, whose genius as an artist was not at issue, for having led a younger generation astray with his abstractions.[11] Barnes, who might have been expected to admire Picasso's neoclassical paintings of the 1920s, saw nothing in this new style except a facile "virtuosity."[12] It should be noted that nearly all of the forty-four paintings and drawings by Picasso in the Barnes collection date to before 1908.

If, during the 1920s, Barnes continued to purchase the works of Renoir and Cézanne—and to a lesser extent Seurat and Picasso—the most important development in that decade was his interest in Matisse. Only after he established relations with the young dealer Paul Guillaume did the work of Matisse come to be so magnificently represented in his collection.[13] In August 1922 Barnes acquired his first panel from the *Three Sisters Triptych* (1907); in December of that year, *The Joy of Life* (1905–06); the following year (1923) saw the arrival of the *Music Lesson* (1917); and in January 1925, four masterpieces, including the *Red Madras Headdress* of 1907 and the *Seated Riffian* of 1912.[14] It is worth pointing out that Barnes had known several of these paintings for over a decade: *The Joy of Life* had belonged to his great friend Leo Stein, in whose apartment he would have seen it in 1912 and 1913; and the *Red Madras Headdress*, owned by Leo's brother and sister-in-law, Michael and Sarah Stein, had come to America in February 1913 for the Armory Show.[15] If Barnes had been unsure of Matisse as a worthy successor to Renoir and Cézanne in the 1910s, he showed no such hesitation in the following decade, when it became clear that Matisse was the single progressive contemporary French painter of stature to work within the colorist, figural tradition that meant so much to him.

The aesthetic coherence that the Barnes collection had assumed by the 1920s was established in the previous decade, and it was one from which Barnes by and large did not deviate. He collected works by Renoir and Cézanne above all, and by Picasso and Matisse selectively; the former between 1901 and 1907, the latter from his Fauve period to the early years at Nice. Only sporadically did he acquire paintings by Van Gogh, Manet, Degas, and Seurat. In the 1920s, with Guillaume's encouragement, Barnes would flirt with other moderns: the *douanier* Rousseau, who had died in 1910; Amedeo Modigliani, whose work Barnes acquired after his death in 1917; and Chaim Soutine, the one living European artist Barnes may be said to have "promoted."[16] But the pillars of his collection remained unchanged: "A great danger that I feel is threatening me," Barnes had confided to Leo Stein as early as July 1914, "is to make my collection either a one, two, or three men affair. I fear the narrowing effect upon my general development."[17] How Barnes came to his "four men affair" and who guided him in his "general development" is the central subject of this essay.

Fig. 44
Albert C. Barnes and William Glackens, c. 1920
Photograph Collection, The Barnes Foundation Archives, Merion, Pennsylvania

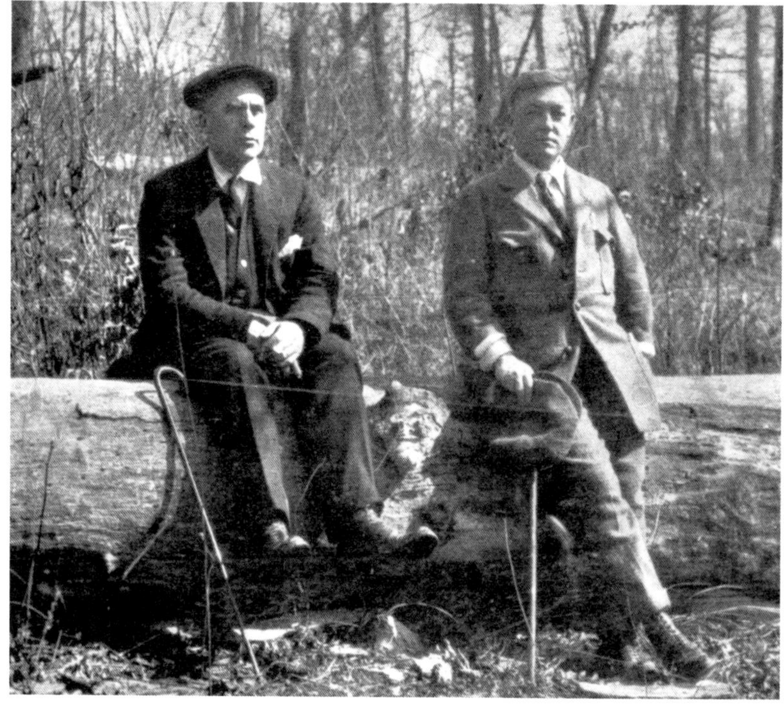

In nearly all accounts of how Barnes formed his collection, the painter William Glackens is given a principal role (Fig. 44). Glackens, two years older than Barnes, had been a classmate of his at Philadelphia's prestigious Central High School, where the teenagers met in 1888 and formed a friendship based on their shared interest in drawing and baseball. In his book *Gist of Art*, the painter John Sloan, another classmate from Central, went so far as to credit Glackens with acquiring "the nucleus of the A.C. Barnes collection of modern pictures."[18] Sloan has Glackens respond to Barnes's boast that he had just spent thousands of dollars in acquiring paintings from the best dealers in New York and Philadelphia with the singeing riposte, "I know what you have. A couple of Millets, red heads by Henner, a Diaz, and fuzzy Corots. They are just stinging you as they do everybody who has money to spend."[19]

As is well known, Glackens made impressive purchases for Barnes in February 1912, and in June of that year Barnes sent a list of these purchases to his lawyer, John G. Johnson, noting that these had been acquired "after studying the matter in collections from various books, with the aid and advice of a life-long friend, who is an artist."[20] In January 1914 it was in Glackens's company that Dr. and Mrs. Barnes first saw the Havemeyer collection in New York,[21] and the following year Barnes publicly acknowledged that "his frequent associations with a life-long friend who combines greatness as an artist with a big man's mind" had been "the most valuable single educational factor" in his appreciation of art.[22]

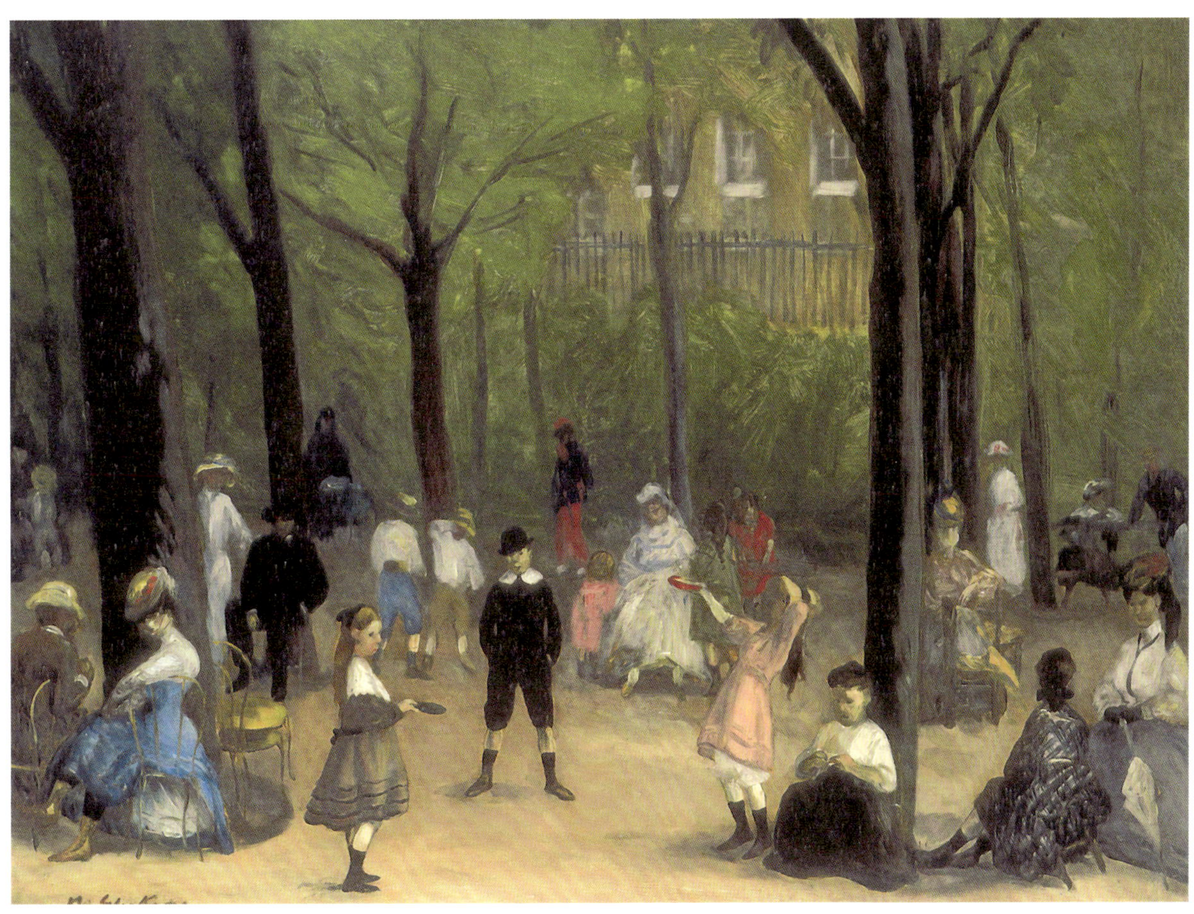

Fig. 45
William Glackens
Luxembourg Gardens, 1906
Oil on canvas
23⅜ × 32⅛ in. (59.4 × 81.6 cm)
Corcoran Gallery of Art,
Washington, D.C.; Museum Purchase,
William A. Clark Fund 37.1

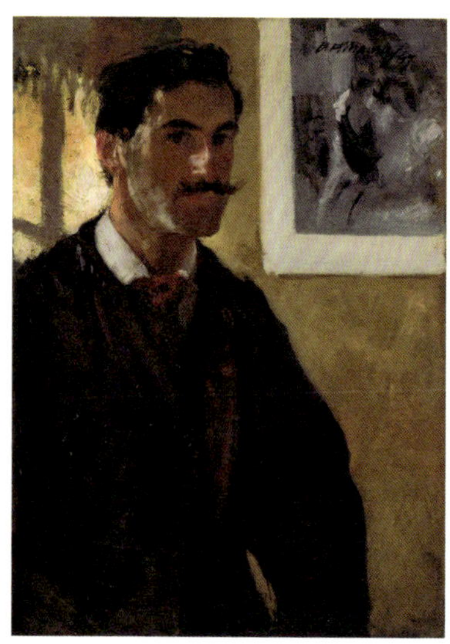

Fig. 46
Alfred Maurer
Self-Portrait, 1897
Oil on canvas
28¾ × 21 in. (73 × 53.3 cm)
Frederick R. Weisman Art Museum at the University of Minnesota, Minneapolis; Gift of Ione and Hudson D. Walker 1953.301

In a life full of strained and broken friendships, Barnes's steadfast affection for Glackens stands as a welcome and all too rare instance of his humanity. Until the end, his admiration for the man and the painter remained undiminished: "I loved Butts as I never loved but half a dozen people in my lifetime," he wrote to Glackens's widow in June 1938; "He was so real, and so gentle, and of a character I would have given millions to possess."[23] Yet it is the case that Barnes's collection exerted a stronger influence on the formation of the painter Glackens than did Glackens on the formation of the Barnes collection. And the most cogent evidence for this is Glackens's work itself, which by 1914 had undergone a profound change (Fig. 45, 47). As sympathetic critics noted, the art of this "lineal descendant" of Manet and Degas had been transformed by his "intelligent study of Renoir."[24] It was at precisely this time that Barnes began to buy late works by Renoir for his collection.

Glackens made only one shopping trip to Paris for Barnes and it fairly exhausted him. Accompanying Glackens in February 1912, and bringing him, almost as soon as their boat docked, to the house of "a Mr. Stein, who collects Renoir, Matisse, etc,"[25] was the "old timer" Alfred Maurer (1868–1932) [Fig. 46]—a former award-winning pupil of William Merritt Chase who had moved to Paris in 1897, and who, around 1910, had abandoned his irreproachable realist manner for a freedom and brightness of form inspired by the Fauves.[26] "Alfy," a good friend of both Leo and Gertrude Stein, was deeply committed to the latest tendencies of modern art in Paris. It was Maurer who introduced the organizers of the Armory Show to the dealer Ambroise Vollard, and it was Maurer who brought collectors such as Sergei Shchukin to the Steins' apartment to see the latest work of Matisse and Picasso.[27] Gertrude Stein claimed, incorrectly, that it was also Maurer who "had selected the first lot of pictures for the famed Barnes collection."[28] Maurer does deserve credit, however, for bringing Barnes to the Steins' apartment on the rue de Fleurus and exclaiming, "So help me God I didn't bring him!" as Barnes started waving his checkbook at Gertrude and chasing her around the dinner table in his eagerness to acquire Picasso's portrait of her, painted six years earlier (Fig. 49).[29]

Maurer's role as Barnes's agent in Paris for the years 1912 and 1913 has been largely overlooked, but research in the Barnes Foundation Archives confirms the importance that Gertrude Stein so eagerly assigned him.[30] After Barnes's first buying trip to Paris in late May 1912, Maurer was informally employed by him both to seek out and vet pictures for the collection and to work with contacts and politicians to overcome the French government's resistance to Argyrol, the silver-nitrate compound used to prevent blindness in newborn infants that was the source of Barnes's fortune.[31] Maurer visited dealers, had photographs sent to Barnes, and encouraged purchases of

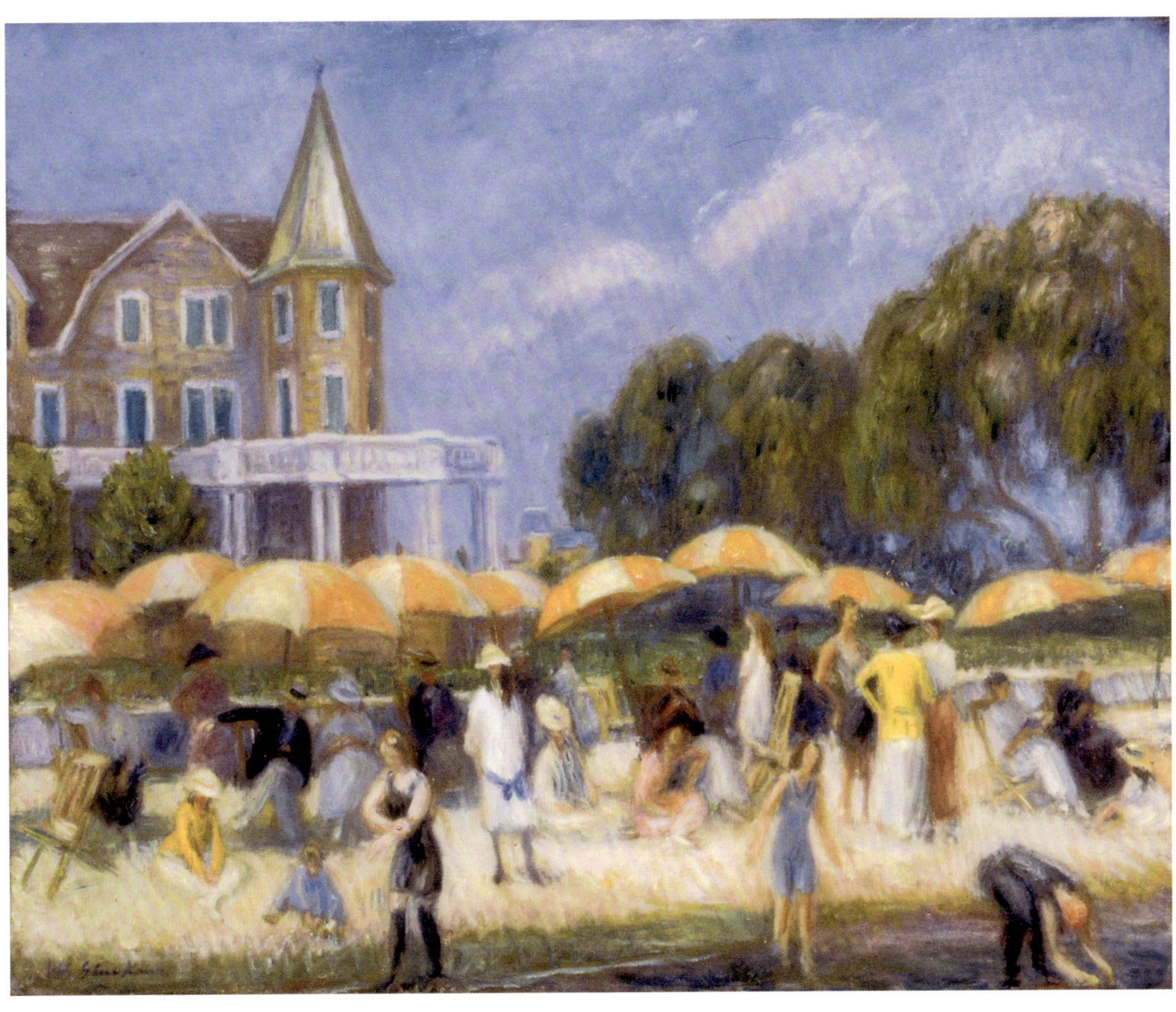

Fig. 47
William Glackens
Beach Umbrellas at Blue Point, c. 1915
Oil on canvas
26 × 32 in. (66.1 × 81.3 cm)
Smithsonian American Art Museum,
Washington, D.C.; Gift of Mr. and Mrs.
Ira Glackens 1968.1

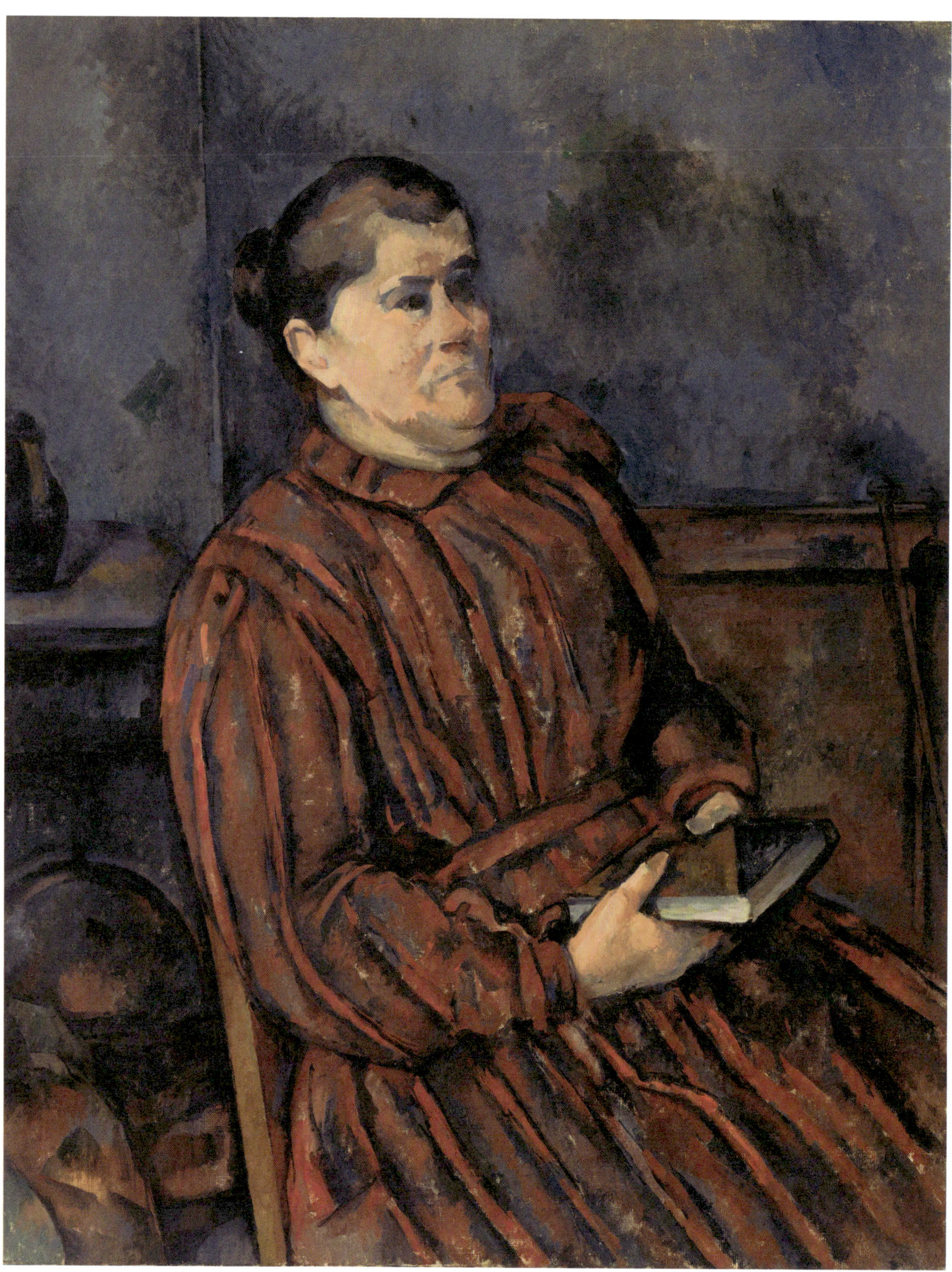

Fig. 49
Pablo Picasso
Gertrude Stein, 1905–06
Oil on canvas
39⅜ × 32 in. (100 × 81.3 cm)
The Metropolitan Museum of Art, New York; Bequest of Gertrude Stein, 1946

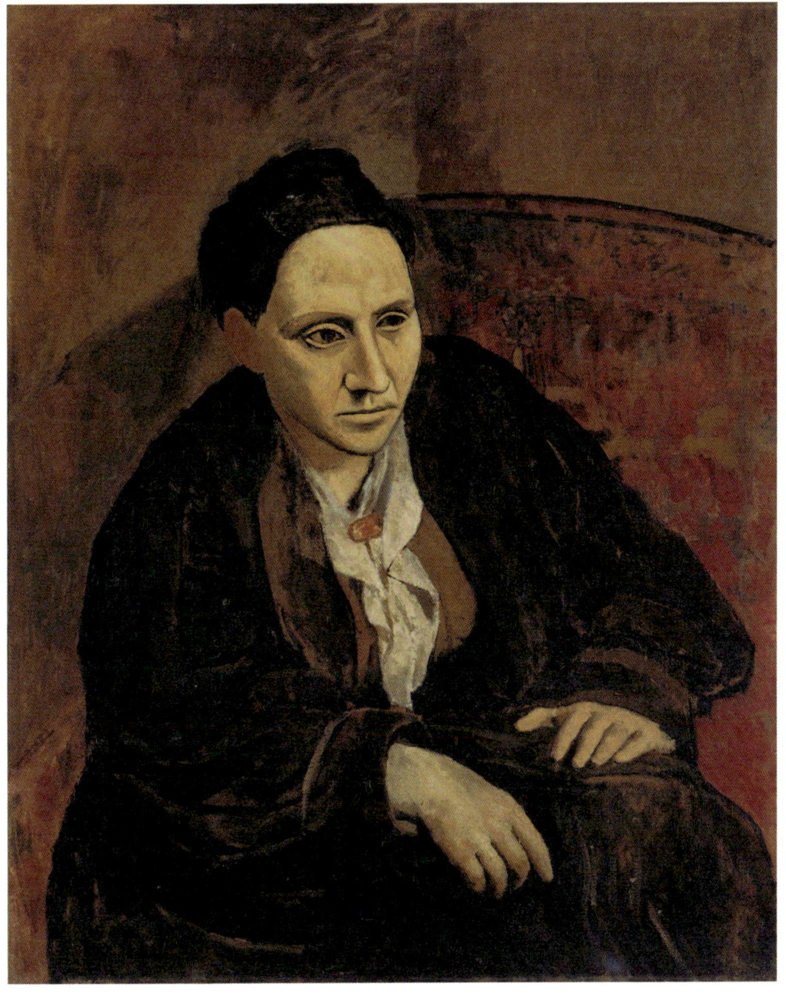

works by Van Gogh, Cézanne, and Renoir.[32] In September and October of 1912 Maurer was responsible for bringing Cézanne's *Woman in a Red-Striped Dress* (*Portrait of a Woman*; Fig. 48) to Barnes's attention, enthusing, "it's as Cézanne as Cézanne can be," and later assuring Barnes that it had "all the qualities of the best Cézanne."[33] Due to Vollard's absolute refusal to send pictures to America on approval—and Barnes's determination never to pay for any work of art before it was safely in his hands—the deal for the *Woman in a Red-Striped Dress* almost foundered: "They are all worse than horse dealers!" wrote an exasperated Maurer in August 1912.[34] It was largely thanks to Maurer's persistence that this painting finally arrived in Merion in April 1915, and it was initially Maurer, and not Barnes, who fully grasped its tough beauty. When it had seemed that negotiations between Barnes and Vollard were at an end, Barnes, in part not to lose face, wrote: "The Cézanne woman is such an unpleasing subject that I shall have to give up the idea of purchasing it and wait for a good still life by the same painter."[35]

Fig. 48
Paul Cézanne
Portrait of a Woman (Portrait de femme), c. 1898
Oil on canvas
36¾ × 28⅞ in. (93.3 × 73.3 cm)
The Barnes Foundation, Merion, Pennsylvania

Maurer may also have been partly responsible for nurturing what would become Barnes's almost religious devotion to Renoir's late work, which was just then beginning to be seen in exhibitions in Paris. "Take a look at some of Renoir's latest things, the very red ones," he wrote to Barnes in November 1912; "Some of them are fine and it's time to buy them."[36] In March of the following year, Maurer reported on Bernheim-Jeune's exhibition of Renoir's late nudes (Fig. 50) with much enthusiasm, noting that a number of these "late things were fine beyond description."[37]

Maurer's advocacy of Renoir's late works in 1912, coupled with Barnes's avidity for them, particularly the bathers and nudes, introduces the role that art criticism and modernist theory may have played in helping to shape Barnes's taste. Barnes tended to dismiss all scholarship in art history and theory as "sentimentalism and antiquarianism sheltered under the cloak of academic prestige," claiming on more than one occasion that "books fail."[38] Early on, at least, he was a voracious student, and he confided in Leo Stein in July 1914, "I have been reading and thinking so damn much about art during the past three years that it has almost become an obsession . . . I have conscientiously read every book on art that has been published during the last few years, from Berenson to Clive Bell's latest."[39] "When he finishes reading a book, the margins are often black with notes," reported the *New Yorker* in September 1928.[40] In the years in which he was forming his collection, Barnes read writers on aesthetics who promoted modern art, and progressive critics who charted an alternative tradition in which certain old masters—El Greco, Velázquez, Rembrandt, and Watteau—as well as the greatest artists of the nineteenth century—Delacroix, Courbet, Manet, Degas, Cézanne, Renoir—appeared as forefathers of the modern movement. Writers such as Julius Meier-Graefe, Clive Bell, Roger Fry, and the young American Willard Huntington Wright expounded new theories of "plastic expression," "significant form," and "design and distortion," which Barnes later appropriated, developed, or discarded in his own writing.[41]

Two themes articulated in modernist aesthetics have obvious implications for Barnes's collecting. First, Bell's "bad science of Claude Monet."[42] For the writers noted above, Impressionism was viewed as an important but transitional movement whose contribution was to have created a new vocabulary of forms and a heightened awareness of the potentialities of color. Impressionism was criticized even by those sympathetic to it for its "excessive accomplishment"[43]—or less politely in the writings of Clive Bell for its "absurd notions of scientific representation."[44] From the vantage point of the 1890s, Impressionism had been too much concerned with the "rapid noting of illusive appearance."[45] As Matisse noted in 1908, "Monet and Sisley had delicate, vibrating sensations; quite close to each other, as a result their canvases are all alike."[46] Impressionism had been

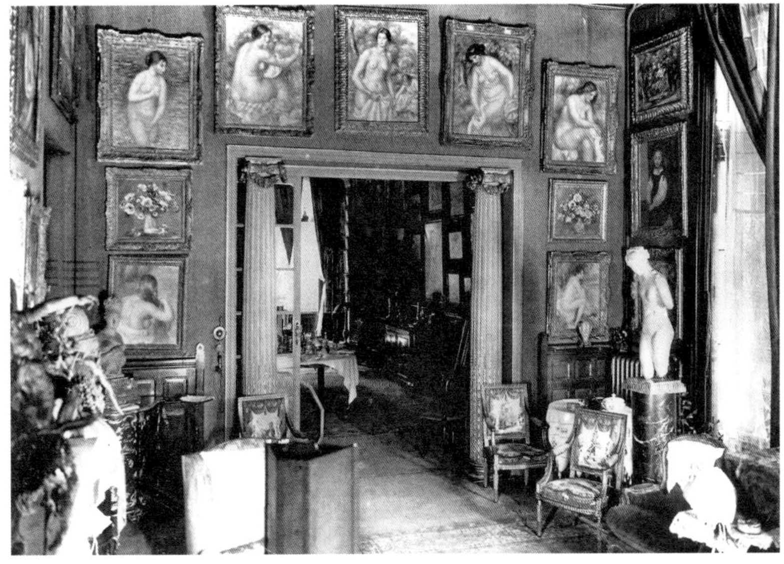

Fig. 50
Collection of Josse and Gaston Bernheim-Jeune at the Bernheim hôtel, 107 Avenue Henri-Martin, Paris, in 1924

too little concerned with structure, form, and composition. Predictably, Barnes was loath to embrace this new orthodoxy completely: "From Impressionism," he claimed, "all that is best in contemporary painting has been developed."[47] Yet he remained skeptical of what he called "the obviousness of [Impressionist] technique," seeing "formula or mannerism" in Impressionist landscapes, and arguing that Monet "falls victim to an interest . . . more photographic than plastic."[48] In his own writings, Barnes came to espouse the party line on Impressionism as a "mere device," harnessed by Renoir and Cézanne for greater ends. The prevailing anti-Impressionist consensus among the advocates of modern art helps explain the scarcity of Monet's work in the Barnes collection—and the absence of Impressionist landscape in general. *Madame Monet Embroidering* (Fig. 51), purchased by Barnes in April 1912, is, after all, among Monet's most Renoiresque compositions.[49] A landscape by Sisley that Glackens had included in his first consignment for Barnes was returned to dealer Joseph Durand-Ruel within the year.[50]

But what of Renoir and Cézanne, the two artists who, according to Barnes, had "left an enriched record of what humanity sees and feels,"[51] and had "created a world richer, fuller, and more meaningful than is revealed to our own unaided perceptions"— the highest goal of painting, present or past?[52] By 1912, it was already something of a cliché to view Cézanne as the father of modern art, and so Barnes was being deliberately provocative when he wrote that Cézanne remained an Impressionist throughout his career.[53] But since the Salon d'Automne of 1904, in which Renoir and Cézanne had each been honored with his own retrospective exhibition, Renoir had also acquired the status of a modern classic, whose genius was most fully engaged, it was claimed, in his recent work. "At the beginning of the present century," Barnes would write in 1925, "Renoir had reached the full control of his powers, and thereafter he deepened and enriched his color-values. . . . In everything he painted there is a more convincing massiveness, and a more powerful three-dimensional rhythm. . . . He left his preceptors constantly further behind, and attained by his own technique to much of the classic spirit of the best Renaissance painting."[54] This view—that Renoir's powers had increased with age—would gain little general acceptance today, but it was an article of faith for artists and critics committed to the progressive and the experimental on the eve of the First World War. Roger Fry, who had purchased Renoir's *Madame Charpentier and Her Children* (1878) for the Metropolitan Museum in 1907, commended the last decade of Renoir's œuvre for "its efflorescence of creative power"; the artist's late nudes were the "consummate realization of plastic relief with the fullest possible intensity of color."[55] Clive Bell stated as axiomatic that since 1900 Renoir had produced works of "completely realized and exquisitely related forms," which far surpassed "even the masterpieces of his middle age."[56] Willard Huntington Wright, whose *Modern Painting: Its Tendency and Meaning* of 1915 both excited and infuriated Barnes,[57] claimed that Renoir had been obliged to abandon the meager aesthetic of Impressionism before he could attain his true stature. *The Bathers* of the late 1880s showed a "greater plenitude of bulging form . . . a purer rhythm" than any work of the previous decade. Wright singled out Renoir's *Bather and Maid* (Fig. 52), which he may have seen at Bernheim-Jeune, as "more extended and conclusive than any of his previous works."[58] Matisse and Picasso—"North Pole, South Pole"—thrilled equally to late Renoir.[59] Matisse may have been influenced by the *Bather and Maid* in *La Coiffure* of 1907 (Staatsgalerie, Stuttgart).[60] And as a young man, Picasso much admired the voluptuous handling of form and color in Renoir's work of the 1890s and early 1900s, an enthusiasm not shared by John Richardson, his present-day biographer, who is frankly mystified by Picasso's preference for the "bloated pink goddesses of Renoir's old age."[61]

Barnes's choices as a collector can thus be seen as broadly consistent with an emerging orthodoxy of modernism—one that was also hostile to Cubism, since with the exception of Wright, whose brother was the Synchromist painter Stanton Macdonald-Wright, none of the other writers mentioned here were initially sympathetic to the movement. For all its popularity today, Impressionism was clearly a secondary consideration for Barnes. In March 1913 a rather desperate Joseph Durand-Ruel urged the collector "to talk to Renoir about Claude Monet and ask his opinion. You would see that Renoir considers Claude Monet the greatest landscape painter of modern times and that his admiration is so great that he cannot even bear discussion of the matter. He places him infinitely above all others, including

Fig. 51
Claude Monet
Madame Monet Embroidering (Camille au métier), 1875
Oil on canvas
25¾ × 22 in. (65.4 × 55.9 cm)
The Barnes Foundation, Merion, Pennsylvania

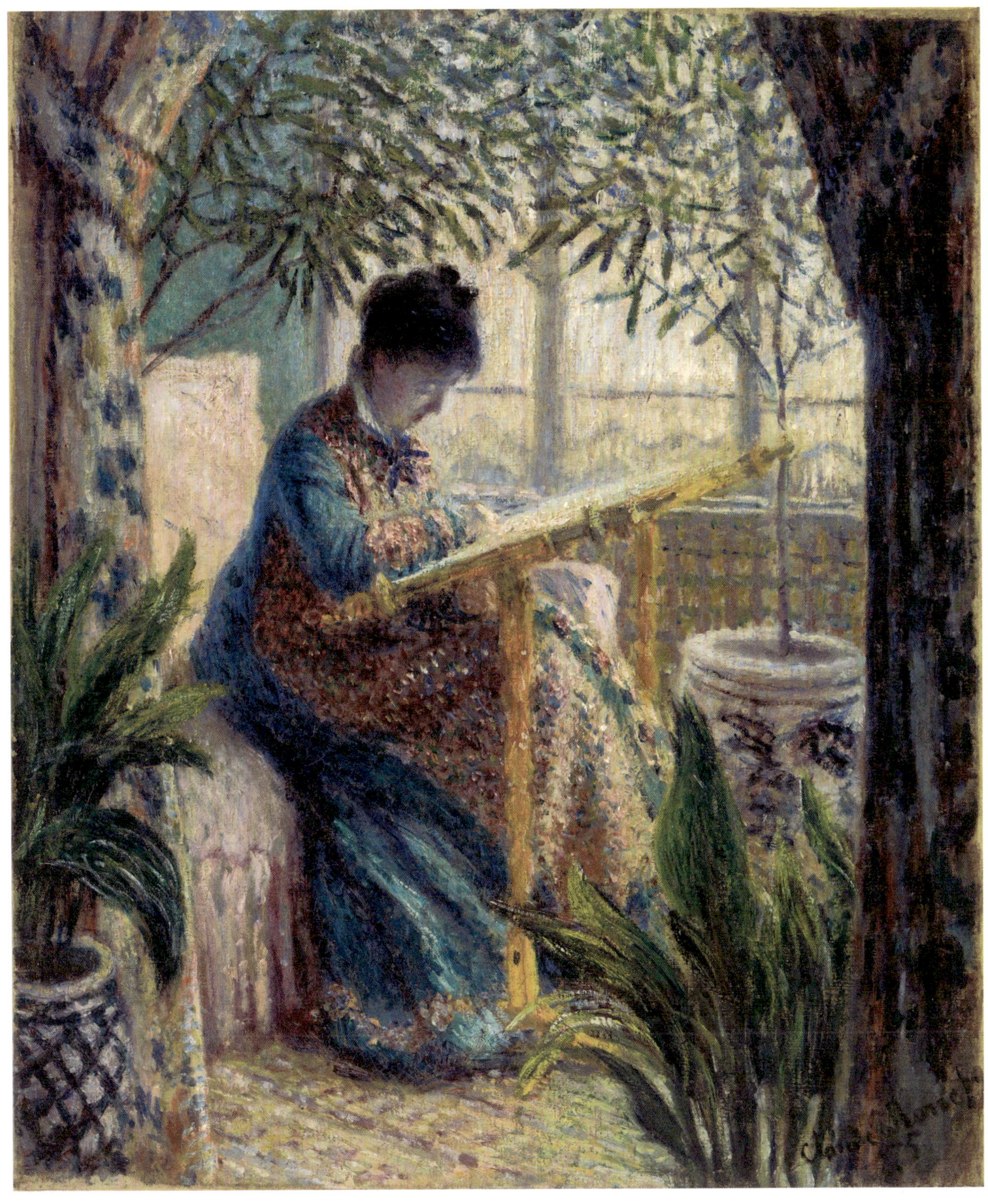

Cézanne."[62] Renoir and Cézanne, jointly the fathers of modern art, take their place as the principal figures in Barnes's collection, because of their perceived classicism, their concern for equilibrium, structure, and composition—with Renoir represented in all periods, but with a marked preference for the late work.

In this context, then, Barnes's taste begins to appear less idiosyncratic or eccentric than is often assumed. His choices, while not consciously predetermined by a specific agenda or ideology, are at least explicable within certain theories of modern art that were in general circulation in the first decades of the twentieth century. A narrower focus allows us to examine more microscopically Barnes's advocacy of the modern movement and his activity as a collector.

How did Barnes, living and working in Philadelphia, gain acquaintance with the major figures of late nineteenth-century French painting? At the outset, in the spring of 1912, Barnes could not easily turn for instruction to existing collections, either public or private. The Metropolitan Museum acquired its first Cézanne only in March 1913, after the Armory Show;[63] the Philadelphia Museum of Art was not installed in Horace Trumbauer's Greek temple overlooking the Schuylkill River until November 1928, and the Museum of Modern Art was not founded until a year later. In April 1915 Barnes would praise the Havemeyer collection as "the best and wisest collection in America," with its "large number of paintings by the men that make up the greatest movement in the entire history of art—the Frenchmen of about 1860 and later, whose work is so richly expressive of life that means most to the normal man alive today."[64] But we also know that he first saw this collection only in the months after January 1914, at a time when his own taste was already formed.[65] Of course, one alternative to looking was reading and, as already noted, Barnes read voraciously. Among the books whose influence he grudgingly recognized, one at least provided him with both practical and philosophical guidance, guidance that he was quite happy to exploit, but less keen to acknowledge.

"With a volume of Meier-Graeffe [*sic*] in my lap and a Cézanne, Van Gogh, or Bonnard propped on a chair," he wrote in 1915, "I have spent months in wading through his verbosity and froth hoping for a ray from it to reflect upon the painting . . ."[66] In 1908 a two-volume translation of the German critic's *Entwicklungsgeschichte der modernen Kunst*, first published in three volumes in 1904, had appeared under the title *Modern Art: Being a Contribution to a New System of Aesthetics*. In April 1912 Barnes, who could read German easily, purchased a copy of this translation from Brentano's bookstore in New York.[67] Despite his unkind reference to the writer's "wordy foam," he granted Meier-Graefe his infectious enthusiasm: "It makes the reader want to learn for himself what the author so joyously sets forth."[68] Meier-Graefe championed the French artists who came to

Fig. 52
Pierre-Auguste Renoir
Bather and Maid (La Toilette de la baigneuse), 1900–01
Oil on canvas
57⅜ × 38½ in. (145.7 × 97.8 cm)
The Barnes Foundation, Merion, Pennsylvania

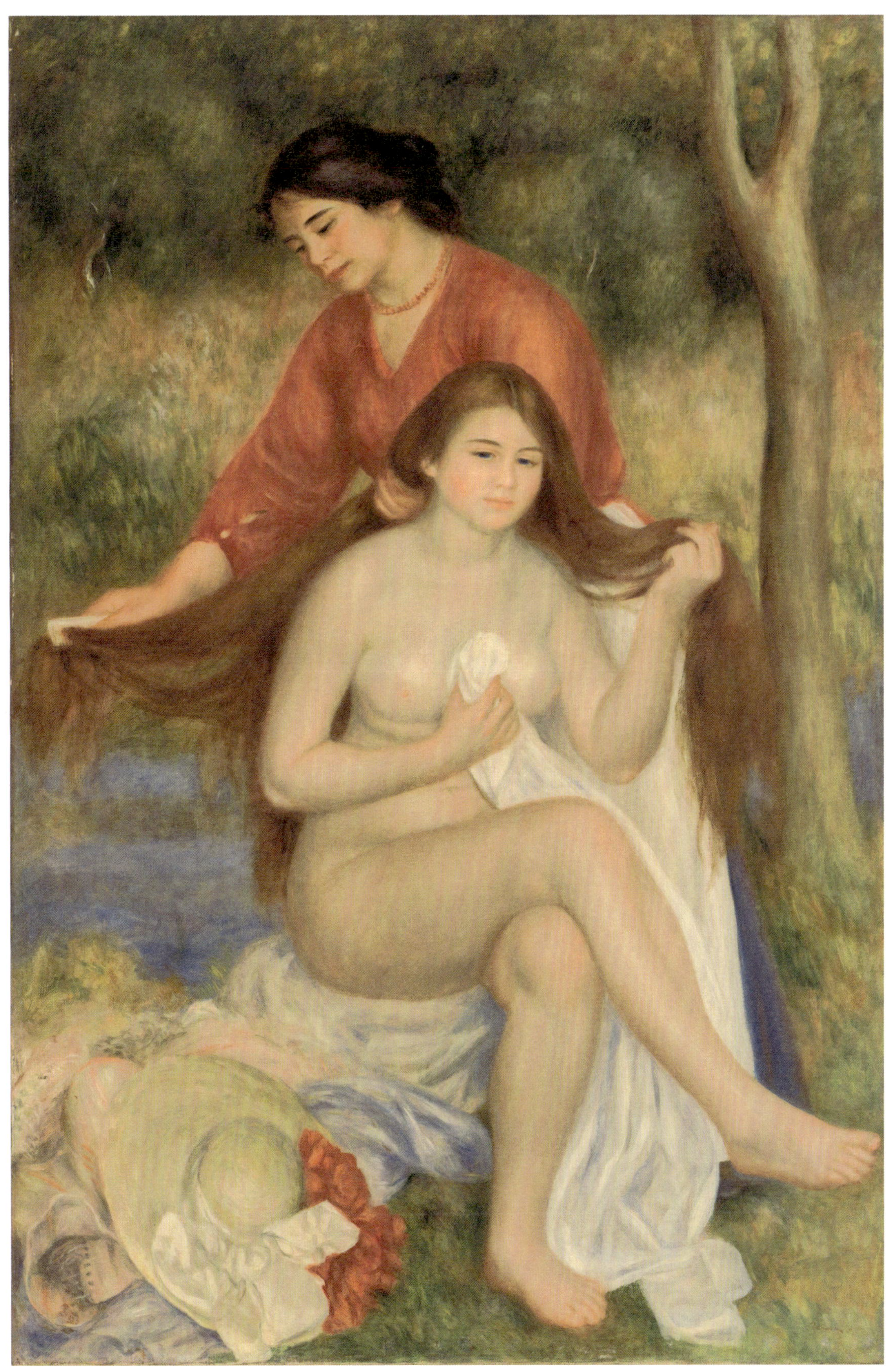

mean so much to Barnes, and whose work Barnes had already started acquiring—literally in the two months before—thanks to Glackens and the Durand-Ruel family.[69] While we cannot credit Meier-Graefe with shaping the Barnes collection, his book can be shown to have been responsible for certain acquisitions, and this throws some light on one of the ways in which Barnes identified paintings for his collection.

Although Meier-Graefe, like Barnes, viewed Manet, Degas, Renoir, and Cézanne as the pillars of the modern movement, he had an overriding passion for Van Gogh. With true feeling Meier-Graefe claimed, "Van Gogh's was animal art, if we so may express it, because it is always absolutely vital, because it is power, and power is always beauty."[70] Not only did Barnes respond to this kind of energetic appraisal, he also noted quite carefully when Meier-Graefe listed works that had not yet entered public collections, and were therefore potentially for sale. Meier-Graefe was particularly impressed by *The Ravine* (Fig. 53), which he considered to be Van Gogh's "masterpiece." "Its intoxicating harmony of rich blue tones" made the painting "a technical model of incalculable value."[71] Barnes must have alerted Maurer to this painting and it was offered to him in the summer of 1912 for 45,000 francs (about $9,000)—"way, way too much" in Maurer's opinion.[72] The picture eventually arrived in Merion in October 1912, and Barnes paid the more acceptable figure of 23,000 francs ($4,430). "While it is the weirdest thing I ever saw," Barnes wrote to Maurer, "I like it."[73]

Thus had Meier-Graefe succeeded in fanning the flame for Van Gogh—it should be remembered that Glackens had returned from Paris in March 1912 with *Joseph-Étienne Roulin*, the finest Van Gogh Barnes would acquire—and in October 1912 Barnes sent the dealer Roger Levesque de Blives a list of pictures by Van Gogh in private collections that he wanted to acquire, each one cited and discussed in Meier-Graefe's chapter on the artist.[74] When Barnes asked Levesque to check into the availability of "two Van Goghs of sulphur-colored houses with deep blue rooves and light blue smoke surrounded with woods of purple red trees"—then in the collection of the critic Théodore Duret—his unusually lyrical description was not merely a flight of fancy: Barnes was copying word for word the description of these works as it appeared in Meier-Graefe's *Modern Art*.[75]

There is a rather touching naiveté in Barnes's assumption that private collections noted in Meier-Graefe's survey could be mined in this way, and it can be shown that he was happy to take his leads however they presented themselves. In his chapter on Renoir, Meier-Graefe had followed the by now rather commonplace stratagem of comparing the French painter to old masters such as Rubens and Hals. In a striking juxtaposition, Meier-Graefe illustrated Renoir's relatively recent *Bathers in the Forest* of 1897 with Fragonard's celebrated

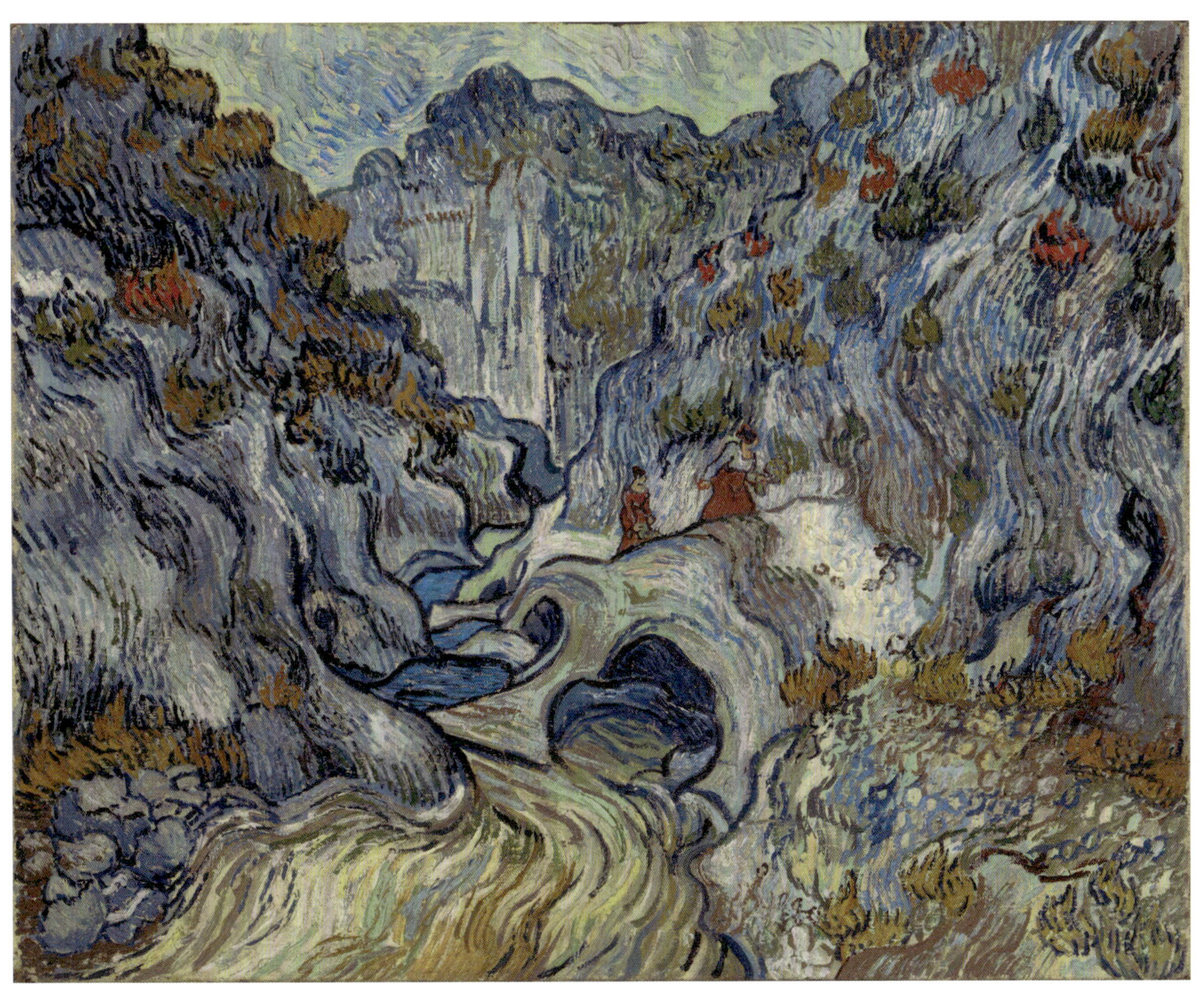

Fig. 53
Vincent Van Gogh
The Ravine, 1889
Oil on canvas
28⅞ × 36¾ in. (73.2 × 93.3 cm)
Kröller-Müller Museum, Otterloo,
The Netherlands

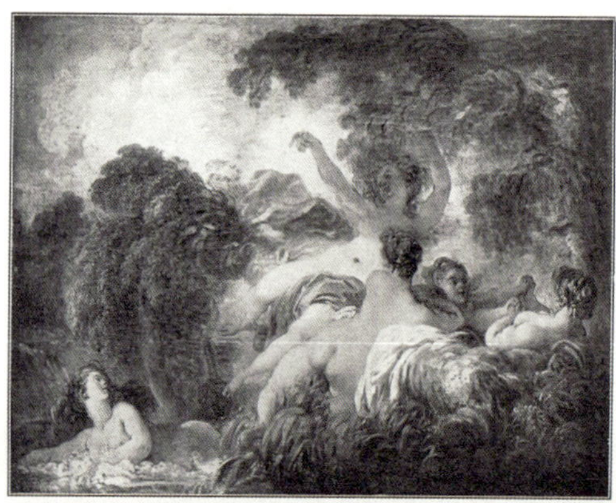

FRAGONARD: WOMEN BATHING (LES BAIGNEUSES)
LOUVRE, PARIS

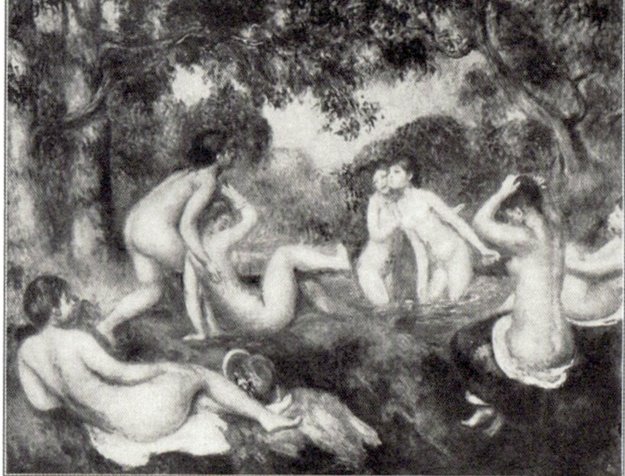

RENOIR: WOMEN BATHING (LES BAIGNEUSES)
BERNHEIM COLLECTION, PARIS

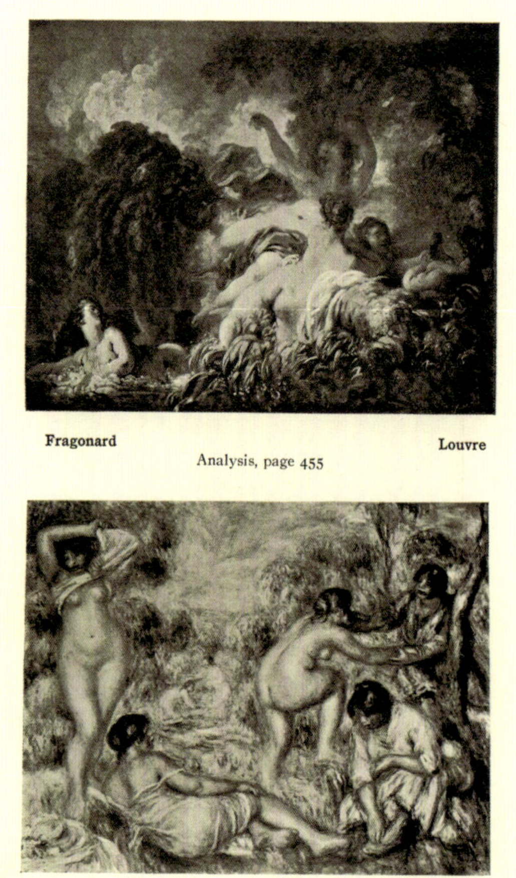

Fragonard Louvre
Analysis, page 455

Renoir Barnes Foundation
Modern versions of the Venetian tradition as it evolved through Rubens.

Fig. 54
Illustration of Fragonard, *Women Bathing*, and Renoir, *Bathers in the Forest*, in Meier-Graefe, *Modern Art*, 1908, vol. I, opposite p. 290

Fig. 55
Illustration of Fragonard, *Women Bathing*, and Renoir, *Bathing Group*, in Barnes, *The Art in Painting*, 1925, p. 180

Fig. 56
Pierre-Auguste Renoir
Apple Vendor (La Marchande de pommes), 1890
Oil on canvas
25¾ × 21½ in. (65.4 × 54.6 cm)
The Barnes Foundation, Merion, Pennsylvania

painting of the same subject in the Louvre (Fig. 54). Consciously or not, this image stuck in Barnes's mind, and when he published *The Art in Painting* in 1925 he used a similar comparison, illustrating the Fragonard with another version of Renoir's Bathers (*Bathing Group*) that he had recently acquired (Fig. 55).[76]

Meier-Graefe's veneration for Renoir—an artist whose late work he admired far more than "the improvisations of the Impressionists"[77]—was not necessary to make a convert of Barnes. Yet Meier-Graefe's lengthy, dithyrambic appreciation of Renoir's fine, but hardly exceptional *Apple Vendor* (Fig. 56), which was reproduced as a frontispiece to his chapter on Renoir, seems to have left its mark on Barnes. From "his most resplendent color period . . . this woodland mystery of fairyland . . . seems to contain the sum of all costly things, and yet remains so true to realities that the effect is not that of a gem, but of the natural envelope of the objects represented."[78] The image (and possibly the description) stayed in Barnes's mind, and he acquired the *Apple Vendor* shortly after reading Meier-Graefe's tomes for the first time.[79]

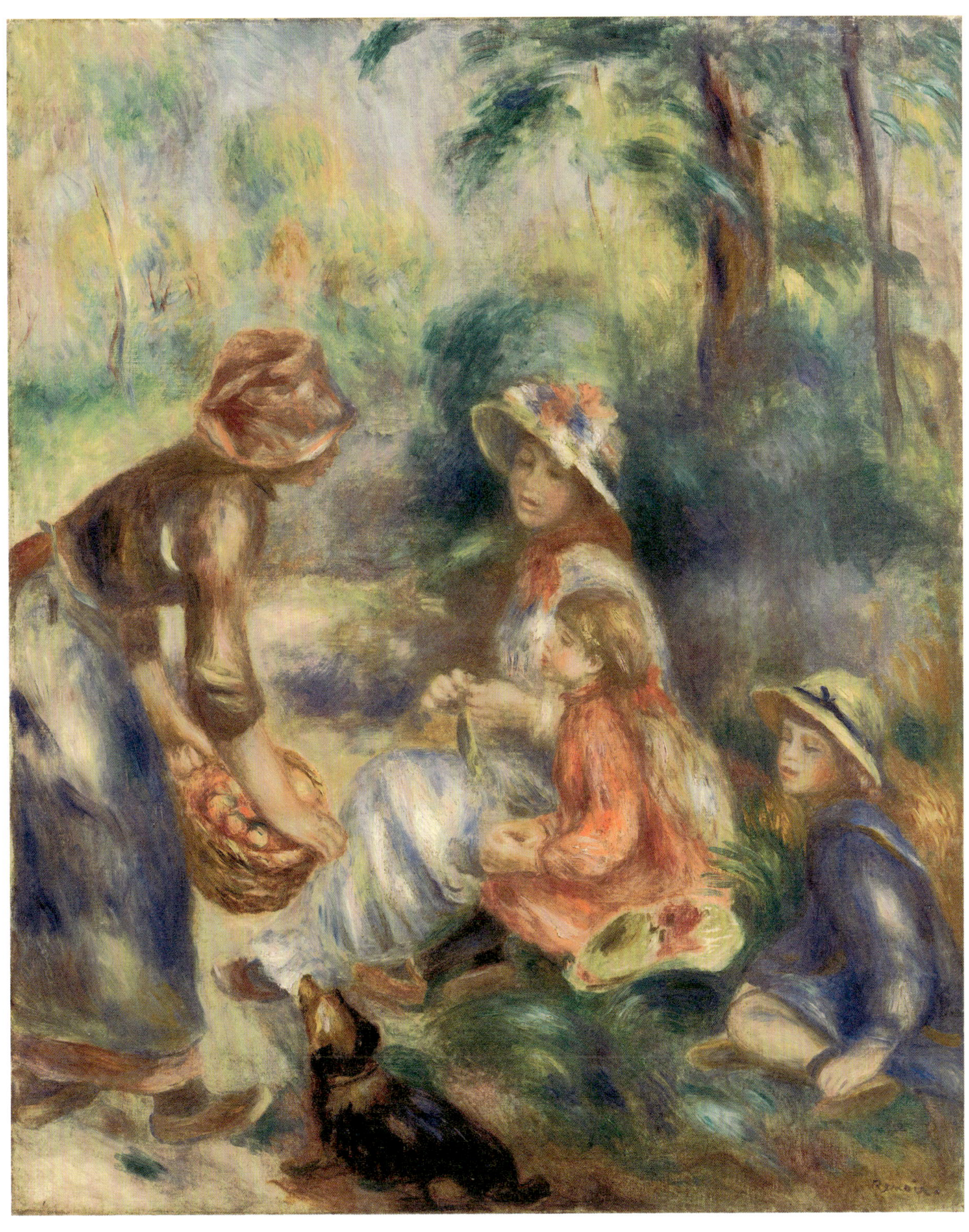

Van Gogh's *Ravine* was returned to its vendor in June 1913 in partial exchange for Renoir's *Luncheon*, and Barnes's brief enthusiasm for Bonnard, Vuillard, and Maurice Denis, again inspired by his reading of Meier-Graefe, also lasted less than a year.[80] This was not unusual. "I have decided not to buy any more Bonnards and Vuillards," Barnes wrote to Maurer in November 1912. "After study of the works of these men which I have, I do not see that they are great men."[81] As for his passion for Van Gogh, he confided to Leo Stein that "he petered out in about a year. . . . Paintings which interested me and which I fairly loved a year ago or even six months ago now leave me cold."[82] Yet Barnes's commitment to Renoir, Cézanne, Picasso, and Matisse never "petered out"; nor did these artists ever "leave him cold." In his absolute assurance of their stature, and in his determination to press forward in collecting and promoting their work, Barnes was indebted above all to one collector whose influence on his early development, while recognized by several scholars, has not received the examination it deserves.[83] This was the man who between 1905 and 1907 could claim to be "unquestionably the most adventurous and discerning collector of twentieth-century painting art in the world": Gertrude Stein's brother, Leo.[84]

Born in 1872, the same year as Barnes, to a Jewish family in Allegheny, Pennsylvania, Leo was the eldest son of a successful businessman, who, having lived briefly in Europe, moved his family to Oakland, California, and made a sizable fortune in cable cars and real estate. Harvard-educated, an early enthusiast of William James and John Dewey, Leo gave up science for aesthetics and in October 1900 went to live in Florence, where he came under Bernard Berenson's cultivated tutelage and started work on a monograph on Mantegna. In September 1902 he left Italy, first for London and then to Paris, where he settled three months later. Abandoning the Italian Renaissance for the modern movement, he decided, after dining one evening with the cellist Pablo Casals, to become a painter himself—hence his decision to move into an apartment with an atelier attached, the legendary 27, rue de Fleurus. Gertrude joined him later that autumn, and his brother and sister-in-law also settled in an apartment on the rue Madame not far away.[85] Dressed in long, monkish gowns of brown cloth, these Jewish expatriates (Fig. 57)—with "their Delphic sandals and scholarly brows"[86]—assumed the aura of authoritative prophets. Before the arrival in September 1907 of Alice B. Toklas, who would become Gertrude's lifelong companion, Gertrude and Leo were, as artist Maurice Sterne archly noted, "the happiest couple on the left bank."[87] After a visit to the Steins, Mary Cassatt confessed that "she had never seen so many dreadful pictures and dreadful people gathered together in one place" and later on referred maliciously to "those receptions where the Steins received in sandals and his wife [Cassatt's mistaken reference to Gertrude] in a garment

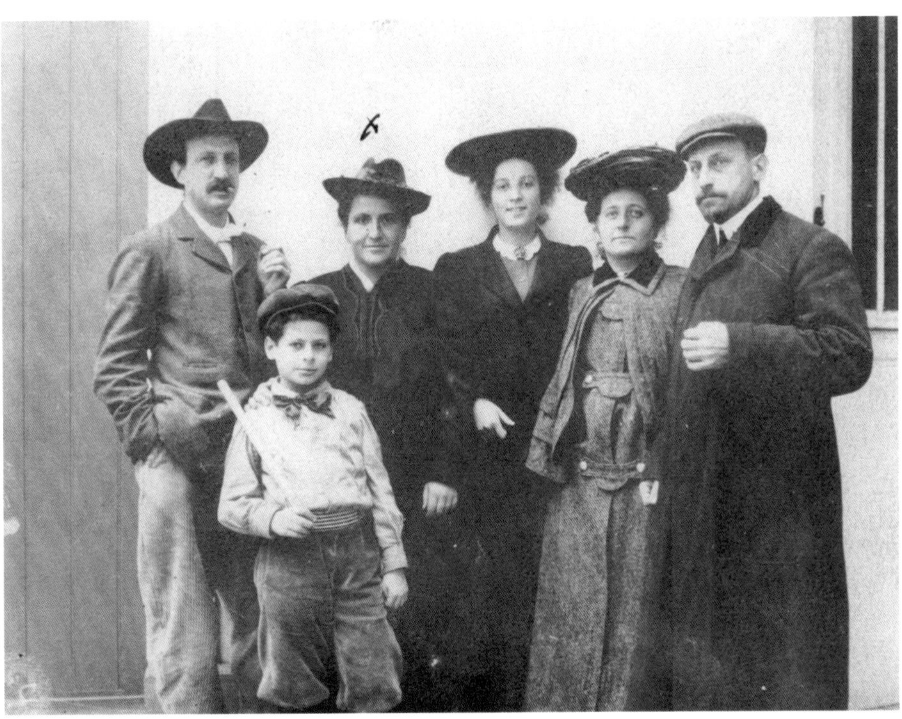

Fig. 57
Leo, Allan, and Gertrude Stein, unidentified woman, Sarah and Michael Stein in the courtyard of 27, rue de Fleurus, c. 1905
Yale Collection of American Literature, Beinecke Rare Book and Manuscript Library, Yale University, New Haven

fastened by a brooch which, were it to give way, might disclose the costume of Eve."[88]

Leo's first acquisitions of major works by Cézanne launched him as a major patron and collector of modern art. In 1904 he acquired *The Conduit* (*The Spring House*; Fig. 59) and the magisterial *Madame Cézanne with a Fan* (1878–88; Foundation E.G. Bührle Collection, Zurich), the latter purchased in November for $1,500: "We is doing business too, we is selling Japanese prints to buy Cézanne," Gertrude informed a friend.[89] Leo was among the first to collect watercolors by Cézanne; through the dealer Clovis Sagot he bought his first Picassos in 1905, going on to acquire (with his sister) some of the artist's finest Blue and Rose period paintings: *Harlequin's Family with an Ape* (1905; Göteborgs Konstmuseum, Gothenburg, Sweden), for which he paid 150 francs ($30); *Girl with a Basket of Flowers* (1905; private collection); and *Boy Leading a Horse* (1906; The Museum of Modern Art, New York).[90] Having encountered Matisse's painting at the Salon d'Automne of 1904, Leo made his first acquisition the following year with *The Woman with the Hat* (1905; San Francisco Museum of Modern Art)—"the nastiest smear of paint I had ever seen."[91] He purchased the extraordinary *Joy of Life* after its exhibition at the Salon des Indépendants in March 1906 for a purported 1,200 francs ($240).[92] In 1907 Stein added Matisse's *Blue Nude: Memory of Biskra* (The Baltimore Museum of Art), painted earlier that year, to his collection of contemporary masterpieces. It was a grouping of works unsurpassed anywhere in the world.

It was at the Steins' apartment on the rue de Fleurus that artists and collectors met each Saturday night. Gertrude and Leo introduced Picasso to Matisse, and it was here, "with a fire no one would have expected," as Mabel Dodge Luhan recalled, that Leo, "this thoughtful, ramish scholar, stood patiently night after night wrestling with the inertia of his guests, expounding, teaching, interpreting."[93] As Picasso perceptively recorded, Leo was rabbinical: a born teacher, who, after his conversion at the Salon d'Automne of 1904, expounded "L'art moderne" with the fervor of a Talmudic scholar (Fig. 58). Manet, Renoir, Degas, Cézanne were the "Big Four: the inspirers of the vital art of today"; Renoir was valued above all for his "absolute color, not as a medium, but as the stuff of art"; Cézanne, "a great mind, a perfect concentration, and great control," was admired for "his remorseless intensity."[94]

The tragedy of this intense and excessively cerebral aesthete/collector was his incapacitating restlessness and an inability to fix upon a subject and exhaust it. Many years later, Matisse recalled a visit to Florence in Stein's company: "Leo was at my feet all the time except in front of great works of art. He'd move a few steps away and come back with the question. What do you think of it? I looked at things with the one idea that I'd have to talk about them."[95] Worse still, Leo's questioning inevitably led from enthusiasm to disenchantment. In his memoirs he recalled: "It happened to me over and over again that I lost interest in very good pictures."[96] Leo's eventual disparagement of Cézanne is perhaps the saddest testimony to this fall from grace: in an epithet that has become notorious, he compared the artist to a "squeezed lemon."[97]

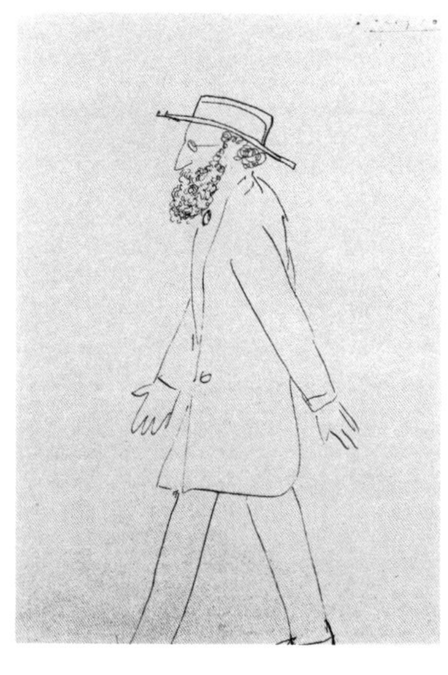

Fig. 58
Pablo Picasso
Leo Stein Walking, 1905
Pen and ink on paper
13¼ × 9¼ in. (33.8 × 23.5 cm)
Private collection

Barnes was probably taken to the Steins' apartment on the rue de Fleurus by Maurer on his second buying trip to Paris: their meeting on December 9, 1912, is appropriately documented by an invoice from Leo to Barnes for his first paintings by Matisse, *Still Life with Melon* (*Dishes and Melon*; Fig. 60) for 3,500 francs and *View of the Sea, Collioure* (1906; The Barnes Foundation) for 900 francs.[98] "The Matisse still-life that I got from you is now one of my favorites and grows daily in my liking," Barnes would write to Leo a few months later.[99] It was presumably on this occasion that Barnes also attempted to buy Picasso's portrait of Gertrude Stein (Fig. 49). Thereafter the two men met in Paris only once more, in June 1913; Barnes did not visit Europe again in the winter of 1913, and by the time he returned to Paris in May 1914, Leo had moved to Settignano, outside Florence.

It is important to note that by 1912 Leo had begun to lose faith in Picasso and Matisse. As he recalled many years later in his autobiography, "By 1910, I had enough of intensive concern with so-called modern art. When my interest in Cézanne declined, when Matisse

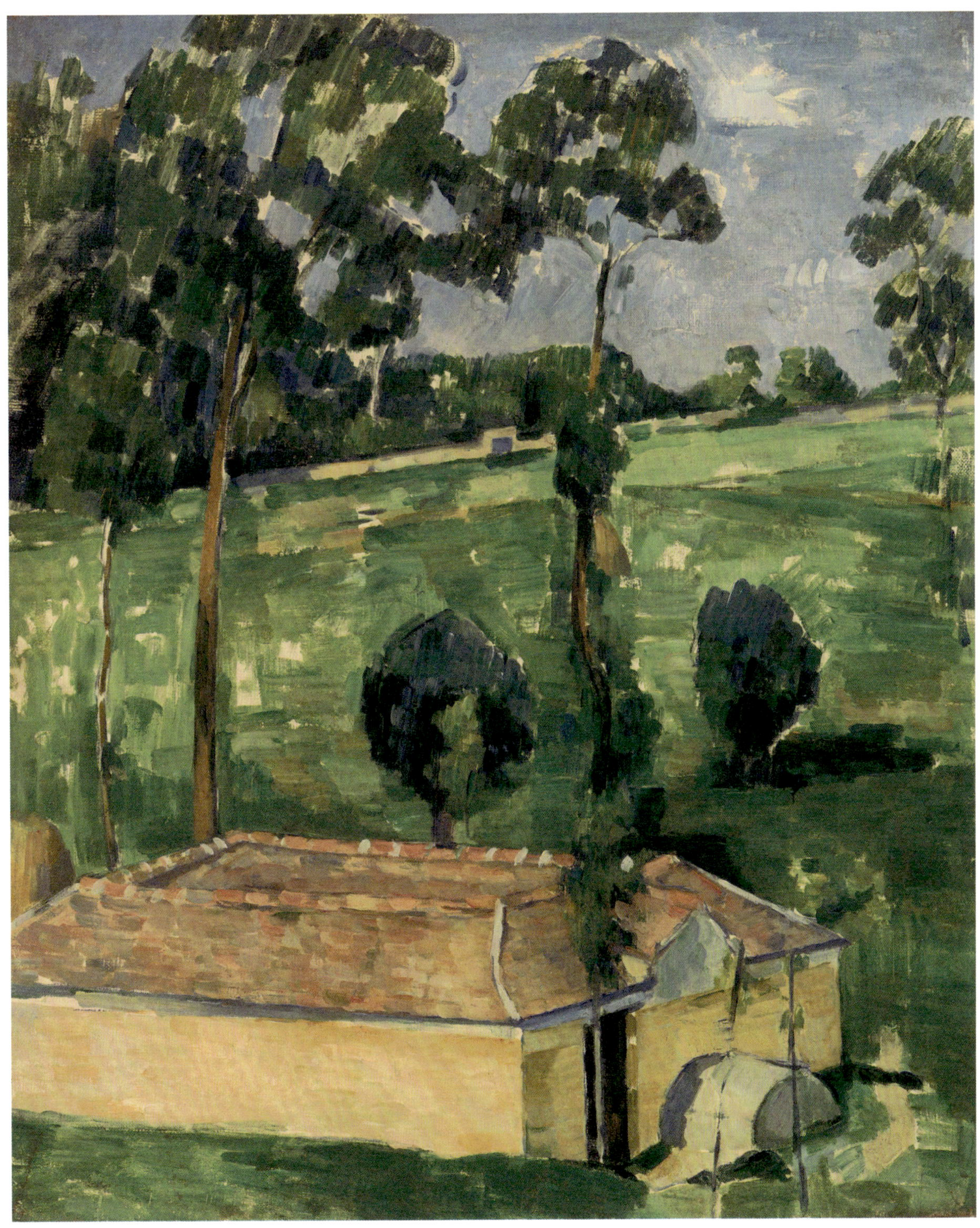

Fig. 59
Paul Cézanne
The Spring House (La Conduite d'eau), c. 1879
Oil on canvas
23⅝ × 19^{11}⁄16 in. (60 × 50 cm)
The Barnes Foundation, Merion, Pennsylvania

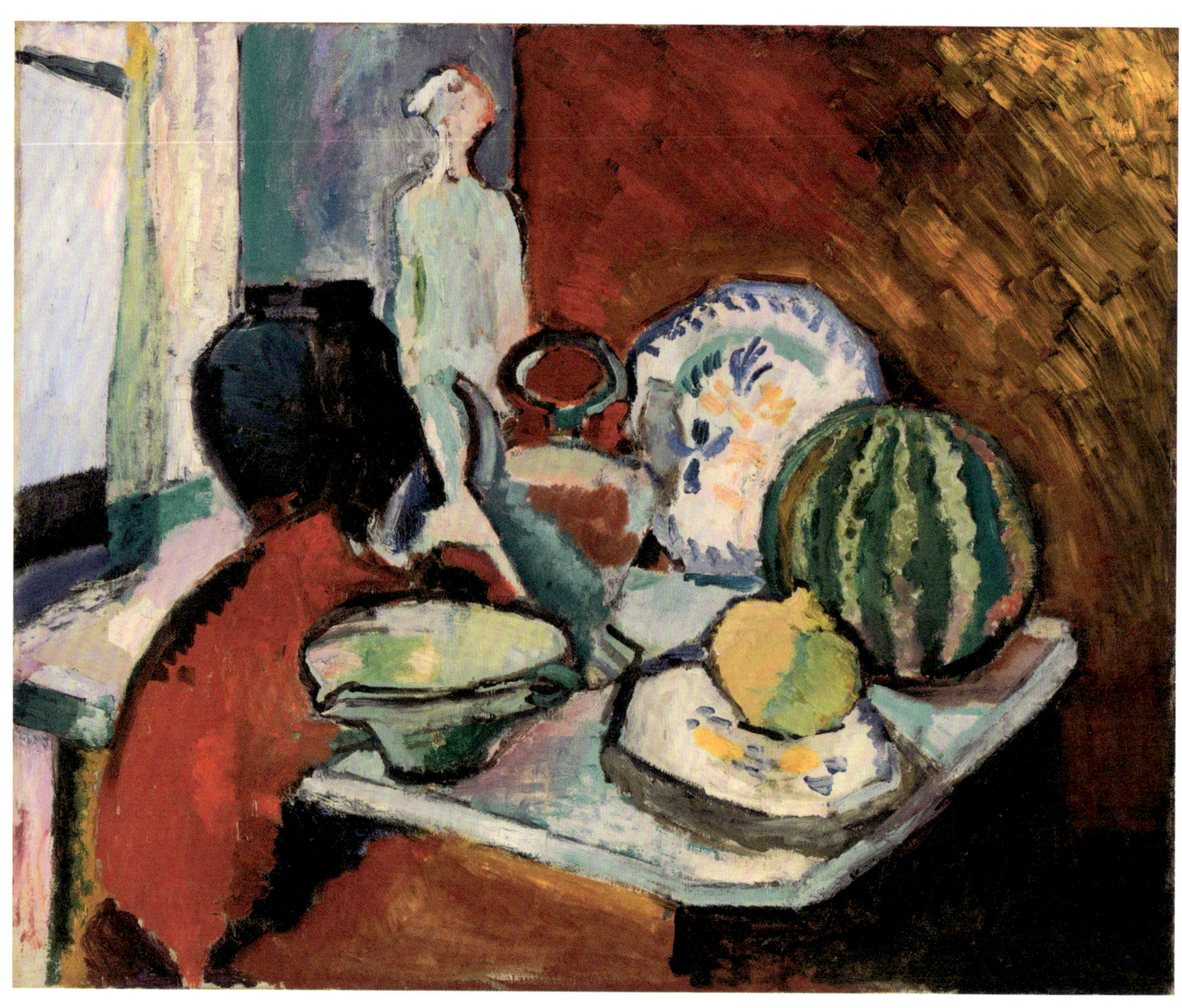

Fig. 60
Henri Matisse
Dishes and Melon (Assiettes et melon),
Fall 1906–September 1907
Oil on canvas
25 9/16 × 31 7/8 in. (65 × 81 cm)
The Barnes Foundation, Merion,
Pennsylvania

was temporarily in eclipse and Picasso turned to foolishness."[100] Just as Gertrude became the high priestess of Cubism, so Leo fulminated against Picasso's most radical shift in style, which he considered "an utter abomination." Convinced that Picasso was one of the greatest illustrators ever born, but that his desire to create "great and original form" through Cubism was thoroughly wrongheaded, Stein argued that Picasso and Gertrude were "using their intellect, which they ain't got, to do what would need the finest critical tact, which they ain't got neither, and they are turning out the most godalmighty rubbish that is to be found."[101] Yet despite his disaffection, Leo remained committed to the early work of both Picasso and Matisse, and above all the study of science and aesthetics—now the "only essential intelligent activities."[102] Furthermore, he simply could not resist proselytizing; 27, rue de Fleurus was "charged with the atmosphere of propaganda," with Leo as a magnetic, if now rather jaundiced, preacher.[103] As late as February 1913 Walter Pach brought the organizers of the Armory show to meet him.[104] Willard Huntington Wright, with whom he discussed aesthetics in Paris and New York, would acknowledge Stein as "one of the ablest and most searching living critics of painting."[105]

And what of Barnes? Both from their correspondence and certain of Barnes's early acquisitions it is clear that, despite Stein's retreat "from the whirlpool of modern art,"[106] he remained a potent influence on his contemporary from Overbook, Pennsylvania. Stein may well have been responsible for consolidating Barnes's attachment to Renoir and Cézanne to the exclusion of any other artist of their generation. On June 22, 1912, *before* Barnes had met the Steins, he had presented a list of his fledgling collection to John G. Johnson, whose collection of early European paintings would become one of the foundations of the Philadelphia Museum of Art. This was the first of the many occasions on which Barnes would alter his will to the disadvantage of the University of Pennsylvania. He was now looking, he wrote, for another "charitable or educational—artistic or otherwise—institution connected with the city" to which he might bequeath his pictures. In this document Barnes listed the names of twenty-four artists, mainly Impressionists and Post-Impressionists: Renoir, Monet, Degas, Cézanne; Morisot, Jongkind, Boudin, Raffaëlli; Van Gogh and Gauguin, Picasso and Bonnard; and the Americans, Glackens, Lawson, and "Maurer in his new key." Matisse's name does not appear. "I have duplicates of most of the works, selected with the idea of representing the versatility of the men."[107] Six months later it would be almost impossible to imagine Barnes drawing up such a list. His collecting had become far more exclusive: "I am convinced I cannot get too many Renoirs," he wrote to Leo Stein in March 1913.[108] Indeed, it was only after his meeting with Stein that Barnes formulated a set of aesthetic priorities—his "four men affair"—that would sustain him over the next two decades.

Stein fostered Barnes's interest in early Picasso, as well as his contempt for Cubism. "Why oh why didn't you give me first chance at buying your early Picassos," Barnes chided Leo in February 1914 when the latter was liquidating part of his collection to finance the move to Italy.[109] Stein introduced him to the work of Matisse—something that Barnes acknowledged, rather tardily, in dedicating his monograph on Matisse to Leo in 1933.[110] And Stein engaged him in lengthy discussions on psychology and aesthetics. In July 1913 Barnes commended Stein for "his many informal, very valuable talks on what to look for in a painting."[111] In February 1914 he urged him, "I hope you'll get busy on the things you can say better than anyone else that I know. You ought to do it: I'll show you how to finance its publication."[112] And in a letter to the painter and editor Guy Pène du Bois the following September, Barnes acknowledged that his present enthusiasm for Renoir's late work had lain dormant two years before, when "even Leo Stein's eloquence had not enough effect to make me buy examples which I now consider the best of all Renoir's period."[113]

Like Barnes, Stein developed a passion for the mature late work of Renoir: he too wrote that Renoir's supreme achievement had been reached in the first decade of the twentieth century. At a time when he had become disenchanted with Cézanne, Picasso, and Matisse, Stein continued to buy late Renoirs from Bernheim-Jeune, insisting, when he and Gertrude split their collection, that all the Renoirs remain with him.[114] Stein's fixed income and the fairly well-established market for Renoirs, early or late, made these acquisitions a great deal less impressive than his previous purchases of Picasso and Matisse. Stein would recall how, possibly around 1907, Braque and Picasso had urged him to look at a Renoir in the window of Hessel's gallery, "a picture of a mother and child with some clothes hanging on a line behind them"[115] (Fig. 61). Unable to get the work out of his mind, Stein marshaled his family into making the purchase with him: "That afternoon I brought the picture home in a cab and sat on a lounge chair opposite till it was so late I thought I should spend the night there."[116] Barnes coveted the painting and made an offer to buy it when he learned that Leo was selling his collection when he left Paris for Settignano in April 1914; he finally acquired it seven years later for the relatively modest sum of $5,000.[117]

Fig. 61
Pierre-Auguste Renoir
Washerwoman and Child
(La Blanchisseuse et son enfant), 1887
Oil on canvas
32 × 25¾ in. (81.3 × 65.4 cm)
The Barnes Foundation, Merion, Pennsylvania

Several of Barnes's early acquisitions testify to the bond between the two men: Stein sold him the first Matisses to enter his collection (see above); as well as Cézanne's *Conduit* and Renoir's *Washerwoman and Child*—both of which had occupied a special place in Stein's collection. Cézanne's *Millstone and Cistern under Trees* (Fig. 62) was sold to Barnes by Stein in May 1914. Even Picasso's *Composition* (1906; The Barnes Foundation), which Barnes purchased from

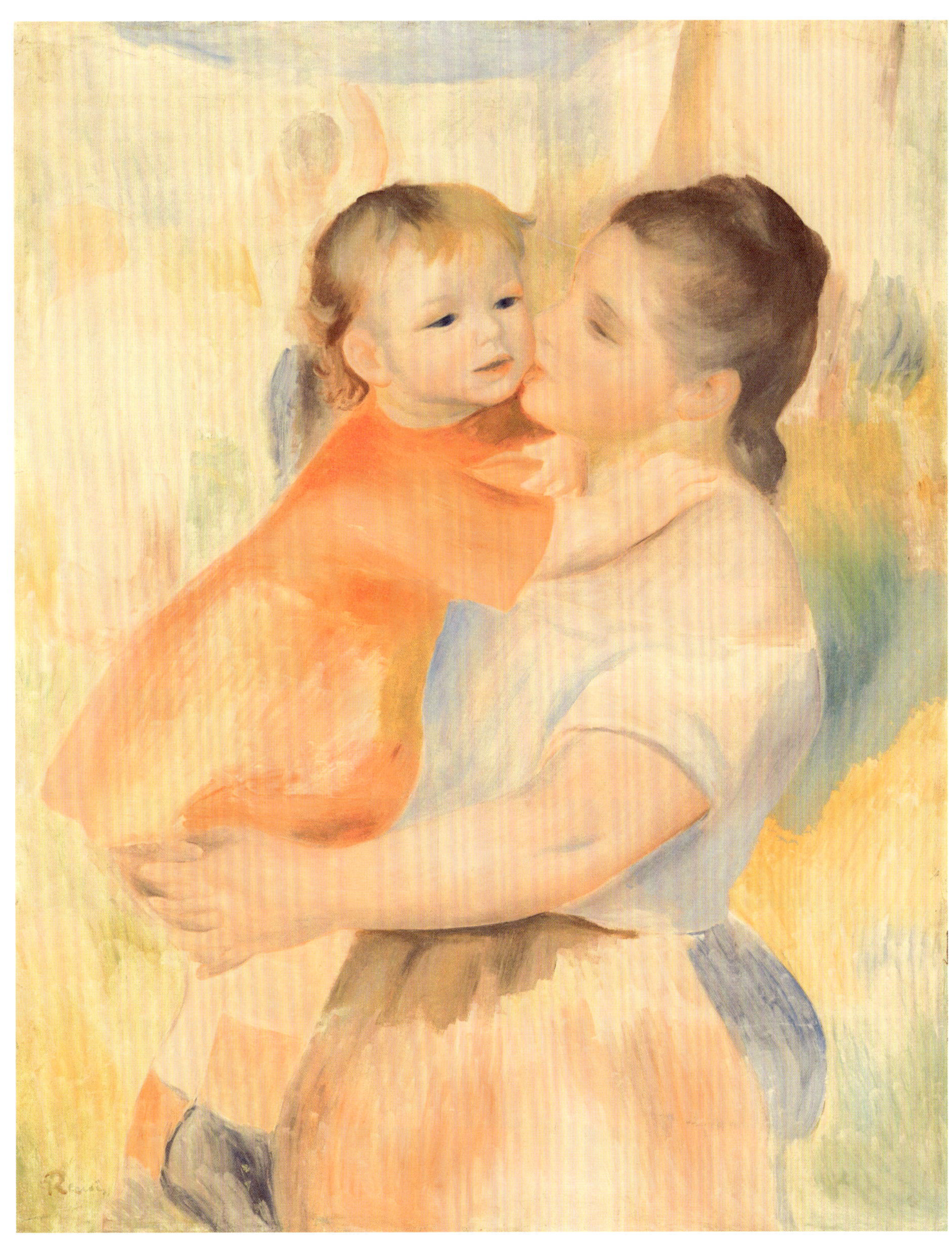

Vollard via Durand-Ruel for a thousand dollars in June 1913,[118] had been one of the last paintings by Picasso of which Leo fully approved. Its genesis may be tracked back to a letter Picasso sent to Leo and Gertrude from Gósol, Catalonia, in August 1906.[119] Barnes had also owned Matisse's *Boy with a Butterfly Net* (1907; The Minneapolis Institute of Arts)—the poignant portrait of Leo and Gertrude's nephew Allan Stein, a record of family holidays in Fiesole and more congenial times, which he later traded in partial payment for Renoir's large *Bather and Maid*.[120]

With his stentorian pronouncements on aesthetics and psychology, his strong opinions and complex formulations, Leo Stein challenged Barnes in a way no other figure could in the years before Barnes met John Dewey and attended his seminars at Columbia University in 1917. A remarkable fondness and candor emerges in Barnes's letters to Stein, an affection and eagerness of discourse between equals that is found nowhere else. Writing to Stein in Settignano in July 1914, Barnes thanks him for his recent letter, "a good substitute for the stimulus that I get from personal contact with your thoughts." Recognizing the fickleness of his own enthusiasms, Barnes confides that Renoir alone never bores him: "I have never experienced from Renoir the ennui or disgust with the platitudinous emptiness and general dam [*sic*] rot that I have found in the work of practically every man represented in my collection." It is "Renoir's joy in painting the real life of red-blooded people and his skill in conveying his sensations to my consciousness" that moves him. As for Cézanne, "he still holds me with a good, strong grip. I love his crudity, his baldness of statement, his apparent lack of skill in the handicraft of painting, and the absolute sincerity of the man. . . . Each year shows a stronger love for him, a recognition of qualities of mind that were his which he was trying to tell to others. I agree with you that Cézanne did not always put virulent enthusiasm in his paintings, and I still stronger agree with you in attributing that as a prime requisite of a great work of art."[121]

These statements, only recently published, are as insightful and carefully formulated as any that Barnes ever committed to print. Writing to Stein, Barnes was also moved to an unwonted confessionalism: "Painting is to a man in proportion as that man is; but the aggravating part to me is that not having been endowed by nature with a strong aesthetic sense, I do not develop along the lines which I feel are right as rapidly as I have gone in other fields." The intimacy between the two is such that it is almost improper to witness their conversation. Barnes concludes his letter: "I have absolutely no social life, and except for a few friends such as Glackens and some of the other artists who drop in on me for a day or two, I am as lonely as you are with your lettuce patch. For that reason and for others more positive and personal, I would like mighty well to get a letter from you once in a while."[122]

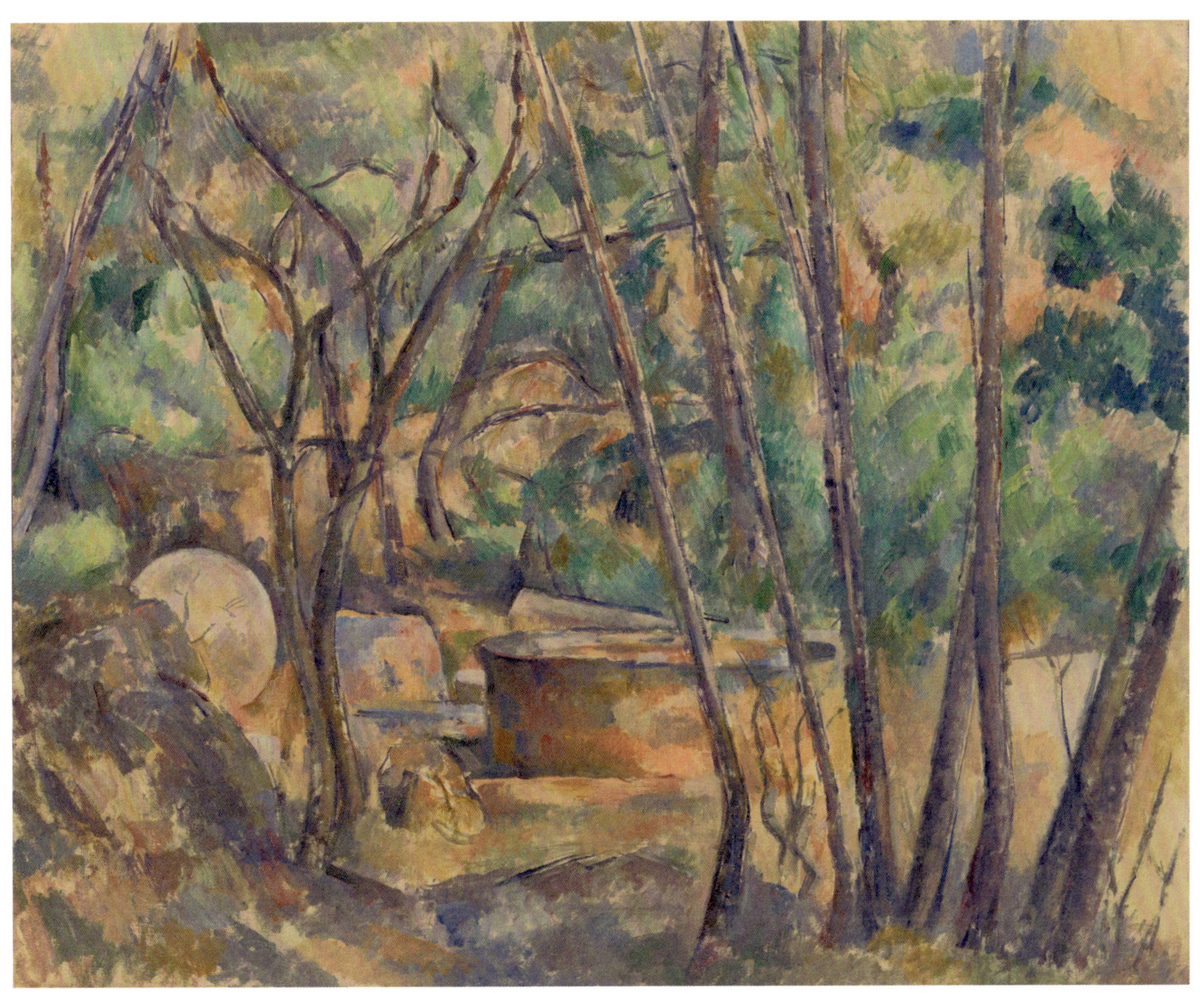

Fig. 62
Paul Cézanne
Millstone and Cistern under Trees
(La Meule et citerne en sous-bois), 1892–94
Oil on canvas
25⅝ × 31⅞ in. (65.1 × 81 cm)
The Barnes Foundation,
Merion, Pennsylvania

A somewhat shorter version of this essay was published as "The Origins of the Barnes Collection, 1912–15," *The Burlington Magazine*, 150, no. 1265 (August 2008), pp. 534–43. I am most grateful to the editor of *Burlington* for allowing it to be reprinted in extended form in this volume. Special thanks to Deborah Lyons and Nicholas Wise for their expert editing.

NOTES

1. Violette de Mazia, "The Lure and Trap of Color Slides in Art Education: The Time-Released Venom of Their Make-Believe," *Vistas* 3, no. 1 (1984–86).
2. Carl W. McCardle, "The Terrible Tempered Dr. Barnes," *Saturday Evening Post,* March 21, 1942; Howard Greenfield, *The Devil and Dr. Barnes: Portrait of an American Collector* (New York: Viking, 1987); John Anderson, *Art Held Hostage: The Battle Over the Barnes Collection* (New York: W.W. Norton and Company, 2003).
3. At the Vischer sale of February 1912, Barnes acquired a painting by Jean-Charles Cazin for $310; at the Anderson sale later in the month, a sketch by Corot for $250; his purchases at the Chase sale of March 1912 included works by Boudin ($725), Forain ($560), and Twachtman ($275); invoices in the Barnes Foundation Archives, Merion, Pa. (hereafter BFA).
4. Glackens acquired twenty works; see Richard J. Wattenmaker et al., *Great French Paintings from the Barnes Foundation: Impressionist, Post-Impressionist, and Early Modern*, exh. cat. (Washington, D.C.: National Gallery of Art, 1993), pp. 6–7, 34–35 and 207 ; see also the account in Ira Glackens, *William Glackens and the Ashcan Group* (New York: Grosset and Dunlap, 1957), pp. 155–60.
5. Barnes's first trip lasted from May 22 to June 13, 1912. The second visit in December was notable for his first meeting with Leo Stein; in his customs declaration (December 23, 1912, BFA), Barnes stated that he had personally acquired twenty-two works on this trip.
6. Barnes to Johnson, January 12, 1915, BFA.
7. Albert C. Barnes, "How to Judge a Painting," *Arts and Decoration* 5 (April 1915), p. 219.
8. Thomas Hart Benton, *An Artist in America* (New York: R.M. McBride and Co., 1937), p. 61; Benton described Barnes as "a Philadelphia patent medicine manufacturer with the manners of Benny the alderman."
9. Albert C. Barnes, "Cubism: Requiescat in Pace," *Arts and Decoration* 6 (January 1916), p. 121.
10. Ibid., pp. 121–22. Marius de Zayas's riposte to this article, "Cubism?" appeared in *Arts and Decoration* 6 (April 1916), pp. 284–86, 308.
11. Barnes, "How to Judge a Painting," p. 219: "My Picassos, painted before he took to having fun with the public with cubes, show a masterly welding of the essences of Greco and Cézanne in a technical manner that Manet and Velazquez would have looked at a second time."
12. Albert C. Barnes, *The Art in Painting* (Merion, Pa.: The Barnes Foundation Press, 1925), p. 328.
13. Anne Distel, "Dr. Barnes in Paris," in Wattenmaker et al., *Great French Paintings*, pp. 38–43; for Guillaume, see C. Giradou, *Les Arts à Paris chez Paul Guillaume*, exh. cat. (Paris: Musée del'Orangerie, 1993).
14. Wattenmaker et al., *Great French Paintings*, pp. 226–35, 238–39, 246–49, 252–57, 258–61.
15. John Rewald, *Cézanne, the Steins and Their Circle* (London: Thames and Hudson, 1987).
16. See Norman L. Kleeblatt, Kenneth E. Silver, and Romy Golan, *An Expressionist*

in Paris: The Paintings of Chaim Soutine, exh. cat. (New York: The Jewish Museum, 1998), pp. 45–46, 198.

17. Barnes to Stein, July 17, 1914, BFA.
18. John Sloan, *Gist of Art: Principles and Practise Expounded in the Classroom and Studio* (New York: American Artists Group, 1939), p. 25.
19. Ibid.
20. Barnes to John G. Johnson, June 22, 1912, BFA.
21. Susan A. Stein, "Chronology," in Alice C. Frelinghuysen et al., *Splendid Legacy: The Havemeyer Collection*, exh. cat. (New York: The Metropolitan Museum of Art, 1993), p. 264; the visit was arranged by Georges Durand-Ruel.
22. Barnes, "How to Judge a Painting," p. 248.
23. Barnes to Edith Glackens, June 3, 1938, in Glackens, *William Glackens and the Ashcan Group*, p. 260.
24. See A. E. Gallatin, *Modern Art at Venice and Other Notes by A.E.G.* (New York, 1910), pp. 63–64; and the same author's reappraisal six years later; idem, "William Glackens," *The American Magazine of Art* 7 (May 1916), pp. 261–62: "In many of his recent portraits and figure compositions the influence that Renoir has exerted on his palette is quite apparent." The shift from Degas to Renoir was first noted in Guy Pène du Bois, "William Glackens, Normal Man," *Arts and Decoration* 4 (September 1914), pp. 404–06: "Like Renoir, he is one of art's most joyous, most careless, most inveterate children."
25. Glackens, *William Glackens and the Ashcan Group*, p. 157.
26. Elizabeth McCausland, *A. H. Maurer* (New York: A. A. Wyn, 1951), p. 115. For a more recent survey of his art, see D. Anderson Deeds, *Alfred Maurer: The First American Modern,* exh. cat. (Minneapolis: Frederick R. Weisman Art Museum, University of Minnesota, 2003).
27. McCausland, *Maurer*, p. 83; see also John Rewald, *Cézanne and America: Dealers, Collectors, Artists and Critics, 1891–1921* (Princeton, N.J.: Princeton University Press, 1989), p. 61.
28. Gertrude Stein, *The Autobiography of Alice B. Toklas* (New York, 1933; repr., New York: Vintage Books, 1990), p. 11.
29. Ibid. and Glackens, *William Glackens and the Ashcan Group*, p. 216.
30. In return, Barnes subsidized the exhibition of Maurer's recent paintings at the Folsom Gallery, 396 Fifth Avenue, New York, which ran between January 15 and 29, 1913. Barnes wrote the introduction to the catalogue (which appeared anonymously), and at his insistence passages from introductions by Clive Bell and Roger Fry for the second Post-Impressionist exhibition at the Grafton Galleries, London, in 1912 were also reprinted; see Barnes to A. H. Folsom, November 11, 1912, December 30, 1912, BFA.
31. Barnes to Maurer, July 12, 1912, BFA, offering a monthly retainer of 250 francs, and March 14, 1913, "I have refrained from bothering you about visits to the dealers, because I would prefer that you confine your energies to the matter of the complications of Argyrol in France."
32. Van Gogh's *Smoker* had been acquired from the dealer Eugène Druet "*par l'intermediare de Monsieur Maurer,*" Druet to Barnes, July 26, 1912, BFA.
33. Maurer to Barnes, September 29 and October 15, 1912, quoted by Joseph Rishel in Wattenmaker et al., *Great French Paintings*, p. 138 n. 2.
34. Maurer to Barnes, n.d. [August 1912], BFA.
35. Barnes to Maurer, November 5, 1912, BFA.
36. Maurer to Barnes, November 19, 1912, BFA.
37. Maurer to Barnes, March 17, 1913, BFA.
38. Barnes, *The Art in Painting*, p. ix; Barnes, "How to Judge a Painting," p. 217: "Books, the usual means of acquiring elementary knowledge, fail."

39. Barnes to Stein, July 17, 1914, BFA; the reference is to the third edition of Bell's *Art* (New York: Frederick A. Stokes, 1913), which in a letter to another correspondent Barnes had praised as "one of the most satisfying books on art recently written.... I would sooner have it for the purpose of learning as much about art as can be learned from any book on the subject," Barnes to Adolph Borie, July 14, 1914, BFA.
40. A.H. Shaw, "De Medici in Merion," *New Yorker*, September 22, 1928, p. 32; note also the comment of the critic Waldemar George, who accompanied Guillaume and Barnes on their museum visits in the 1920s. "Barnes never stopped bombarding us with questions . . . and wrote down all our answers," quoted in Distel, "Dr. Barnes in Paris," p. 39.
41. See Rewald, *Cézanne and America*, pp. 237–46.
42. Bell, *Art*, p. 208.
43. George Moore, *Modern Painting* (London: Walter Scott, 1893), p. 85.
44. Bell, *Art*, p. 191.
45. Moore, *Modern Painting*, p. 84.
46. Matisse, "Notes d'un peintre," *La Grande Revue*, December 25, 1908, in Jack D. Flam, ed., *Matisse on Art* (New York: Phaidon, 1973), p. 36.
47. Barnes, *The Art in Painting*, p. 249.
48. Albert C. Barnes, "Renoir and Cézanne," in Dewey et al., *Art and Education* (Merion, Pa.: The Barnes Foundation Press, 1929), pp. 136, 141; Barnes, "The Transition to Modern Painting," ibid., p. 134.
49. Wattenmaker et al., *Great French Paintings*, p. 7.
50. Barnes to Joseph Durand-Ruel, February 28, 1913, BFA; the Sisley was valued at 7,000 francs.
51. Albert C. Barnes, "Renoir: An Appreciation," *The Dial*, 157 (January–June 1920), p. 165.
52. Albert C. Barnes, "Cézanne: A Unique Figure Among the Painters of His Time," *Arts and Decoration* 12 (November 1920), p. 40.
53. Barnes, *The Art in Painting*, p. 252.
54. Ibid., pp. 268–69.
55. Roger Fry, "The Last Works of Renoir," *Atheneum* 4702 (June 1920), pp. 771–72.
56. Clive Bell, *Since Cézanne* (London: Chatto and Windus, 1922), pp. 66 and 71.
57. "I misjudged Wright whose book I have just finished. In my second reading I found a great many things that I have never been able to find in any other book," Barnes to Stein, January 12, 1916, BFA.
58. Willard Huntington Wright, *Modern Painting: Its Tendency and Meaning* (New York: John Lane, 1915), pp. 106–25.
59. On Matisse's and Picasso's veneration for Renoir's late work, see A. de Butler, "Revoir Renoir," 2 vols. (Ph.D. diss., Université de Paris 8, 2006), vol. 1, pp. 251–356.
60. Anne Distel and Christopher Riopelle in Wattenmaker et al., *Great French Paintings*, p. 83.
61. John Richardson, *A Life of Picasso, Volume I, 1881–1906* (New York: Random House, 1991), p. 423.
62. Durand-Ruel to Barnes, March 3, 1913, BFA.
63. Cézanne's *View of the Domaine Saint-Joseph*, c. 1888, acquired from Vollard on March 30, 1913, for $6,700, was the first painting by the artist to enter an American museum; see Rebecca A. Rabinow, ed., *Cézanne to Picasso: Ambroise Vollard, Patron of the Avant-Garde*, exh. cat. (New York: The Metropolitan Museum of Art, 2006), p. 341.
64. Barnes, "How to Judge a Painting," p. 246.
65. See note 21.

66. Barnes, "How to Judge a Painting," p. 217.
67. Invoice for $10.50, April 1, 1912, BFA. In a letter of June 22, 1912, to John G. Johnson, Barnes noted that he had bought his paintings in Paris, "after studying the matter in collections and from various books (Meier-Graefe, Holmes etc)." In a letter to his customs broker of July 8, 1912 (BFA), Barnes referred to "the most authoritative book on modern art, the author of which is J. Meier-Graefe."
68. Barnes, "How to Judge a Painting," p. 248.
69. For a recent introduction to Meier-Graefe, see Catherine Krahmer, ed., *Kunst ist nicht für Kunstgeschichte da: Briefe und Dokumente, Julius Meier-Graefe* (Göttingen: Wallstein, 2001).
70. Julius Meier-Graefe, *Modern Art: Being a Contribution to a New System of Aesthetics*, transl. Florence Simmonds and George William Chrystal, vol. 1 (New York: G.P. Putnam's Sons, 1908), p. 205.
71. Ibid., pp. 211–12.
72. Maurer to Barnes, n.d. [August 1912], BFA.
73. Barnes to Maurer, October 14, 1912, BFA.
74. Barnes to Levesque, October 14, 1912, BFA. He also asked Levesque to track down a number of works by Cézanne, "which I know can be bought," illustrated in the August issue of *Les Arts*.
75. Meier-Graefe, *Modern Art*, p. 270.
76. Barnes, *The Art in Painting*, p. 180.
77. Meier-Graefe, *Modern Art*, p. 292.
78. Ibid., p. 201.
79. François Daulte, *Auguste Renoir: Catalogue raisonné de l'oeuvre peint* (Lausanne: Durand-Ruel, 1971), no. 586. Barnes purchased *Apple Vendor* from Durand-Ruel in December 1914 for $10,000, paying $4,000 in cash and returning Renoir's *The Braid* (c. 1886–87; Museum Langmatt, Sidney and Jenny Brown Foundation, Baden), acquired the previous May, for the remaining $6,000.
80. Barnes paid the dealer Levesque 30,000 francs for *The Luncheon*, with Van Gogh's *Ravine* valued at 23,000 francs against the purchase; see Distel and Riopelle in Wattenmaker et al., *Great French Paintings*, p. 54.
81. Barnes to Maurer, November 12, 1912, BFA.
82. Barnes to Stein, July 17, 1914, BFA.
83. John Rewald was the first to stress Leo Stein's influence on Barnes: "While there is no absolute proof . . . at least it can be said that Barnes's preferences show remarkable parallels to those of Leo. His vast collection was to be built around the two artists who were Leo's favorites, Renoir and Cézanne, to whom, among the younger artists, he added especially Matisse, a knowledge of whom he always connected with Leo Stein"; Rewald, *Cézanne and America*, p. 63. Rewald was unable to consult the Barnes Foundation Archives, the one lacuna in his otherwise superbly documented account; see also Wattenmaker in *Great French Paintings*, pp. 8–9, and Mary Ann Meyers, *Art, Education, and African-American Culture: Albert Barnes and the Science of Philanthropy* (New Brunswick, N.J.: Transaction Publishers, 2004), pp. 31–40.
84. Richardson, *Life of Picasso*, p. 396.
85. Rewald, *Cézanne and America*, pp. 53–87; see also Brenda Wineapple, *Sister, Brother: Gertrude and Leo Stein* (New York: G.P. Putnam's Sons, 1996).
86. "*Leurs pieds nus sont chausses de sandals delphiques/Ils lèvent vers le ciel des fronts scientifiques*"; Guilaume Apollinaire, *Chroniques d'art, 1902–1918*, ed. Leroy Clinton Breunig (Paris, 1960), p. 53.
87. Sterne in Charlotte Mayerson, ed., *Shadow and Light: The Life, Friends and Opinions of Maurice Sterne* (New York: Harcourt, Brace and World, 1952), p. 48.

88. Cassatt's comments are cited in Rewald, *Cézanne and America*, pp. 72–73.
89. Gertrude and Leo Stein to Mabel Foote Weeks, November 1904, quoted in ibid., p. 55.
90. Richardson, *Life of Picasso*, pp. 393–401.
91. Leo Stein, *Appreciation: Painting, Poetry and Prose* (New York: Crown Publishers, 1947), p. 158.
92. Hilary Spurling, *The Unknown Matisse: A Life of Henri Matisse, the Early Years, 1869–1908* (New York: Alfred A. Knopf, 1998), pp. 342–43, 345.
93. Mabel Dodge Luhan, *Intimate Memoirs* (New York, 1935), vol. 2, pp. 321–22; partially cited in Rewald, *Cézanne and America*, p. 64.
94. Leo Stein to Mabel Foote Weeks, n.d. [January–February 1905], in Leo Stein, *Journey Into the Self*, ed. Edmund Fuller (New York: Crown Publishers, 1950), pp. 15–16.
95. P. Courthion, "Conversations avec Henri Matisse," unpublished typescript, 1979, Getty Research Institute, Brentwood, Los Angeles; see also Jack Flam, *Matisse: The Man and His Art, 1869–1918* (Ithaca, N.Y.: Cornell University Press, 1986), pp. 206–07.
96. Stein, *Appreciation*, pp. 164–65.
97. Leo Stein, *The A-B-C of Aesthetics* (New York: Boni and Liveright, 1927), p. 267; see the discussion in Rewald, *Cézanne and America*, pp. 259, 261, n. 34.
98. Invoice, from Durand-Ruel et fils, December 12, 1912, BFA: "M Matisse, Nature morte, Purchased December 9, 1912, from M. Stein., 27, Rue de Fleurus, 890 ff."
99. Barnes to Stein, March 30, 1913, Yale Collection of American Literature, Beinecke Rare Book and Manuscript Library, Yale University, New Haven, Leo Stein Collection.
100. Stein, *Appreciation*, p. 166.
101. Leo Stein to Mabel Weeks, Februry 4, 1913, reprinted in Stein, *Journey Into the Self*, p. 53.
102. Ibid., p. 51.
103. Stein, *Appreciation*, p. 84.
104. Rewald, *Cézanne, the Steins and Their Circle.*
105. W.H. Wright, "The Aesthetic Struggle in America," *The Forum* (February 1916), cited in Rewald, *Cézanne and America*, p. 245.
106. As he characterized the Armory show in a letter to Mabel Weeks (February 4, 1913), see Stein, *Journey Into the Self*, p. 48.
107. Barnes to Johnson, June 22, 1912, BFA.
108. Barnes to Stein, March 1913, BFA.
109. Barnes to Stein, February 9, 1914, Beinecke Library, Yale.
110. "To Leo Stein, who was the first to recognize the genius of Matisse and who, more than twenty years ago, inspired the study which has culminated in this book"; Albert C. Barnes and Violette de Mazia, *The Art of Henri-Matisse* (New York and London: Scribner, 1933), p. v.
111. Barnes to Stein, July 2, 1913, BFA.
112. Barnes to Stein, February 1914; quoted in Wattenmaker et al., *Great French Paintings*, p. 9.
113. Barnes to Guy Pène du Bois, September 1, 1914, BFA.
114. As Stein wrote to Mabel Weeks on April 4, 1914: "I am going to Florence a simple minded person of the "Old School" without a single Picasso, hardly any Matisses, only 2 Cézanne paintings and some aquarelles, and 16 Renoirs"; quoted in Irene Gordon, ed., *Four Americans in Paris: The Collections of Gertrude Stein and Her Family* (New York: The Museum of Modern Art, 1970), p. 29; Richardson, *Life of Picasso*, p. 397 n. 66.
115. Stein, *Journey Into the Self*, p. 18.

116. Ibid., pp. 18–19.

117. "If the two Renoirs—Mother with child and the little nude standing in water—are to be sold, you can probably do better with me than with the dealers," Barnes to Stein, February 9, 1914, cited at note 110 above. For its purchase in May 1921, see Barnes to Stein, May 9, 1921, BFA. Barnes was now acting as the agent for selling the remainder of Stein's collection (thirty-four paintings, including sixteen by Renoir, noting (ungenerously), "I had not seen your pictures since 1913 and was very much surprised as [to] the slight, unimportant character of nearly all of them." For the background to these final sales, see Stein, *Journey Into the Self*, pp. 83–87.

118. Invoice, June 12, 1913, BFA.

119. Richardson, *Life of Picasso*, pp. 448–49, 454–55; and Jeffrey S. Weiss in Wattenmaker et al., *Great French Paintings*, p. 200.

120. Barnes sold the Matisse to the dealer Etienne Bignou in December 1935 for $6,000 toward the cost of Renoir's *Bather and Maid*, acquired for $50,000; see Riopelle in Wattenmaker et al., *Great French Paintings*, p. 80 n. 6.

121. Barnes to Stein, July 17, 1914, BFA. This three-page, single-spaced letter is one of the most expressive testaments of aesthetic faith ever written by a collector.

122. Ibid. This letter was first published in Colin B. Bailey, "The Origins of the Barnes Collection, 1912–15," *The Burlington Magazine*, 150, no. 1265 (August 2008), pp. 534–43.

A Need for Portraits: John Sloan, Robert Henri, and John Butler Yeats

AVIS BERMAN

Lecture given on May 23, 2007

National Academy Museum and School of Fine Arts

New York City

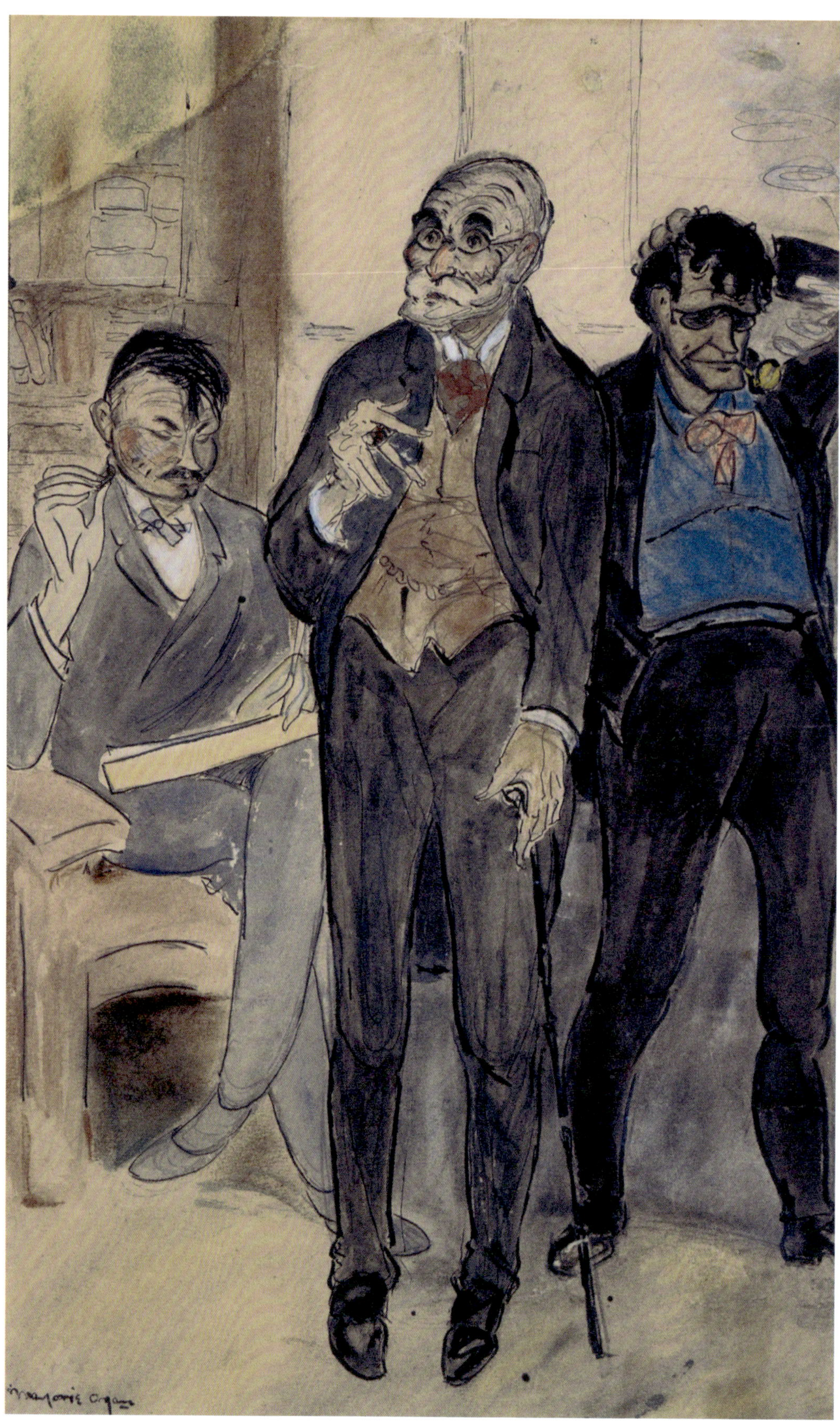

A Need for Portraits: John Sloan, Robert Henri, and John Butler Yeats

AVIS BERMAN

In analyzing artists through their portraits, we first turn to likenesses painted on canvas, etched on a plate, or exposed on a negative. But equally compelling in the study of artists and why they make the images they do are those portraits deduced and composed from the examination of their psychological and social motivations. This sort of assessment is especially revealing in the case of the American painter and printmaker John Sloan (Fig. 65). Sloan could not have matured into the artist he was without the catalytic and interlocking relationships he sustained with two other forceful personalities–the painters Robert Henri and John Butler Yeats. The transformative power of the personal and intellectual friendships formed by these artists—friendships that became central experiences, opened doors to new worlds, provided essential support and inspiration, and were the impetus to intense rounds of portrait-making—does much to explain mysterious and lesser-known facets of Sloan's life and work. The three men's interactions also had more general consequences for American art—they prompted drawings, paintings, and prints produced by a number of outstanding artists in Sloan and Henri's orbit.

A close examination of Sloan's background and early history gives clarity to the reasons that his later friendships mattered so highly to him and why they shaped the development of his art. Sloan depended on charismatic male figures—indeed, father figures—in order to repair familial damage and replace what he lacked in his own past.

Sloan (1871–1951) was born in Lock Haven, in central Pennsylvania, the only son of Henrietta Ireland Sloan and James Dixon Sloan (Fig. 64). He was the eldest child, and was followed by two sisters, Elizabeth and Marianna. Henrietta Sloan was from the Philadelphia area. She had been a schoolteacher, and her wealthy relatives felt that she had married beneath her. James Sloan's family business, building furniture and coffins, had failed, and James, a Civil War veteran, eked out a living as a freelance photographer and a bicycle repairman, but neither occupation had the potential for

Fig. 63
Marjorie Organ
Portrait of Henri, Yeats, and Sloan, n.d.
Gouache and black ink on paper
19½ × 12¼ in. (49.5 × 31.1 cm)
Museum of Art, Fort Lauderdale,
Nova Southeastern University, Florida;
Bequest of Ira Glackens 91.40.61

high earnings. In the household in which John Sloan grew up, little physical affection was expressed,[1] and his mother's gloomy religiosity and prim decorum were aped by his sisters, who were raised as conventional females.[2]

James Sloan was a well-intentioned man, but he could not manage money. He was, said his son, "a total wreck in business."[3] In 1877 the family lost their home and, as a result, they moved in with Henrietta's parents, the Irelands, in Germantown, Pennsylvania, outside of Philadelphia, while the unemployed James Sloan looked for work. Although unsuccessful in his search, through Ireland family connections he was eventually given a job as a traveling salesman for a publisher of books and greeting cards, a job that further demeaned his dignity.

With that sporadic income, the Sloans were able to move from Germantown to Philadelphia, where John Sloan went to Central High School, and met and became friends with William Glackens and Albert C. Barnes, the future inventor and businessman who would amass one of the great collections of modern art. In 1883 James Sloan left his sales job to establish a related business—a stationery store, again financed by his wife's family. Along with being a poor manager, he was kind and extended credit to his customers—a kindness that disappointed his wife and daughters. These experiences lay behind the mature John Sloan's staunch belief that commercial success often equaled spiritual and creative failure.[4] In 1887 the stationery business was forced to close, and James Sloan resorted to doing odd jobs and raising chickens in the backyard. His perceived personal inadequacies and financial collapse precipitated a depression and mental breakdown. James Sloan was never able to work again and spent the

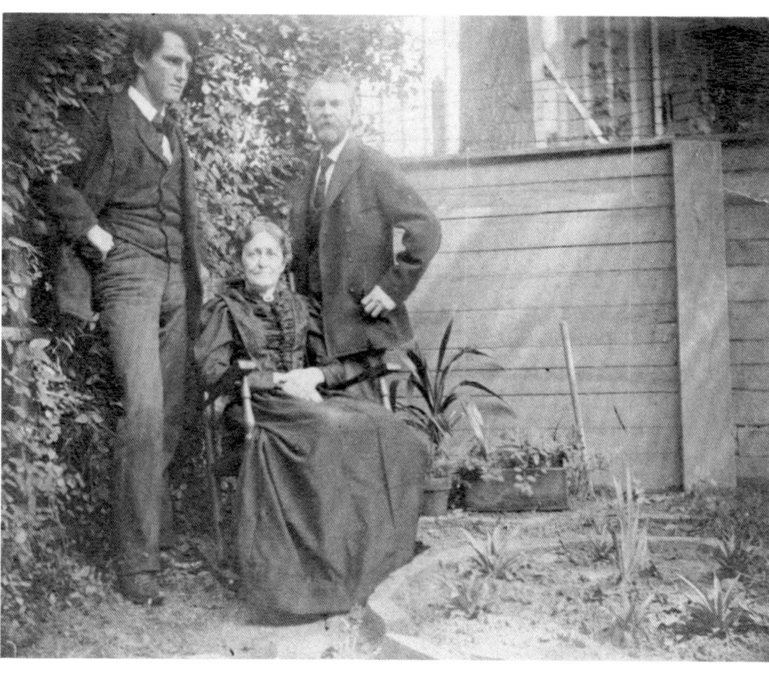

Fig. 64
John Sloan, Henrietta Ireland Sloan, and James Dixon Sloan in the yard at 1921 Camac Street, Philadelphia, 1898
John Sloan Manuscript Collection, Delaware Art Museum, Wilmington; Gift of Helen Farr Sloan, 1978

Fig. 65
Gertrude Käsebier
John French Sloan, c. 1907
Platinum print
8¹⁄₁₆ × 6 in. (20.5 × 15.3 cm)
National Portrait Gallery, Smithsonian Institution, Washington, D.C.
NPG 78.246

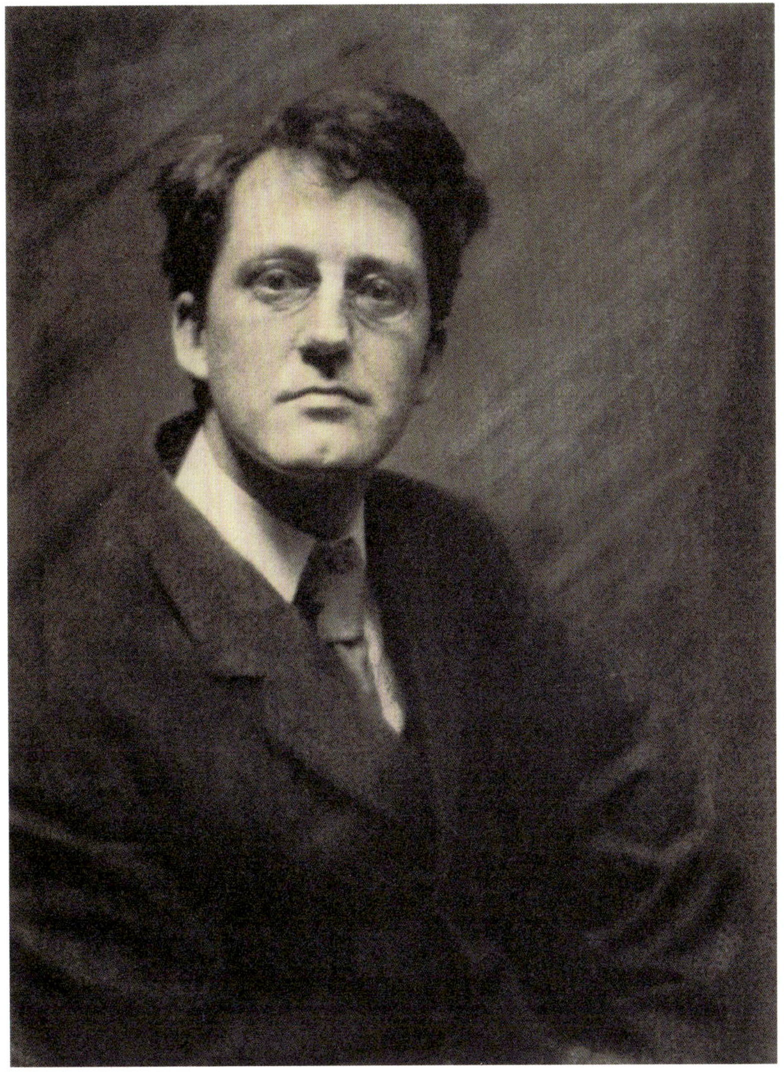

rest of his life tending chickens and raising vegetables in the garden. At age sixteen, John Sloan had to drop out of school to support his mother, father, and sisters. In a reversal of roles, John Sloan was elevated to head of the family; his father, who could no longer protect or care for him, was further humiliated. Such responsibility for the rest of his family was an open-ended affair, and would last for decades. After Sloan married in 1901, his wife, Dolly, persuaded him that he could not remain his family's sole support, and one of Sloan's sisters did begin working around that time. However, letters exist from Sloan's father dated as late as 1909, 1910, and 1911 thanking his son for money that he had sent.[5] According to John Butler Yeats, Sloan sent his family at least twenty dollars every month, which probably amounted to about fifteen percent of his early income.[6]

Although Sloan's father was physically present in the household, he was absent as a force, especially when measured against the ruling values and mores of his mother and sisters. John Sloan was profoundly affected by, and would continue to suffer from, paternal deprivation—an emotional condition that the psychiatrist James Herzog has labeled "father hunger."[7] Herzog contends that when a child's need for an active father is not satisfied, and consequently the need for closeness with a father that encourages a boy to feel secure in developing a masculine identity is thwarted, it becomes nearly impossible for a man to form a full and fulfilling relationship with an adult partner.[8] This deficiency crippled Sloan's relationships with women during the formative period of his youth. For Sloan, alleviating father hunger was also paramount to his development as a creative artist. But in that sphere, he was able to repair the damage he had suffered and blossom creatively by seeking and successfully establishing relationships with replacement fathers. Sloan himself testified that his father's collapse was a traumatic event that he continually revisited: "After that [James Sloan's loss of his business] my father was really broken in spirit," he noted. "This gentle intelligent man walked with his head bowed all the rest of his life. I don't think I was ever bitter about going without a college education, but I cannot bear to remember the look of melancholy defeat on my father's face when he had to tell me the family had decided I must leave school."[9]

As his father might have, Sloan initially accepted a post as an errand boy at the office of the Ireland family lawyer. But he mustered enough initiative to get a job at a book and print dealer's shop, where he could read in his spare time and draw; there he taught himself to etch. In 1890 he was asked by A. Edward Newton, the proprietor of a fancy stationery store, to join his establishment, where he would design and illustrate calendars, Christmas cards, bookmarks, and matchboxes.[10] This position naturally appealed to Sloan because he could work as a graphic artist, but employment in a stationery store might also have been part of an effort to embrace and connect with his father, who had been a stationer—the one business he had owned and in which he had briefly been the boss. Sloan did not yet think of himself as a fine artist—he had not conceived of the idea that he could be one, although he did learn how to use oil paint by studying a manual. Sloan painted only one canvas in 1890, an earnest self-portrait. He took care to write on the back, "Stretcher made by father for this painting."[11]

After a year and a half with Newton and a few months as a freelance designer, Sloan was hired as an illustrator by the *Philadelphia Inquirer* in early 1892.[12] There he renewed his acquaintance with Glackens, who was also drawing for the newspaper at the time. Another recruit for the *Inquirer*'s art department was Everett Shinn, and when he, Glackens, and Sloan transferred to the rival *Philadelphia Press*, they worked with George Luks, who was yet another illustrator-reporter. Their careers as artists were some years in the

Fig. 66
Gertrude Käsebier
Robert Henri, c. 1907–08
Platinum print
8¼ × 6¼ in. (21 × 15.9 cm)
Delaware Art Museum, Wilmington;
Gift of Helen Farr Sloan, 1978

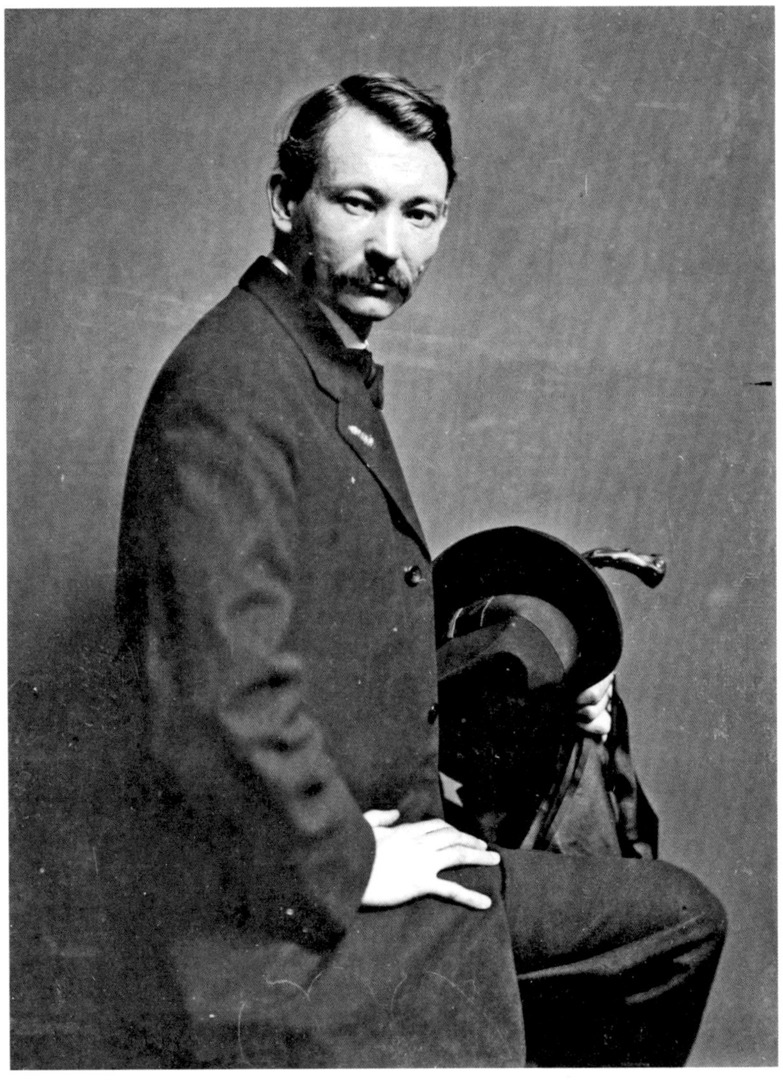

future. Although Sloan was in a better situation than he was before, he was still navigating without a map. But their destinies were altered after their introduction to Robert Henri (1865–1929) [Fig. 66], whom Sloan met at a party in the sculptor Charles Grafly's studio in December 1892 and ever after credited as the person who redirected his life. Sloan referred to him as "the emancipator," "the Abraham Lincoln of American art," and most significantly, "my father in art."[13] Henri was only six years older than Sloan, but he was already a trained painter, and he had lived in Paris, where he had seen the work of the old masters firsthand. He was free from the chains of family responsibilities, he was exciting, he was glamorous, and he knew how to light the fire of ambition. Sloan caught Henri's fire—here was a charismatic father figure who had everything Sloan needed and had lacked before. Henri exuded confidence: he could help Sloan realize his talents and abilities and guide him toward the right kind of success—to paint for himself alone. Sloan, Henri, and the painter Joe Laub shared a studio at 806 Walnut Street from 1893 to 1894. Sloan repeatedly said that Henri could make anyone want to be a painter, and he was chiefly responsible for getting Sloan to be one.[14]

In his compilation of Sloan and Henri's correspondence, the art historian Bennard Perlman astutely observed, "Henri made a habit of testing Sloan's friendship and devotion by saddling him with various responsibilities: instructing Henri's art classes, seeing that his paintings were delivered to various exhibitions, even overseeing the . . . move of Henri's studio" from one building to another.[15] Although Sloan did grumble in his diaries about the grunt work that fell to him, he nonetheless habitually accepted those tasks with a degree of pleasure: assisting Henri was a means of restaging a relationship with his father, which this time would have a happy ending. Sloan was subconsciously comforted by having a decisive man like Henri rely on him because it was a mark of attention and trust (Fig. 67).

In the mid-1890s, because of his family responsibilities and newspaper work, Sloan was not painting regularly, and before he met Henri he had only managed to finish a few portraits and a landscape or two. Under Henri's influence, he tried something different—some dark, uningratiating pictures of Philadelphia, such as *Philadelphia Stock Exchange* (c. 1897–98; Delaware Art Museum, Wilmington), which reflected an immersion in the older man's gods—Velázquez, Goya, and Manet—as well as his espousal of urban subject matter. "All my instruction in painting came from Henri, but indirectly, not in class," Sloan said. "When I started to paint a few portrait studies he gave me criticisms, and . . . [when] I began to paint city life pictures, . . . [they] aroused his real enthusiasm."[16] Henri's friendship came as a great shaft of light, illuminating new possibilities and sweeping away some of Sloan's cultural isolation.

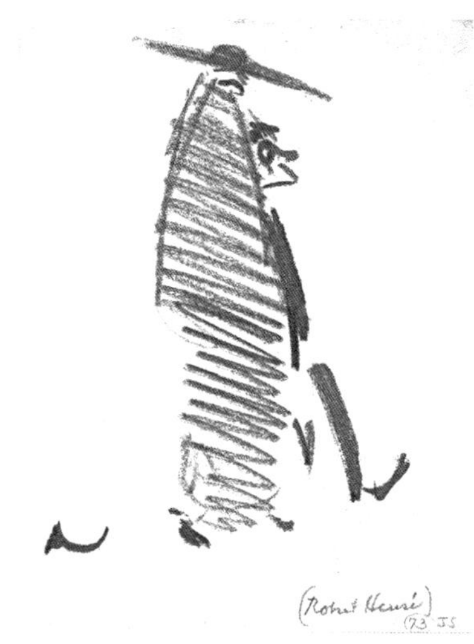

Fig. 67
Robert Henri
Caricature of Henri and Sloan Walking, n.d.
Crayon on paper
6¼ × 4⅞ in. (15.9 × 12.4 cm)
Delaware Art Museum, Wilmington; Gift of Helen Farr Sloan

Sloan looked to Henri for guidance on such paintings as *Independence Square, Philadelphia* (1900; Collection of Abby and Alan D. Levy, Los Angeles) and *East Entrance, City Hall, Philadelphia* (Fig. 68). When Sloan asked what he thought of the latter, Henri gave it his blessing, writing,

> It pleases me mightily just as it is—fine value of height, and carrying up. cuts [*sic*] off much to my taste and is sure to come out a rival of the "Square" [*Independence Square, Philadelphia*] if you get the figures below to give as much of that eternal business of life—going in and coming out, as you get the eternal park loitering sense in the other.
>
> It seems to me that you will surely get another thing out of it.[17]

Henri's critique was prescient. "That eternal business of life"—the going in and coming out of the human tide—would become a hallmark of Sloan's most striking work. And he created it most often and most incisively when there was a like-minded companion or mentor

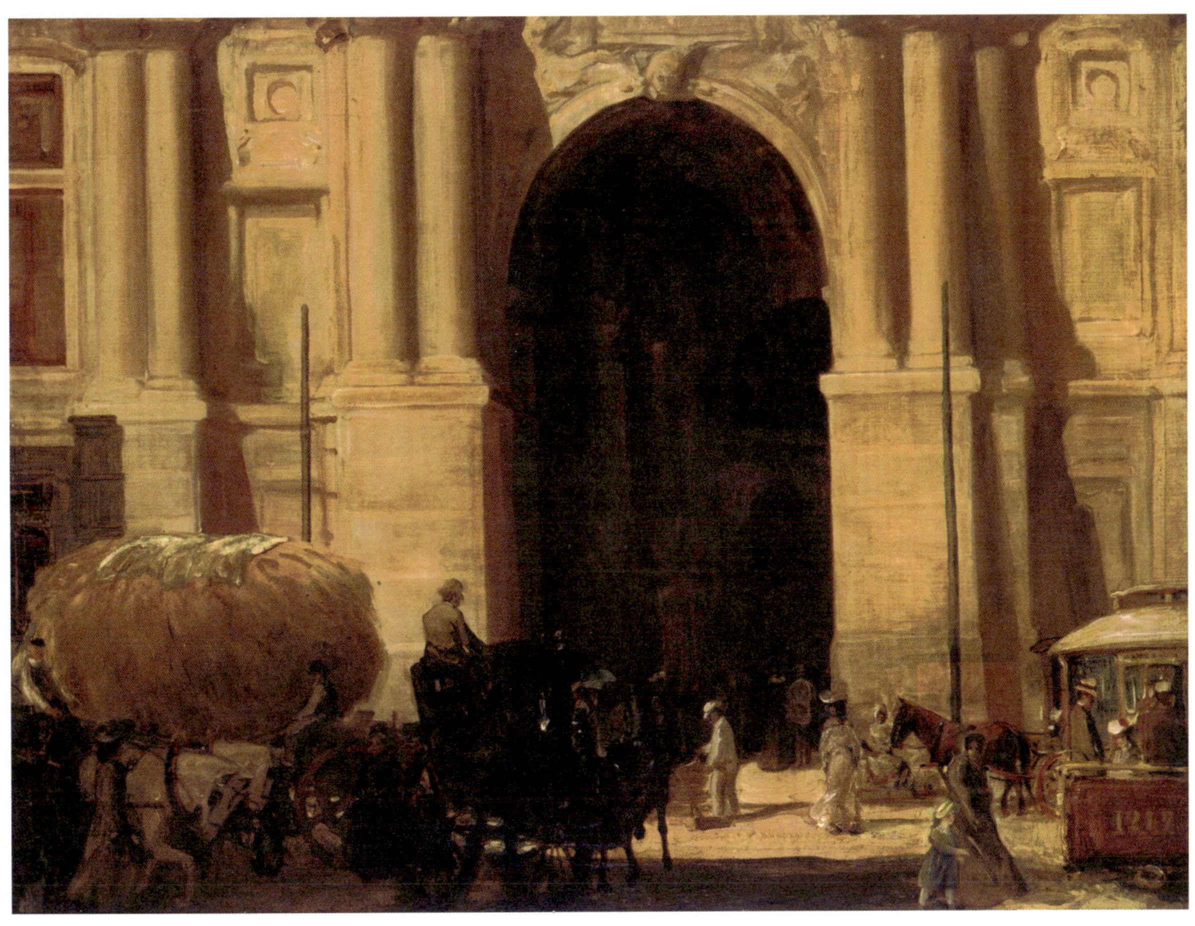

Fig. 68
John Sloan
East Entrance, City Hall, Philadelphia,
1901
Oil on canvas
27¼ × 36 in. (69.2 × 91.4 cm)
Columbus Museum of Art, Ohio;
Howald Fund Purchase 1960.006

nearby, whenever his father hunger was sated. Sloan confirmed this, saying that his "city paintings were inspired by Henri's doctrine of painting with an emotional concept."[18]

Henri's paternal attention to Sloan declined after his marriage in June 1898 to Linda Craige, a former student who was from an upper-crust Philadelphia family. The couple spent a fourteen-month honeymoon in Europe and, upon their return in September 1900, they moved to New York. Henri correctly sensed that his career would improve in Manhattan and successfully applied for a teaching job there.

By the time the Henris were back from their wedding trip, Sloan was living with twenty-two-year-old Anna M. Wall, known as Dolly for her small stature—she was only four feet nine (Fig. 69). Tellingly, Sloan met and became involved with Dolly within thirty days of Henri's marriage and departure, and one can only suspect to what degree that this massively self-destructive choice of a mate was in reaction to Henri's perceived abandonment of him. Indeed, in a letter to Henri in 1898 explaining his attachment—Henri had cautioned Sloan about getting involved with Dolly in case she would deflect him from becoming an artist—Sloan wrote as a partial explanation, "of course when you 'jumped into harness and flew the coop' I was in the blues."[19] Henri suggested keeping Dolly as a mistress, but Sloan was determined to marry her, which was a disaster of his own choosing. Dolly Sloan's parents, who were poor immigrants, had died when she was a child. Her life was hardscrabble, and she was a woeful alcoholic and a manic-depressive by the time she was an adolescent.[20] Her illnesses were never cured, but Sloan, in his role as all-responsible father, evidently thought he could handle someone in her mental condition. He tended to infantilize her, as did John Butler Yeats, who described her as a "child woman." In her letters to her husband, Dolly was complicit in promoting this image, constantly referring to herself as "your little girl," "your little baby girl," and "your baby girl."[21]

Dolly was thrown out of her brother's house at the age of fifteen, and she had to survive on the street.[22] By the time Sloan met her, she was working in a brothel, though she also had a job in the accounting department of a large store. Perhaps because he had no role model for how to conduct himself as a man, Sloan had been afraid of women since he was a teenager. He did not know how to judge women and, fearing maternal engulfment, he had had no real relationships with any.[23] In his unpublished notes, he compared going to Europe, which he never attempted, with "being caught by a scheming woman."[24] He saw both endeavors as financial traps, as reprises of his long support of his mother and sisters.

In 1898 Sloan worked nights at the newspaper and kept late hours. He used the fact of his schedule to rationalize his courtship of Dolly, who, unlike more conventional women, would see him after his shift in the press room ended. In unpublished notes, Sloan described their

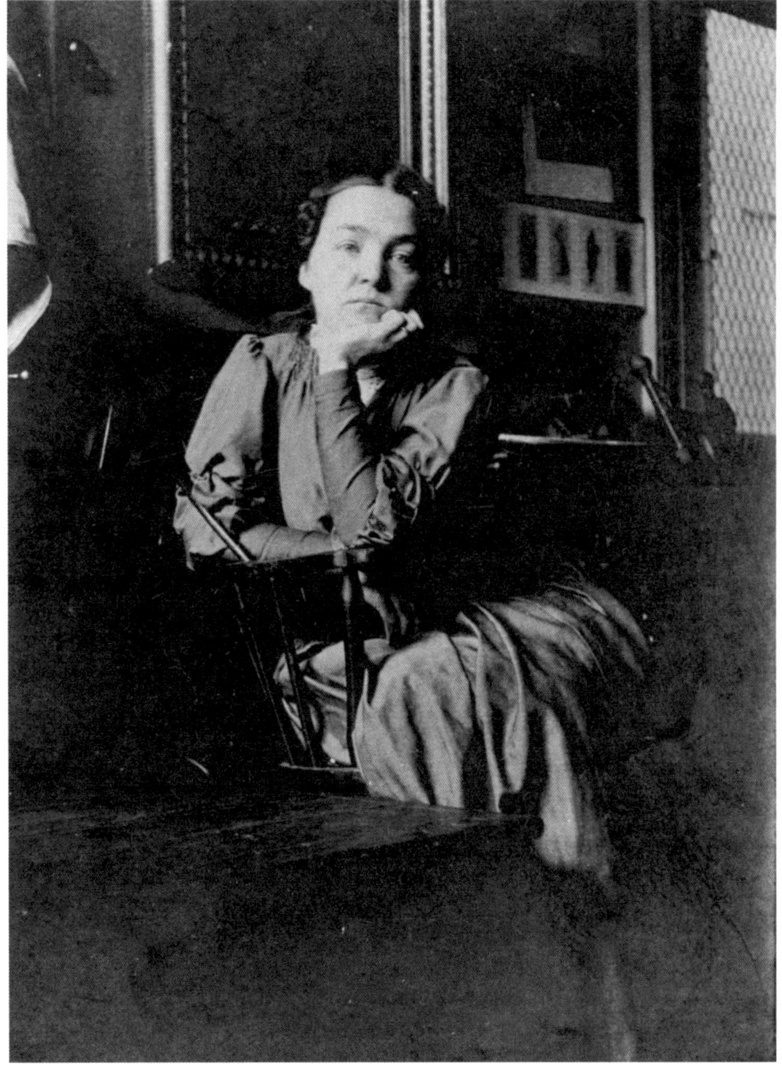

Fig. 69
Dolly Sloan, c. 1906
John Sloan Manuscript Collection, Delaware Art Museum, Wilmington; Gift of Helen Farr Sloan, 1978

typical meeting as follows: "I used to call her up at her boarding house around eleven at night when I got out of the newspaper office & then we'd go drink ale until three or four in the morning at some chop & oyster house."[25] On these outings, Sloan tolerated and accepted Dolly's drinking. But in these same notes, written after more than twenty-five years of marriage, he also said, "If I could press a button with my foot right now that would remove liquor from the world, I'd do it." His diaries are littered with an anagram which, unscrambled, meant "wife drunk."[26] In his diaries and other writings, Sloan was honest enough to record himself consuming plenty of liquor—he drank to forget the miseries of his union with Dolly.

Without Henri nearby, Sloan's paintings reflected his lack of focus. Missing Henri's tutelage, he created fewer of the city scenes that Henri had advocated. In 1903, Sloan lost his job at the *Philadelphia Press*, and in April 1904, he and Dolly moved to New York, where not only Henri, but Glackens, Shinn, and Luks had already relocated. At first the Sloans moved into the same building as the Henris—the Sherwood Building at Fifty-seventh Street and Sixth Avenue. This was the first and last time Sloan lived uptown; in September 1904, the Sloans moved to 165 West Twenty-third Street, and Sloan's life as an unsurpassed chronicler of New York life began.

Sloan had willingly settled into a less than ideal marital relationship, but one compensation was the romance of living in New York. Sloan spoke of the city as if it were Cleopatra or Helen of Troy. Manhattan, he wrote, "is a massive creation, heaped upon one small island—ambiguous, evasive, ever changing and always fascinating, like a woman's smile."[27] For Sloan, there was an equation between New York and womanhood. The central figure in so many of his paintings is a blooming, vibrant woman who is something less than innocent or virginal.[28] His images of women are always contemporary in their costumes and attitudes, and he and they enjoy their attractiveness, but the artist does so from a distance. Although realistically rendered, Sloan's female figures are fantasies in that they are the wish fulfillment of his desires, painted realizations of the independent dream woman he had prevented himself from having.

Sloan also began to paint more once he relocated to Manhattan for the simple reason that Henri was steadily organizing exhibitions between 1904 and 1906 that included him, and he had few other outlets to show his work. His first New York genre painting was *The Coffee Line* (1905; Carnegie Museum of Art, Pittsburgh), a vignette showing a line of cold and hungry men queuing up at Madison Square. Compared with the livelier treatment of the same subject in *Spring, Madison Square* (1905–06; Chazen Museum of Art, University of Wisconsin, Madison), begun about eight months later, it is still more like a Philadelphia picture in its subdued mood. Even more advanced in style and handling is the complex group of figures and fluid, swirling movement of *The Picnic Grounds* (Fig. 70), begun in June 1906 and completed in the autumn of the same year. However, in February 1907, Sloan worked on it again "to get it into shape" for the National Academy of Design's annual exhibition, which opened the next month.[29]

The Picnic Grounds was accepted by the Academy's jury without incident and was part of the March 1907 exhibition, but events did not usually proceed so felicitously between the Academy and Sloan, Henri, and their allies in art. One hundred years ago, the National Academy of Design was the most powerful artists' society in New York and hence in the country. With so few galleries for younger artists in existence, acceptance to its exhibitions could mean the difference between survival and failure. Henri was tireless in maneuvering his friends into shows, and was a political firebrand whom Sloan described as a "philosophical anarchist."[30] He had been safely elected

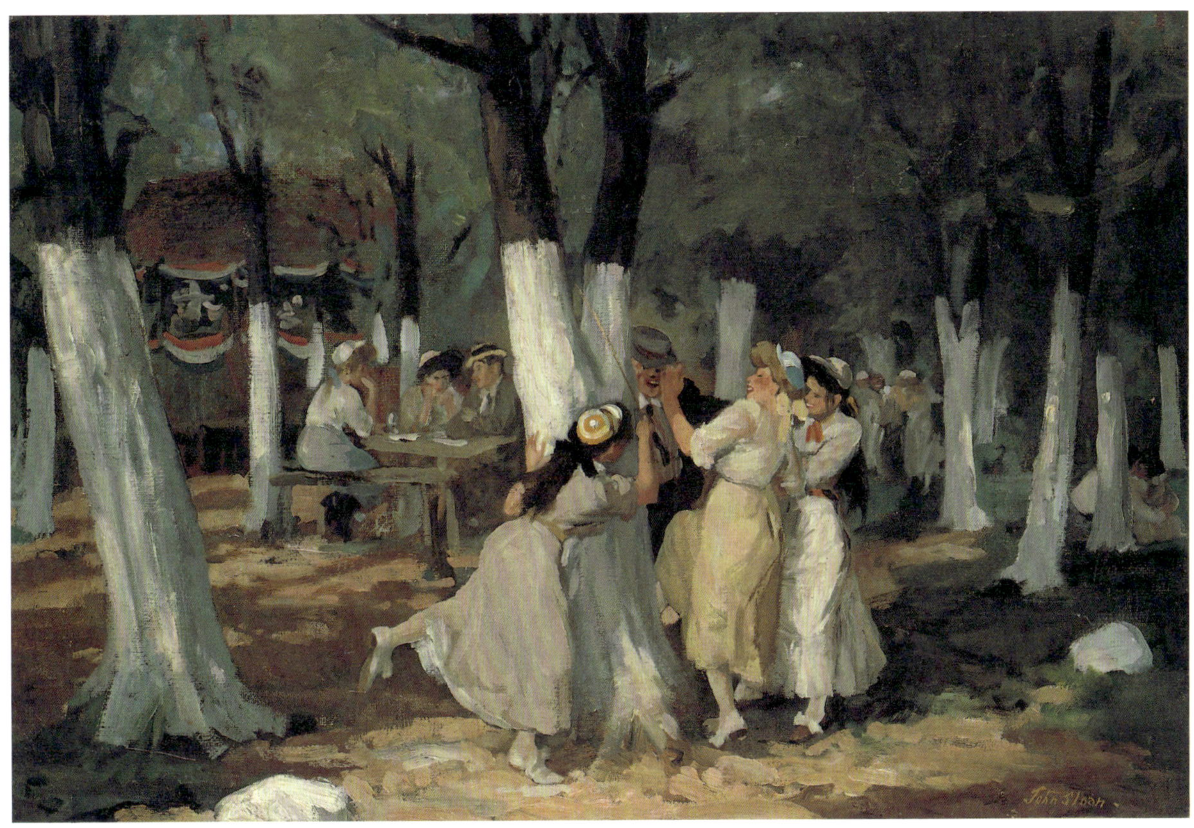

Fig. 70
John Sloan
The Picnic Grounds, 1906–07
Oil on canvas
24 × 36 in. (61 × 91.4 cm)
Whitney Museum of American Art, New York; Purchase 41.34

to the Academy; if he challenged the institution, he would risk his own standing and livelihood. Yet he was determined to do so when his friends were not allowed to exhibit there. In March 1907, when Henri was a member of the Academy's jury, his own paintings were snubbed, and Sloan's other submission was rejected, as were canvases by Glackens, Luks, and Shinn. Henri removed two of his own paintings in protest, and the group decided to mount an exhibition of their own. Henri became the leader who selected the participating artists—himself, Sloan, Glackens, Luks, and Shinn, as well as Arthur B. Davies, Ernest Lawson, and Maurice Prendergast. The group, of course, would eventually become known as The Eight, and their exhibition was a vital step in the struggle to democratize the process by which American artists could put their work before a wider audience. Normally, much of what transpired in art circles did so in the face of public indifference, but the birth of The Eight was noticed. Henri was a well-known artist, his friends were seasoned journalists, and the affair generated splashy headlines in the New York papers.

Sloan and Henri were especially close again by 1907—and Sloan's painting reflected their renewed bond in both proficiency and amplitude[31]—because Linda Henri had died in December 1905 at the age of thirty. Henri could not work in his studio or bear to be alone, so in early 1906 he temporarily moved in with the Sloans.[32] Linda was esteemed by Sloan because she had always been kind to Dolly, and as a memorial to the times they had enjoyed together, Sloan created the ineffable etching *Memory* (Fig. 71). For all his adroitness at depicting crowds, Sloan was an intimist of a high caliber when it came to depicting himself and his friends. Seeking to comfort the distraught Henri and commemorate the many convivial evenings the Sloans and Henris had spent together, he began *Memory* in January 1906.[33] The day after he started making the sketch for the plate, Sloan, in conscious recognition of Henri's paternal role in his life, wrote that he was working on his "Family" group.[34] *Memory* is a moving evocation of the two couples' friendship in the tradition of the conversation piece, a portrait in which the sitters are involved in their normal, everyday activities. In Sloan's informal rendering, memory permeates every aspect of the image. The scene is Henri's New York studio, and the table around which everyone sits came from his old rooms in Philadelphia, where Sloan was reborn as an artist through Henri's motivating force. Henri and Sloan are drawing, and Dolly Sloan gazes into the distance while Linda Henri reads aloud. Sloan's keen visual retentiveness is apparent in each figure's typical posture and gesture, and Henri himself was astonished to see that Sloan had noticed and recorded Linda's habit of rolling her fingers as she read.[35] Memory, as a title and as a subject, is a gloss on Sloan's own artistic processes. Although often classified as a transcriber of what he saw—men and women enjoying the small pleasures of their urban surroundings—Sloan actually memorized the raw material that he noticed during his travels around the city and, once back in his studio, he selected and abstracted details from his original observations. For him, memory was sharper, more vivid, and more real than a mere visual record because the impressions that remained were more likely to be the essence of the thing itself. This densely layered etching is an exaltation of recalled experience.

An event that would prove important for Sloan and Henri was the arrival of John Butler Yeats in the United States in December 1907. Born in County Down, Ireland, Yeats (1839–1922) [Fig. 72] was for many years known merely as the father of two magnificent sons—the incomparable William Butler Yeats, perhaps the arch-poet of the twentieth century, and Jack Yeats, a pioneering modernist painter. John Butler Yeats (referred to hereafter as "JBY" to avoid confusion with William and Jack), also had two remarkable daughters, Susan Mary and Elizabeth Corbet Yeats, known to everyone as Lily and Lollie. They worked as textile artists, rare book binders, and publishers.

John Butler Yeats was far more than a father to genius. He was a ravishing personality in his own right, and his eloquent letters and conversation make it easy to identify the source of his children's gifts.

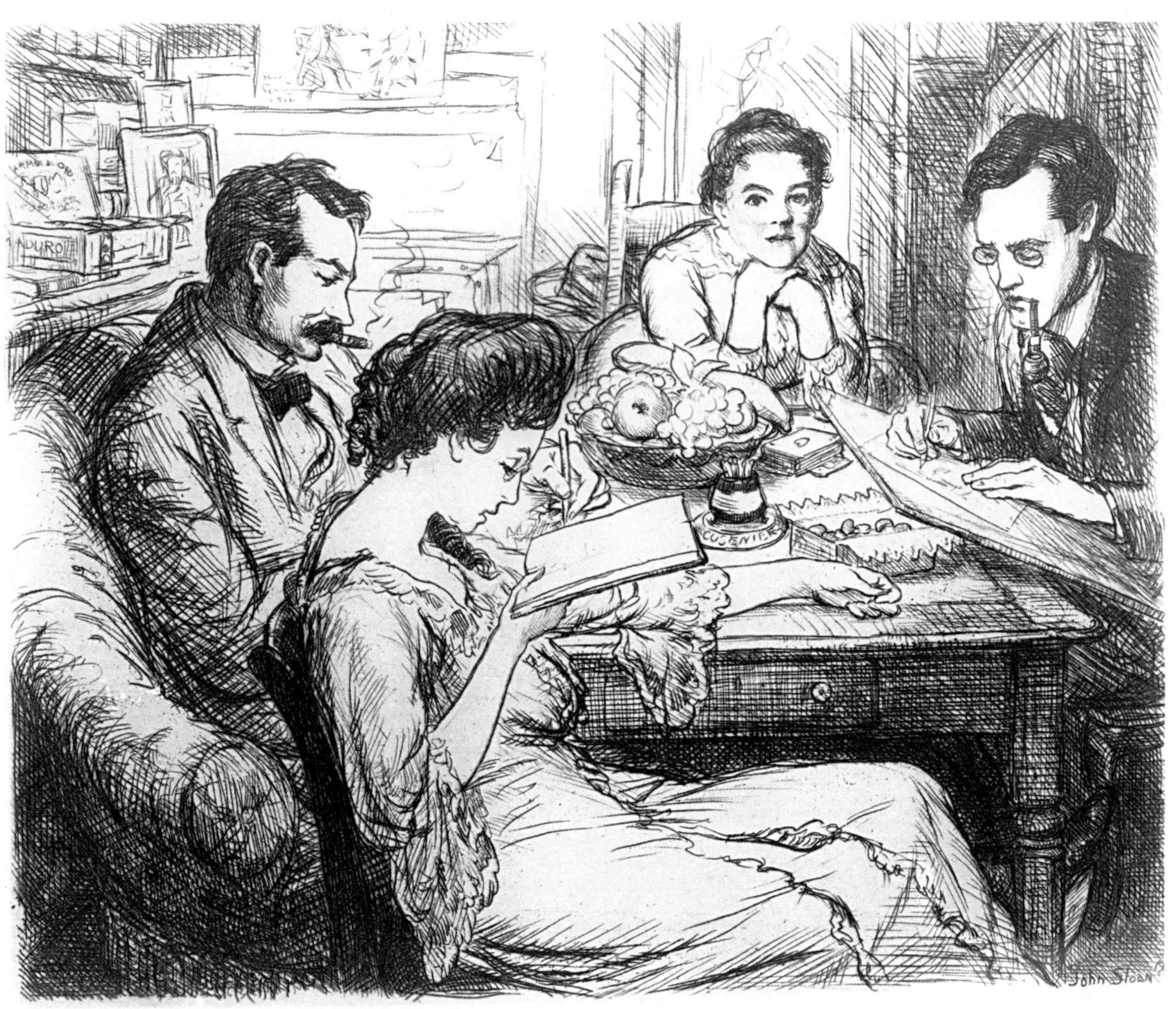

Fig. 71
John Sloan
Memory, 1906
Etching on paper
Sheet: 9 9/16 × 12 5/8 in. (24.3 × 32.1 cm)
Whitney Museum of American Art, New York; Purchase 31.825

JBY began life somewhat conventionally, taking his degree from Trinity College in Dublin in 1862. That year, he traveled to County Sligo to visit George Pollexfen, an old school friend. He met George's sister, Susan Pollexfen, and proposed to her. They were married in 1863, when JBY was studying law at the King's Inns; he took honors and was on his way to what looked like a shrewd career as a barrister. He suddenly abandoned the law to pursue his heart's desire—to become an artist, specializing in portraiture, and moved his family to London to pursue his new vocation.[36]

JBY had undoubted talent, but the decision horrified the relentlessly business-like Pollexfens. His wife, Susan, who had expected a more comfortable existence and had no interest in aesthetic matters, lived in a permanent state of despondency. Even though Yeats painted steadily, he was unable to demand money for his portraits, or follow up on money owed. He used up his inheritance and incurred debts, and, like John Sloan's father, was deemed a failure by the world at

Fig. 72
Alice Boughton
John Butler Yeats, December 1907
Photograph courtesy Library of Congress Prints and Photographs Division, Washington, D.C.; Gift, Everett Boughton, 1945

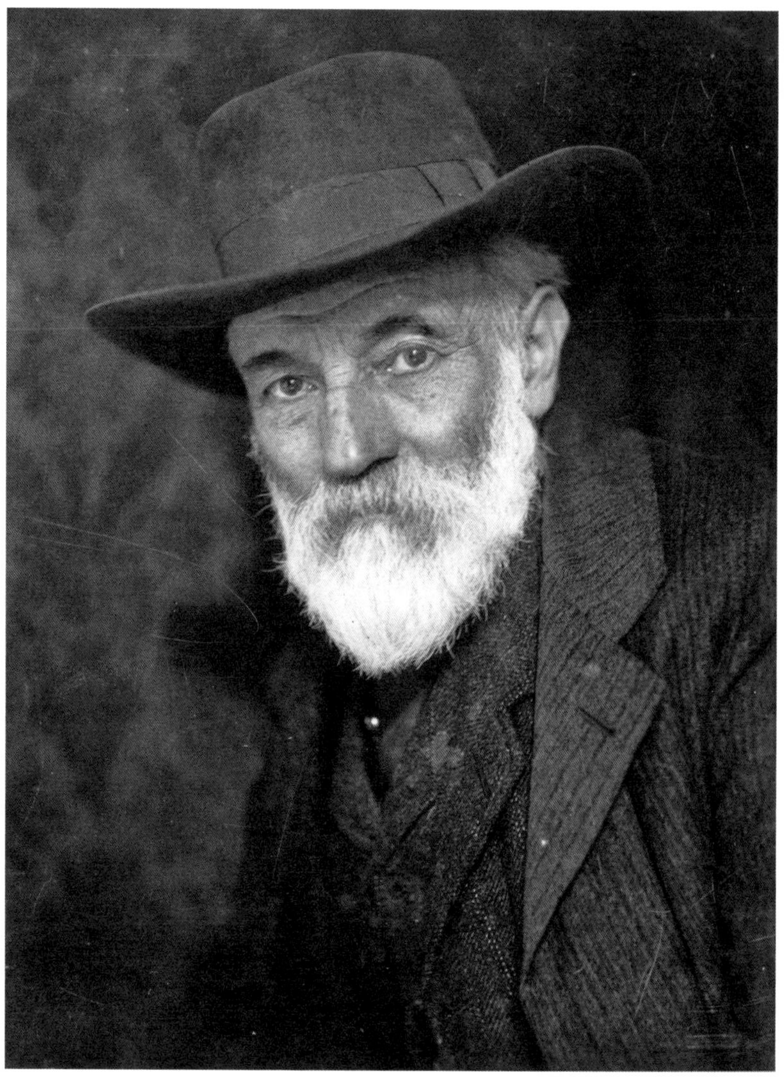

large. Writing about how such opposites produced their vastly articulate children, JBY mused, "The Pollexfens are as solid and powerful as the sea cliffs, but hitherto they are altogether dumb. . . . By marriage to a Pollexfen, I have given a tongue to the sea cliffs."[37] And at one point, when he was in New York and William sent him some much-needed cash as a surprise, JBY wrote to his daughter Lily, "It may be endlessly debated whether Willie is a Pollexfen or a Yeats . . . . It was like a Yeats to send this money and make no fuss about it. It was like a Pollexfen to have it to send."[38]

Yeats's choice of art over the law was not the absurdity that the Pollexfens thought. He was the opposite of a society portraitist, preferring to paint the artists, writers, politicians, and thinkers he knew rather than the rich and titled. This seemingly foolish idea of assembling his own gallery of the mightiest minds in Ireland—sitters who could not afford to pay for paintings—secured his future reputation as the visual historian of the Irish Renaissance. With sensitivity and discernment, he painted and drew such intellectual luminaries of the Celtic Revival as John O'Leary, George Russell, Douglas Hyde, Lady Augusta Gregory, John Millington Synge, George Moore, and of course Jack and William Butler Yeats. When Robert Henri went to Ireland for the first time during the summer of 1913, he visited the National Gallery of Ireland in Dublin, and wrote to Sloan about Yeats's merits as a portraitist. As JBY proudly told a friend, "He was a week in Dublin and saw all my portraits and prefers them to [Sir William] Orpen's. . . . So there. I am in my 75th year and life is just beginning."[39] Yeats, who had considered Orpen his primary rival in Dublin,[40] continued to trumpet Henri's compliments to everyone he knew, including his son Jack, for whom he added the detail, "[Henri] says that I am the most modest portrait painter he ever met."[41]

Yet especially after Susan Pollexfen Yeats's death in 1900, which he blamed on his own shortcomings as a provider, JBY felt the need to justify his decision of choosing art over the law. He made his children the reason:

> I ought to have stayed in Dublin and worked hard for success, for that was the voice of prudence. But had I been a success as a lawyer, my son would have grown up an ordinary citizen of Dublin. Because I turned artist and lived in London among wild men and poets . . . my sons are now distinguished men, not of the sort called prudent, my second an artist and writer, and my eldest son a poet of the highest importance to Ireland.[42]

Because of his training, Yeats had a formidable education, far more extensive than the American artists he met, and they respected him for his store of learning, his ability to quote from literature and philosophy, and his readiness to apply them to argument and insight about their own work.[43] But he was looked down on in Dublin, and in 1907 he was desperate. Old guilt, both financial and emotional, dogged him, as well as the specter of his sons rapidly eclipsing what small reputation that he had.

In January 1908, a large Irish exhibition was to open in New York at which the Yeats sisters would be selling their embroideries, and forty-two-year-old Lily, the elder of the two daughters, was slated to attend the event in person. At the last minute, JBY decided to join her. On December 29, 1907, they sailed into New York Harbor for what was ostensibly a six-week holiday abroad. Both father and daughter reveled in Manhattan's spectacle, and they extended their visit. Lily took ship for Ireland on June 6, 1908. But John Butler Yeats evaded repatriation, permanently exchanging the "hopeless insolvency"[44] of Ireland for the hopeful penury of New York.

Yeats intended to return to his Dublin studio when he left for Manhattan, but as his letters home make clear, he was excited by the possibilities of a new life and made up his mind quickly. As early as

January 13, 1908, two weeks after his arrival, he wrote home to his daughter Lollie that he would not leave New York if he "could help it, because I am convinced that fortune awaits me here."[45] If not fortune, he did gain the freedom to read, write, sketch, stroll, drink wine, smoke cigars, and philosophize, unfettered by the debts and family responsibilities that plagued him in Dublin. He also looked at the wealth around him and prophesied—somewhat faultily, as it turned out, to Jack Yeats, "[T]here will be a need for portraits here and for that I shall come in handy."[46]

JBY's impulse to flee his birthplace had invigorating consequences for American art. His presence would spur many drawings, paintings, and prints produced by a number of outstanding artists, most notably John Sloan. And, because he was as adept at character sketches in words as he was at those composed with a pencil or a brush, Yeats wrote to family and friends in Ireland and England constantly about his expanding set of acquaintances, and his letters are a treasury of information on the lives of the many Americans he knew.

At the age of sixty-eight—and this at a time when no social safety net existed for someone who would today be classified as an illegal alien—JBY, exhibiting lunatic optimism, opted for a life of insecurity. He believed he could triumph in New York as a portrait painter, writer, and lecturer, ever postponing his departure. At first his activities (and Lily's) were orchestrated and subsidized by his patron, John Quinn. A redoubtable lawyer and a leading collector of modern art, Quinn was an admirer of William Butler Yeats, and helped the rest of the family as a measure of his regard; he was tickled by JBY, but expected him to go back to Ireland. JBY affected to live by his art, writings, and speeches, but Quinn paid his debts whenever they grew too great, and then received original manuscripts from W. B. Yeats in return.[47]

But after years of delays, even the extraordinarily indulgent Quinn had had enough of his aged charge, and JBY slipped into a long and ultimately victorious maneuver of perpetually deferring his return to Ireland. Quinn commissioned Yeats to paint a self-portrait, for which he would pay him a large sum of money and passage home. But JBY outwitted him. The self-portrait, never finished, became his "Penelope's web."[48] Whenever it got perilously close to completion, he would scrape it out and start again. Its main utility, JBY discovered, was its magnificence as an excuse for doing or not doing whatever he pleased. But for Quinn, it became an albatross.

Sloan and Henri were not among Quinn's acquaintances, so Yeats was destined to enter their circle through other people and circumstances. First, John Butler Yeats arrived in New York just six weeks before the debut of The Eight. As has been noted, Henri and the other artists who formed The Eight were out to create a sensation. They knew how to attract attention and had well-placed friends in the newspaper world. Charles FitzGerald, art critic of the *Evening Sun*, who would later become Glackens's brother-in-law, was a champion of The Eight. Frederick J. Gregg, who also reviewed art for the *Evening Sun*, was similarly partisan. The Eight's exhibition ran for two weeks, and an article about the show appeared every day of its run. Henri noted "the great crowds all day" in his diary for the opening of the show on February 3, 1908, as well as an evening celebration with the Glackenses, the Shinns, Maurice Prendergast and his brother Charles, Ernest Lawson, Charles FitzGerald, and Charles Johnston, another Irish newspaper writer.[49]

From the onset of his arrival in New York, JBY was a devotee of the various papers and constantly clipped articles to send home to Ireland. As an artist, a news hawk, and a friend of the journalists involved, JBY was keenly aware of The Eight. He read the *Sun* and had personal ties to FitzGerald and Gregg. Gregg had been a schoolmate of William Butler Yeats at Erasmus Smith High School in Dublin,[50] and JBY had done a painting of FitzGerald, the son of an Irish oculist who admired the artist's portraits, when he was a little boy. The two critics renewed their acquaintance with JBY soon after he was settled, as did Charles Johnston, who had been close to William Butler Yeats in school as well. The first member of The Eight whom Yeats met was George Luks. JBY and Lily were introduced to Luks in April or May 1908 after Luks had painted a portrait of Gregg. Lily "regarded him with horror and would not have met him without his wife to keep him sober," Yeats wrote home.[51] "His wife, his 2nd—the other divorced him and has the children—requires all his judgment to keep him from breaking out into drink. He is very amusing and can imitate to perfection all the instruments in a brass band. . . . One of his pictures is a cat with all her kittens, really a wonderful thing." JBY did not neglect to appraise Luks as an artist: "In his painting there is a lot of sensuality (that is good) and humour of the farcical sort, and a very strong imaginative feeling for the mystery of chiaroscuro."[52]

Gregg was a great friend of Quinn, and after Gregg began touting Luks's talents as a portraitist to him, JBY was incensed, feeling that his territory had been invaded. However, in July 1908, he wrote to his daughters, "Last night John Quinn was praising Gregg's portrait done by Lucks [*sic*] in three sittings. I saw it and well!! . . . I have begged Quinn to get himself painted by Lucks and he says he will."[53]

Luks's portrait of Quinn, now in the National Portrait Gallery in Washington, D.C., exists because JBY maneuvered Quinn into commissioning it. Quinn admitted some second thoughts about the canvas, writing to Lily, "My artist friends all praise [the portrait] and say it is 'magnificent,'. . . . But I don't consider it a good <u>portrait</u>."[54] Then JBY teased Quinn into commissioning a portrait by him to prove that he could produce a more agreeable likeness than Luks.[55]

Although Sloan was known to Yeats from the newspaper accounts, at first he was no more than a passing colleague. The two first met in December 1908, according to one of Yeats's letters to Lily.[56] But the encounter apparently did not make an impression, because Sloan recorded in his diary for July 22, 1909, that he had just met Yeats. According to that account, the Henris and the Sloans were introduced to Yeats at a dinner given by the writer and editor Mary Fanton Roberts. A loyal supporter of the Henri group, Roberts edited *The Craftsman*, a magazine published by the furniture-maker Gustav Stickley, who also attended this gathering for Yeats. Another guest at the 1909 evening was Frederick King, the literary and drama editor of the *Literary Digest*, who was shortly to change Yeats's life.[57] Yeats and Henri gravitated to each other first. As JBY wrote,

> Lately I have made a pleasant acquaintance, Henri, a well-known artist of the real sort (you know I don't admire all artists, and least of all the successful ones) last Thursday. I was with him practically from 4 o'clock till 11 o'clock. He is doing well, though he won't exhibit at the Academy here, and is in permanent rebellion against all the recognized leaders. He is a big man with black hair and black eyes. In a slow way, avoiding emphasis or brilliancy, he talks very amusingly, in his talk a lot of personal quality. He is about 40 or 45, very big and well made. When he sits in a chair he looks all shoulders and legs. His wife looks about 19, says she is Irish . . . very pretty and nice and innocent, and I should say was a model, an exceedingly good figure. She has a beautiful complexion and rich auburn hair in great quantity [Fig. 73].
>
> He does lots of portraits, fashionable ladies life size, also dancers, extraordinary looking creatures, half naked, and not very young.[58] He has been a good deal in both France and Spain. On art matters we agree. You'd love the man, he is so big and wise and kind. I first met him at dinner. . . . I am sure he gets continual amusement out of his wife's ignorance of the social conventions.[59]

As JBY reported, Henri had remarried, in May 1908, just before he left to take his painting class on a tour of Europe. Legend has it that he kept the wedding a secret because he didn't want his boatload of eager female students to defect from the class. Unlike Henri's first wife, Linda, her successor, Marjorie Organ, was rather crude, which did not help win acceptance among Henri's friends. Yeats was present at another dinner party when she announced in a loud voice that she had eaten so much that she was going to loosen her corsets.[60] Marjorie Henri's conversation was laced with New York slang, and Yeats barely understood her. "She never even by accident talks English," JBY wrote. "We all, even the women who hate her, find her most amusing. She is also thoroughly kindhearted and staunch."[61] But given where she had come from, Marjorie Organ Henri was entirely remarkable and her faux pas understandable. She was born in Ireland in 1886, and she and her family came to the United States thirteen years later. She went to school for about a year before dropping out to

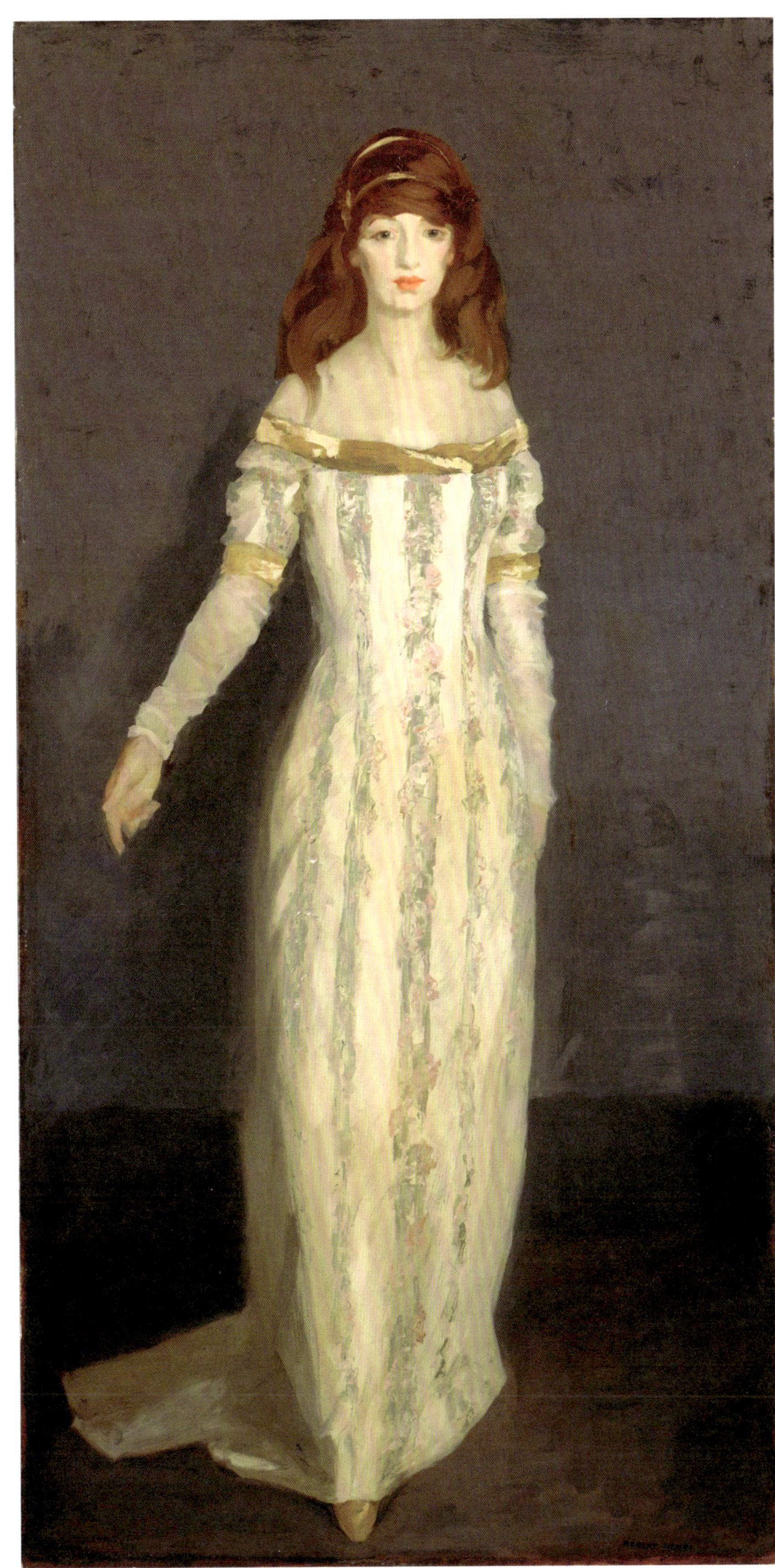

Fig. 73
Robert Henri
The Masquerade Dress, 1911
Oil on canvas
76½ × 36¼ in. (194.3 × 92.1 cm)
The Metropolitan Museum of
Art, New York; Arthur
Hoppock Hearn Fund, 1958

become a newspaper cartoonist. At the age of sixteen, she was on the staff of the *New York Journal*, drawing caricatures and writing and originating comic strips. She was the only woman on the staff, and with her youth and beauty, one can hardly imagine the innuendos and harassment she had to endure. JBY marveled that by the time she left the paper to marry Henri, she was making a stunning salary for the times—$50 a week—and it is her incisive caricature of the three men [Fig. 63] that captures the essence of each, and is not the least of the works of art that Yeats's presence in America inspired.

On August 12, 1909, Henri recorded another dinner with JBY, the Sloans, and King. Added to the party this time was the swiftly ascending artist George Bellows, Henri's favorite student. On August 19, Yeats visited Henri's studio, as he did again on August 26, with Bellows.[62] On August 16, 1909, JBY reported that he was dining with the Sloans at home for the first time.[63] Dolly became an immediate favorite of his, and he championed her despite her flaws. He drew her portrait more than forty times. But in September, Henri was still in the forefront of Yeats's acquaintance. He proudly wrote to Lily, "I see a good deal of Henri, the artist, and he is a great comfort."[64]

Although he followed The Eight's artistic exploits in the newspapers and befriended the leaders of the group, Yeats was somewhat cut off from the bohemian enclaves in which he would feel most at home. Since his arrival nearly two years before, he had lodged at the Grand Union Hotel, on East Forty-second Street, which was in a commercial area remote from artists' neighborhoods. But in August 1908, he was brought by Frederick King, first as a dinner guest, and then, nearly a year later, in autumn 1909, just after he met Sloan and Henri, as a permanent resident, to 317 West Twenty-ninth Street, in the Chelsea district. This was the address of a boardinghouse run by three French sisters, Marie, Josephine, and Celestine Petitpas, where the rooms were cheaper, the food and wine were better, and entertaining conversation was prized.

At this establishment Yeats was admired, and his status changed. No longer merely a superannuated father to famous sons, he soon held court at his own table and attracted writers, artists, singers, and other creative personalities to join him there—one of his Petitpas conquests was Isadora Duncan. Sketching people every night while he presided indoors near the fire or in the backyard garden on warm nights, Yeats wrote to Dublin, "The liveliness every evening . . . keeps my mind bright."[65]

Fig. 74
John Sloan
Yeats at Petitpas', 1910–c. 1914
Oil on canvas
26⅜ × 32¼ in. (67 × 81.9 cm)
Corcoran Gallery of Art, Washington, D.C.; Museum Purchase, Gallery Fund 32.9

Another virtue of Yeats's new lodging was its location. It was six blocks from the Sloans' apartment at 165 West Twenty-third Street, and a pleasant walk to Robert and Marjorie Henri at 10 East Twentieth Street. Once the move was made, in October of 1909, Sloan could—and did—become much more friendly. On October 4, 1909, Yeats stopped by to see Sloan, who wrote that he "enjoyed his company

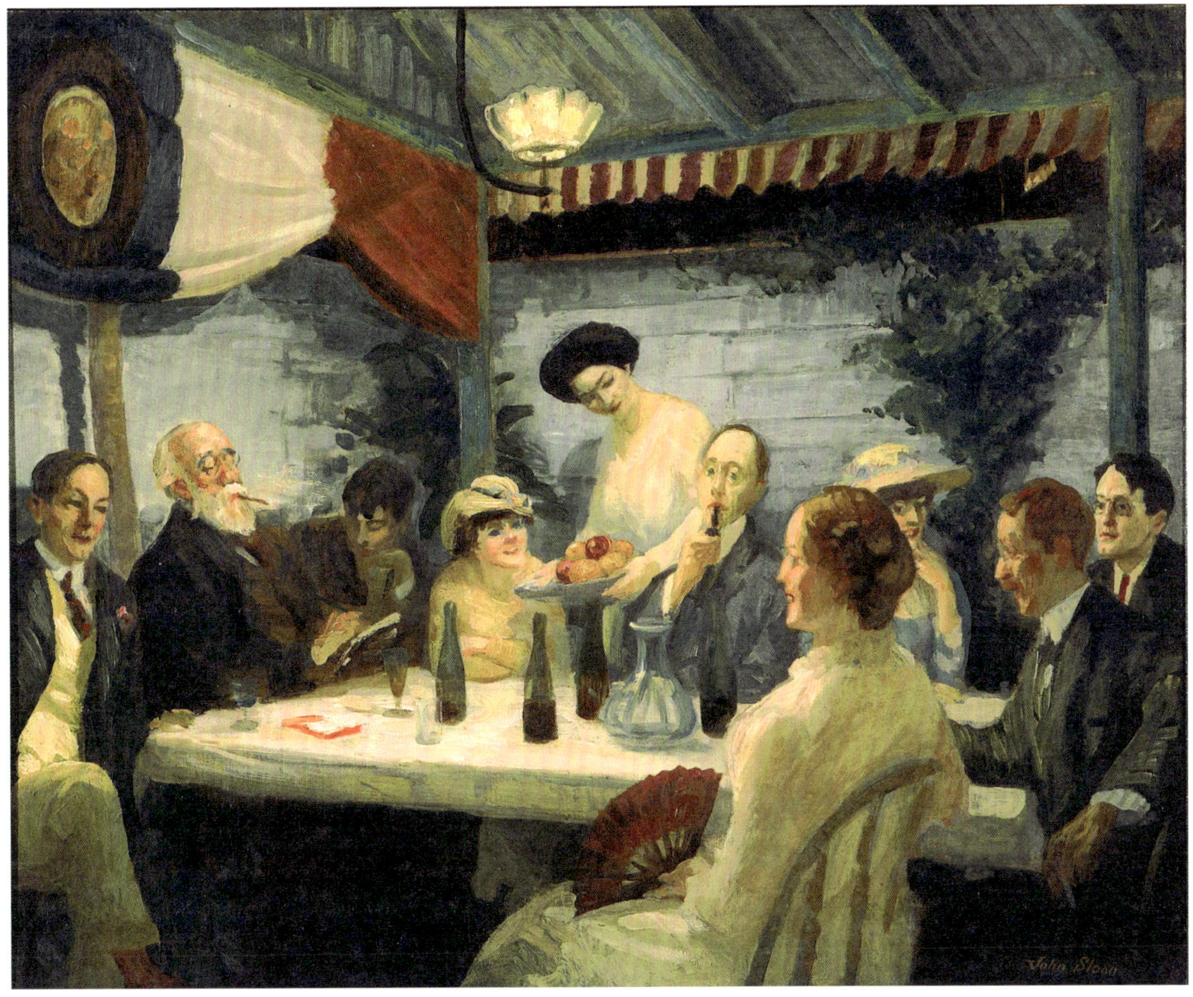

Pictured around the table, from left to right: Van Wyck Brooks, John Butler Yeats, Alan Seeger, Dolly Sloan, Celestine Petitpas, Robert Sneddon, Eulabee Dix, John Sloan, Frederick A. King, and Vera Jelihovsky Johnston (in foreground)

very much. He is a fine unspoiled old artist gentleman. His vest is slightly spotted; he is real."[66] That night Sloan ate at the Petitpas' dining room for the first time.

The most ambitious painting to document John Butler Yeats's American stay and impact was Sloan's *Yeats at Petitpas'* (Fig. 74). Of all the artists who knew Yeats, Sloan was the one most affected by him, and the painting was created when their friendship, which would last until the older man's death in 1922, evolved from a happy acquaintance to a more intense association. The two formed a bond that was paternal and filial as well as artistic. Yeats, who was perennially buoyed by youth, was seeking a replacement son who would return his affection and whose reputation would not overwhelm his, as had happened in Dublin once William Butler Yeats's genius was acknowledged. And Sloan still needed a mentor to bloom—he craved the attention of a charismatic male figure as an improvement on his own father to assuage the old trauma. Henri had been Sloan's first surrogate father, but Henri no longer required as much devotion as before, and with Marjorie Henri on the scene, there was tension. Another father substitute would be required to keep father hunger at bay. Sloan, who was childless yet needed to act like a responsible father himself, was eager to adopt JBY, who Henri said was "an old man who had run away from home."[67]

Meals at the Petipas' boardinghouse were cheap, but the Sloans were still too poor to eat there very often, and they invited Yeats to their apartment instead. In a typical message to Lily, Yeats wrote on October 22, 1909, "I have just now had a 'phone from the Sloanes to come and dine with them in 23rd St., quite near. The Henris will be there, so it will be all delightful, and of course no ceremony. . . . His art is of Jack's school, that is it is life and its humors, on this occasion New York life."[68] Henri's pleasure in that unpretentious evening of artists enjoying themselves was recorded in a sketch that Sloan preserved (Fig. 75). This passage marks the first time that JBY compared John Sloan with Jack Yeats. Indeed, the similarity of spirit between some of the Henri group's work—mainly that of Sloan and the early Everett Shinn—and Jack Yeats's is noticeable, and obviously engaged JBY. All of them had looked at Manet and Degas, and Jack Yeats was apparently familiar with the British painter Walter Sickert. There was a shared concentration on crowd scenes, street life, the theater, and other popular entertainment. The resemblance of the American paintings to his son's work might well be the reason why JBY could appreciate their contemporariness, despite the fact that he was seventy years old, and his own artistic training in the 1870s had involved a Ruskinian emphasis on Pre-Raphaelite technique and detail.

Though the paternal relationship between Sloan and the elder Yeats was genuine, JBY was not above using Sloan as a means of attracting Jack's attention and manipulating him to communicate more—he knew that Lily would show Jack his letters. (Coincidentally, Sloan was born in 1871, the same year as Jack, and Henri in 1865, the same year as W. B. Yeats. And within the Sloan family, John Sloan was known as Jack—he often signed his letters to Dolly and his parents "Jack.") Cajoling again for a response, in November of 1909, JBY wrote to Jack and his wife that they should visit New York for a month or two. "Jack's work would be received by the artists here with enthusiasm," he reported, "by men like Henri and John Sloan,

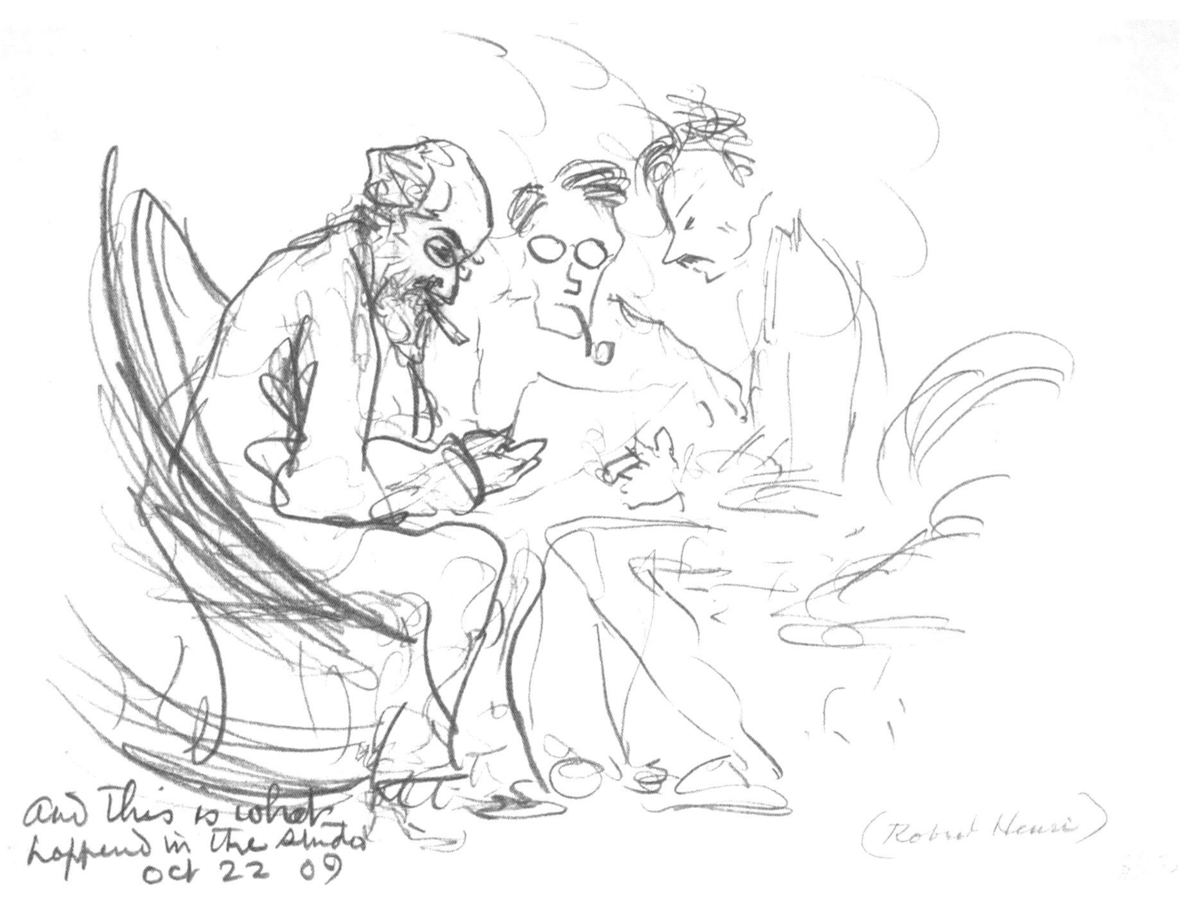

Fig. 75
Robert Henri
"And This Is What Happened
in the Studio, Oct 22 09"
Pencil on paper
6⅞ × 9⅜ in. (17.5 × 23.9 cm)
Delaware Art Museum, Wilmington;
Gift of Helen Farr Sloan

Glackens, and by Charles Fitzgerald. . . . Tomorrow . . . I am to dine with John Sloan and his wife. Henri and his wife are to be there. . . . Jack and he [Henri] would be great friends."[69] Yeats tried wooing his son in a similar fashion in early 1910, writing, "I am delighted with your book [his latest exhibition catalogue]. . . . I wish you saw the joy with which Henri hailed it reading every word of it. . . . John Sloane was also greatly pleased, and sighed with envy for your talent."[70] But no bid for Jack's filial devotion worked. Although the Yeats daughters wrote faithfully, and W.B. Yeats could be drawn into corresponding if the subject engrossed or irritated him, Jack was the one Yeats family member who remained impervious to his father's epistolary blandishments.[71]

On December 9, 1909, Henri started painting a portrait of JBY (Fig. 76),[72] as part of a campaign by Yeats's artist-friends to promote him as a desirable speaker. One of the ways devised for Yeats to earn money was for him to lecture on the famous figures of the Irish literary renaissance whom he had known so intimately. Dolly Sloan had endeared herself to JBY by successfully organizing talks and collecting fees for him, without complaint or wish for anything for herself. Yeats's next lecture, on J.M. Synge—who had just died suddenly of Hodgkin's disease at the age of thirty-eight and was thus of enormous interest—was to take place in Henri's Gramercy Park studio on December 14, 1909,[73] and the portrait would be unveiled as part of the festivities. Henri was so enthusiastic, Yeats wrote to Lollie, that he decided "to do a full length portrait of me, which will make its glorious appearance on [the] night of lecture." Henri rethought the idea of the full-length canvas, but the painting is typical in his insistence on speed to convey energy and a particular look or impression. JBY evidently agreed, writing, "Henri's portrait of me is, I think, very life-like—full of vitality and color."[74]

On January 18, 1910, Sloan painted a small, tender oil sketch of Yeats and Henri (*My Two Friends–Yeats and Henri*; whereabouts unknown), which he made on the spot when the Henris and Yeats were sketching together at the Sloans' apartment.[75] JBY described their companionable evening in words. Proud to be counted as a peer, he wrote,

> Last night I dined at John Sloan's (an artist with whom Jack would have so much sympathy). He produced after dinner sheets of drawing paper and, all of us being artists, we set to work to make drawings of each other and of everybody, John Sloan himself doing a painting—talk and laughter going on all the time. I do enjoy these kinds of meetings. They are unlike anything anywhere else in the world. Regretfully we broke up at a mere one o'clock, and this in New York where people start early.[76]

JBY's warm acceptance by the Henri group was made manifest in early 1910, when he became a confidant and witness to their work as prime movers behind the Exhibition of Independent Artists, the first

Fig. 76
Robert Henri
John Butler Yeats, 1909
Oil on canvas
32¼ × 26⅜ in. (81.9 × 66.9 cm)
Hirshhorn Museum and Sculpture Garden, Smithsonian Institution, Washington, D.C.; Gift of the Joseph H. Hirshhorn Foundation, 1966

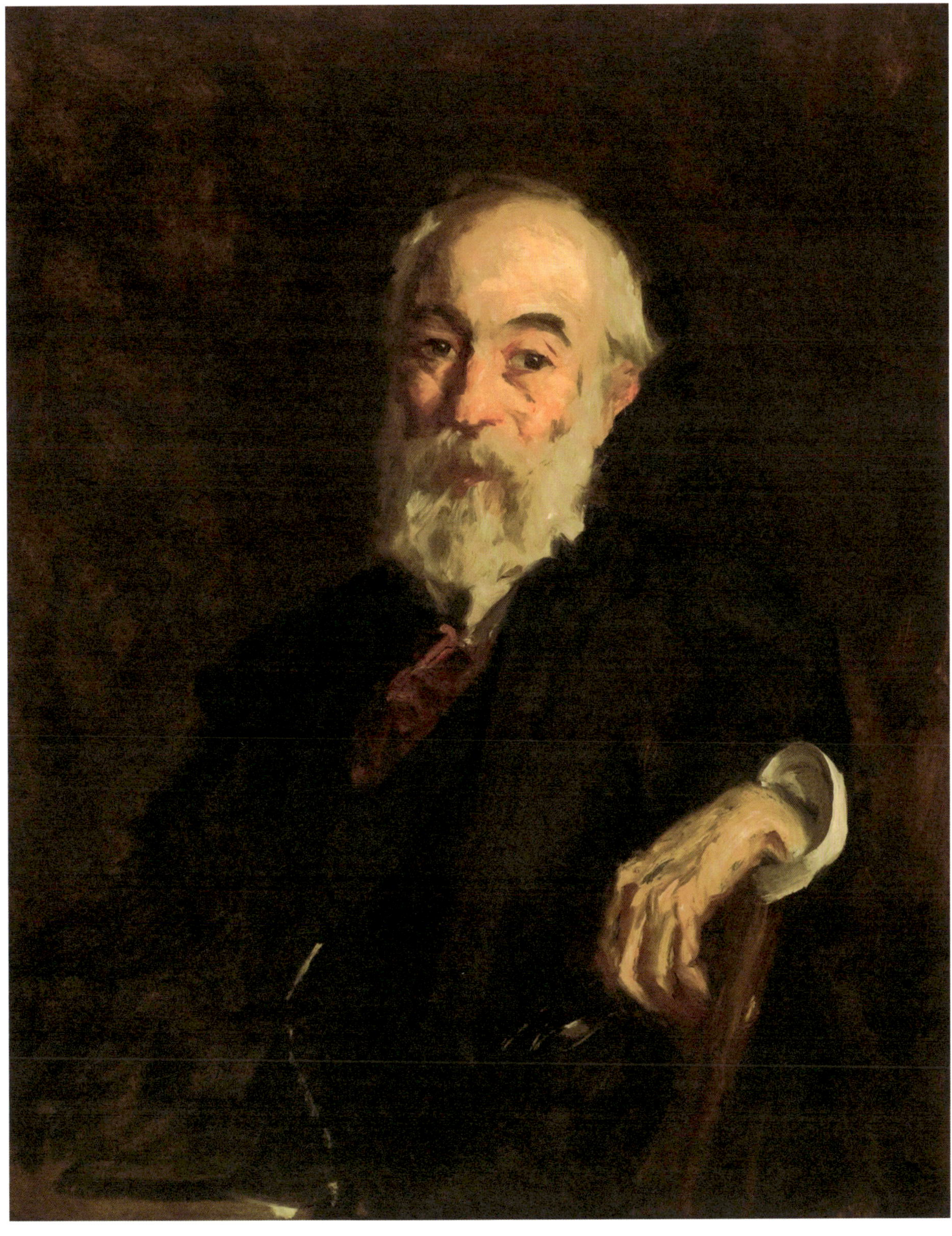

Fig. 77
John Butler Yeats
John O'Leary, 1904
Oil on canvas
44⅛ × 34¼ in. (112 × 87 cm)
National Gallery of Ireland, Dublin;
Presented, Mr. C. Sullivan, in memory of Mr. J. Quinn, 1926

large-scale invitational show of progressive artists, and the Henri group's next assault on the Academy. The Independents exhibition was the bridge between The Eight's 1908 exhibition and the Armory Show of 1913—with 103 painters and sculptors participating free of juries and prizes, it too was a landmark in American art. All of The Eight except Luks entered pictures, as did Edward Hopper, Stuart Davis, Bellows, Walt Kuhn, Rockwell Kent, Morton Schamberg—and John Butler Yeats. Sloan first mentioned the show in his diary on January 3, 1910, brought it up with Henri and JBY the next day at Petitpas', and the initial organizational meeting took place on January 10, 1910.[77] The galvanizing insult, however, occurred in March, when *Pigeons* (1910; Museum of Fine Arts, Boston) and *Three A.M.* (1909; Philadelphia Museum of Art), Sloan's submissions to the Academy's annual exhibition, were rejected. Sloan knew in advance that *Three A.M.* was doomed. "One girl in her shift cooking, the other gossiping over a cup of tea," he wrote. "Quite too much for them." But when *Pigeons*, a rooftop scene with no one unclothed, was refused, he decided he had "evidently underrated it." Sloan realized that the Academy had "cut me off from the exhibition game: must find some way to show the things." Dolly immediately telephoned the news to the Henris, and the Sloans were shocked to learn that the jury had also rejected one of Henri's portraits of Marjorie as well as his first version of Salomé—*Salomé Dancer* (1909; Mead Art Museum, Amherst College, Massachusetts).[78]

On March 12, 1910, JBY reported everyone's reactions to Lily: "Henri's chief pictures have been kicked out of the Academy. He is angry and though he fights against this—feeling rather depressed. He had been getting on lately so triumphantly, selling his pictures also. I feel for him."[79] Four days later, he wrote of being comrades in shared fury: "Just now we are all boiling with indignation. The Academy has thrown out Henri, Sloan and Luks, &c., so they and their friends, the party of Eight, are putting their money together in order to hold an exhibition of their own. Henri is undoubtedly the finest painter in America."[80]

JBY did his part to help his friends. He told John Quinn about the exhibition, which was to open on April 1, 1910, and induced him to send the organizers a check for his own exhibiting expenses. The latter act was as much a testament to Quinn's reflexive generosity toward artists as JBY's persuasiveness, because Quinn expressed his disapproval of the exhibition's format and scope. In a letter to the English artist Charles Shannon, he said that he had refused Sloan's entreaties to borrow seascapes by Shannon and landscapes by the Irish painter Nathaniel Hone because the "artists who organized it meant well, but they made the mistake of allowing anybody who claimed to be an artist and who was willing to pay the fee to send, one, two or three pictures."[81] Given Quinn's jaundiced view, Sloan

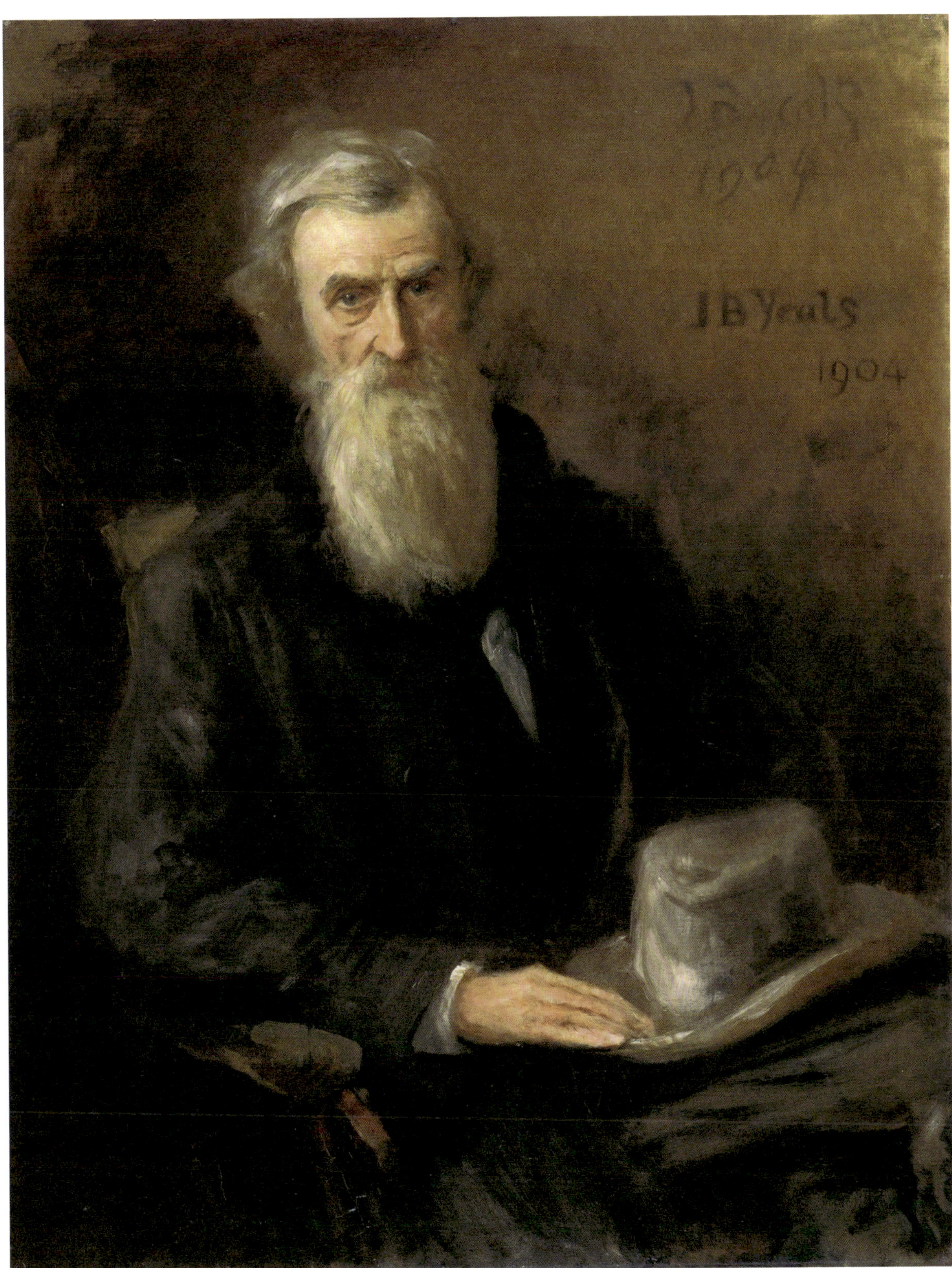
J B Yeats
1904

had to be content with borrowing seven works by JBY that Quinn owned, most importantly the oil portrait of John O'Leary (Fig. 77).[82] The exhibition caused such a stir that JBY even dared to brag to W. B. Yeats about what he counted as a mark of success—having his work among a "rebel body just launched in antagonism to the Academy here"[83] and in an "exhibition of the cleverest artists in America."[84] He was ready with a more realistic appraisal when he wrote to Lily, whom he knew would not judge him as coldly as his sons: "[M]y O'Leary looks very well and not badly hung. It looks perhaps a little conservative among these more riotous works round about, where if they paint an eye they do the whole thing, lids, iris, eyelashes, with two strokes of a big black brush."[85]

Throughout 1910 Sloan and Yeats's relationship deepened. JBY liked to walk around the city for several hours a day and Sloan began to accompany him on these strolls. The two would talk about life, art, and literature, and Yeats would call Sloan's attention to paintable subjects. Among the well-known canvases that resulted from their forays is *Scrubwomen, Astor Library* (1910–11; Munson-Williams-Proctor Arts Institute, Utica, New York), which came out of visits both men paid there on May 25 and May 26, 1910.[86]

The Sloans and JBY became even closer over the summer of that year. One of the mysteries of the painting *Yeats at Petitpas'* is why Henri, whose income permitted him to be a regular at the gatherings at the boardinghouse and whom Yeats had so recently characterized as "undoubtedly the finest painter in America," is not among the dramatis personae in the composition. But the Henris departed for four months in Europe on May 31, 1910. The Sloans were in New York for the summer and, with few others left in the city, their friendship with Yeats intensified. JBY, likewise too impoverished to go elsewhere for extended periods, told Lily on June 5 that when he needed company, "not far off are the Sloans. I can always retreat to them if I want to be cheered up."[87] There was also a sense, benign but nonetheless marked, of staking a primary possessive claim on Yeats's affections. The Henris traveled more in general, and the Sloans were there to take up the slack, although Yeats never lost his regard for Henri. Dolly Sloan in particular made herself indispensable to JBY, mending his clothes, finding him lecture venues, and generally cheering him up. In June 1910 JBY coaxed Quinn into buying a large number of Sloan's prints for $340.[88] Despite Yeats's repeated pleadings, Quinn would never buy a painting by Sloan or Henri—he was committed to the European avant-garde. But he continued to buy etchings from Sloan through 1916,[89] and because he yielded to JBY's intercession, Quinn is always credited as being "the first collector who took an interest in Sloan's etchings."[90]

The Sloans were so grateful to Yeats for getting Quinn to notice them that they commissioned him to draw pencil portraits of themselves (Fig. 78).[91] Pencil drawing was a medium JBY resorted to more frequently as his energy and concentration waned. Pencil was less demanding than oil, and it was more suited for work in his small room in the boardinghouse, which lacked the space for a real studio. However, JBY's work lost some of its penetrating astringency in that medium—the pencil portraits tend to be sweeter than his corresponding work in oil.

Yeats was thrilled with the Sloans' windfall from Quinn, crowing to Lily, "Now they feel themselves in funds and so often come and dine here. I love them both, and am a different man since I have got their studio to go to."[92] The Sloans and JBY also went to an outdoor performance of Shakespeare's *As You Like It*. The company was the Coburn Shakespearean Players, acted and managed by Charles Coburn, who later moved to Hollywood and became a beloved character actor in the movies. Sloan was so taken with the experience of watching a comedy *en plein air* that he completed *The Coburn Players* (1910; The Dayton Art Institute, Ohio) in just one day—and the painting is notable for its quick, impressionistic brushwork.

Because Sloan could visit the Petitpas establishment more often, he was able to observe the social dynamics of JBY's table. The sense of rebirth, or at least of new adventures, was shared by both men, because Sloan began the group portrait that was to become *Yeats at Petitpas'* on August 2, 1910, his thirty-ninth birthday. He made the setting accurate—the diners, listening to Yeats, smoking, chatting, and sketching, sit in the canopied back garden as a respite from the heat indoors during the stifling summer weather. As he did for Henri in *Memory*, Sloan placed JBY in the confines of a cozy space and immortalized the magic of being in his company. "Like the intimates in *Memory*," John Loughery observes, "these people know and like each other enough to be carried along by the rhythm of the evening. They trust Yeats to hold them together."[93]

The selection of the people in *Yeats at Petitpas'* naturally had its fortuitous element—several sitters who happened to be frequenting JBY's table during that particular summer and autumn of 1910 would depart before the end of the year—but in general Sloan chose his cross-section of Yeats's friends with care and logic. Almost every person in the composition—Van Wyck Brooks, Alan Seeger, Dolly Sloan, Celestine Petitpas, Robert Sneddon, Eulabee Dix, Frederick A. King, Vera Jelihovsky Johnston, and Sloan himself—have symbolic value. Each represents or illuminates distinctive facets of JBY's history and interests. Sloan's own position at the table is lower, provisional, and deferential. Like a dutiful son, Sloan cedes pride of place to Yeats and to Van Wyck Brooks and Alan Seeger, the two bright young men flanking him, but his seat also allows him to study the scene at its best angle. Edged out of the pictorial space by Frederick King, the man on his left, Sloan offers a clue to knowing viewers that it was not possible for him to be a regular at the establishment. Indeed, King deserved to be in the foreground of any account of the Petitpas' establishment because he was the one who discovered the place and brought Yeats there.[94]

Brooks, then a fledgling writer, had already been sketched by Yeats in 1909, and the older man was encouraging him in his dream of becoming a historian of American culture. As Brooks put it, "I had never been touched by anyone's intellect until . . . I met J.B. Yeats,—the old Irish artist in whom I found a master."[95] Yeats introduced Brooks to Sloan and, in the 1950s, when he was a celebrated literary figure, Brooks became Sloan's first biographer. With his history as Yeats's sitter, Brooks was an incarnation of his master's art in practice and inclination. He was someone of promise, an American version of the Dublin intelligentsia whom Yeats had excelled at painting a decade before. In turn, writes Brooks's biographer, Raymond Nelson, JBY was beloved by Brooks and Sloan as a "new incarnation of Falstaff, reliving the sweet excitement of his youth through an assembly of American Prince Hals."[96]

Whereas Sloan got on well with Brooks, he did not particularly care for Seeger, a recent Harvard graduate whom he thought priggish. However, he was of visual interest to the artist because he looked like Aubrey Beardsley.[97] Seeger was a poet, and therefore Yeats claimed a special understanding of him on the grounds that he had raised one. In 1912 Seeger moved to Paris, and became an ardent Francophile. An idealist and a patriot, he enlisted in the Foreign Legion in 1914 and was killed in action in 1916; he left behind a prophetic poem, "I Have a Rendezvous with Death," that became a staple of anthologies for decades. He was also the brother of composer Charles Seeger and the uncle of the folk singer Pete Seeger. Sloan was a pacifist and held no brief for the military, and though he finished *Yeats at Petitpas'* well before World War I, it was not exhibited until autumn 1916. Sloan did not let his politics disfigure his portrayal. Indeed, Yeats praised him for it, noting that Seeger was the figure in the painting most

> sympathetically rendered. . . . Seeger is sitting as I so often saw him, courteously attentive yet himself silent, his head drooping forward, all of him in deep shadow —a man with a poet's soul. . . . It was characteristic of Sloan to introduce this note of tender appreciation into that noisy scene. One is tempted to think he is psychic and knew what must happen.[98]

In contrast to Seeger's self-containment, Sloan emphasized Dolly Sloan's extroversion by the animated thrust of her face and head. Yeats's fondness for Dolly gave her a confidence in his presence that is reflected in her joyous expression. Celestine Petitpas, who serves the meal, warranted equal prominence in the canvas. The youngest, friendliest, and Yeats's favorite of the three sisters, Celestine provides a pleasing contrast to the seated group, and her crown of dark hair

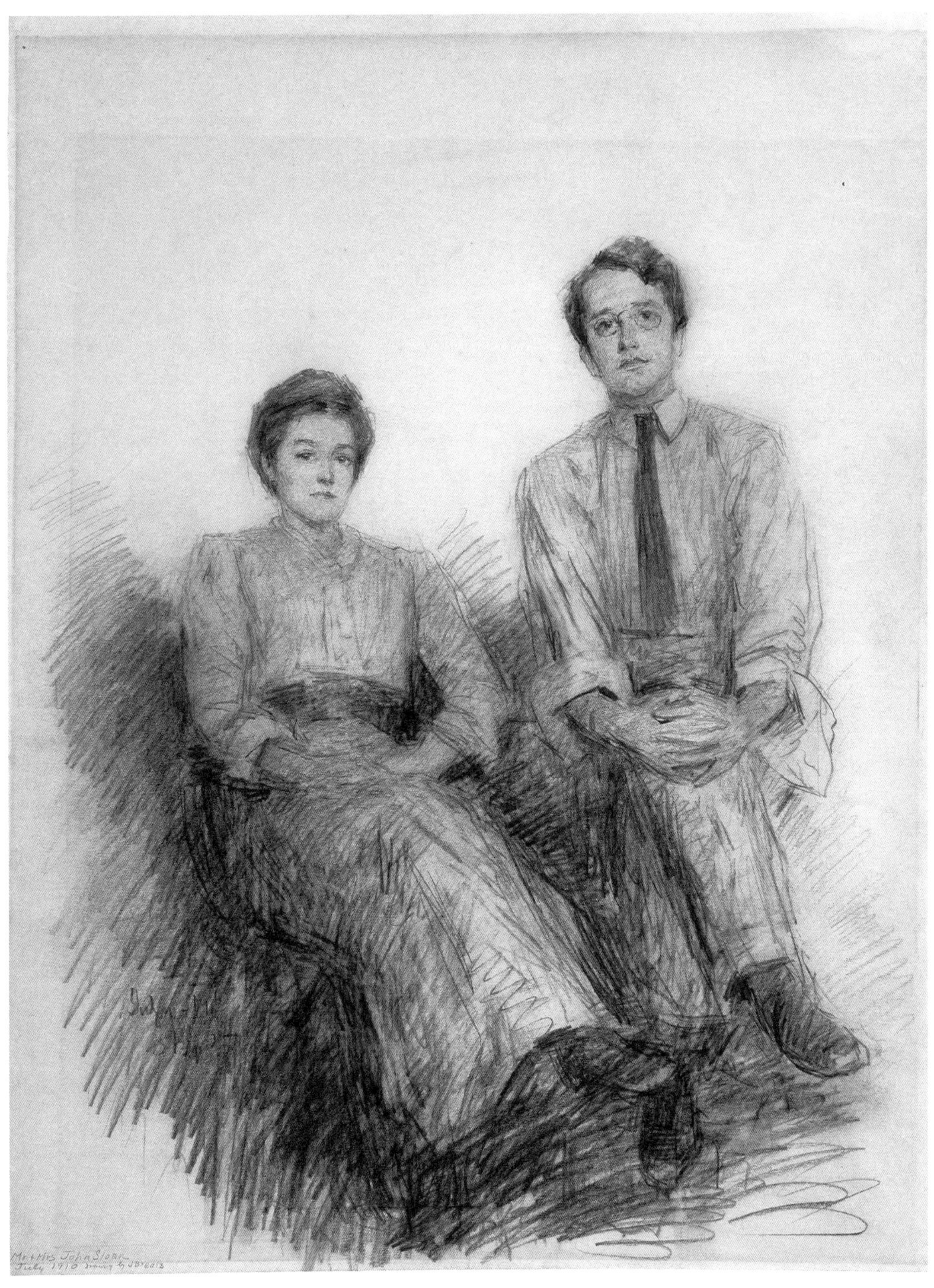

Fig. 78
John Butler Yeats
John and Dolly Sloan, 1910
Pencil on board
17 7/16 × 13 7/16 in. (44.3 × 34.1 cm)
Delaware Art Museum, Wilmington;
Gift of Helen Farr Sloan, 1977

leads the eye to the lanterns and the French tricolor bunting draped across the wall.

Sloan's decision to obscure the figure and face of Eulabee Dix, an artist who specialized in portrait miniatures, is telling. She met JBY at Petitpas' in 1908 and Sloan in the summer of 1910, just before he began to work on *Yeats at Petitpas'*. Pretty, determined, skilled, self-absorbed, and grasping, Dix captivated and maddened Yeats. But he remained friendly enough with her to visit her in Buffalo, New York, after she married and moved there in late 1910. Dix was an exemplar of an artist neither Yeats nor Sloan wanted to be. Whereas JBY had difficulty getting commissions for his portraits, Dix secured many. Yeats could barely obtain $15 or $20 for a drawing and at this point Sloan had not yet sold a single oil painting; she charged hundreds of dollars for her flattering likenesses. While Yeats and Sloan preferred to portray friends and colleagues, Dix concentrated on the social elite.

Unlike Yeats, Sloan, or Henri, Dix had no interest in collegiality except as it served her. She bragged that she got $500 from Quinn for a miniature of his niece, whom she met through JBY, and when Yeats made a sketch of her in 1910, she would only pay him $5 for it.[99] Yet Yeats respected her ability to thrive as an independent woman. After her marriage, when Dix fought to maintain a career in the face of her in-laws' disapproval, JBY took her part. (Perhaps the old man identified with her: Dix's struggle and ensuing conflicts could have reminded Yeats of what happened to him when he quit the law and its steady income to become a painter.)

Yeats's friendship with Dix, or more likely, his inability to resist her appeals, resulted in several paintings by better-known artists. He said of Dix, "She has a clinging way like ivy which we know always kills the tree to which it attaches itself."[100] By attaching herself to Yeats, she was able to arrange being painted by Robert Henri *twice*.

At the end of December 1910 Dix married attorney Alfred Becker. Because, she recalled, "Henri always wanted to paint a bride,"[101] she posed for Henri in her wedding dress on December 17 and 19,[102] and the result was *Portrait of Eulabee Dix (Becker) in Wedding Gown* (Museum of Nebraska Art, Kearney). Dix's ambition was stifled after marriage, and in October 1911, nearly a year later, because she was tall and thin—a physical type that he favored as a model—Henri painted her again, with an even better outcome—*Lady in Black Velvet (Portrait of Eulabee Dix Becker)* (Fig. 79). Throughout the teens, Dix clung to Henri by letter, hounding him about the portraits. She wanted him to give them to her at no charge, and he was not going to do any such thing.[103] As late as 1921, JBY, who was now referring to her as "that Mrs. Becker," was telling Lily that she was pursuing Henri. However, he predicted that she would have better luck

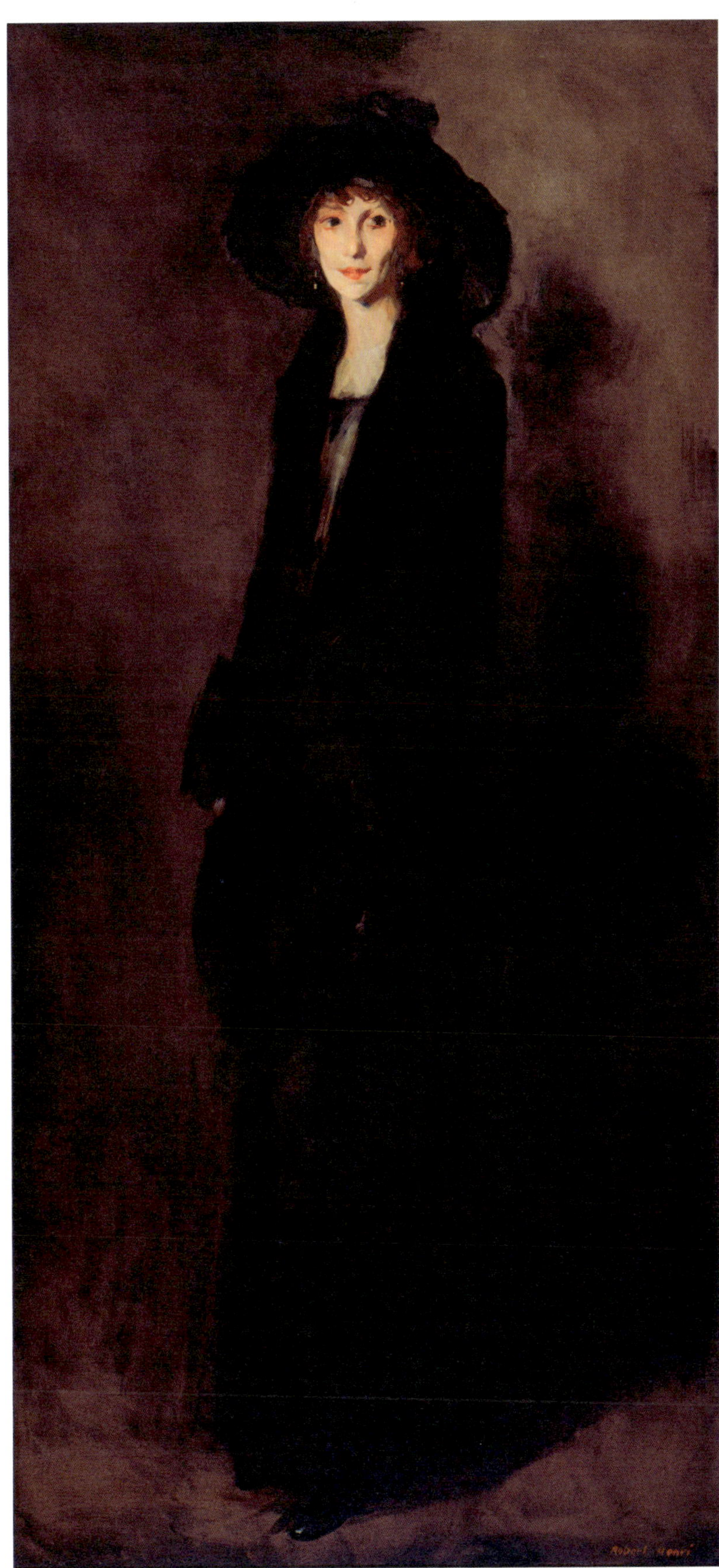

Fig. 79
Robert Henri
Lady in Black Velvet
(Portrait of Eulabee Dix Becker), 1911
Oil on canvas
77½ × 36¹⁵⁄₁₆ in. (196.9 × 93.8 cm)
High Museum of Art, Atlanta; Gift
in memory of Dr. Thomas P. Hinman
through exchange and general funds
73.55

wangling a free canvas out of Charles Hawthorne, who had painted her in 1920, because "Hawthorne has not Henri's obstinacy."[104]

Seated in the foreground in *Yeats at Petitpas'* closest to the viewer is Vera Jelihovsky Johnston. Both Vera Johnston and her husband, Charles (not pictured), were links to William Butler Yeats and his immersion in the occult. Charles Johnston was a writer, translator, and a teacher of Sanskrit, and he, like Gregg, had been a schoolmate of W. B. Yeats in Dublin. Together they pursued their interest in theosophy and Eastern philosophy; Johnston became a member of the Theosophical Society first and introduced W.B. Yeats to Madame Helena Blavatsky, one of its founders.[105] Vera herself was Blavatsky's niece. They had known John Butler Yeats in London and Dublin, and they were among his earliest friends to see him again in America. Although JBY was skeptical of mysticism, he believed in palmistry, clairvoyance, and other psychic feats, and he often asked Vera Johnston to tell his fortune. Painting, poetry, female beauty, the conflict between family demands and professional ambition, the promise of the new world intercut with memories of Ireland and the dominating brilliance of his older son—all these themes in *Yeats at Petitpas'* are suggested and summarized in the faces and figures of a few men and women by an artist expert in applying the tradition of a conversation piece to his own vivid purposes.

The art historian Paul B. Franklin has proposed that the antecedents of the composition and iconography of *Yeats at Petitpas'* are paintings of *The Supper at Emmaus* by Caravaggio, Rembrandt, and Velázquez, as well as depictions of *The Last Supper* by Leonardo da Vinci and Andrea del Sarto.[106] But Sloan is arguably indebted to more secular and contemporary artistic models. Closer inspirations for *Yeats at Petitpas'* are the memorials to artistic creativity by Henri Fantin-Latour, particularly his *Homage to Eugène Delacroix* (1864; Musée d'Orsay, Paris), which amounts to an artistic manifesto, and *An Atelier in the Batignolles* (1870; Musée d'Orsay), a portrait of Manet surrounded by his friends. Fantin's *The Corner of the Table* (1872; Musée d'Orsay) is compositionally almost identical to *Yeats at Petitpas'*. Like Fantin, Sloan assembles the central figure's spiritual family to indicate the breadth of his cultural legacy. In each case, despite an indifferent outer world, within the intimate venue presented in the painting, the achievement of the artist is unassailable.

Yeats and Sloan remained close for another year or two, but Sloan's increasing dedication to Socialism and lacerating temper about it made their communications difficult. These differences, exacerbated by the onset of World War I, further estranged them. As Yeats remarked, "Sloan has gone pacifist, which means that he is at war with everybody."[107] Also, Yeats astutely pointed out weaknesses in Sloan's work and was not afraid to criticize him. They did reconcile in 1918 and by the time JBY died on February 22, 1922, at the age

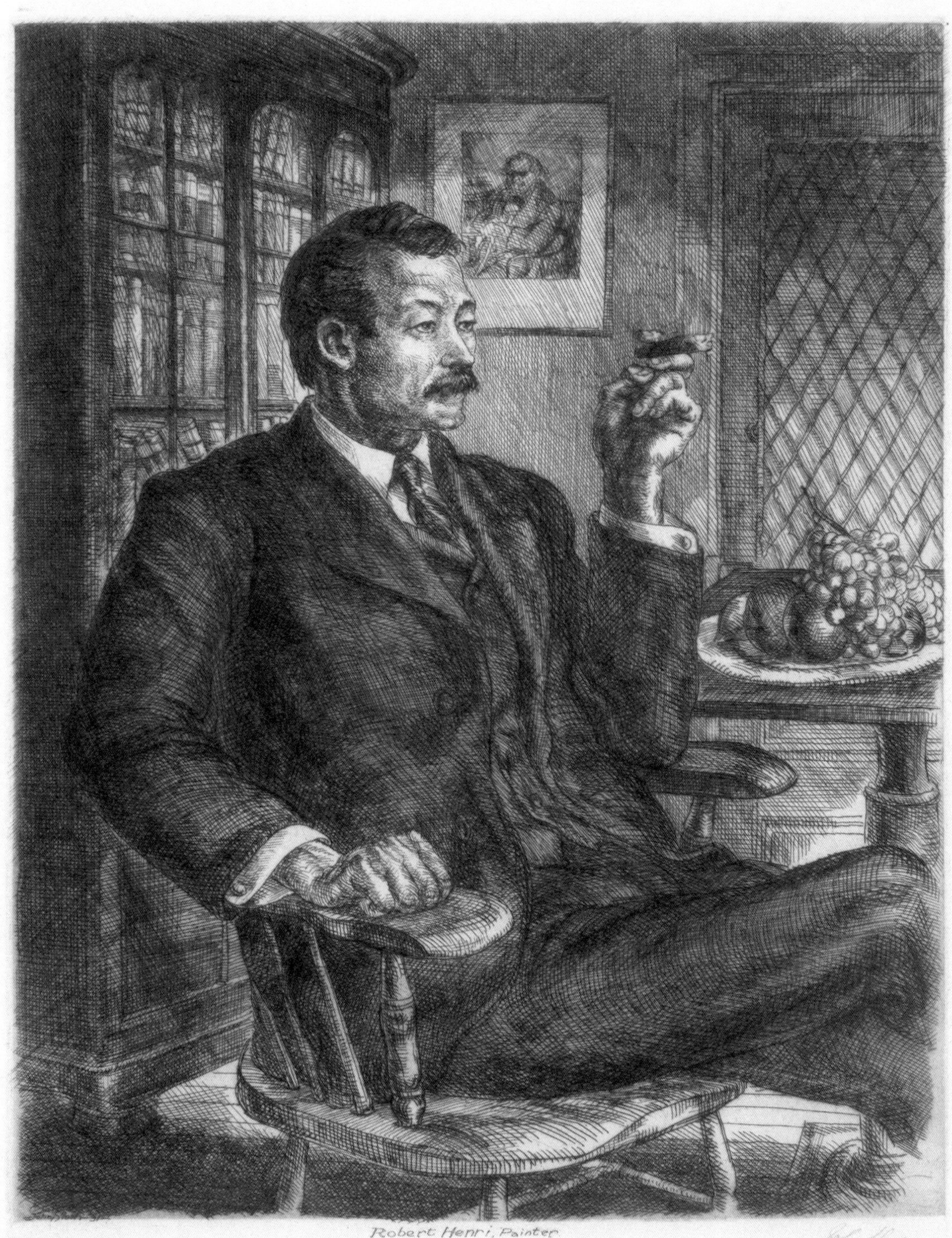

Fig. 80
John Sloan
Robert Henri, Painter, 1931
Copper plate etching, ink on paper
14 × 11 in. (35.6 × 27.9 cm)
Delaware Art Museum, Wilmington;
Gift of Helen Farr Sloan, 1998

of eighty-three, both Sloans were grief-stricken. John Sloan wrote to Lily Yeats, "[T]hey each [the other mourners] felt as I did, that they had lost their father—I assure you my own father's death was not so great a loss to me. I was never as near to him as to John Butler Yeats."[108]

Sloan was equally affected by Robert Henri's death from prostate cancer in 1929. Two years later, as a memorial, he made an etching of Henri. *Robert Henri, Painter* (Fig. 80) was based on some early drawings and an etching of him from 1902–04, but more significant, Sloan only painted a portrait of his own father, James Dixon Sloan, once, in 1903 (Fig. 81). John Sloan did not employ this pose or angle again for a male portrait ever again, except when creating his likenesses of Robert Henri, first sketchily from 1902 to 1904, and then in handsome detail in 1931. The latter fulfilled what John Butler Yeats defined as the quintessence of a "perfect" portrait—it was "an embodied dream of the sitter."[109]

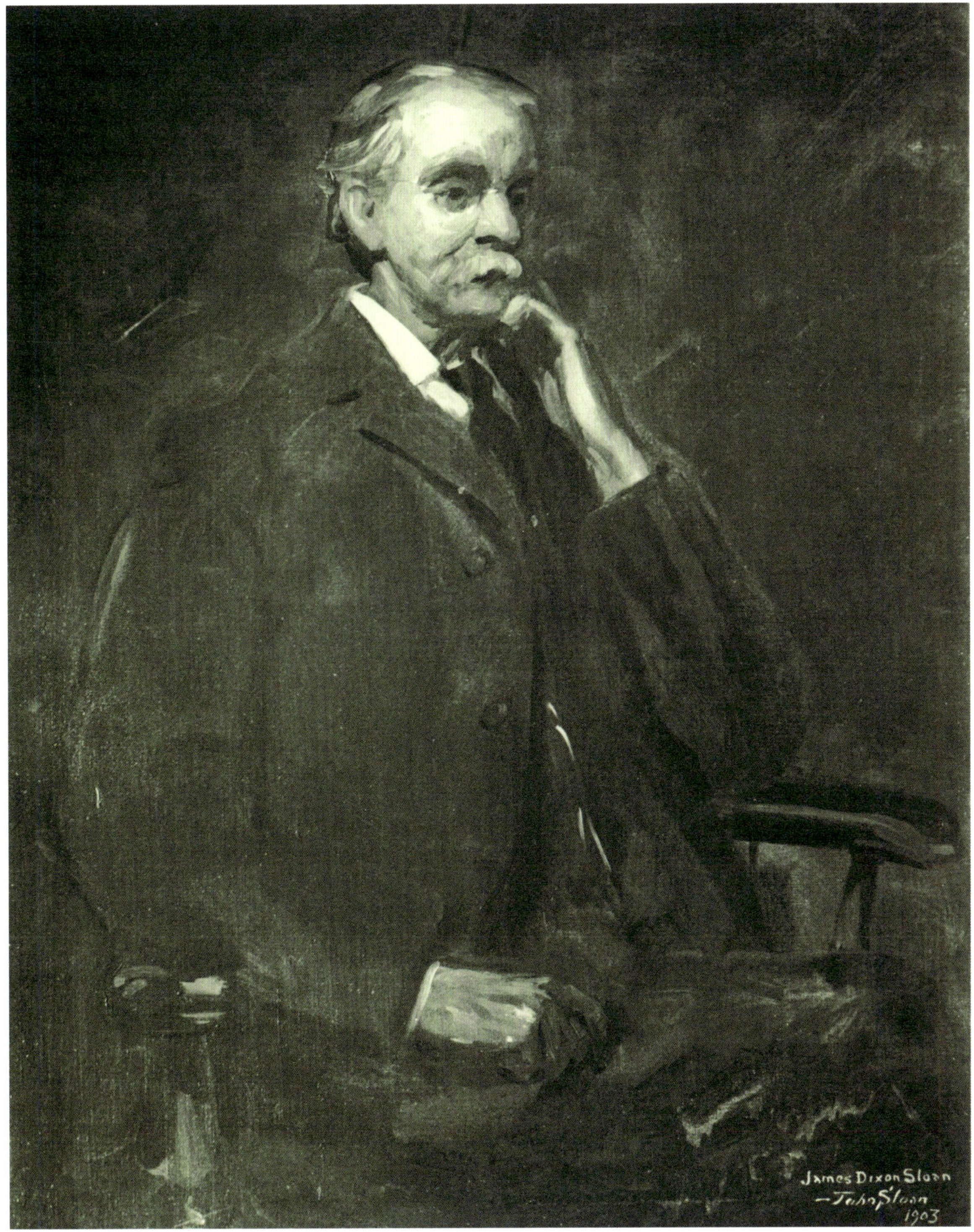

Fig. 81
John Sloan
James Dixon Sloan, My Father, 1903
Oil on canvas
36⅛ × 27⅛ in. (91.7 × 68.9 cm)
Annie Halenbake Ross Library, Lock Haven, Pennsylvania

In composing this essay about long-ago artistic friendships, I like to think of the results as a commemoration of my friendships with Ira and Nancy Glackens and with Helen Farr Sloan, who urged me to look into the subject of her husband's relationship with John Butler Yeats. I am enormously grateful to the Sansom Foundation for encouraging me to pursue this research and for supporting it so unstintingly. I am also delighted to pay tribute to the most selfless of scholars, the late William M. Murphy, whose matchless biography, *Prodigal Father: The Life of John Butler Yeats (1839–1922)*, I happened upon with intense pleasure more than twenty years ago. Dr. Murphy gave me permission to examine his typewritten transcriptions of John Butler Yeats's letters from archives and libraries in the United States and Europe for their references to John Sloan, Robert Henri, and other American artists. This article could not have been written without my taking advantage of the monumental labors that the Murphy Transcriptions represent. I also wish to thank Ellen Fladger, Archivist and Head of Special Collections, at Schaffer Library, Union College, for her help and professionalism during the time I was consulting the Murphy Transcriptions. Similarly, I am grateful to Sarah Cash and Emily D. Shapiro at the Corcoran Gallery of Art, Washington, D.C., for sharing their institution's research files on *Yeats at Petitpas'* with me, and to Heather Campbell Coyle, of the Delaware Art Museum, Wilmington, for her tireless assistance in sifting through the collections of the John Sloan Archives. Kristen J. Nyitray, Special Collections & University Archives, Stony Brook University, and Barbara J. MacAdam, Hood Museum of Art, Dartmouth College, were also kind enough to answer my requests for information fully and swiftly.

NOTES

1. Sloan first publicly acknowledged "the Puritan standoffishness—no love expressed, all repression" he endured as a boy in 1922. John Sloan to Lily Yeats, February 7, 1922, quoted in Joseph Hone, ed., *J.B. Yeats: Letters to His Son W.B. Yeats and Others, 1869–1922* (New York: E.P. Dutton, 1946), p. 289.
2. John Loughery, *John Sloan: Painter and Rebel* (New York: Henry Holt, 1995), p. 3.
3. John Sloan, *Gist of Art: Principles and Practise Expounded in the Classroom and Studio* (New York, 1939; repr., New York: Dover, 1977), p. 3.
4. Ibid., p. 27.
5. James Dixon Sloan to John Sloan, February 9, 1909, December 4, 1910, and April 19, 1911, John Sloan Archives, Delaware Art Museum, Wilmington (hereafter JSA), Boxes 19–20.
6. John Butler Yeats (JBY) to Rosa Butt, January 11, 1911; JBY to Lily Yeats, May 25, 1915, William Murphy Transcriptions, Schaffer Library, Union College, Schenectady, N.Y. (hereafter WMT). The original letters of JBY to Rosa Butt are in the Bodleian Library, Oxford University, and those to his children are in the Yeats Collection, National Library of Ireland, Dublin.
7. See James M. Herzog, *Father Hunger: Explorations with Adults and Children* (Hillsdale, N.J.: The Analytic Press, 2001). I am grateful to Herbert Cogan for calling my attention to this reference.
8. Ibid., pp. 2, 22, 88, 310.
9. John Sloan, autobiographical sketch, undated, JSA, Box 251.
10. Van Wyck Brooks, *John Sloan: A Painter's Life* (New York: E.P. Dutton, 1955), p. 8. Newton later became one of the best-known book collectors in America.
11. Quoted in Rowland Elzea, *John Sloan's Oil Paintings: A Catalogue Raisonné*, part 1 (Newark: University of Delaware Press, 1991), p. 41.

12. In his biography of Sloan, John Loughery (p. 20) reported that the artist's first signed illustration for the *Inquirer* appeared on February 16, 1892.
13. John Sloan, unpublished notes about Robert Henri, 1949, p. 12, JSA, Box 252; Sloan, *Gist of Art*, p. xiii.
14. Sloan, *Gist of Art*, p. 6.
15. Bennard B. Perlman, ed., *Revolutionaries of Realism: The Letters of John Sloan and Robert Henri* (Princeton, N.J.: Princeton University Press, 1997), p. 158.
16. Quoted in Elzea, *Sloan's Oil Paintings*, part 1, p. 17.
17. Robert Henri to John Sloan, June 15, 1901, quoted in Perlman, *Revolutionaries*, p. 53.
18. Sloan, unpublished notes about Robert Henri, 1949, p. 12, JSA.
19. John Sloan to Robert Henri, October 1, 1898, quoted in Perlman, *Revolutionaries*, p. 31.
20. Brooks, *Sloan*, p. 35. Brooks first met the Sloans in 1910.
21. See for example, Dolly Sloan to John Sloan, July 28, 1909, and February 6, 1910, JSA, Boxes 19–20.
22. Loughery, *Sloan*, pp. 49–50.
23. John Sloan, miscellaneous unpublished notes, 1920s and 1930s, JSA, Box 249; Brooks, *Sloan*, p. 9; see also Herzog, *Father Hunger*, pp. 51–53, on the fear of maternal engulfment.
24. Sloan, unpublished notes about Robert Henri, 1949, p. 11, JSA; Brooks, *Sloan*, p. 9.
25. Sloan, miscellaneous unpublished notes, 1920s and 1930s, JSA, Box 249.
26. Brooks, *Sloan*, p. 35.
27. John Sloan, "Souls of Our Cities," *New York Times Magazine*, February 25, 1925.
28. See, for example, the etching *Turning Out the Light* (1905) and the paintings *Sixth Avenue and Thirtieth Street* (1907; Philadelphia Museum of Art), *South Beach Bathers* (1907–08; Walker Art Center, Minneapolis), *Chinese Restaurant* (1909; Memorial Art Gallery, University of Rochester), *Three A.M.* (1909; Philadelphia Museum of Art), *Sunday, Women Drying Their Hair* (1912; Addison Gallery of American Art, Phillips Academy, Andover, Mass.), and *Sunday Afternoon in Union Square* (1912; Bowdoin College Museum of Art, Brunswick, Maine).
29. John Sloan, diary, February 25, 1907, quoted in Bruce St. John, ed., *John Sloan's New York Scene: From the Diaries, Notes and Correspondence 1906–1913* (New York: Harper and Row, 1965) (hereafter *JSNYS*), p. 197.
30. Sloan, unpublished notes about Robert Henri, 1949, p. 9, JSA.
31. In 1907 Sloan painted, among other oils, *The Cot* (Bowdoin College Museum of Art), *Easter Eve* (private collection), *The Wake of the Ferry No. 2* (The Phillips Collection, Washington, D.C.), *Hairdresser's Window* (Wadsworth Atheneum, Hartford, Conn.), and *Sixth Avenue and Thirtieth Street.*
32. Bennard B. Perlman, *Robert Henri, Painter* (Wilmington: Delaware Art Museum, 1984), p. 87.
33. Sloan, diary, January 14, 1906, *JSNYS*, p. 6.
34. Sloan, diary, January 15, 1906, ibid.
35. James Kraft, *John Sloan: A Printmaker* (Washington, D.C.: International Exhibitions Foundation, 1984), p. 31.
36. Unless otherwise stated, all information about John Butler Yeats's life and work is drawn from William M. Murphy, *Prodigal Father: The Life of John Butler Yeats (1839–1922)* (Ithaca, N.Y.: Cornell University Press, 1978).
37. Quoted in William M. Murphy, *Family Secrets: William Butler Yeats and His Relatives* (Syracuse, N.Y.: Syracuse University Press, 1995), p. 3.
38. Ibid., p. 4.

39. JBY to Rosa Butt, November 21, 1913, WMT.
40. Hone, *J.B. Yeats,* p. 36.
41. JBY to Jack Yeats, December 16, 1913, WMT.
42. JBY Memoirs I, unpublished transcript, p. 9, WMT.
43. Sloan, unpublished notes about Robert Henri, 1949, p. 1, JSA.
44. JBY to Isaac Yeats, July 1, 1909, WMT. The same phrase is also quoted from a letter JBY wrote to William Butler Yeats in Murphy, *Prodigal Father*, p. 330.
45. JBY to Lollie Yeats, January 13, 1908, WMT; also quoted in Murphy, *Prodigal Father*, p. 328.
46. JBY to Jack Yeats, July 22, 1915, WMT.
47. Murphy, *Prodigal Father*, pp. 432–35; John Quinn to WBY, April 24, 1915, WMT.
48. Helen Vendler, "J.B.Y.," *New Yorker*, January 8, 1979, p. 66.
49. Robert Henri, diary, February 3, 1908, Robert Henri Papers, Archives of American Art, Smithsonian Institution (AAA), microfilm reel 886.
50. Sam McCready, *A William Butler Yeats Encyclopedia* (Westport, Conn.: Greenwood Press, 1997), pp. 170–71.
51. JBY to Rosa Butt, January 10, 1909, WMT.
52. Ibid.
53. JBY to Lollie and Lily Yeats, July 19, 1908, WMT. Luks painted a portrait of JBY in watercolor (ex-collection IBM Corporation; present whereabouts unknown) during this period too.
54. John Quinn to Lily Yeats, December 20, 1908, WMT.
55. JBY's 1908 portrait of John Quinn is also in the National Portrait Gallery, Washington, D.C.
56. JBY to Lily Yeats, December 2, 1908, WMT.
57. Sloan, diary, July 22, 1909, *JSNYS*, p. 324.
58. Yeats is referring to Henri's very recent paintings, *Salomé Dancer* (1909; Mead Art Museum, Amherst College, Amherst, Mass.) and *Salomé (No. 2)* (1909; John and Mable Ringling Museum of Art, Sarasota, Fla).
59. JBY to Rosa Butt, August 1, 1909, WMT; JBY to Lily Yeats, July 30, 1909 [pmk], WMT.
60. JBY to John Quinn, January 9, 1910, WMT. JBY's original letters to John Quinn are in the John Quinn Memorial Collection, Rare Books and Manuscript Division, New York Public Library (NYPL).
61. JBY to Lily Yeats, February 9, 1910, WMT.
62. Henri, diaries, August 12, 19, 26, 1909, AAA, reel 886. George Bellows reconstructed these and other social occasions with the Henris and Yeats in a drawing, *Night at Petitpas'* (1914; Boston Public Library), and the lithograph *Artists' Evening* (1916), published in the July 1916 issue of *The Masses.*
63. JBY to Lily Yeats, August 16, 1909, WMT.
64. JBY to Lily Yeats, September 3, 1909, WMT.
65. JBY to Lily Yeats, September 10, 1908, WMT.
66. Sloan, diary, October 4, 1909, *JSNYS*, pp. 338–39.
67. James C. Young, "Yeats of Petitpas'," *New York Times Book Review and Magazine,* February 19, 1922.
68. JBY to Lily Yeats, October 22, 1909, WMT; part of this passage was quoted in Murphy, *Prodigal Father*, p. 360. Yeats wrote "Sloan" and "Sloane" interchangeably throughout his letters mentioning the artist.
69. JBY to Jack and Mary Cottenham Yeats, November 23, 1909, WMT.
70. JBY to Jack Yeats, January 9, 1910, WMT.
71. See Murphy, *Family Secrets*, pp. 265–327, for an essay on Jack Yeats that discusses his silences and his distance from his father.

72. Henri, diary, December 9, 1909, AAA, reel 886.
73. JBY to Lollie Yeats, December 13, 1909, WMT.
74. JBY to Lily Yeats, December 17, 1909, WMT.
75. Sloan, diary, January 18, 1910, *JSNYS*, p. 376.
76. JBY to Lily Yeats, January 19, 1910, WMT.
77. Sloan, diary, January 3, 4, 10, 1910, *JSNYS*, pp. 371–74.
78. Sloan, diary, February 24 and March 9, 1910, *JSNYS*, pp. 391, 395–96.
79. JBY to Lily Yeats, March 12, 1910, WMT.
80. JBY to Lily and Lollie Yeats, March 16, 1910, WMT.
81. John Quinn to Charles Shannon, April 12, 1910, John Quinn Memorial Collection, NYPL, reel 37.
82. JBY to John Quinn, March 21, 1910, WMT.
83. JBY to William Butler Yeats, April 7, 1910, quoted in Hone, *J.B. Yeats*, p. 129.
84. JBY to William Butler Yeats, April 8, 1910, WMT.
85. JBY to Lily Yeats, April 10, 1910, WMT.
86. Sloan, diary, May 25, May 26, and June 1, 1910, *JSNYS*, pp. 426, 429.
87. JBY to Lily Yeats, June 5, 1910, WMT.
88. John Sloan to John Quinn, June 27, 1910, NYPL, reel 37.
89. See the correspondence between Sloan and Quinn in ibid.
90. Helen Farr Sloan, "Introduction," in Helen Farr Sloan, ed., *John Sloan's New York Etchings* (New York: Dover, 1978), p. viii.
91. JBY to Lily Yeats, July 5, 1910, WMT. Yeats drew John and Dolly Sloan separately and together, and the various sketches and finished drawings are in the collection of the Delaware Art Museum as a gift of Helen Farr Sloan, Sloan's second wife.
92. JBY to Lily Yeats, June 16, 1910, WMT.
93. Loughery, *Sloan*, p. 161.
94. JBY to Lily Yeats, August 12, 1908, WMT.
95. Paul B. Franklin, "Pilgrim Father, Native Son: John Butler Yeats, John Sloan, and the Making of a Friendship in New York City," in Janis Londraville, ed., *Prodigal Father Revisited: Artists and Writers in the World of John Butler Yeats* (West Cornwall, Conn.: Locust Hill Press, 2003), p. 294.
96. Raymond Nelson, *Van Wyck Brooks: A Writer's Life* (New York: E.P. Dutton, 1981), p. 68.
97. Sloan, diary, July 22, 1910, *JSNYS*, p. 442.
98. John Butler Yeats, "John Sloan's Exhibition," *The Seven Arts*, 2 (May–October 1917), p. 259.
99. JBY to Lily Yeats, December 23, 1910, WMT.
100. Ibid.
101. Eulabee Dix, typescript of unpublished memoirs, p. 108, Eulabee Dix Papers, Special Collections, Library and Research Center, National Museum of Women in the Arts, Washington, D.C., Box 2.
102. Henri, diary, December 17, 1910, AAA, reel 886.
103. See, for example, Henri to Eulabee Dix Becker, October 20, 1912, Eulabee Dix Papers, Box 1.
104. JBY to Lily Yeats, January 24, 1921, WMT. Yeats prophesied correctly–she did extract the painting from Hawthorne.
105. McCready, *Yeats Encyclopedia*, pp. 205–06.
106. Franklin, "Pilgrim Father," p. 295.
107. JBY to Lollie Yeats, April 7, 1917, WMT.
108. Sloan to Lily Yeats, February 7, 1922, quoted in Hone, *J.B. Yeats*, p. 289.
109. Quoted in Sloan, *Gist of Art*, p. 105.

How the American Impressionists and Realists Kept the Wolf from the Door

H. BARBARA WEINBERG

Lecture given on December 4, 2008

New-York Historical Society

New York City

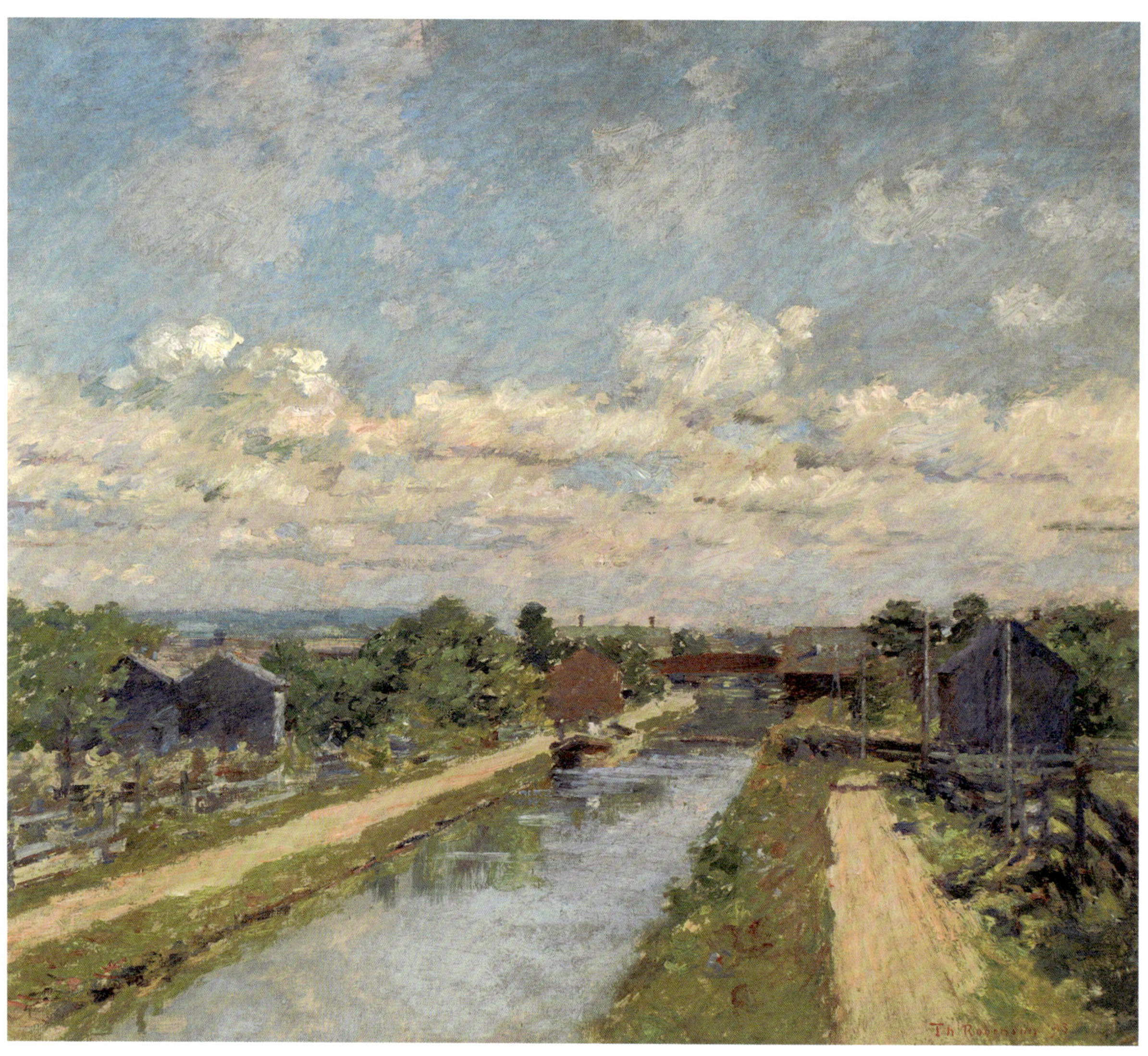

Fig. 82
Theodore Robinson
Port Ben, Delaware and Hudson Canal, 1893
Oil on canvas
28¼ × 32¼ in. (71.8 × 81.9 cm)
Pennsylvania Academy of the Fine Arts, Philadelphia;
Gift of the Society of American Artists as a memorial to Theodore Robinson

How the American Impressionists and Realists Kept the Wolf from the Door

H. BARBARA WEINBERG

When we think of the American Impressionists, we think first of their sunlit landscapes and scenes of carefree leisure, while we associate the American Realists, also known as the Ashcan painters, with their earthy images of New York's streets, amusements, and characters.[1] Yet painting such pictures was only one of many professional activities that occupied these artists and yielded only limited monetary rewards. Many American Impressionists and Realists led much more complicated professional lives than we generally acknowledge, and became what we might now call master multitaskers in order to keep the wolf from the door.

We may not recognize how little economic success these two groups of artists had during their movements' prime years—about 1885 to 1900 for the American Impressionists and about 1900 to 1915 for the Realists. There has been little study of the patronage of either group,[2] and monographs tend to emphasize their now-popular paintings and remain silent or elusive about how they made a living. This essay begins to delineate a socio-economic profile of several New York-based American Impressionists and Realists, with a focus on some of the financial frustration they faced as painters and how this affected the paths they chose in their professional lives.

With respect to the value of money, which provides a context for the discussion of prices and artists' earnings: In the United States in 1901 the annual income for a household (4.9 individuals) was $750; in New York State it was $675 (no statistics exist for New York City alone).[3] The value of the dollar remained fairly constant until inflation surged in 1918–19, at the end of World War I.[4]

Apart from the pioneering expatriates Mary Cassatt and John Singer Sargent, who explored Impressionism in Paris in the late 1870s, Americans began to adopt the style in the mid-1880s. They were led by William Merritt Chase in New York and by Theodore Robinson and others who worked in Claude Monet's orbit at Giverny in France. However, patronage lagged as most American collectors pursued old master, French academic, and Barbizon paintings. Those who became interested in French Impressionism as a result of major exhibitions held in Boston in 1883 and New York in 1886 took little interest in the American version.[5] In fact, patronage for most American art was weak. In the late 1880s, the painter John Joseph Enneking complained: "Art has always had a hard time in America. 'No one buys an American picture,' the dealers say, and they're about right. We all have to teach or paint potboilers to make a living."[6]

The first New York dealer committed to promoting American art exclusively was William Macbeth, who opened his gallery in 1892, exhibiting works by Winslow Homer, Arthur B. Davies, and the older Hudson River School painters. The few collectors who sought American pictures preferred Tonalism, which echoed the poetic Barbizon style; Macbeth served that interest by showing paintings by George Inness, Homer Dodge Martin, and Alexander H. Wyant. After 1900, a few established dealers such as M. Knoedler and Company, Kraushaar Galleries, and Montross Gallery, and some newer establishments, such as Milch Galleries, joined Macbeth in endorsing American art, including American Impressionism.

Thus, it was not until almost fifteen years after their style had emerged in New York and Giverny that the American Impressionists found a consistent market for their works. From 1897 to 1917, the organization known as Ten American Painters was an important forum for several New York and Boston Impressionists, although their creative energy had by then begun to fade.[7] Collectors such as William T. Evans, John Gellatly, George A. Hearn, Alexander C. Humphreys, Samuel T. Shaw, and others began to acquire American Impressionist works.[8] Appreciation of the style was not universal, however. For example, in 1898 the Metropolitan Museum's Art Committee declined the gift from the Society of American Artists of the recently deceased Theodore Robinson's *Port Ben, Delaware and Hudson Canal* (Fig. 82), declaring that the canvas "represented a class of painting that should not be encouraged."[9]

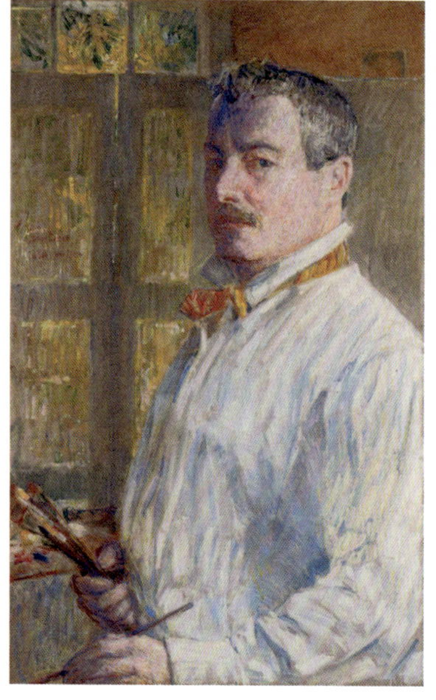

Fig. 83
Childe Hassam
Self-Portrait, 1914
Oil on canvas
32⅞ × 20¾ in. (83.5 × 52.7 cm)
American Academy of
Arts and Letters, New York

Lacking reliable patronage for their paintings during their peak years, the leaders of American Impressionism were obliged to turn to portraiture, mural commissions, illustration, printmaking, or teaching in order to make a living. The principal exception was Childe Hassam (1859–1935) [Fig. 83], who depended entirely on marketing his huge output of oils and watercolors.[10] Hassam's colleague J. Alden Weir noted in a letter of November 1910: "He produces more canvases than any man I know, thirty or forty in a season seem nothing to him. I wish I had that power. I count on six or eight and think I am doing well."[11] No venue was too minor or obscure to escape Hassam's interest, from the parlor of Florence Griswold's boardinghouse

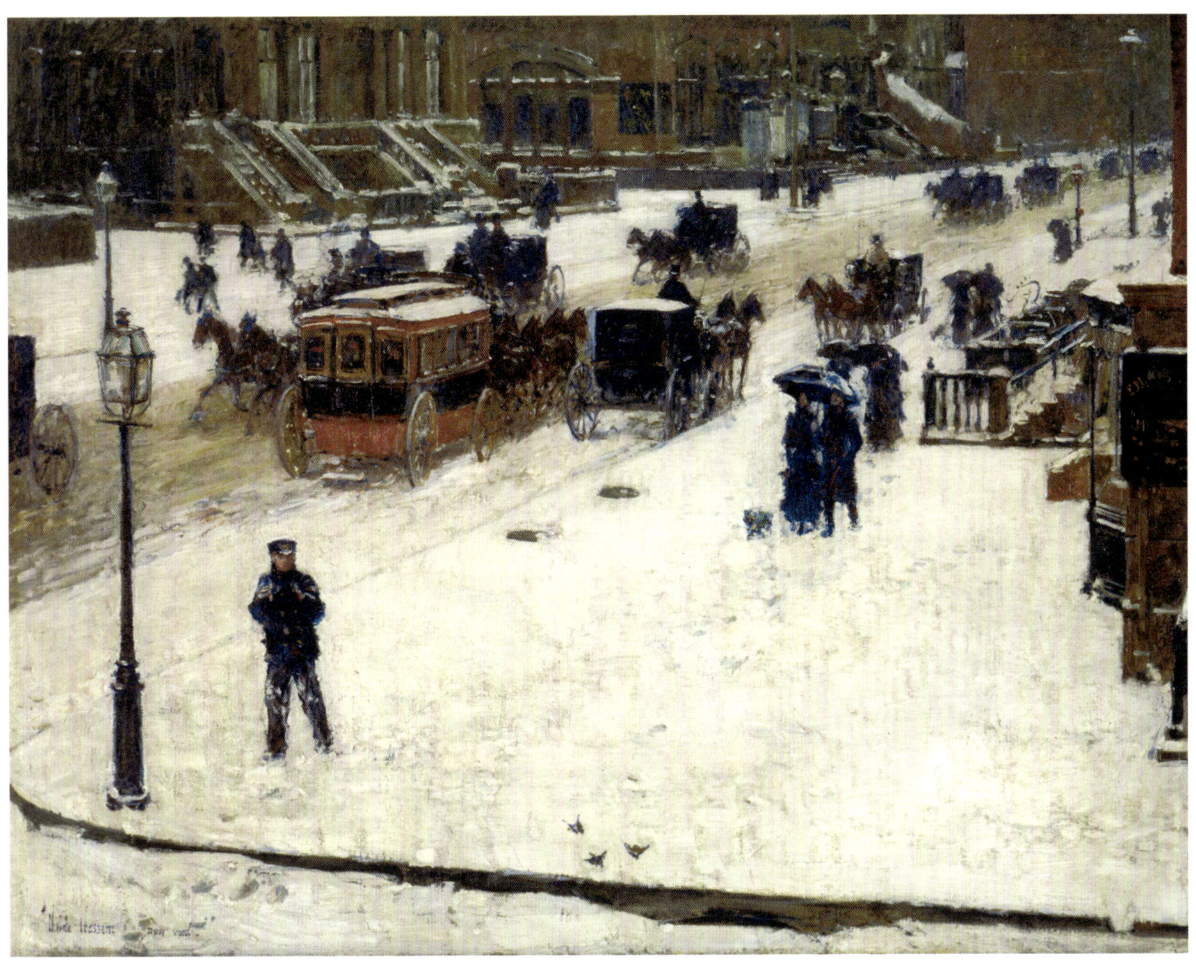

Fig. 84
Childe Hassam
Fifth Avenue in Winter, c. 1892
Oil on canvas
22 × 28 in. (55.9 × 71.1 cm)
Carnegie Museum of Art, Pittsburgh; Purchase 00.2

in Old Lyme, Connecticut, to the Gallery on the Moors in East Gloucester, Massachusetts, to the midwinter exhibition at the Haydon Art Club in Lincoln, Nebraska. In 1900 the Carnegie Institute bought his *Fifth Avenue in Winter* (Fig. 84) out of its 1899 Annual International Exhibition for $800. This was one of the earliest museum purchases of an American Impressionist painting, and according to Hassam himself, was "a large price for a painting in those days."[12] Also in 1900 the Cincinnati Art Museum purchased *Pont Royal, Paris* (1897). After 1900 Hassam had many dealers representing him simultaneously, and by 1911, his paintings were included in almost every major public collection in the United States. When he died in 1935, his gross estate, which mainly comprised stocks and bonds, exclusive of the many works of art he bequeathed to the American Academy of Arts and Letters, was appraised at $212,710, equivalent to about $3.35 million in 2010.[13]

Hassam's associates were much less successful financially as painters, which meant they had to pursue other ventures. Theodore

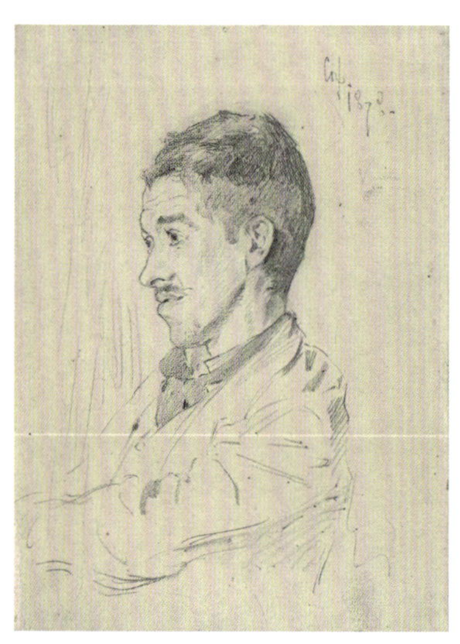

Fig. 85
Kenyon Cox
Theodore Robinson, 1878
Pencil on paper
11 × 8½ in. (27.9 × 21.6 cm)
The Metropolitan Museum of Art, New York; Gift of Raymond J. and Margaret Horowitz, 2007

Robinson (1852–1896) [Fig. 85] was born into a large family of modest circumstances in Vermont and raised in the Midwest. His father was a farmer, a minister, and later, a clothing merchant.[14] Robinson received instruction in Chicago and New York before going to Paris to study in 1875. Back in New York in 1881, he taught at Mrs. Sylvanus Reed's Boarding and Day School for Young Ladies, instructed a private class, and worked on various decorative projects. He saved enough money to be able to return in 1884 to France where he became a mainstay of the American art colony at Giverny, spending half of each year there between 1887 and 1892. Robinson adopted Monet's techniques, his appreciation of familiar subjects, and his commitment to expressing the essence of a place. It is not known how Robinson made a living during these years.

In December 1892 Robinson returned permanently to the United States, where he lived a frugal bachelor's existence with support from several teaching assignments: a class in Napanoch, New York, for the Brooklyn Institute of Arts and Sciences in summer 1893; a class for the Brooklyn Art School at Evelyn College in August 1894; a class at the Pennsylvania Academy of the Fine Arts in Philadelphia as a substitute for Robert Vonnoh in January 1895; and a class in Vermont between May and November 1895.

For his French paintings, Robinson received a few awards, including the $300 Webb Prize from the Society of American Artists in 1890 for *Winter Landscape* (1889; Terra Foundation for American Art, Chicago) and its $1,500 Samuel T. Shaw Purchase Prize in 1892 for *In the Sun* (1891; whereabouts unknown). In 1892, he sold the first, small version of *The Layette* (1892; Corcoran Gallery of Art, Washington, D.C.) to the New York banker Henry G. Marquand for his Boston business partner; and *Le Débâcle* (1892; Scripps College, Claremont, California) to the insurance and real-estate mogul John Gellatly for $400.[15] In 1893, Robinson sold a watercolor to the railroad magnate Collis P. Huntington; two paintings, including *The Watering Pots* (1890; Brooklyn Museum) for $270, to Frank L. Babbott, the director of the Chelsea Jute Mills; and one of his three versions of *Valley of the Seine* (Fig. 86) to the dry-goods merchant George A. Hearn. Robinson wrote in his diary on May 25, 1893: "Sold my 'Valley of the Seine' to Hearn for $700. I had asked 1200 . . . it was perhaps too much." But he added, "It is the largest price I've yet received for a landscape."[16] On August 17, 1893, Robinson wrote to Monet: "I am happy to be after all a little bit more successful, I mean regarding monetary affairs. I am selling enough now to live modestly, and I think that it will continue. It is true that I do not have very large expenses. It is agreeable nevertheless to be a bit sure of the future, especially at my age."[17]

Robinson's diary reveals a preoccupation with money and how to earn it without sacrificing his integrity. On October 12, 1892, he

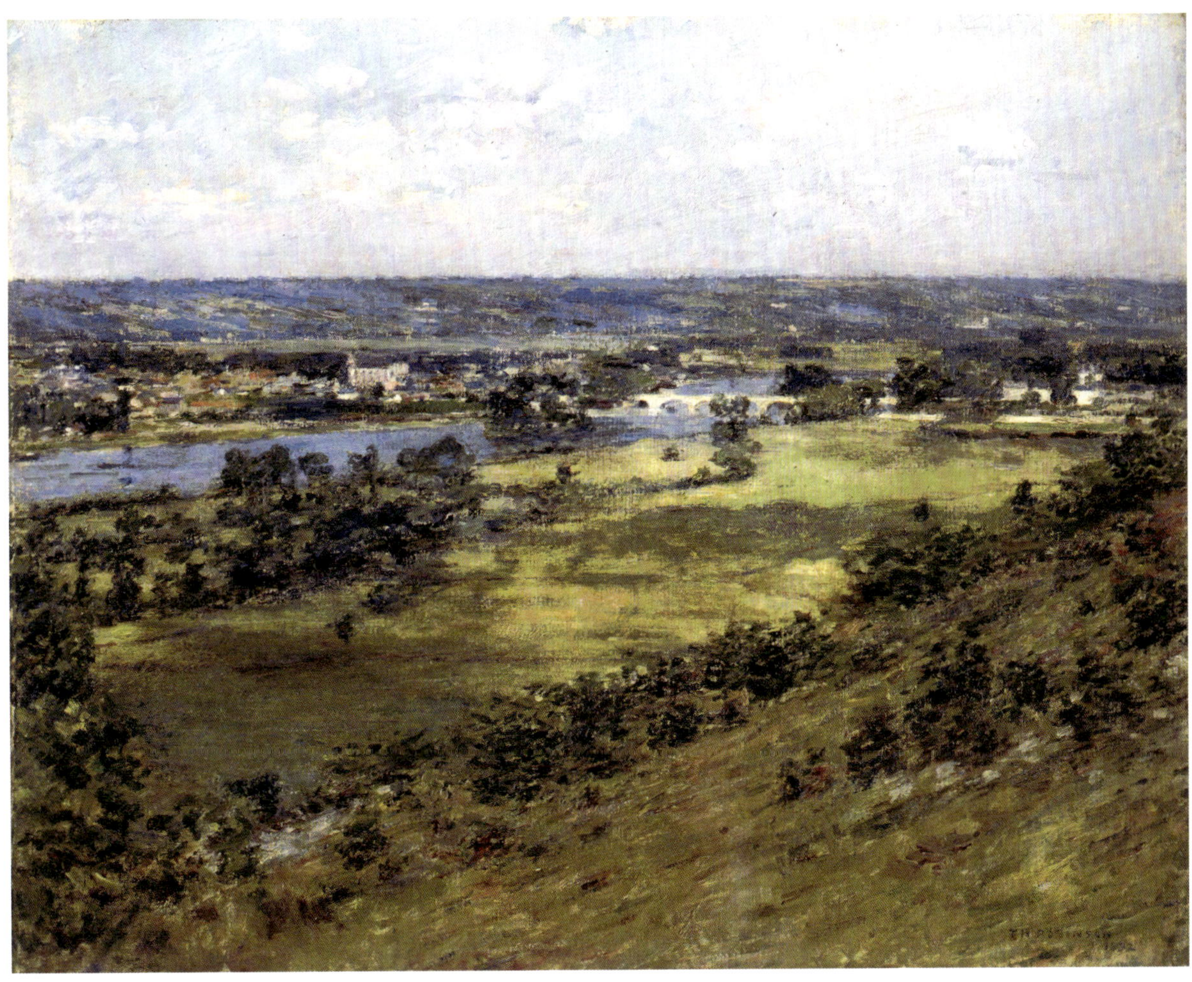

Fig. 86
Theodore Robinson
Valley of the Seine, 1892
Oil on canvas
25¾ × 32⅜ in. (65.4 × 82.2 cm)
Addison Gallery of American Art, Phillips Academy, Andover, Massachusetts; Museum Purchase 1934.3

remarks that he likes the American painter Louis Paul Dessar and mentions Dessar's success: "He has no fear of the banal, of doing the 'already done,' which is perhaps one secret of his prosperity." On October 27, 1894, he notes: "I must try and devise some scheme of my own to avoid illustrating as others do, viz. stories or sketches, but do something in my own line that will interest the public." Robinson also recorded his own annual income during those years:

> Dec. 31, 1892: I have been fortunate in 1892 financially more money than ever I made in one year—about ~~$3500~~ Receipts 2852.
>
> Dec. 31, 1893: Casting up accounts, I find I have received this year 3307. dols. against 2852. dols. for last yr. Considering the hard times I ought not to complain—it is the most I ever received in one year by considerable.
>
> Dec. 31, 1894: Financially a bad year. I have rec'd $1080.25 and spent 1387.66 a deficit in the budget of $307.41.
>
> Dec. 31, 1895: Amount of income the past year (1895) $1,817.08.[18]

Robinson had more difficulty selling his American subjects than his French scenes. On February 19, 1895, during his first solo exhibition at the Macbeth Galleries in New York, he jotted in his diary: "Macbeth's man called—an offer of $225 for the 'New England Brook' which I took. . . . This is the first to sell of my American canvases—and marks a date." Robinson annotated the diary entry on March 4: "The above was only a 'nibble'—and nothing came of it."[19] His painting *November* (1892; private collection), however, did sell from the Macbeth show—to a "Mrs. Stone," who paid $350 for it. Robinson wrote in his diary on March 4: "I'm glad one thing sold for MacBeth's account—he will be encouraged."[20] On May 4, 1895, he noted in his diary that he was often asked what his lowest price would be for a particular work, and on October 25, 1895, he acknowledged that he would accept any price offered, given the dearth of recent sales.

Robinson died in April 1896 at the age of forty-three of asthma, which had plagued him since childhood. Just before his death, he sold *Autumn Sunlight* (1888; Florence Griswold Museum, Old Lyme, Connecticut) to A.P. Yorston. However, he did not live to see works in his "own line" attract the interest of private and public collectors, which they began to do by the time of his March 1898 estate sale, held at the American Art Association in New York.[21]

Robinson's friend John H. Twachtman (1853–1902) [Fig. 87] also died before the art market embraced American Impressionism.[22] He was born in Cincinnati, the son of German immigrants of modest resources. From 1868 to 1880, he was a peripatetic student in Cincinnati, Munich, and New York, often supplementing his income by teaching and returning to Cincinnati whenever money ran out. In 1881 Twachtman married Martha Scudder, with whom he would raise a large family. With financial help from his father-in-law, a prominent Cincinnati physician, he went, with his wife and child, to study in Paris and to travel in Europe from 1883 to 1886; two more children were born in Europe.

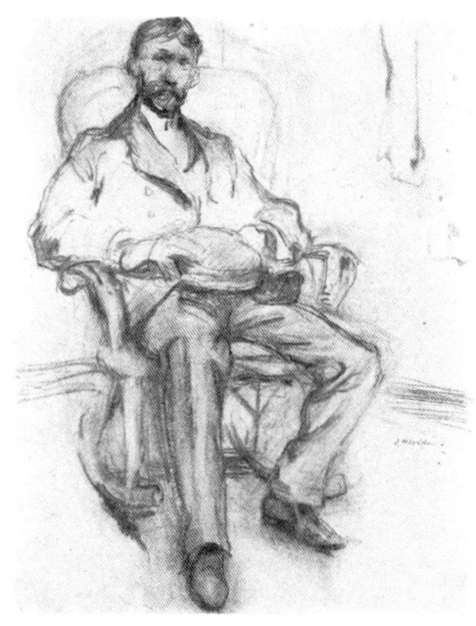

Fig. 87
J. Alden Weir
John Henry Twachtman, c. 1895
Charcoal on paper
9 15/16 × 7 15/16 in. (25.2 × 20.2 cm)
National Portrait Gallery,
Smithsonian Institution,
Washington, D.C. NPG 87.236

In the summer of 1888, Twachtman rented a house for himself and his family in Branchville, Connecticut, near his close friend and colleague J. Alden Weir, whom he had met in New York ten years earlier.[23] From 1889 until his death in 1902, Twachtman found steady income by commuting to New York to teach drawing from plaster casts at the Art Students League. He also taught cast drawing at the Cooper Union (1894–1902); gave classes in Cos Cob, Connecticut, either alone or with Weir, almost every summer between 1890 and 1899; taught in Norwich, Connecticut, in the summer of 1898; and made illustrations for *Scribner's* (1889–93) and other publications.

In February 1889, Twachtman and Weir held a joint exhibition and auction of eighty-four works at the Fifth Avenue Art Galleries in New York. The sale total was $7,300, of which Twachtman's share was about half; only nine of his works brought $100 or more.[24]

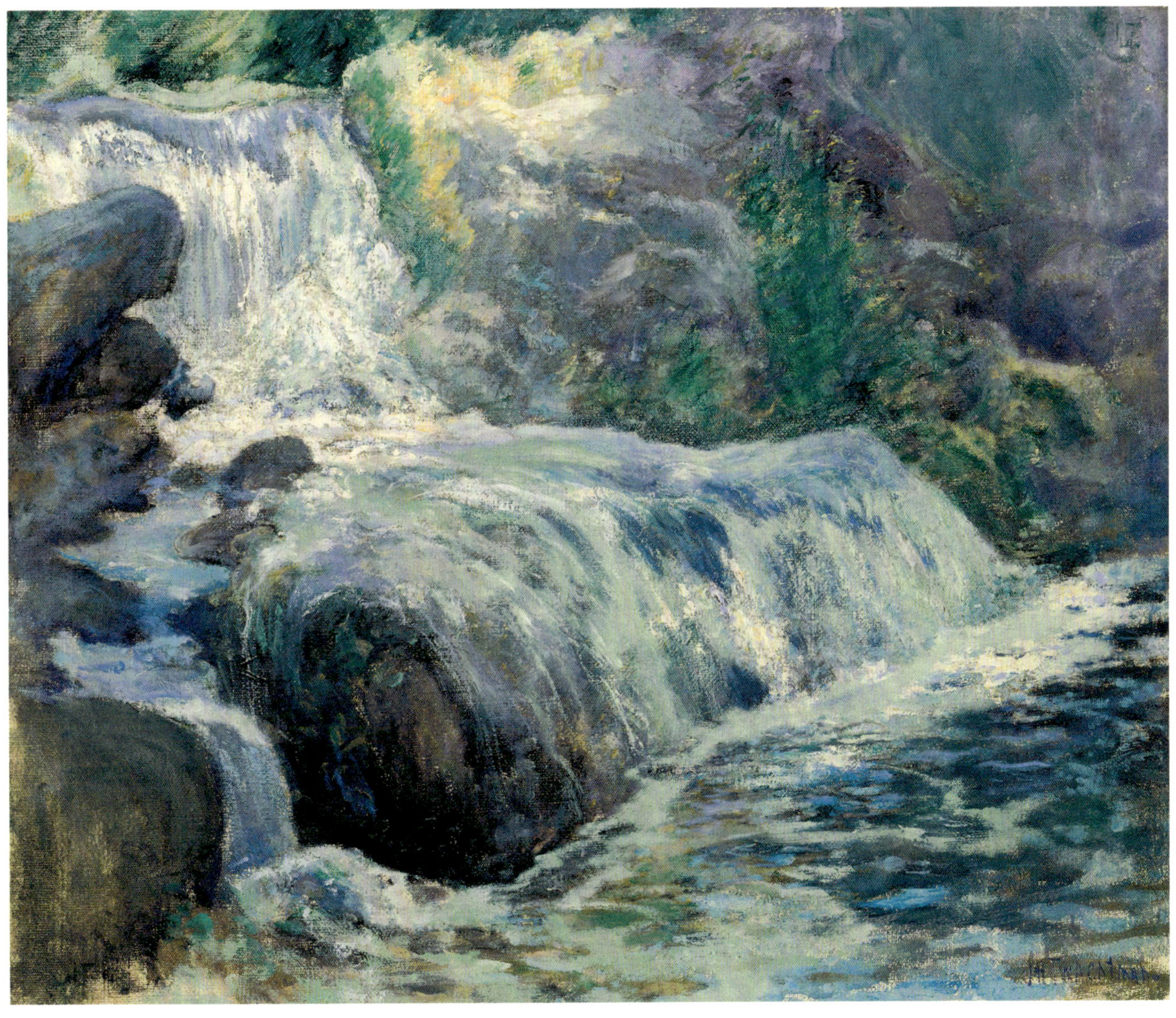

Fig. 88
John H. Twachtman
Waterfall, 1895–99
Oil on canvas
25⅛ × 30¹⁄₁₆ in. (63.8 × 76.4 cm)
Cincinnati Art Museum;
Annual Membership Fund Purchase

Notwithstanding these modest results, the proceeds (perhaps with a contribution from his father-in-law) enabled Twachtman to purchase three acres and a house in Greenwich, Connecticut, which became his home and headquarters in fall 1889.[25] The only other painting by Twachtman auctioned during his lifetime was *Autumn Afternoon* (c. 1894–95; private collection), which appeared in December 1900 at the American Art Galleries; it is not known whether he consigned it himself.[26] Twachtman was never economically secure and his financial problems were amplified by his poor health and by the fact that he had a family to support.[27]

Twachtman did receive two commissions—from Dr. Charles Cary of Buffalo in 1894 and from Major William A. Wadsworth of Geneseo, New York, in 1895—for views of Niagara Falls and Yellowstone Park, respectively. Otherwise, he found his inspiration in the Connecticut countryside and, between 1900 and 1902, in Gloucester,

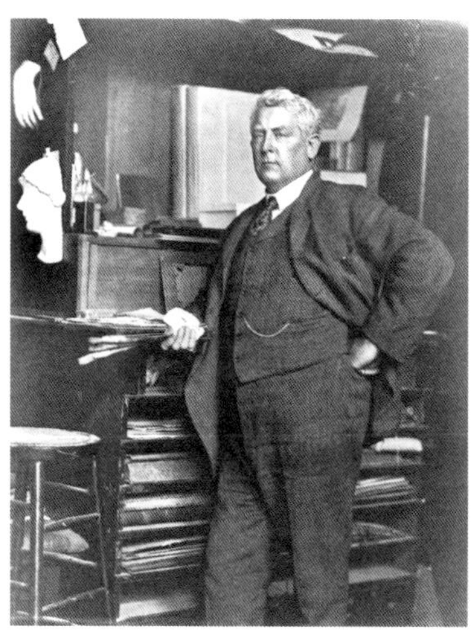

Fig. 89
J. Alden Weir in His Studio, n.d.
Smithsonian American Art Museum, Washington, D.C.; Peter A. Juley & Son Collection

Massachusetts. With their muted tonal harmonies, textured brushwork, and poetic aspect, his pictures were among the most radical and distinctive produced by any American Impressionist. He showed widely and steadily and gained his fellow artists' esteem and support but enjoyed little critical acclaim or commercial success. In the spring of 1895, Weir urged the Pennsylvania Academy's managing director, Harrison S. Morris, to purchase Twachtman's paintings, but Morris declined, saying: "The public is still apathetic in buying at all [after the depression of 1893], and 'Impressionism' as they name whatever is too sincere for them to understand, has few votaries among the non-elect. Alack-a-day, it takes a generation or two for the public to grow up to a big idea."[28] Over dinner at the Players Club in December 1895, Twachtman told Robinson that he had made merely $1,000 from the sale of pictures that year.[29] (Robinson himself had made $1,817.08, and had no wife or family to support.) The only painting that Twachtman sold to a museum was *Waterfall* (Fig. 88), which was acquired by the Cincinnati Art Museum in 1900. When Twachtman died at the age of fifty in 1902, he left a wife and four children. Ironically, his March 1903 estate sale was remarkably successful, reflecting collectors' change of heart about American Impressionism.[30]

J. Alden Weir (1852–1919) [Fig. 89] was born into comfortable middle-class circumstances, the son of a well-known painter and art teacher at West Point, Robert W. Weir.[31] After lessons with his father and studies in New York and Paris, Weir settled in New York in 1877 and began teaching at the Cooper Union the following year and at the Art Students League in 1885. He also received a few commissions and sold a few paintings. For example, in 1884, Ichabod T. Williams, a collector who made his fortune in the lumber business, purchased *The Muse of Music* (1882–84; Fine Arts Museums of San Francisco) for $1,500. Weir also acted as an art agent and adviser for the banker Henry G. Marquand and for the silver-mine owner Erwin Davis, who acquired among other works paintings by Barbizon artists and by Diego Velázquez, Gustave Courbet, Édouard Manet, Jules Bastien-Lepage, Inness, and Twachtman. In 1882, Weir resold to Davis "a very fine picture" that he had bought in a gallery for $560, receiving the purchase price plus a 153-acre farm in Branchville, Connecticut, that would be his summer home for thirty-seven years.[32] Also in 1882, Weir became engaged to Anna Dwight Baker, the nineteen-year-old daughter of a prominent and wealthy Connecticut family.

In the winter of 1882–83, Weir made $1,300 teaching a class of young women and was receiving more portrait commissions. He was confident enough in his financial situation to marry in April 1883 and then to enjoy a leisurely honeymoon in Europe. Upon their return, the couple moved into a small apartment on West Tenth Street. However, when in 1886 they wished to purchase a house on East Twelfth Street, Weir needed to appeal to his mother-in-law for a loan. When

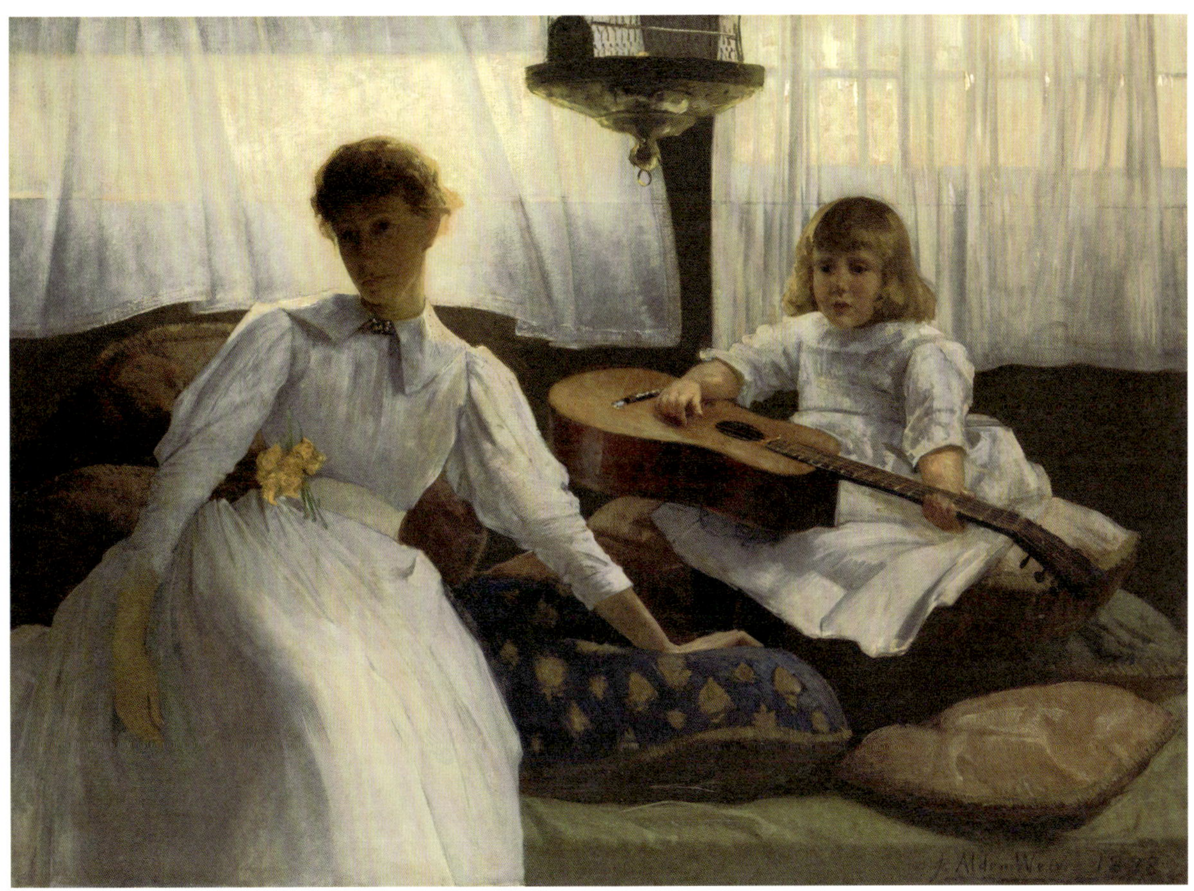

Fig. 90
J. Alden Weir
Idle Hours, 1888
Oil on canvas
51¼ × 71⅛ in. (130.2 × 180.7 cm)
The Metropolitan Museum of Art, New York; Gift of several gentlemen, 1888

photography undermined the popularity of portraits, Weir turned to floral still lifes, pastels, drypoints, and etchings. In 1888, a $2,000 award for *Idle Hours* (Fig. 90) in the Fourth Annual Prize Fund Exhibition at the American Art Association boosted Weir's income and morale. However, from the 1889 auction of works that he held with Twachtman, Weir made only about $3,800. Sales included *Lengthening Shadows* (1887; private collection); *The Miniature* (1888; Heckscher Museum of Art, Huntington, New York); and three paintings purchased by Smith College: *Oriana* (1888), *The Delft Plate* (1888; Museum of Fine Arts, Boston), and a floral still life.[33]

Weir had expressed disdain for Impressionism while he was an art student in Paris, grumbling, for example, that the 1877 French Impressionist exhibition "was worse than the Chamber of Horrors."[34] By the early 1880s, however, he had come to admire Manet's works, which influenced his own still-life and figure paintings. By about 1890–91, he was finally inspired by the Connecticut countryside, his association with Robinson, Twachtman, and Hassam, and his study of Japanese prints to adopt a lighter palette, broken brushwork, and informal compositions. Initially, however, Weir did not receive any financial benefits from his Impressionist efforts. When Anna Baker

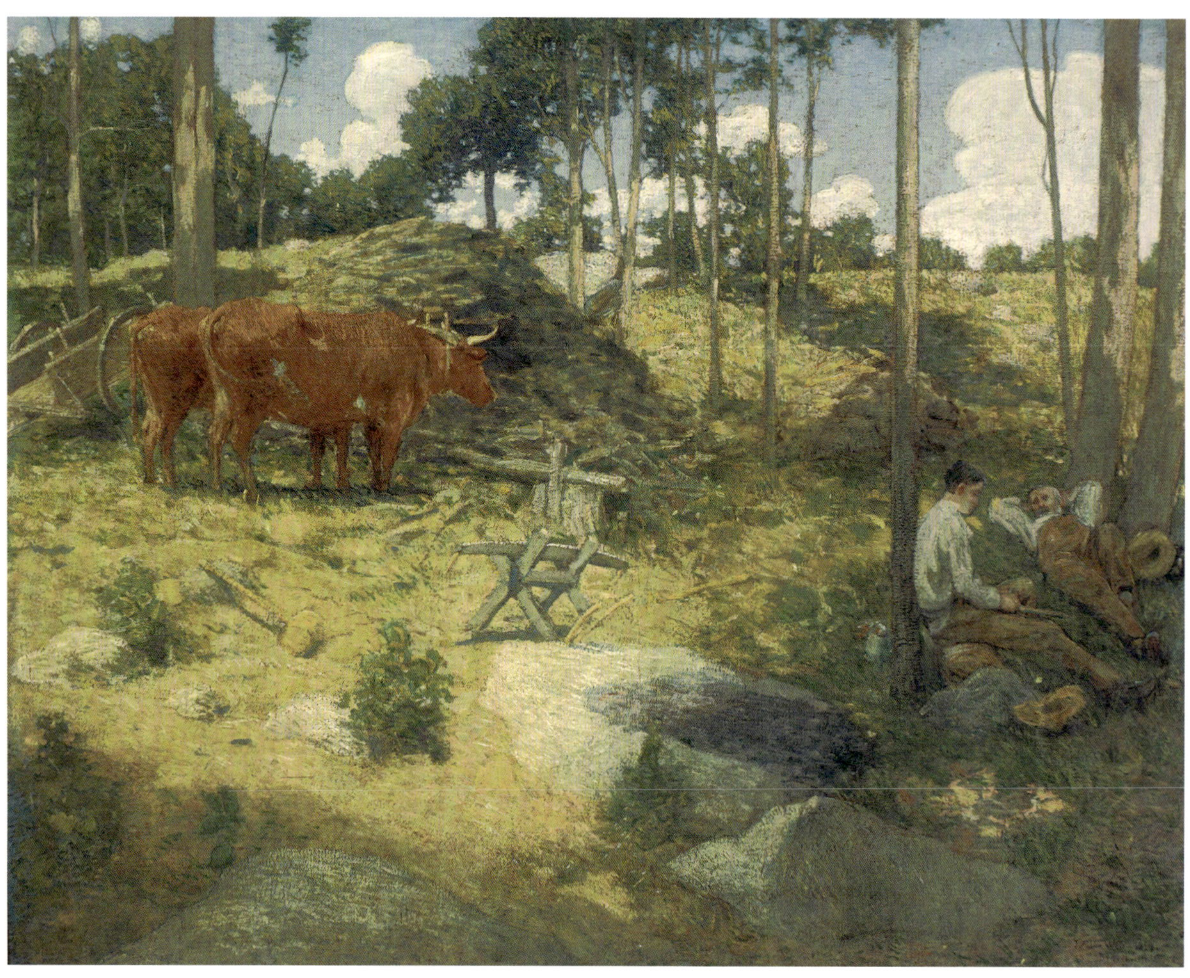

Fig. 91
J. Alden Weir
Midday Rest in New England, 1897
Oil on canvas
39⅝ × 50⅜ in. (100.7 × 128 cm)
Pennsylvania Academy of the Fine Arts, Philadelphia; Gift of Isaac H. Clothier, Edward H. Coates, Dr. Francis W. Lewis, Robert C. Ogden, and Joseph G. Rosengarten

Weir died in February 1892 from puerperal fever, just after the birth of her fourth child, Weir wrote to his mother-in-law: "When we were first married my income was much larger than it is now, having of late striven for other things in which Anna gave me strength and encouragement, and we were both ambitious, we often talked of the time when we would look back on these hard times and smile at them."[35] Weir's conversion to Impressionism in the early 1890s had not been to his economic advantage.

As American Impressionism gained some favor with collectors, Weir's fortunes improved. In 1897, his old friend Charles Erskine Scott Wood, a West Pointer and a Portland, Oregon, attorney and author, began to purchase Weir's works and also began to build a West Coast market for them. Wood sold several paintings on Weir's behalf, including *The Open Book* (1891; Smithsonian American Art Museum, Washington, D.C.), which brought $2,000, and *The Green Bodice* (c. 1896–98; The Metropolitan Museum of Art, New York) to the contractor and engineer Edward F. Milliken.[36] In 1898, five

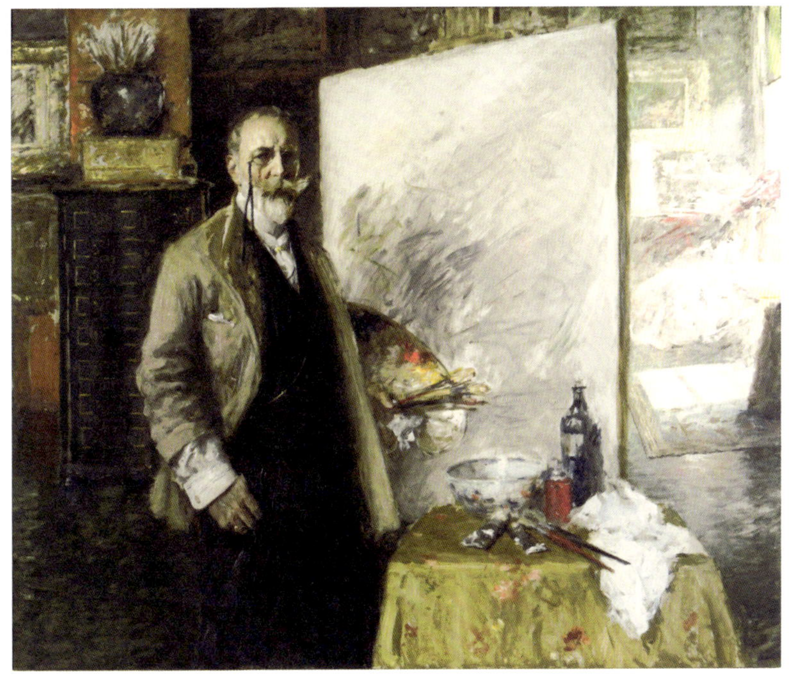

Fig. 92
William Merritt Chase
Self-Portrait: The Artist in His Studio, 1916
Oil on canvas
52 × 63 in. (132.1 × 160 cm)
Richmond Art Museum, Richmond, Indiana; Gift of Warner M. Leeds and Art Association Purchase

collectors gave Weir's *Midday Rest in New England* (Fig. 91) to the Pennsylvania Academy. By January 1899, Weir was able to give up teaching, except for the summer classes he taught in Branchville until 1901, and to make a living as a painter.

Although William Merritt Chase (1849–1916) [Fig. 92] appeared to be an artist-gentleman, his family background was modest and his finances were always tenuous.[37] Born in Indiana, Chase was the eldest son of a small-scale farmer who later worked as a merchant in Indianapolis. After studies in New York, Chase joined his family in St. Louis, where they had moved and where he supported himself by painting still lifes. In 1872, he eagerly responded to an offer from several local art patrons to subsidize his study abroad with a total of $2,100, in exchange for copies of paintings he would make for each of them and his advice on acquisitions. From his six years at the Munich Royal Academy and the influence of the Munich School realist Wilhelm Leibl, Chase acquired a painterly technique and an appreciation of saturated colors and dramatic chiaroscuro. He was rewarded with a commission for family portraits from his principal instructor, Karl von Piloty; the 1877 purchase of his *Ready for the Ride* (1877; The Union League Club, New York) by the New York art dealer Samuel P. Avery; and an invitation to return to New York in 1878 to teach at the newly founded Art Students League for a salary of $50 per month.

In New York, Chase debuted as a painter, teacher, and a man of style. He staffed his professional quarters in the Tenth Street Studio Building with a full-time servant and decorated it with his own pictures and his collections of bric-a-brac, paintings, and furniture.

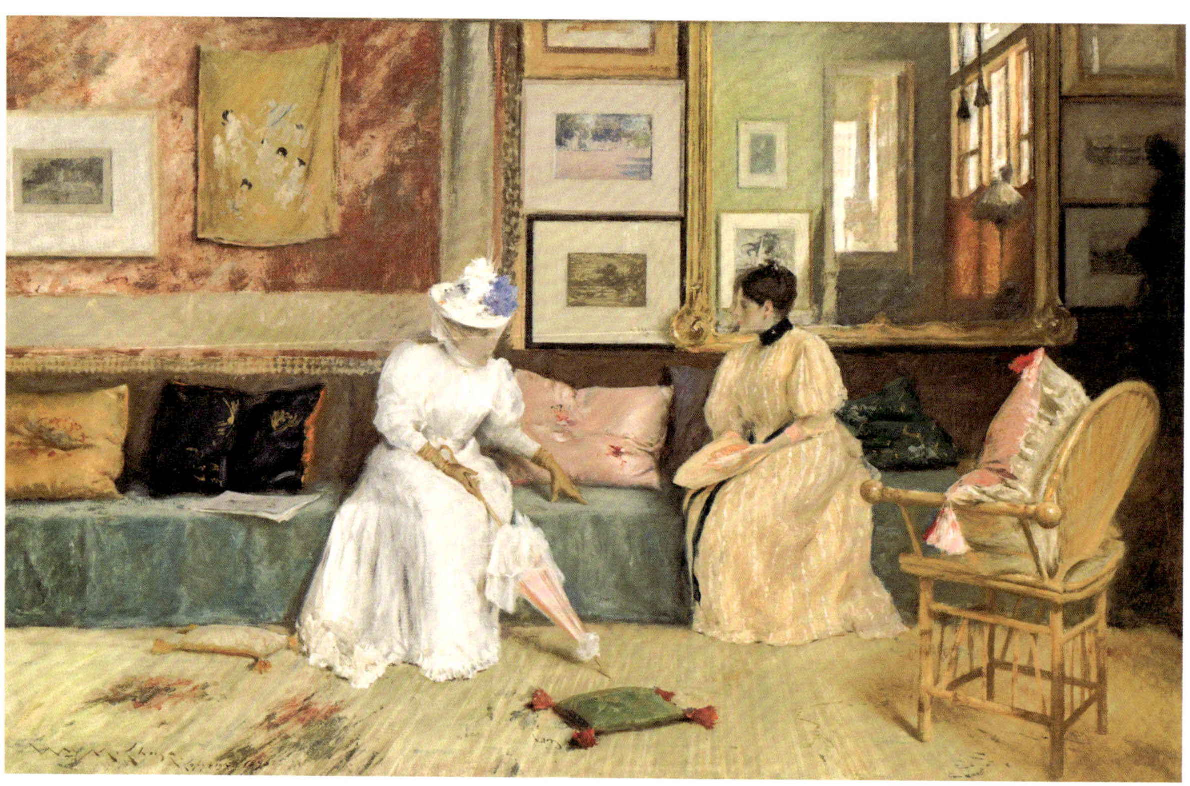

Fig. 93
William Merritt Chase
A Friendly Call, 1895
Oil on canvas
30⅛ × 48¼ in. (76.5 × 122.6 cm)
National Gallery of Art, Washington, D.C.; Chester Dale Collection

Such refinement impressed potential patrons. In 1886, Chase married Alice Gerson and started a family that would eventually include eight children. Even the stylish clothing they all wear in his many pictures of them suggests good taste and great expense.

Chase matured into a prolific, versatile master. His brilliant, homegrown Impressionism is apparent in splendid park scenes of the mid- and late 1880s and ravishing Shinnecock views of the 1890s, but the monetary rewards from his paintings were variable. For example, in 1895 he won the lucrative Samuel T. Shaw Purchase Prize of $1,500 at the Society of American Artists exhibition for *A Friendly Call* (Fig. 93). He was also the best-represented New York Impressionist in the collection of Thomas B. Clarke, then the leading patron of American art. But Clarke's pictures by Chase were almost all modest in scale, and seven of them sold for an average price of only $170 in Clarke's epochal February 1899 auction—when Winslow Homer's *Eight Bells* (1886; Addison Gallery of American Art, Phillips Academy, Andover, Massachusetts) brought $4,700 and Inness's *A Gray Lowery Day* (1877; Davis Museum and Cultural Center, Wellesley College, Wellesley, Massachusetts) sold for $10,150, breaking all previous auction records for an American painting.[38]

Portrait painting was essential to Chase's income.[39] He had positioned himself as a society portraitist, often painting likenesses of his students as samples and showing them widely, as in the case of *Portrait of Dora Wheeler* (1883; The Cleveland Museum of Art), which appeared in Munich and Paris, or donating them to leading institutions, as in the case of *Lady in Black* (1888), which he gave to the Metropolitan Museum of Art in 1891. As a result, portraits of fashionable women became his stock-in-trade. By the 1890s, Chase had increased his prices. The artist Reynolds Beal, who studied with Chase at Shinnecock during the 1890s, wrote: "Chase gets $750.00 for a head and shoulders. $1500.00 for a half length, and $2,000.00 for a full length, and often paints them in one sitting, even a full length."[40] As the scholar Ronald G. Pisano has documented: "A few known prices for portraits include $500 for a bust length, posthumous portrait painted after a photograph of William Skinkle in 1892; $2000 for a full-length, standing portrait of Irene Dimmock, c. 1900; and $1000 for a waist-length portrait of Dr. John Sparhawk Jones in 1906."[41]

Chase's still lifes, such as *An English Cod* (1904), which the Corcoran Gallery of Art purchased in 1905, and *Still Life: Fish* (Fig. 94), which George A. Hearn purchased for the Metropolitan Museum of Art in 1908—sold for $1,000 or $2,000 each.[42] Although these canvases helped to pay the bills, Chase worried that he would be known to future generations only as "a painter of fish, a painter of fish."[43] Chase's success with portraits of people and fish is suggested by the fact that the first of his paintings acquired by Smith College was *Woman in Black* (c. 1890) and the first two of his paintings acquired by the Pennsylvania Academy were *Portrait of Mrs. C. (Lady with*

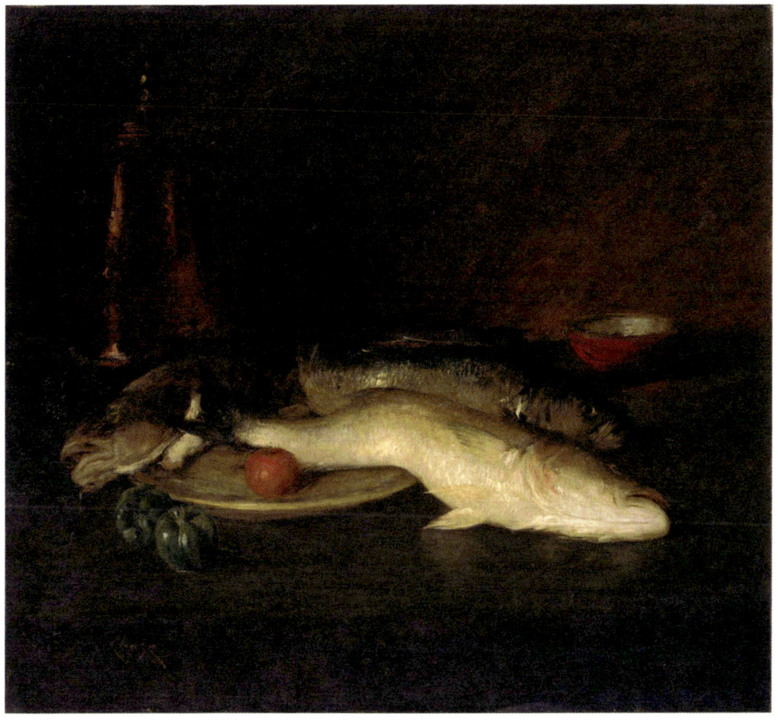

Fig. 94
William Merritt Chase
Still Life: Fish, by 1908
Oil on canvas
40⅛ × 45¹⁄₁₆ in. (101.9 × 114.5 cm)
The Metropolitan Museum of Art, New York; George A. Hearn Fund, 1908

a White Shawl) (Fig. 95), purchased in 1895, and *Still Life, Fish* (c. 1903), purchased in 1904.

Chase was not represented by a dealer. In response to financial pressures, he intermittently sent large groups of his own works and other property to auctions in New York, always with disappointing results. In 1887, his first New York exhibition and sale—which included ninety-eight pictures, eighty of which were oils—received extensive publicity and generally favorable reviews at Moore's Art Gallery. However, the works were "cruelly sacrificed" at the two-night auction, which yielded a total of only $8,646, or less than $90 for each lot.[44] History repeated itself in Chase's 1891 auction at Ortgies Fifth Avenue Art Galleries with sixty-seven lots. The preview generated favorable publicity, but the sale, which yielded a total of only $5,565, was deemed by the *Art Amateur* to be "The Slaughter of Mr. Chase's Pictures."[45] In January 1896, having given up his New York home and his studio in the Tenth Street Studio Building, Chase consigned the contents, including sixty-six of his own paintings, to a four-evening auction at the American Art Galleries. The highest price for one of his paintings was only $610—for *Old Road to the Sea (Shinnecock Hills)* (1895; The Cleveland Museum of Art).[46]

Chase did enjoy financial success in the early twentieth century. By the 1910s, he would be making about $35,000 per year, but his expenditures, which included gifts of tuition money to his students and purchases of art, sometimes from his students, almost always outstripped his income. His financial mainstay was teaching, and he was one of his generation's leading and most esteemed teachers—rivaling Thomas Eakins—and one of its most active. In addition to teaching at the Art Students League (1878–96), he taught at the Brooklyn Art Association (1887, 1891–96) and the Shinnecock Hills Summer School of Art (1891–1902) in Southampton, New York, and signed on for brief stints at the School of the Art Institute of Chicago and the Hartford Art School in Connecticut.[47] Although he vowed to give up teaching in the fall of 1896 to devote himself to painting, in October he took everyone by surprise by opening the Chase School of Art, which was renamed the New York School of Art in 1898 and is now Parsons The New School of Design.[48] Chase taught there until falling out with his fellow teacher Robert Henri in November 1907. He also commuted from New York to Philadelphia to teach at the Pennsylvania Academy from 1896 to 1909.

Fig. 95
William Merritt Chase
Portrait of Mrs. C.
(Lady with a White Shawl), 1893
Oil on canvas
75 × 52 in. (190.5 × 132.1 cm)
Pennsylvania Academy of the Fine Arts, Philadelphia; Joseph E. Temple Fund

As the American Impressionists were coming into their own financially, they were challenged by a group of younger artists, the New York Realists, who would come to be known as the Ashcan School. Their leader, Robert Henri, and his associates were committed to portraying modern urban life in a more frank and vital way than

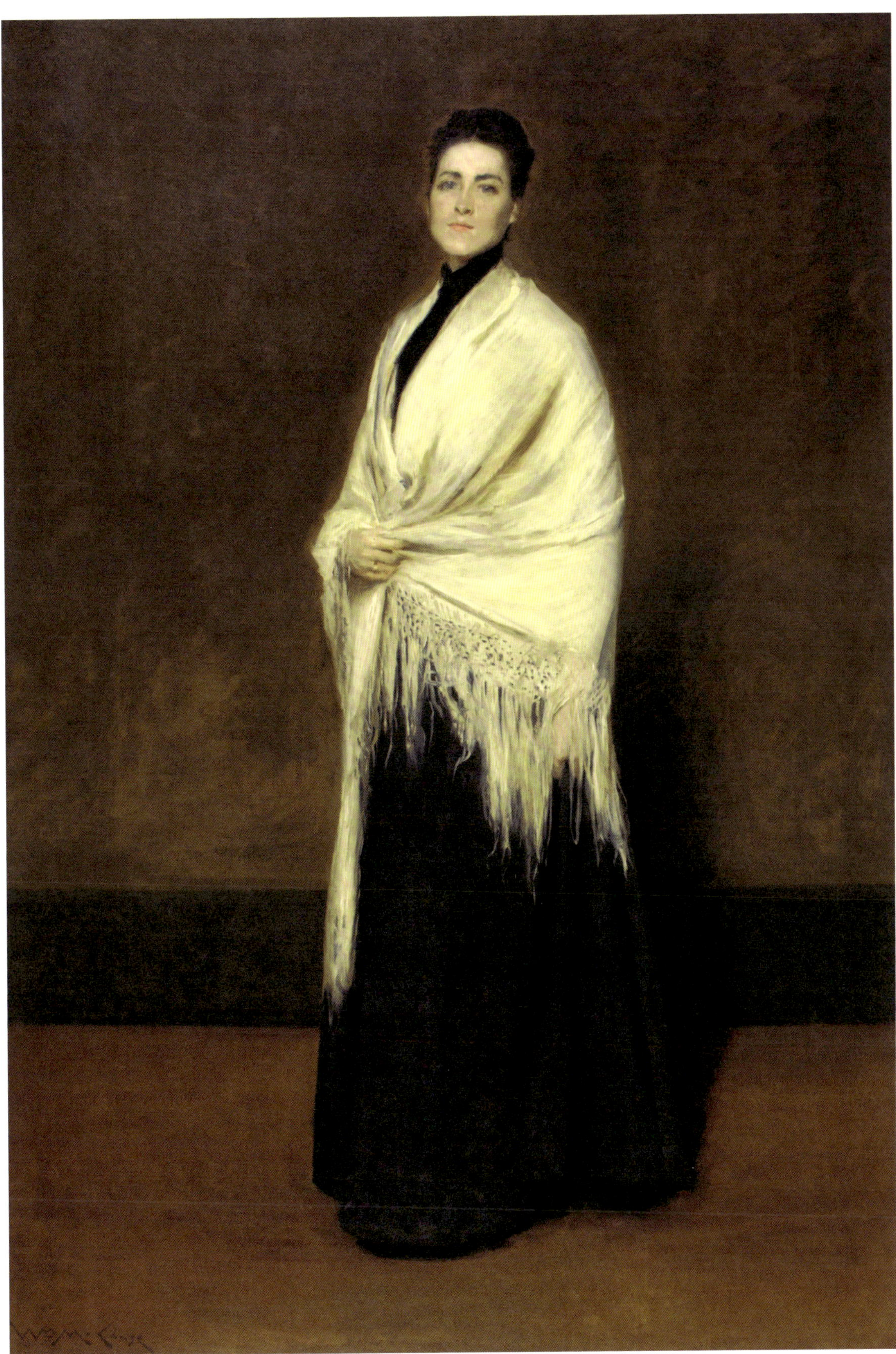

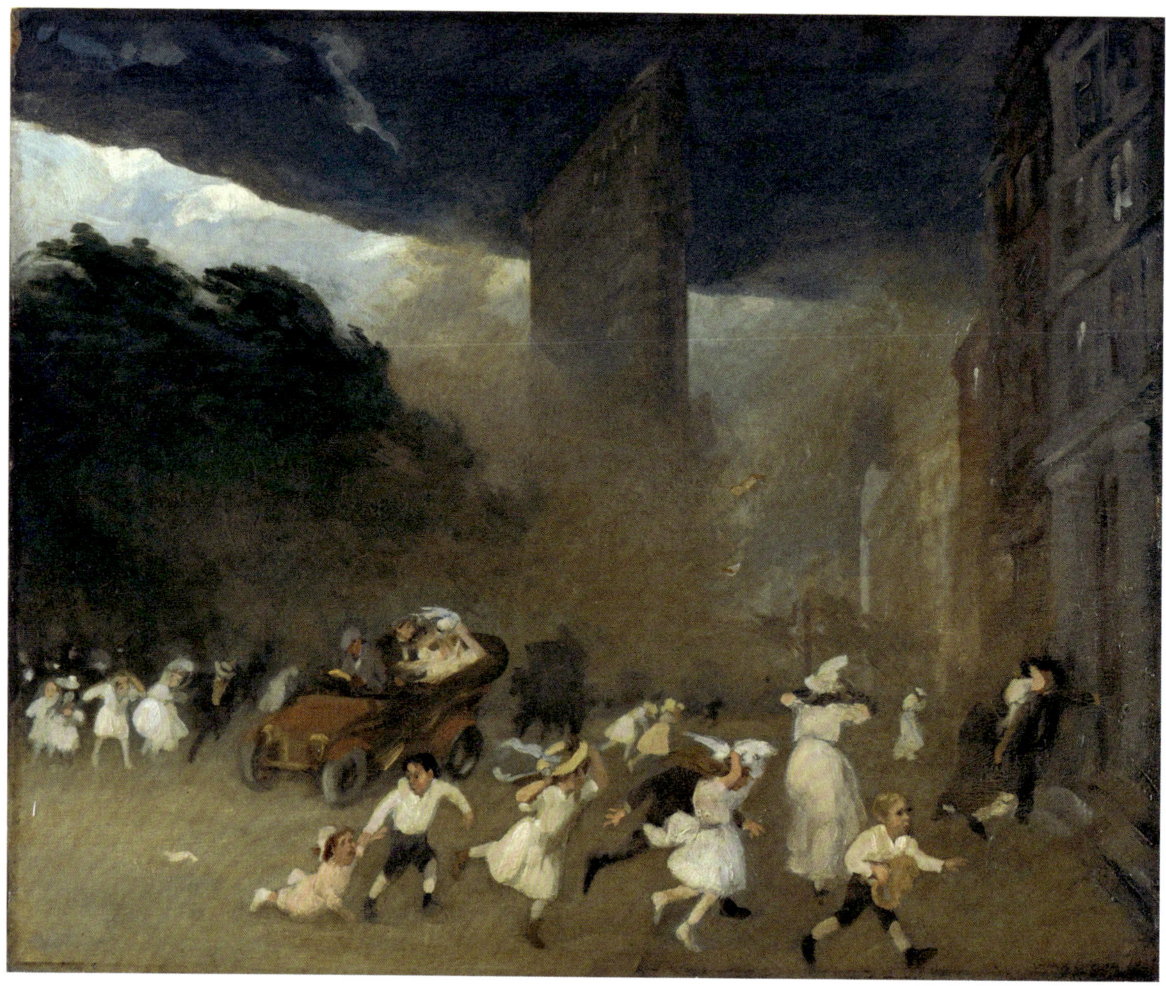

Fig. 96
John Sloan
Dust Storm, Fifth Avenue, 1906
Oil on canvas
22 × 27 in. (55.9 × 68.6 cm)
The Metropolitan Museum of Art, New York; George A. Hearn Fund, 1921

Fig. 97
William Glackens
Central Park, Winter, c. 1905
Oil on canvas
25 × 30 in. (63.5 × 76.2 cm)
The Metropolitan Museum of Art, New York; George A. Hearn Fund, 1921

Fig. 98
Everett Shinn
London Music Hall, 1918
Oil on canvas
10 × 12 in. (25.4 × 30.5 cm)
The Metropolitan Museum of Art, New York; George A. Hearn Fund, 1921

the Impressionists preferred. While the Realists pictured the seedier aspects of urban existence, they themselves largely led pleasant middle-class lives, enjoying the city's restaurants and bars, theater, and vaudeville, and popular nearby resorts. They painted their most interesting works between about 1900 and 1915, but they, like the American Impressionists, experienced a lag in patronage. The Metropolitan Museum's pattern of acquiring the Realists' paintings was emblematic of this delayed response. The museum purchased Henri's *Spanish Gypsy* (Fig. 101) from the artist for $1,500 in 1914, but did not acquire paintings by his colleagues until 1921, when it purchased four works: George Luks, *The Old Duchess* (1905) from Kraushaar Galleries for $3,000; John Sloan, *Dust Storm, Fifth Avenue* (Fig. 96) from Kraushaar Galleries for $1,500; William Glackens, *Central Park, Winter* (Fig. 97) from Montross Gallery for $800; and Everett Shinn, *London Music Hall* (Fig. 98) from M. Knoedler for $800.[49] Like the American Impressionists, the Realists faced a weak market for their paintings and had to pursue other ventures during their prime professional years.

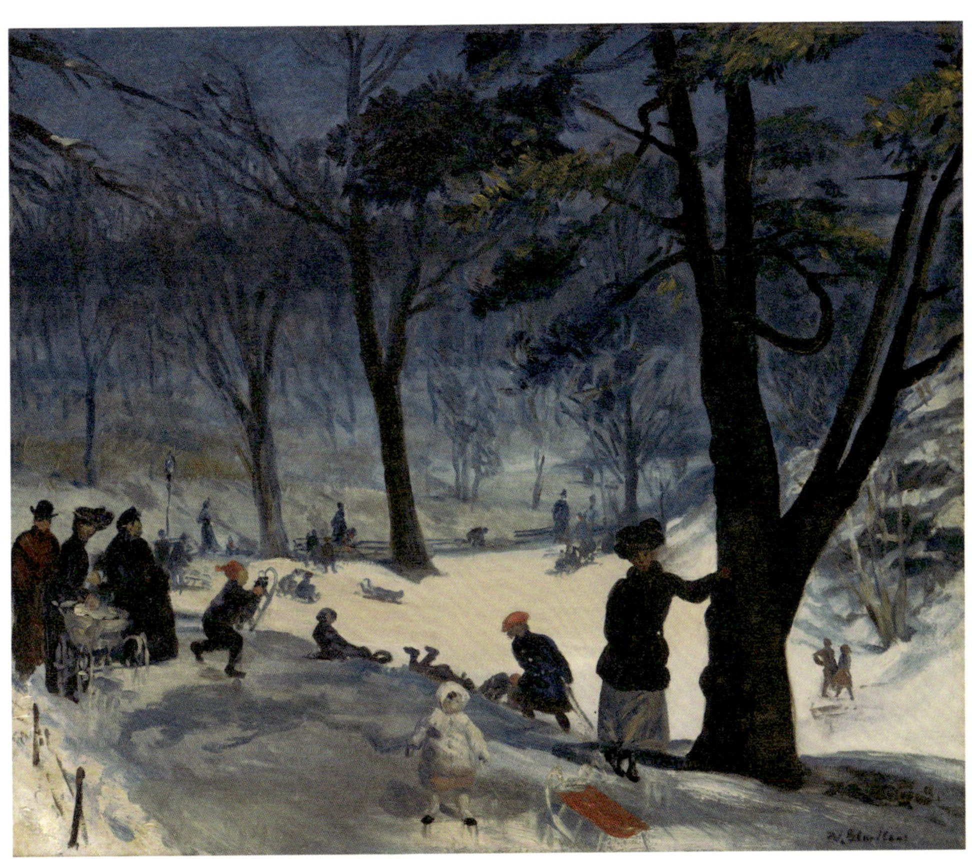

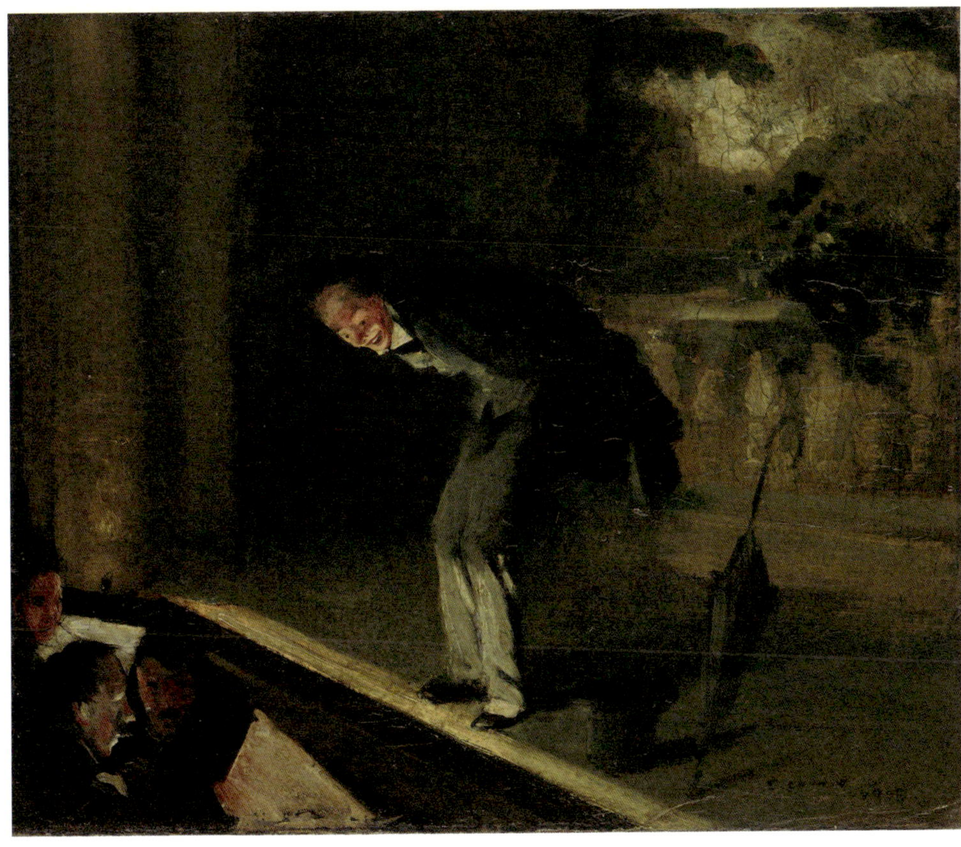

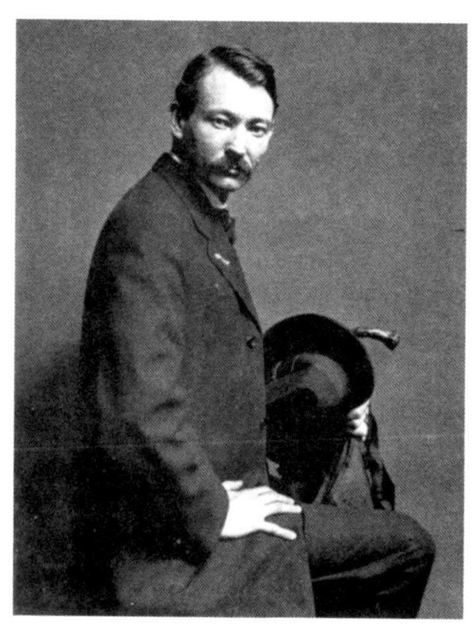

Fig. 99
Gertrude Käsebier
Robert Henri, c. 1907–08
Platinum print
8¼ × 6¼ in. (21 × 15.9 cm).
Delaware Art Museum, Wilmington;
Gift of Helen Farr Sloan, 1978

Robert Henri (1865–1929) [Fig. 99] was born in Cincinnati.[50] His mother was from a respected Southern family and his father was a riverboat gambler turned successful real-estate speculator, whose legal troubles complicated his family's lives. Henri studied in Philadelphia and Paris between 1886 and 1892. He then taught in various venues in and around Philadelphia and, during several trips to France, in and around Paris. In 1900 he moved to New York City and began two years of teaching at the Veltin School, an exclusive finishing school for girls, for $100 per month. In June 1898, he married Linda Craige, who had been his student in Philadelphia. Often ill, she was treated for a variety of ailments, and died of gastritis in December 1905. In May 1908, Henri married another student, Marjorie Organ. An immigrant from Ireland at the age of thirteen, at the time of their marriage she worked as a cartoonist at the *New York Journal*, earning a generous salary of $50 per week. The Henris had no children to support.

Henri would energize and inspire his Realist colleagues and would be involved with four key independent exhibitions: a group show at the National Arts Club in 1904 (Henri, Glackens, Luks, Sloan); the landmark exhibition of The Eight at the Macbeth Galleries in 1908 (Henri, Glackens, Luks, Shinn, and Sloan, along with Arthur B. Davies, Ernest Lawson, and Maurice Prendergast); the Exhibition of Independent Artists in 1910 (Henri, Glackens, Shinn, Sloan); and the Armory Show in 1913 (Henri, Glackens, Luks, Sloan).[51] He was himself a versatile, prolific, and successful artist, selling important paintings to public institutions and private collectors. Among such sales were *La Neige* (1899), purchased in 1899 by the Musée du Luxembourg, Paris; *Snow in New York*, purchased in 1902 by A. J. Crawford, now in the National Gallery of Art, Washington, D.C. (Fig. 102); *Laughing Child* (1907), purchased from the exhibition of The Eight by Gertrude Vanderbilt Whitney, now in the Whitney Museum of American Art, New York; *Young Woman in Black* (1902), awarded the Norman W. Harris prize of $500 and purchased in 1910 by the Art Institute of Chicago; *The Equestrian* (1909), purchased in 1910 by the Carnegie Institute, Pittsburgh; *Catharine* (1913), purchased in 1913 by William J. Johnson, now in the National Gallery of Art, Washington, D.C.; *The Spanish Gypsy* (Fig. 101), purchased in 1914 by the Metropolitan Museum of Art, New York); and *Gertrude Vanderbilt Whitney*, purchased in 1916 by Gertrude Vanderbilt Whitney, now in the Whitney Museum of American Art, New York (Fig. 100). Henri's *Girl in White Waist*, purchased in January 1904 for $2,000 by the Carnegie Institute from its annual exhibition, was his first full-length portrait to enter a museum collection; it was later destroyed in transit to the Art Institute of Chicago.

Notwithstanding Henri's sales and success as a painter, it was teaching that gave him economic security, along with pleasure from

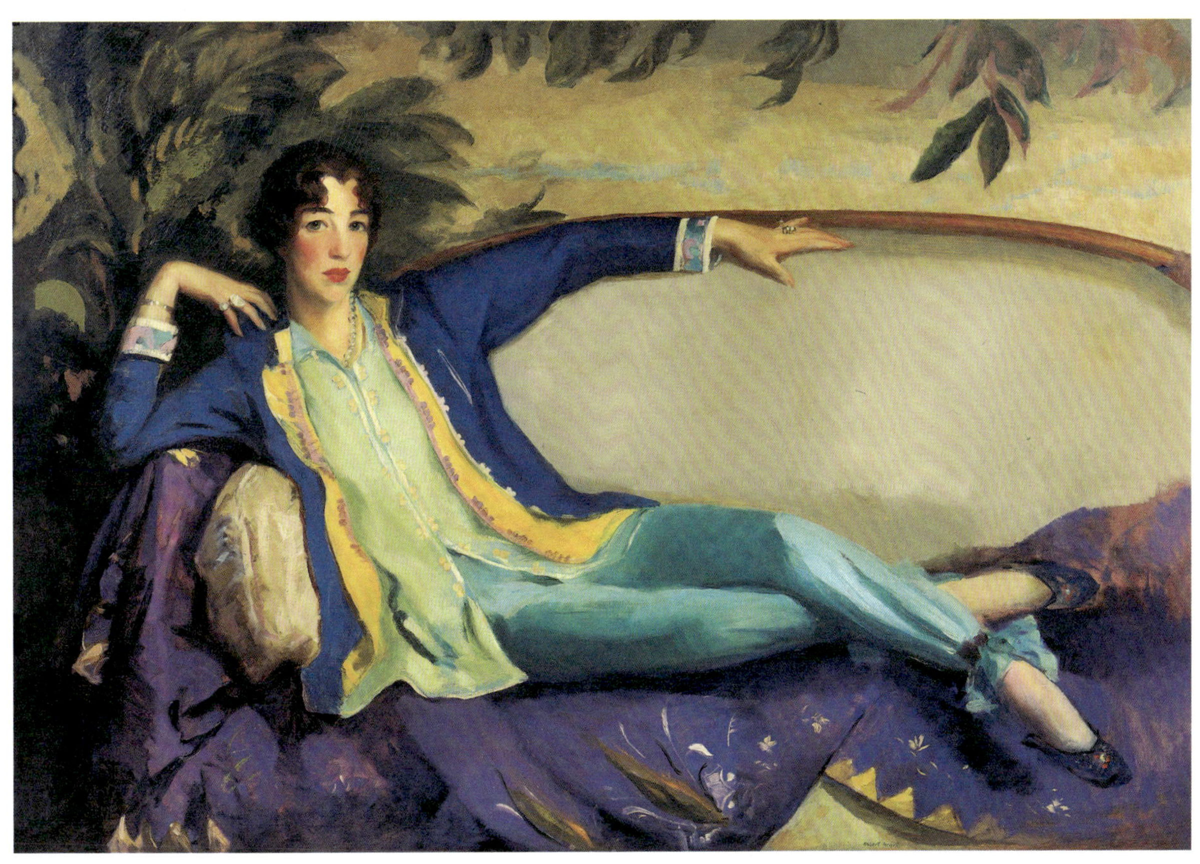

Fig. 100
Robert Henri
Gertrude Vanderbilt Whitney, 1916
Oil on canvas
50 × 72 in. (127 × 182.9 cm)
Whitney Museum of American Art,
New York; Gift of Flora Whitney Miller
86.70.3

Fig. 101
Robert Henri
The Spanish Gypsy, 1912
Oil on canvas
40¾ × 33 in. (103.5 × 83.8 cm)
The Metropolitan Museum of Art, New York; Arthur Hoppock Hearn Fund, 1914

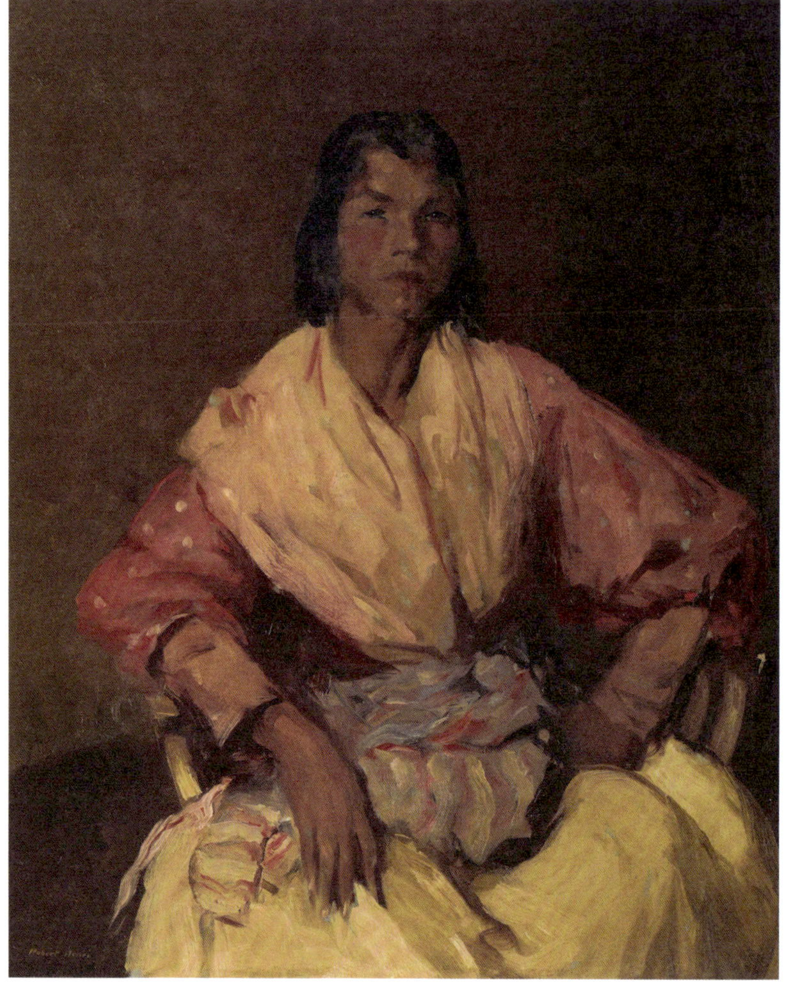

instructing others and expressive independence as an artist. Between November 1902 and 1908, he taught at the New York School of Art; between 1909 and 1912 at his own Henri School of Art; from 1911 to 1916 at the Modern School of the Ferrer Society; and from 1915 to 1927 at the Art Students League. He also offered private classes at various times and in various places at home and abroad. Although teaching and occasional portrait commissions provided a regular income, Henri had some lean years and struggled financially, particularly during the later 1910s.

As a matter of principle, Henri detached painting from financial rewards. In his book, *The Art Spirit* (1923), a compilation of his philosophy and practices, he is quoted as saying: "I am not interested in art as a means of making a living, but I am interested in art as a means of living a life."[52] In another place in the same volume, he remarked: "'What's the use of it if you are not making money out of it?' is a too common question. To what distinction an artist's labors are raised the moment he does happen to make money out of them!

Fig. 102
Robert Henri
Snow in New York, 1902
Oil on canvas
32 × 25¾ in. (81.3 × 65.5 cm)
National Gallery of Art, Washington, D.C.; Chester Dale Collection

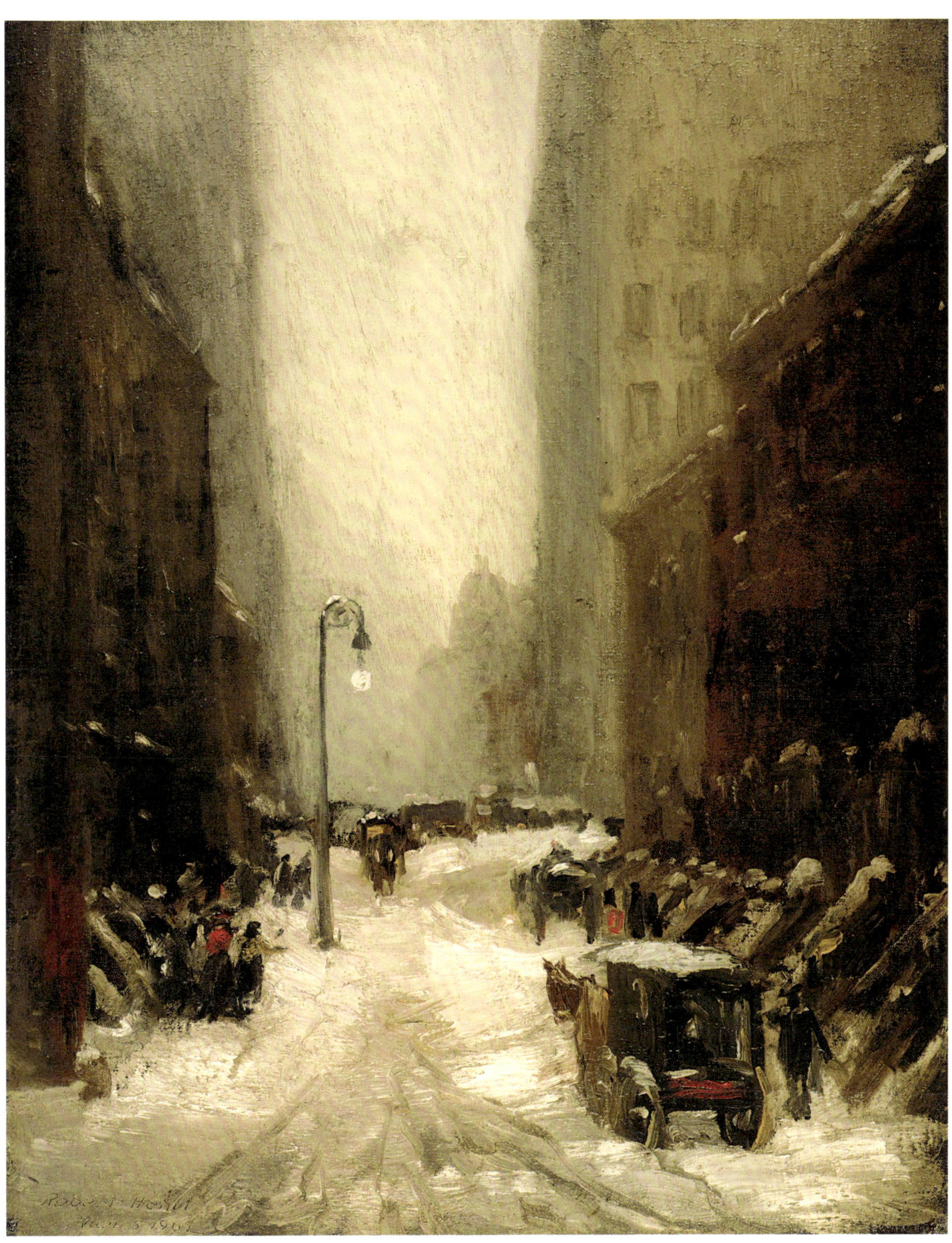

Very false values. I say this and I know as well as any the difficulties of making sufficient money and the necessity of making it in order to live and go on."[53]

William Glackens (1870–1938) [Fig. 103] had a similar dual-track career, but instead of teaching, he worked as an illustrator.[54] Glackens was born into a middle-class family in Philadelphia. His father, the son of an Irish immigrant, was employed by the Pennsylvania Railroad. After graduating in 1890 from the prestigious Central High School, Thomas Eakins's alma mater, Glackens became an artist-reporter for the *Philadelphia Record* and then for the *Philadelphia Press*, working there with Luks, Shinn, and Sloan, all of whom joined the staff by 1895. These four artists, along with Henri, whom Glackens met at the Pennsylvania Academy in 1892, would work together at several Philadelphia newspapers and gather to study, share studios, and travel. They would all settle in New York by 1904.

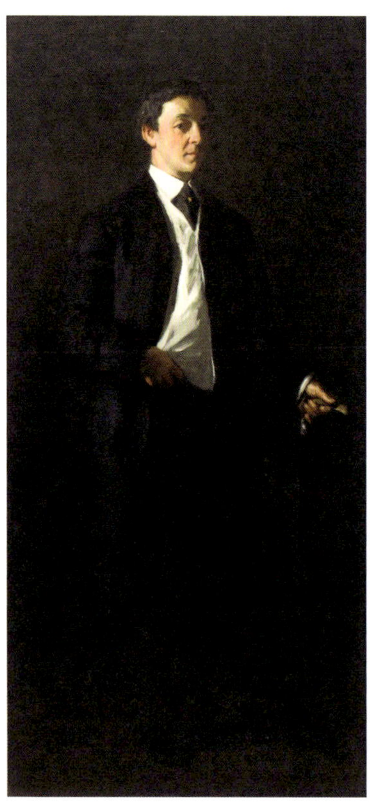

Fig. 103
Robert Henri
William Glackens, 1904
Oil on canvas
78 × 38 in. (198.1 × 96.5 cm)
Sheldon Museum of Art,
University of Nebraska, Lincoln;
NAA—Thomas C. Woods Memorial

In 1896, Glackens, along with Luks, became the first of these Philadelphia artist-reporters to move to New York. For about two years, he drew illustrations for the *New York World* and *New York Herald* and did a great deal of freelance work for books and magazines, including *Century*, *Collier's*, *Harper's Weekly*, *Saturday Evening Post*, and *McClure's*, for which he covered the Spanish-American War. In fact, Glackens's most pointed commentaries on urban realities appear in his illustrations. His paintings, including *Hammerstein's Roof Garden* (1902; Whitney Museum of American Art, New York) and *At Mouquin's* (1905; The Art Institute of Chicago), focus instead on cheerful bourgeois entertainments.

Although Glackens made a good living from illustration, his marriage in February 1904 to Edith Dimock, an art student and the daughter of a wealthy Connecticut textile manufacturer, alleviated any financial worry. While Edith's parents did not support the couple, her father would sometimes slip Edith a hundred-dollar bill when he visited,[55] and they left a substantial inheritance after their deaths in 1917. Glackens and his wife were able to raise two children; live comfortably in good neighborhoods; travel often to Europe, particularly France; and spend summers at various seaside resorts.

Another bit of good luck was that in 1910 or 1911, Dr. Albert C. Barnes, Glackens's former schoolmate at Central High School, began to seek his advice on collecting, which then focused on Barbizon paintings. By early 1912, Glackens, along with the painter Alfred Maurer, began to acquire modern paintings for Barnes, traveling to Paris to build what would become an extraordinary collection of European Impressionist, Post-Impressionist, and modernist works by Renoir, Degas, Manet, Cézanne, Gauguin, Van Gogh, Matisse, Picasso, and others.

Before 1915 Glackens sold few of his own paintings and received few portrait commissions. One of his rare recorded early sales was *Flying Kites, Montmartre* (Fig. 104), which he sold to Mrs. Richard

Fig. 104
William Glackens
Flying Kites, Montmartre, 1906
Oil on canvas
23¾ × 32 in. (60.3 × 81.3 cm)
Museum of Fine Arts, Boston;
The Hayden Collection—
Charles Henry Hayden Fund 38.7

Fig. 105
William Glackens
The Bathing Hour, Chester, Nova Scotia, 1910
Oil on canvas
26 × 32 in. (66 × 81.3 cm)
The Barnes Foundation,
Merion, Pennsylvania

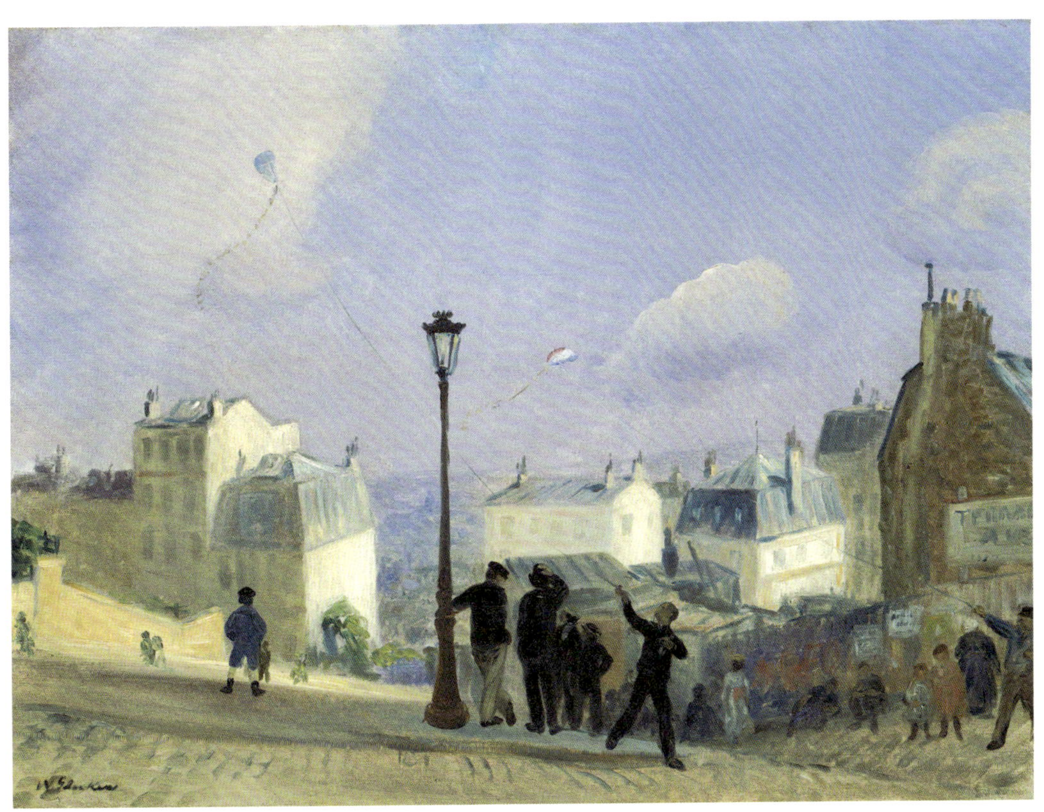

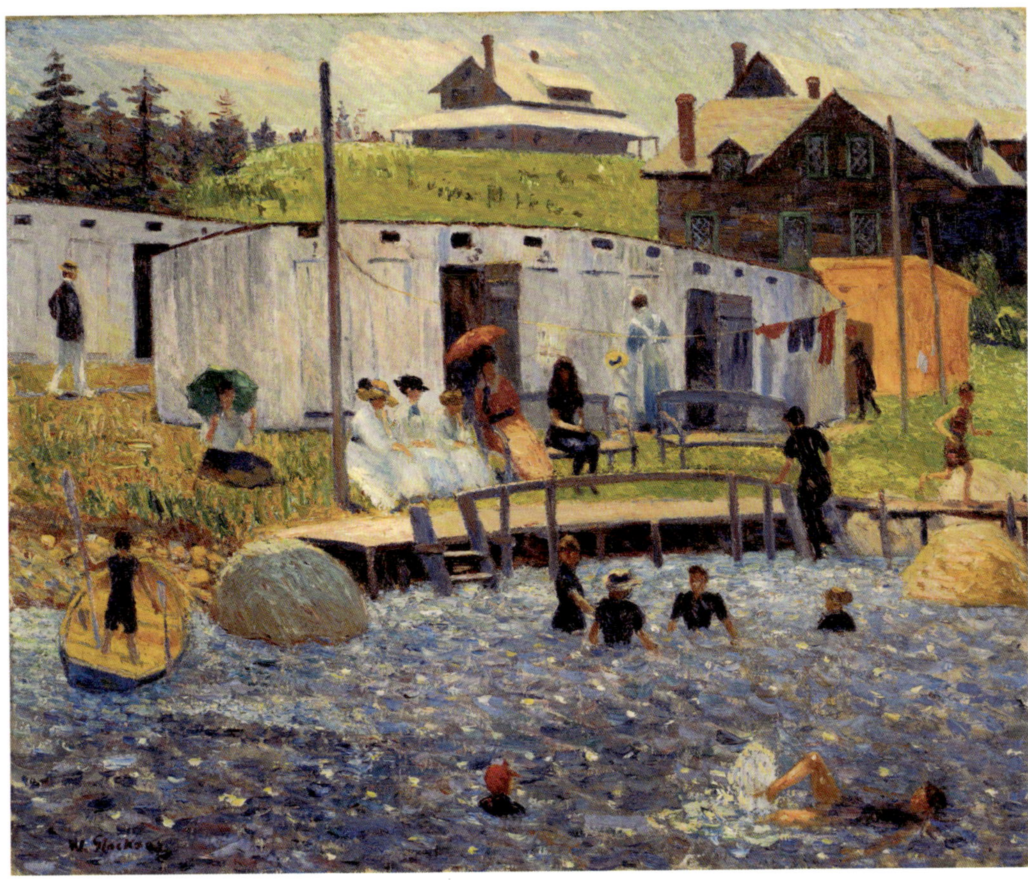

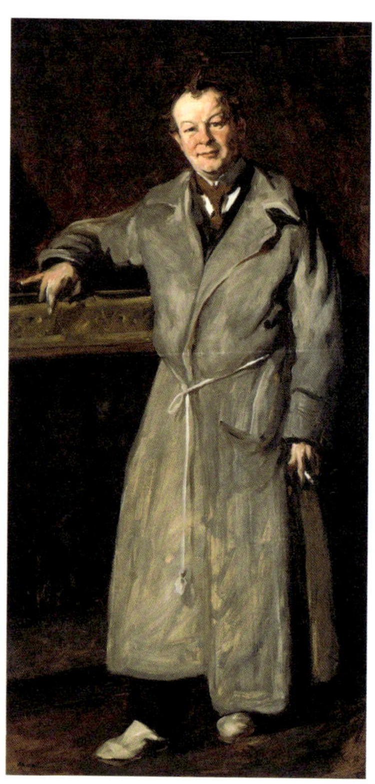

Fig. 106
Robert Henri
George Luks, 1904
Oil on canvas
76½ × 38¼ in. (194.3 × 97.2 cm)
National Gallery of Canada, Ottawa

Fig. 107
George Luks
Woman with Goose, 1907
Oil on wood
19½ × 15⅝ in. (49.5 × 39.1 cm)
Whitney Museum of American Art, New York; Gift of Gertrude Vanderbilt Whitney 31.288

E. Dwight of New York in 1908. His works reflect his steadily increasing emulation of Impressionism, and, especially after 1910, of Renoir, a taste he shared with Barnes. Glackens's subjects also shifted from city scenes to studio models, still lifes, and images of seaside recreation. His *Family Group* (1910–11; National Gallery of Art, Washington, D.C.) and *The Bathing Hour, Chester, Nova Scotia* (Fig. 105), both of which appeared in the Armory Show, demonstrate his new style and subject preferences. Barnes became Glackens's principal patron, acquiring seventy-one of his works, a mixed blessing because they were "seen by scarcely anyone but the Foundation's two hundred students," as Glackens's son, Ira, complained in 1957.[56] Although his debt to Renoir was often disparaged, Glackens was well regarded during his lifetime and won awards at several major expositions and exhibitions.

George Luks (1866–1933) [Fig. 106] cultivated his reputation for being a character and often invented or concealed biographical details.[57] He is believed to have been born in 1866 in the lumber town of Williamsport, Pennsylvania, to cultured immigrant parents. His father was a physician and apothecary from Gdańsk, Poland; his mother was the well-educated daughter of a Bavarian army officer. Luks studied briefly at the Pennsylvania Academy in 1883 or 1884 and studied and visited museums and galleries in Munich, Paris, and London in 1889. Back in Philadelphia, he worked as an illustrator for several magazines and newspapers. In December 1895, he traveled to Cuba as an artist-reporter for the *Philadelphia Evening Bulletin*, but was fired in March 1896 for absenteeism and drunkenness. In April 1896, relocating to New York, Luks found a job as a cartoonist at Joseph Pulitzer's *New York World*, drawing a second version of the hugely successful *Yellow Kid* comic strip that its originator, Richard F. Outcault, had moved from the *World* to William Randolph Hearst's *New York Journal American*.[58] Luks began to focus more on painting by 1899, and in 1904 he began selling his work through Macbeth Galleries. From the 1908 show of The Eight, he sold *Woman with Goose* (Fig. 107) to Gertrude Vanderbilt Whitney. Exemplified by this canvas, Luks's earthy urban subjects and dark palette make his relative success as a painter seem remarkable. He had his first one-artist show at Macbeth's in April 1910 and another at Kraushaar's in 1913.

In 1914, Luks initiated what would become a twenty-year association with *Vanity Fair* as an illustrator. He moved to a large house in Washington Heights, where he gave art lessons to Edward Wales Root, who had been an editor at the *New York Sun* and who would become a leading collector of early twentieth-century American art, including Luks's paintings. Upon his death, Root bequeathed his collection to the Munson-Williams-Proctor Arts Institute (Utica, New York), where it became the cornerstone of the institution's holdings.[59] Other key patrons were Arthur Egner, a Newark, New Jersey,

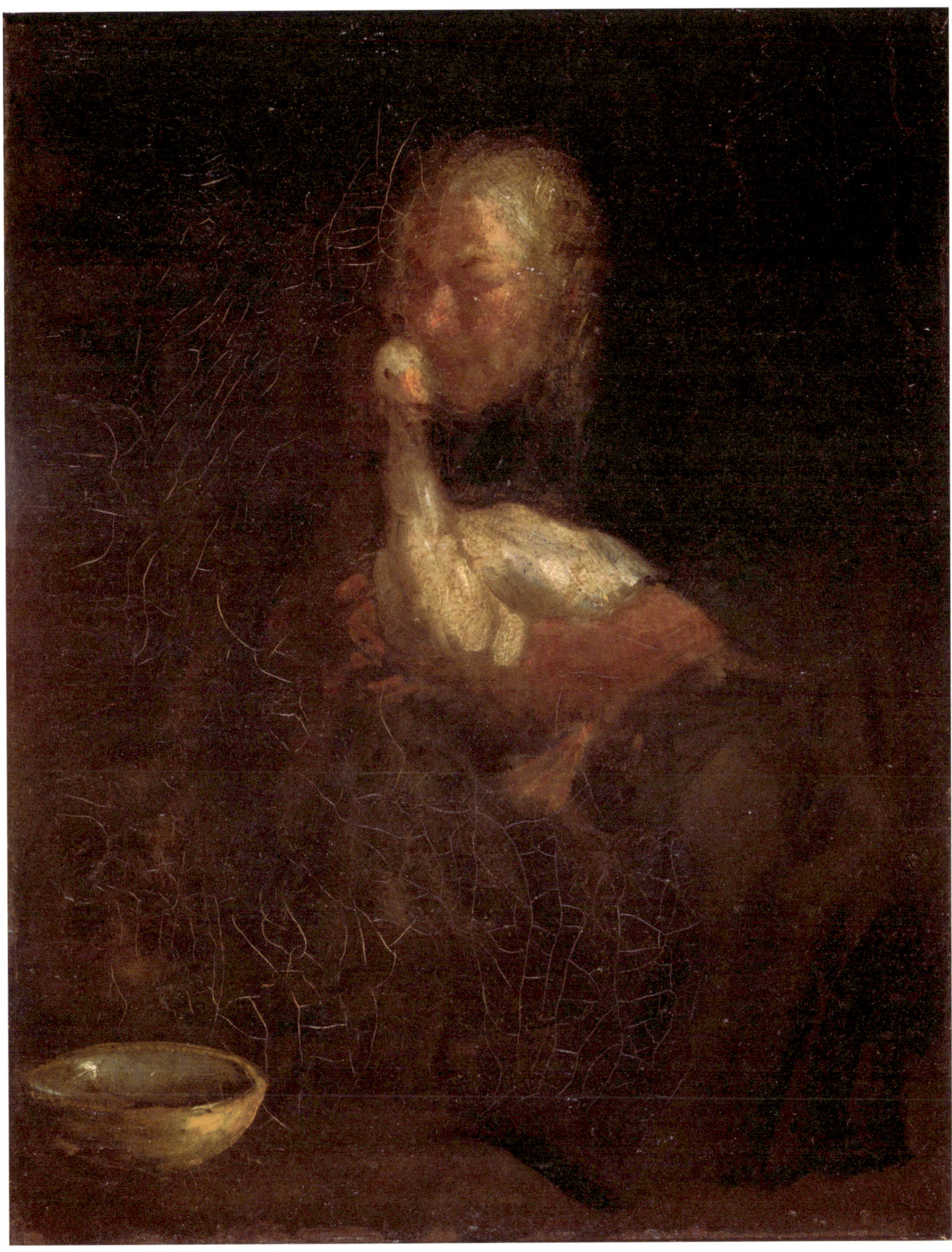

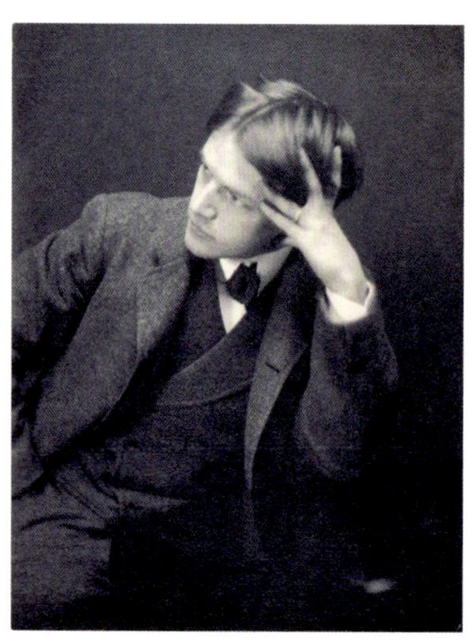

Fig. 108
Zaida Ben-Yusuf
Everett Shinn, c. 1901
Platinum print
7 5/16 × 5 5/8 in. (18.6 × 14.3 cm)
ARTnews Collection

lawyer, who may have traded his professional services for Luks's pictures; Duncan Phillips, the well-to-do son of the co-founder of Pittsburgh's Jones and Laughlin steelworks; and the lawyer John Quinn. Luks was also a popular portraitist, numbering among his sitters Root's father, Senator Elihu Root, Quinn, and Antoinette Kraushaar, his dealer's daughter.

After a stint at the Art Students League from 1920 to 1924, where his critiques were deemed too ribald for the classroom, Luks started his own school on East Twenty-second Street. He said of teaching: "This pays all my living expenses and so I don't have to care if my paintings sell or not."[60] In the early or mid-1920s, Luks divorced his second wife and fell ill—probably as a result of his longstanding abuse of alcohol. He remarried in 1927 to a woman who was forty years his junior and died in 1933 from injuries sustained in a barroom brawl.

Everett Shinn (1876–1953) [Fig. 108], the youngest of the Philadelphia group, was the son of a bank teller and was raised as a Quaker near rural Woodstown, New Jersey, about thirty-five miles south of Philadelphia.[61] At the age of fourteen, Shinn began two years of study at Philadelphia's Spring Garden Institute, a technical school, and then took a job at the Thackery Gas Fixture Works. Between 1893 and 1897, he worked as an illustrator for Philadelphia newspapers and took evening classes at the Pennsylvania Academy. By 1897 he had decided to join the art department of the *New York World*, where, instead of the $17 per week he earned at the *Philadelphia Inquirer*, he received a salary of $19 per week. In early 1898, Shinn married Florence ("Flossie") Scovel, an artist (and later, a spiritual teacher and writer) who earned a good living as an illustrator. In 1899, Shinn left the *New York World* for a more lucrative job as an art editor at *Ainslee's Magazine*.

Shinn also began making pastels, which he exhibited and sold in a variety of outlets ranging from the Pennsylvania Academy to the home of the decorator Elsie de Wolfe. De Wolfe introduced Shinn to the architect Stanford White, who arranged his first solo exhibition at Boussod, Valadon & Company, and promoted his work among his friends. Between 1900 and 1910, Shinn made and successfully marketed, at prices up to $500 each, pastels of cheerful scenes in London, Paris, and New York.[62] Shinn supplemented his income by teaching illustration at the New York School of Art. He also began to paint lighthearted subjects, particularly of popular entertainments, in oil. From the 1908 exhibition of The Eight, he sold *Girl in Blue* (now titled *Revue*; Fig. 109) to Gertrude Vanderbilt Whitney, who also bought four chalk drawings and a monotype when the exhibition traveled to the Pennsylvania Academy.

After 1910, Shinn increasingly put aside drawing and painting and committed himself to decorative projects. De Wolfe helped him get work decorating houses, and David Belasco and Stanford White

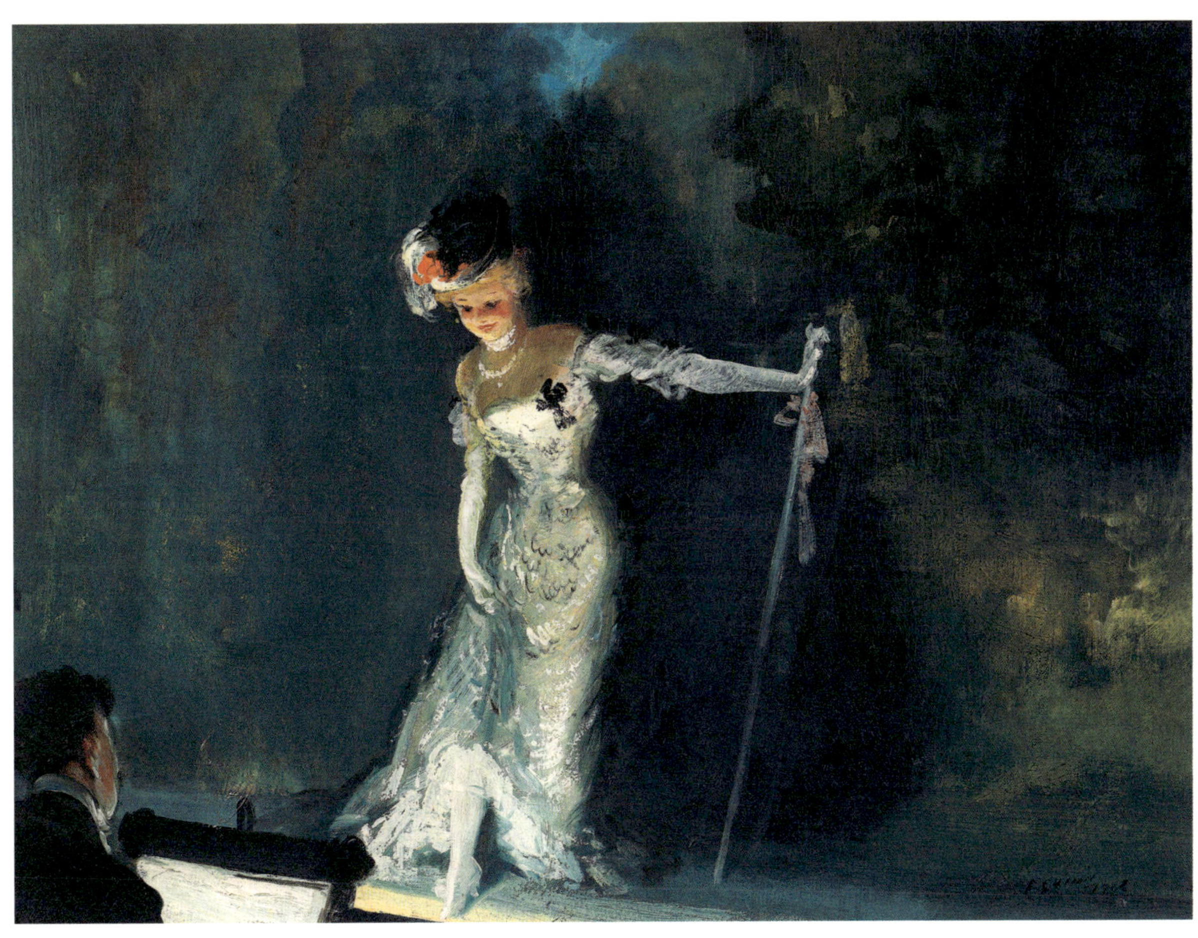

Fig. 109
Everett Shinn
Revue, 1908
Oil on canvas
18 × 24 in. (45.7 × 61 cm)
Whitney Museum of American Art,
New York; Gift of Gertrude Vanderbilt
Whitney 31.346

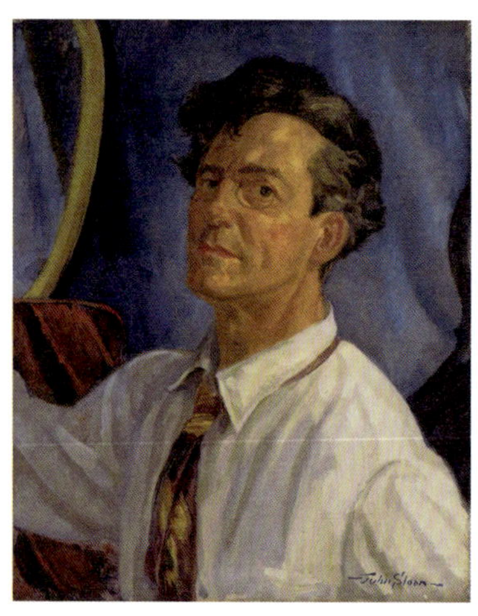

Fig. 110
John Sloan
Self-Portrait, Working, 1916
Oil on canvas
22 × 18 in. (55.9 × 45.7 cm)
Hood Museum of Art,
Dartmouth College,
Hanover, New Hampshire;
Gift of John and Helen Farr Sloan

proffered commissions for murals, including eighteen for the Belasco Theatre in New York. Shinn found other venues for his talents as a decorator, ranging from the Council Chambers in Trenton's City Hall (1911) to the Oak Bar at New York's Plaza Hotel (1944). Between 1917 and 1923, he also worked as a set designer and later as artistic director for several early film companies in New York, sometimes for high pay. His financial security was compromised only by his four marriages and three divorces, which cost him substantial alimony payments and several expensive houses.[63]

John Sloan (1871–1951) [Fig. 110] was born into a struggling family in Lock Haven, Pennsylvania, and grew up in Philadelphia.[64] Although his mother was the daughter of a well-to-do paper merchant, his father earned only a modest living, first as a traveling salesman for a paper company and then as the proprietor of a small stationery store. In 1884, Sloan entered Central High School, where he met Glackens and Barnes, but he left school in April 1887 to support his family by running errands and working as a cashier in a shop selling books and prints. In 1888 he taught himself to etch with Philip Gilbert Hamerton's *Etcher's Handbook* (1871) and sold his prints for $5 each.

Etching would ultimately rival painting as Sloan's principal creative medium and would provide him with a steady income. In 1901, for example, he undertook a series of fifty-one etched illustrations for an edition of the French novelist Paul de Kock, a set of which with some miscellaneous prints he would sell to John Quinn for $340 in June 1910.[65] Sloan's only sale from the 1913 Armory Show was an etching, *The Picture Buyer*, which William Macbeth, the subject of the print, purchased for $10.[66] Etching would also bring about Sloan's first award, a bronze medal at the 1915 Panama-Pacific International Exposition in San Francisco.

Sloan's formal art instruction was limited to an evening drawing class at the Spring Garden Institute in the winter of 1890–91 and night classes at the Pennsylvania Academy in 1891 and 1892. During this time he continued to work as an illustrator for several Philadelphia newspapers. Under Henri's guidance, he began to paint oils in 1897 and to exhibit them in 1900. In 1898, Sloan met Anna Maria ("Dolly") Wall, who had been orphaned at age three, and who, after a complicated youth, had been working as a bookkeeper and as a prostitute in a brothel, where Sloan met her. They married in 1901 and moved in April 1904 to New York, where Sloan worked as a freelance illustrator for *Century*, *Collier's*, *Saturday Evening Post*, and other magazines.

Sloan also taught, substituting for Henri at the New York School of Art in 1906; providing instruction one day a week at Pittsburgh's Art Students League in the fall of 1907; serving now and then on the faculty of New York's Art Students League from 1916 to 1938; and

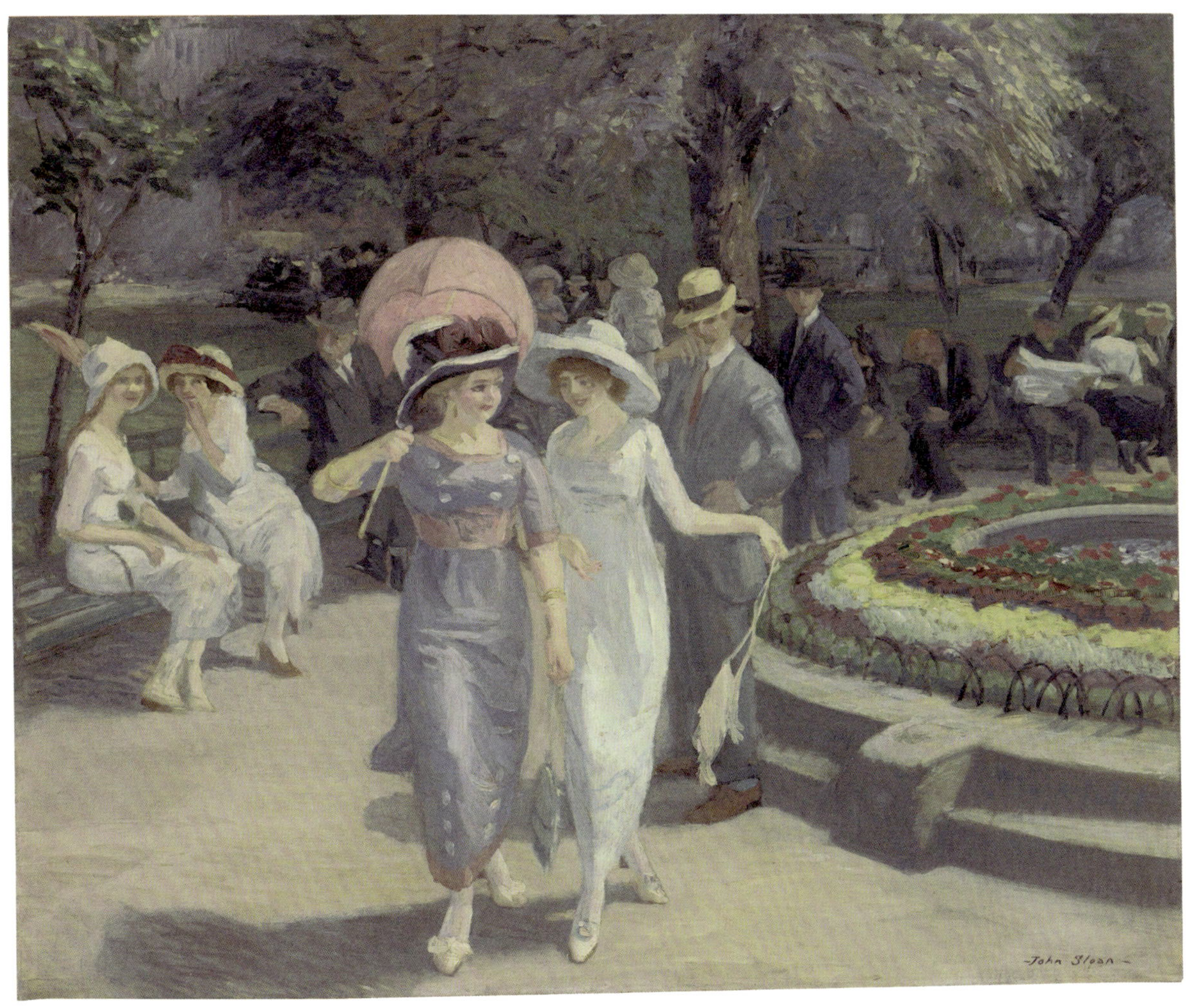

Fig. 111
John Sloan
Sunday Afternoon in Union Square, 1912
Oil on canvas
26⅛ × 32⅛ in. (66.4 × 81.6 cm)
Bowdoin College Museum of Art, Brunswick, Maine; Bequest of George Otis Hamlin

taking on private students from time to time to help make ends meet. Between 1910 and 1916, his most reliable income came from work on Socialist Party newspapers, particularly *The Masses*, where he was art editor from 1912 to 1916.

Sloan painted and exhibited his works steadily. He participated in all four of the major independent exhibitions; enjoyed the interest of Gertrude Vanderbilt Whitney, who hosted his first solo exhibition in her studio in January 1916; and he also became associated with Kraushaar Galleries in 1916. Yet he made very little money from his paintings and those that he sold before 1920 were not the urban scenes that later defined his reputation. He sold one painting—of a woman at a shooting gallery (whereabouts unknown)—to a friend for $50 in 1901; obtained a $2,000 commission in 1911 to paint portraits of Gottlieb Storz, an Omaha brewer, and his wife (The Durham Museum, Omaha); sold *Nude, Green Scarf* (1913) in 1913 to Barnes, who, according to Barnes's biographer, "drove a very hard bargain";[67] and sold *Clown Making Up* (1910; Phillips Collection, Washington, D.C.) to Duncan Phillips in 1919.

In 1921 Sloan made his first sale of a painting to a major museum when the Metropolitan purchased *Dust Storm, Fifth Avenue* (Fig. 96) for $1,500. In 1928, Sloan's friends purchased *The Lafayette* (1927) for $5,000 and donated it to the Metropolitan. In order to meet his and Dolly's hospital bills in 1923, Sloan sold twenty paintings to the businessman George Otis Hamlin for $5,000. These included *The Cot* (1907) and *Sunday Afternoon in Union Square* (Fig. 111), which Hamlin would bequeath to the Bowdoin College Museum of Art in Brunswick, Maine, along with many other works by Sloan.[68]

In a section of his 1939 book *Gist of Art* entitled "You Can't Make a Living at Art," Sloan confirmed the importance of his artistic multitasking: "That I am alive, it hurts me to confess, does not prove that one can make a living at art. . . . I have been able to scratch enough together to pay the rent from the time when it was twelve dollars a month including gas, to a time, not so far away, when it was two hundred and fifty a month. I didn't make a living from the pictures I made for myself, but by illustrating and teaching."[69] Sloan may have been an extreme case with respect to the paucity of paintings sales, but he was speaking for almost all the leading American Impressionists and Realists who became master multitaskers, even during their best years, in order to keep the wolf from the door.

NOTES

1. The author acknowledges with gratitude the assistance of Elizabeth Athens and Katie Steiner, her research assistants at the Metropolitan Museum of Art, 2007–09, and the generous advice of the following scholars: D. Frederick Baker on William Merritt Chase; Avis Berman on Ashcan patronage; Susan G. Larkin and Sona Johnston on Theodore Robinson; Lisa N. Peters on John H. Twachtman; and Judith Hanson O'Toole on George Luks. The following colleagues kindly provided images for her lecture: Susan Faxon and James M. Sousa (Addison Gallery of American Art, Phillips Academy, Andover, Mass.); Judith A. Barter and Denise Mahoney (The Art Institute of Chicago); Ayanna Burrus (Carnegie Museum of Art, Pittsburgh); Margot Chvatal (Christie's, New York); Julie Aronson (Cincinnati Art Museum); Mark Cole (The Cleveland Museum of Art); Sarah Cash (Corcoran Gallery of Art, Washington, D.C.); Elaine Mehalakes and Sandra Hachey (Davis Museum and Cultural Center, Wellesley College, Wellesley, Mass.); Sarah Swain (The Durham Museum, Omaha); Timothy Anglin Burgard (Fine Arts Museums of San Francisco); Amy Kurtz Lansing (Florence Griswold Museum, Old Lyme, Conn.); Lisa Chalif and William Titus (Heckscher Museum of Art, Huntington, N.Y.); Alicia Longwell (Parrish Art Museum, Southampton, N.Y.); David Brigham and Barbara Katus (Pennsylvania Academy of the Fine Arts, Philadelphia); Sharon L. Kennedy and Laurie J. Sipple (Sheldon Art Museum, University of Nebraska, Lincoln); Jessica Nicoll and Louise Laplante (Smith College Museum of Art, Northampton, Mass.); Elizabeth Kennedy and Ariane Westin-McCaw (Terra Foundation for American Art, Chicago); John Wilson (Timken Museum of Art, San Diego); Ruby Hagerbaumer (Joslyn Art Museum, Omaha); Elizabeth Mankin Kornhauser (Wadsworth Atheneum, Hartford, Conn.); Anita Duquette, Barbara Haskell, and Sasha Nicholas (Whitney Museum of American Art, New York).
2. See Teresa A. Carbone, "'An Imitation Is Worth Nothing': Patronage of the First American Impressionists," lecture, Wadsworth Atheneum Collectors' Council, Hartford, Conn., December 1991; Gwendolyn Owens, "Art and Commerce: William Macbeth, The Eight, and the Popularization of American Art," in *Painters of a New Century: The Eight and American Art*, exh. cat. (Milwaukee: Milwaukee Art Museum, 1991), pp. 61–85; William H. Gerdts, "Collectors of American Impressionism," in *Masterworks of American Impressionism from the Pfeil Collection*, exh. cat. (Alexandria, Va.: Art Services International, 1992), pp. 31–38; Rebecca Zurier, *Picturing the City: Urban Vision and the Ashcan School* (Berkeley: University of California Press, 2006), p. 36; Michael E. Crane, "'Recognition of Modernity': Detroit Collects Contemporary American Art in the Early Twentieth Century," *Bulletin of the Detroit Institute of Arts* 82, no. 1/2 (2008), pp. 30–45.
3. U.S. Bureau of Labor Statistics, "100 Years of U.S. Consumer Spending." http://www.bls.gov/opub/uscs/1901.pdf. This includes farm households.
4. U.S. Bureau of Labor Statistics, Consumer Price Index. ftp://ftp.bls.gov/pub/special.requests/cpi/cpiai.txt.
5. *Foreign Exhibition, Boston, 1883, Official Catalogue*, comp. C. B. Norton, secretary (Boston: G. Coolidge, 1883); *Works in Oil and Pastel by the Impressionists of Paris*, exh. cat. (New York: American Art Association, 1886). Pioneering New York collectors of French Impressionism include Mrs. H.O. Havemeyer, wife of the sugar magnate, the silver-mine owner Erwin Davis, and the businessman Albert Spencer. Leading Chicago collectors were the dry-goods merchant Potter Palmer and his wife, Bertha.
6. Enneking, quoted in Hamlin Garland, *Roadside Meetings* (New York: Mac-

millan, 1930), p. 27; cited in Ulrich W. Hiesinger, *Childe Hassam: American Impressionist* (New York and Munich: Prestel-Verlag, 1994), p. 63.

7. William H. Gerdts et al., *Ten American Painters*, exh. cat. (New York: Spanierman Gallery, 1990).
8. See William H. Truettner, "William T. Evans, Collector of American Paintings," *American Art Journal* 3, no. 2 (Autumn 1971), pp. 50–79; Linda Henefield Skalet, "The Market for American Painting in New York, 1870–1915" (Ph.D. diss., Johns Hopkins University, 1980).
9. "Refused Offered Picture," *New York Times,* December 30, 1898, p. 1.
10. Key sources on Hassam are Hiesinger, *Childe Hassam*; H. Barbara Weinberg et al., *Childe Hassam, American Impressionist*, exh. cat. (New York: The Metropolitan Museum of Art, 2004).
11. J. Alden Weir, Windham, Conn., to C.E.S. Wood, November 13, 1910, C.E.S. Wood Papers, Henry E. Huntington Library and Art Gallery, San Marino, Calif.
12. Hassam interview with DeWitt McClellan Lockman, January 31, 1927, p. 23, DeWitt McClellan Lockman Papers, New-York Historical Society; Archives of American Art, Smithsonian Institution, microfilm reel 503.
13. "Petition in the Matter of the Tax Upon the Estate of Frederick Childe Hassam, April 30, 1936, Schedule A," Surrogate's Court, Suffolk County, New York. See also "Hassam Estate Is Appraised at $212,710," *East Hampton Star,* July 9, 1936, p. 2.
14. Key sources on Robinson are Theodore Robinson Diaries, 1892–95, Frick Art Reference Library, New York; *Theodore Robinson*, exh. cat. (New York: Owen Gallery, 2000); Susan G. Larkin, *The Cos Cob Art Colony: Impressionists on the Connecticut Shore*, exh. cat. (New York: National Academy of Design; New Haven and London: Yale University Press, 2001); Sona Johnston, *In Monet's Light: Theodore Robinson at Giverny*, exh. cat. (Baltimore: Baltimore Museum of Art, 2004).
15. Gellatly offered Robinson $300 for the painting on December 20, 1892, but Robinson wrote in his diary the next day: "Gellatly arrived early and took the canvas—Marie at little bridge—at my figure—$400—wished me to 'keep shady'—not tell anyone." Robinson Diaries, Frick Library.
16. Robinson's diary entry for January 21, 1894, notes his visit to Hearn's home: "In the dining room is my 'Valley of the Seine' between two Boudins. Mr. H. hoped I would not object to its position and cracked a bottle of wine (champagne) which we drank." Robinson Diaries, Frick Library.
17. Robinson, New York, to Claude Monet, August 17, 1893, Getty Research Library, The Getty Research Institute, Los Angeles (860757), reproduced in Johnston, *In Monet's Light*, p. 206.
18. Susan G. Larkin kindly provided transcriptions from Robinson's Diaries, Frick Library.
19. John I.H. Baur, *Theodore Robinson, 1852–1896*, exh. cat. (New York: Brooklyn Museum, 1946), p. 70, no. 153. The current location of the painting is unknown.
20. *November* was sold at Christie's, New York, May 26, 1999, lot 66.
21. *Oil Paintings and Studies by the Late Theodore Robinson to be sold . . . March 24* (New York: American Art Association, 1898), annotated copy, Department of American Paintings and Sculpture, The Metropolitan Museum of Art, New York.
22. Principal sources on Twachtman are Lisa N. Peters, "John Twachtman and the American Scene in the Late Nineteenth Century: The Frontier Within the Terrain of the Familiar" (Ph.D. diss., City University of New York, 1995); Lisa N. Peters, *John Henry Twachtman: An American Impressionist*, exh. cat. (Atlanta: High Museum of Art, 1999); Lisa N. Peters, with contributions by John Nelson and Simon Parkes, *A 'Painter's Painter'*, exh. cat. (New York: Spanierman Gallery, 2006).

23. Lisa N. Peters, "'Spiritualized Naturalism': The Tonal-Impressionist Art of J. Alden Weir and John H. Twachtman," in Ralph Sessions et al., *The Poetic Vision: American Tonalism*, exh. cat. (New York: Spanierman Gallery, 2005), p. 87, n. 3: "The two artists probably met in New York City in late 1878 or early 1879, when both began to show at the Society of American Artists and became members of the Tile Club."
24. *Catalogue of paintings in oil and pastel by J. Alden Weir and J.H. Twachtman to be sold at auction* (New York: Fifth Avenue Art Galleries, 1889); "The Weir-Twachtman Paintings," *New York Times*, February 3, 1889.
25. Lisa N. Peters mentioned Dr. Scudder's help in a telephone conversation with the author, October 16, 2008.
26. Peters, *A 'Painter's Painter'*, p. 150.
27. According to Peters, *Twachtman*, 1999, Twachtman's children were Alden (b. March 5, 1882); Marjorie (b. June 1884); Elsie (c. late 1885–late 1894 from scarlet fever); Eric Christian (May 12, 1890–September 25, 1891); Quentin (b. September 6, 1892); Violet (b. May 23, 1895); and Godfrey (b. early December 1897).
28. Dorothy Weir Young, *The Life and Letters of J. Alden Weir* (New Haven: Yale University Press, 1960), p. 179.
29. Robinson diary, December 17, 1895, Frick Library.
30. "Twachtman Picture Sale," *New York Times*, March 25, 1903, p. 5.
31. The principal sources on Weir are Young, *Weir*; Doreen Bolger Burke, *J. Alden Weir: An American Impressionist* (Newark: University of Delaware Press, 1983).
32. "Yesterday I went out for a walk & visited a gallery where I found a very fine picture which I could not resist the temptation of buying for which I paid $560 & last evening I had an offer for it from a gentleman who saw it, of the price & a farm of 150 acres in Connecticut." J. Alden Weir, June 15, 1882, to Anna Dwight Baker, Anna Dwight Baker Papers, quoted in Elizabeth Milroy, "The Land of Nod: J. Alden Weir and His Connecticut Neighbors," in Nicolai Cikovsky Jr., et al., *A Connecticut Place: Weir Farm, An American Painter's Rural Retreat*, exh. cat. (Wilton, Conn.: Weir Farm Trust, 2000), p. 32. Weir acquired additional land in 1907, bringing the total to 283 acres.
33. *Catalogue of paintings in oil and pastel by J. Alden Weir and J. H. Twachtman*; "The Weir-Twachtman Paintings."
34. Weir, Paris, April 15, 1877, to Mr. and Mrs. Robert W. Weir, quoted in Young, *Weir*, p. 123.
35. Quoted Young, *Weir*, p. 180.
36. In February 1902, Milliken sold *The Green Bodice* at American Art Galleries, New York, for $1,125 to George A. Hearn, who gave it to the Metropolitan Museum in 1906.
37. For this essay, key sources on Chase were Ronald G. Pisano, *A Leading Spirit in American Art: William Merritt Chase, 1849–1916*, exh. cat. (Seattle: Henry Art Gallery, University of Washington, 1983); Keith L. Bryant, *William Merritt Chase: A Genteel Bohemian* (Columbia: University of Missouri Press, 1991); Annette Blaugrund, *The Tenth Street Studio Building: Artist-Entrepreneurs from the Hudson River School to the American Impressionists*, exh. cat. (Southampton, N.Y.: Parrish Art Museum, 1997); Barbara Dayer Gallati, *William Merritt Chase: Modern American Landscapes, 1886–1890*, exh. cat. (New York: Brooklyn Museum of Art, in association with Harry N. Abrams, 1999); Kimberly Orcutt, *Painterly Controversy: William Merritt Chase and Robert Henri*, exh. cat. (Greenwich, Conn.: Bruce Museum, 2007).
38. H. Barbara Weinberg, "Thomas B. Clarke: Foremost Patron of American Art from 1872 to 1899," *American Art Journal* 8 (May 1976), p. 72.
39. Ronald G. Pisano, *William Merritt Chase: Portraits in Oil—The Complete*

Catalogue of Known and Documented Work by William Merritt Chase (1849–1916), vol. 2 (New Haven and London: Yale University Press, 2006).

40. Reynolds Beal Papers, 1874–1939, Mr. and Mrs. Wayne Morrell, Archives of American Art, Smithsonian Institution, microfilm reel 286, frame 10.
41. "Ronald G. Pisano Project Files for the Catalogue Raisonné of William Merritt Chase," Kellen Archives Center for Parsons The New School of Design, New York; courtesy of D. Frederick Baker.
42. George A. Hearn, New York, to Bryson Burroughs [the Metropolitan's curator], April 6, 1908: "I . . . intend to propose Chase's 'Still Life' which was in the Montross Exhibition. He himself says that it is the best thing he has every [*sic*] done, and I understand all the Artists are very enthusiastic about it. I myself think it a great picture." The Metropolitan Museum of Art Archives, New York.
43. Bryant, *Chase*, p. 234.
44. Bryant, *Chase*, pp. 136–37, and associated notes.
45. "The Slaughter of Mr. Chase's Pictures," *Art Amateur* 24, no. 5 (April 1891), pp. 115–16.
46. *Paintings, studio appointments, curios, bric-a-brac belonging to William Merritt Chase, N.A.* (New York: American Art Association, 1896). Chase's last lifetime auction was held in 1912 at the American Art Association, New York.
47. "A Great Artist and His Work," *Indianapolis Sunday Star*, April 4, 1909, reported that Chase made $1,000 a month for a few hours of weekly service at the Art Students League, a claim that is likely to have been exaggerated.
48. Ronald G. Pisano, "Chronology," in *William Merritt Chase: Landscapes in Oil—The Complete Catalogue of Known and Documented Work by William Merritt Chase (1849–1916)*, vol. 3 (New Haven and London: Yale University Press, 2009), p. 162.
49. Because the value of the dollar declined in 1918–19, the Luks was equal in value to the Henri in today's dollars. The Glackens brought the lowest price considering that it is 25 × 30 inches and the Shinn—at the "special price" of $800—is only 10 × 12 inches.
50. The principal sources on Henri are William Innes Homer, with the assistance of Violet Organ, *Robert Henri and His Circle* (Ithaca, N.Y., and London: Cornell University Press, 1969); Bennard B. Perlman, *Robert Henri: His Life and Art* (New York: Dover Publications, 1991).
51. See *Loan Exhibition of Pictures by Robert Henri, William Glackens, George Luks, Arthur B. Davies, and Maurice Prendergast* (New York: National Arts Club, 1904); *Exhibition of Paintings by Arthur B. Davies, William J. Glackens, Robert Henri, Ernest Lawson, George Luks, Maurice B. Prendergast, Everett Shinn, John Sloan* (New York: Macbeth Galleries, February 3–15, 1908); Judith Zilczer, "The Eight on Tour, 1908–1909," *American Art Journal* 16, no. 3 (Summer 1984), pp. 20–48; *Catalogue, Exhibition of Independent Artists, From April 1st to 27th 1910, Galleries, 29-31 East Thirty-Fifth St., N.Y.*; *The Fiftieth Anniversary of the Exhibition of Independent Artists in 1910*, exh. cat. (Wilmington: Delaware Art Center, 1960); *Catalogue of International Exhibition of Modern Art* (New York: Vreeland Advertising Press, 1913).
52. Robert Henri, *The Art Spirit*, comp. Margery Ryerson (1923; repr., New York: Harper and Row, 1984), p. 158.
53. Henri, *The Art Spirit*, pp. 177–78.
54. The principal sources on Glackens are Ira Glackens, *William Glackens and the Ashcan Group* (New York: Grosset and Dunlap, 1957); William H. Gerdts, *William Glackens*, with essay by Jorge H. Santis (Fort Lauderdale, Fla: Museum of Art, Fort Lauderdale, in association with Abbeville Press, 1996).
55. Gerdts, *Glackens*, p. 98, n. 84.

56. Glackens, *William Glackens and the Ashcan Group*, p. 257.
57. The principal sources on Luks are Everett Shinn, "Everett Shinn on George Luks: An Unpublished Memoir," *Archives of American Art Journal* 6, no. 2 (April 1966), pp. 1–12; Stanley L. Cuba, Nina Kasanof, and Judith H. O'Toole, *George Luks: An American Artist*, exh. cat. (Wilkes-Barre, Pa.: Sordoni Art Gallery, Wilkes College, 1987); Mark Andrew White, "Luks, George Benjamin," *American National Biography Online* (Feb. 2000), http://www.anb.org/articles/17/17-00538.html, accessed October 2, 2007. The June 1870 census shows Luks's age as three years old, which would make his birth date 1866, rather than 1867, the year that is sometimes given.
58. Both versions of the cartoon ceased publication in 1898.
59. *The Best Kind of Life: Edward W. Root as Teacher, Collector and Naturalist*, exh. cat. (Clinton, N.Y.: Emerson Gallery, Hamilton College, 2007); https://my.hamilton.edu/college/emerson_gallery/Root/default.html; Aline B. Saarinen, "Prologue," in *Edward Wales Root Bequest*, exh. cat. (Utica, N.Y.: Munson-Williams-Proctor Arts Institute, 1961), unpaginated.
60. *George Luks: An American Artist*, p. 43.
61. The principal sources on Shinn are Edith DeShazo, *Everett Shinn, 1876–1953: A Figure in His Time* (New York: Clarkson N. Potter, 1974); Janay Wong, *Everett Shinn: The Spectacle of Life*, exh. cat. (New York: Berry-Hill Galleries, 2000).
62. Account book, Shinn Papers, Archives of American Art, Smithsonian Institution, Box 1, folders 49–50.
63. In 1912, Shinn divorced Florence and was required to pay her $4,800 in alimony. The following year he married Corinne Baldwin, with whom he had two children. When that marriage ended in divorce in 1921, his ex-wife kept their elaborate house in Palenville, N.Y., and the children. In 1922 Shinn married Gertrude Chase and lived in Westport, Conn., but they divorced in 1932 and Gertrude got the Westport house. His final marriage, which lasted from 1933 to 1942, was to Paula Downing, who was more than thirty years his junior.
64. The principal sources on Sloan are John Sloan, *Gist of Art: Principles and Practise Expounded in the Classroom and Studio* (New York: American Artists Group, 1939); Bruce St. John, ed., *John Sloan's New York Scene: From the Diaries, Notes and Correspondence 1906–1913* (New York: Harper and Row, 1965); Rowland Elzea, *John Sloan's Oil Paintings: A Catalogue Raisonné*, 2 vols. (Newark: University of Delaware Press; London and Toronto: Associated University Presses, 1991); John Loughery, *John Sloan: Painter and Rebel* (New York: Henry Holt, 1995); Avis Berman, *Rebels on Eighth Street: Juliana Force and the Whitney Museum of American Art* (New York: Atheneum Publishers, 1990).
65. St. John, *Sloan's New York Scene*, pp. 437–38.
66. Loughery, *Sloan*, p. 186.
67. William Schack, *Art and Argyrol: The Life and Career of Dr. Albert C. Barnes* (New York: Thomas Yoseloff, 1960), pp. 77–78. Schack's claim that Barnes was Sloan's first customer is untrue.
68. *The Art of John Sloan, 1871–1951*, exh. cat. (Brunswick, Maine: Bowdoin College, 1962). Hamlin, a businessman who had become friendly with Sloan in Philadelphia, was originally from Maine. He had a house in Boothbay Harbor and a relationship with the Bowdoin College Museum of Art, to which he bequeathed nineteen of Sloan's paintings and one hundred and eighty-nine of his prints in 1961. The bargain price of $5,000 that Hamlin paid for twenty paintings in 1923 upset John Kraushaar, who spun to the press the story that the price was $20,000. As a result, Sloan was audited by the Internal Revenue Service for reporting only $8,885 in income that year. Hamlin gave the twentieth painting, Sloan's *Wind on the Bay* (1915; private collection) to a friend, Dr. Alvin G. Dujart.
69. Sloan, *Gist of Art*, p. 32.

Collateral Damage: George Bellows and the Great War

CAROL TROYEN

Lecture given on December 3, 2009

New-York Historical Society

New York City

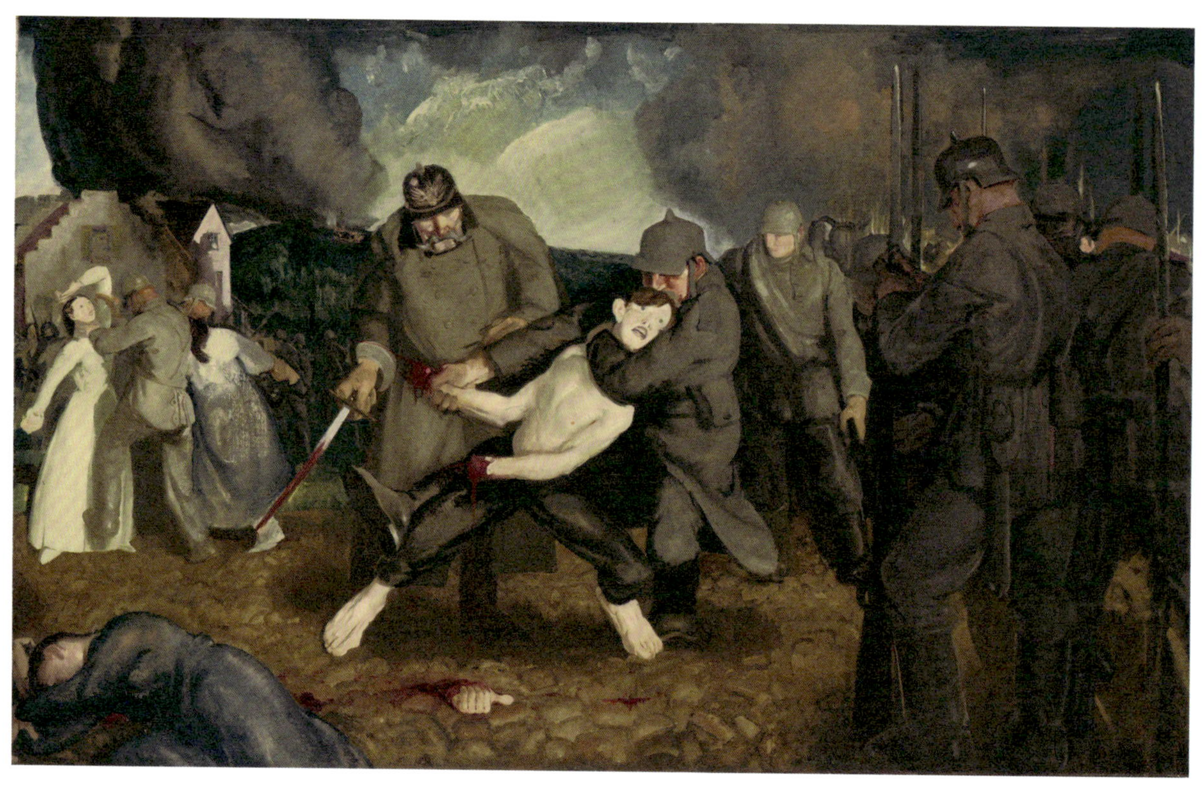

Fig. 112
George Bellows
The Germans Arrive, 1918
Oil on canvas
49½ × 79¼ in. (125.7 × 201.3 cm)
National Gallery of Art, Washington, D.C.;
On Deposit—Promised Gift of Ian and
Annette Cumming

Collateral Damage: George Bellows and the Great War

CAROL TROYEN

On the evening of April 2, 1917, President Woodrow Wilson, who had been re-elected under the campaign slogan, "He kept us out of war," beseeched Congress to bring the United States into the conflict. What came to be called The Great War had been going on in Europe for more than two years at that point, with tens of thousands of deaths on both sides, and little resolution. President Wilson called for America's intervention after Germany resumed unrestricted submarine warfare, and the Allies intercepted the "Zimmerman telegram," in which Germany urged Mexico to ally with the Central Powers and attack the United States. Congress declared war on April 4, 1917, and by June, significant numbers of American troops had reached France.

Like much of the rest of the population, the American artistic community had been divided on the subject of the country's involvement. While most advocated neutrality,[1] their sentiments were generally pro-Allies and they participated in a number of efforts in support of those nations. In May 1915, for example, members of the Authors' Club of New York, among them William Dean Howells, Booth Tarkington, and Theodore Roosevelt, contributed books and manuscripts to be sold for the benefit of Belgian citizenry.[2] Just before America entered the war, a group of prominent artists and writers donated brief essays, poems, sketches, and illustrations to an anthology titled *For France*. Most of the submissions were pro-France in a general way, honoring the glories of French landscape, culture and history, and expressing gratitude for the country's gifts to the world. Robert Henri's *Night, Fourteenth of July* (1897; Sheldon Museum of Art, University of Nebraska-Lincoln), a painting celebrating Bastille Day, and Otis Skinner's essay, "What the Actor Owes to France," are typical examples. Only a few of the contributions referred to the war itself.[3]

Once the United States entered the war, the divide became sharper. Some artists, like John Sloan, remained pacifists. Sloan called his one effort to produce a war-related subject, the etching *Tank Corps*

(1918; Philadelphia Museum of Art), "a failure" and canceled the plate. His heart simply wasn't in the subject. As he said, "The propaganda motive was a mistake . . . I felt uncomfortable about it."[4] Other artists became fiercely pro-Allies. Childe Hassam, for example, wrote furious letters to the editor of the *New York Times* excoriating Germany.[5] He also celebrated America's entry into the war with a series of exuberant, ultra-patriotic paintings of the flags—America's and those of her allies—that were hoisted along Fifth Avenue during parades and rallies.

By and large, the Stieglitz circle of artists kept their heads down. Alfred Stieglitz had spent much of the previous decade challenging America's cultural patrimony, exhibiting the European avant-garde in his gallery 291, a pursuit that would not have been well received in wartime. The Americans associated with the gallery were personally loyal to Stieglitz, who was of German descent and remained a great admirer of German culture.[6] A few shared Stieglitz's views, notably Marsden Hartley. Always impolitic, Hartley was excited by the displays of nationalism and military might he saw in Berlin. His paintings from this period are full of admiration for German pageantry and for the debonair uniforms worn by the soldiers. Even after Germany had completed its brutal march through Belgium, in August 1914, he wrote home to insist "how nice the Germans are . . ."[7]

George Bellows (1882–1925), who was by this time highly successful as a painter of sporting and urban subjects, was initially opposed to American involvement in the war. He made this viewpoint clear in *Christ in Chains*, a 1917 cartoon he produced for the radical magazine *The Masses*. It shows Christ in prison stripes, jailed for "language tending to discourage men from enlisting in the United States Army."[8] But once the United States was fully involved, Bellows changed his views. He identified himself, somewhat cryptically, as "a patriot for beauty. I would enlist in any army to make the world more beautiful. I would go to war for an ideal far more easily than I could go for a country. Democracy is an idea to me, it is the Big Idea."[9] Then, along with his colleague Eugene Speicher, he volunteered for the Tank Corps, although he was thirty-five years old and a husband and father. He was never called up.

In fact, few American artists enlisted, or served.[10] Rather than going overseas, most threw themselves into the propaganda effort, raised funds for the war, or engaged in other patriotic activities. Artists manufactured camouflage, not only for the soldiers but also for their wagons, ambulances, and other vehicles. Painters and illustrators produced large-scale landscapes for soldiers to use for target practice. Sculptors aided doctors in designing models for facial surgery and devised masks for the seriously disfigured.[11] But artists made their greatest contributions by providing inspiring, patriotic imagery for parades and designing posters that were meant to incite anger at

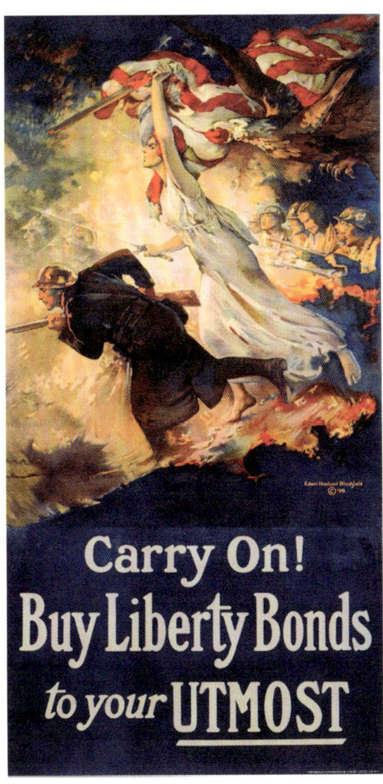

Fig. 113
Edwin Blashfield
Carry On! Buy Liberty Bonds to Your Utmost, 1918
Lithographic poster
76 × 39 in. (193 × 99.1 cm)
Image © Swim Ink LLC/Corbis

the enemy, sell Liberty Bonds, and encourage enlistment (Fig. 113). (James Montgomery Flagg's "Uncle Sam Wants You" is probably the best-known recruitment poster to come out of the war.) Many donated works of art to be sold for relief funds and other purposes.

Patriotic activities were staged all across the country, perhaps nowhere more energetically than in New York, where they began even before the United States entered the war. The biggest prewar rally was the Preparedness Day parade in May 1916, a twelve-hour event in which nearly 140,000 people marched up Fifth Avenue beneath decorations provided by Edwin Blashfield, Charles Dana Gibson, Frederick MacMonnies, and others. Gibson would later head the Division of Pictorial Publicity (under the National Committee on Public Information), which was created to organize artistic activities for the war effort.[12]

Parades soon became a constant feature of the "public information" campaigns all over the country. New Yorkers, for example, cheered the marchers in the Wake Up America parade in April 1917, the Liberty Loan Drive parades in April and October 1918, the Red Cross parade in May 1918, and parades to welcome war commissioners from Britain, France, Italy, and Russia. In *Blue Devils, Fifth Avenue* (1918; The Phillips Collection, Washington, D.C.), George Luks documented the arrival of the "Blue Devils," a unit of French soldiers who marched down Fifth Avenue to the strains of the Marseillaise during the April Liberty Loan parade.

Artists played a significant role in creating decorations for these events. For the Fourth Liberty Loan Drive, which took place in September and October of 1918, celebrated architect Thomas Hastings designed an "Altar of Liberty" for Madison Square; it sometimes served as a reviewing stand. Storefront decorations along Fifth Avenue were coordinated by the "Window Display Bureau" with contributions by A.C. Goodwin, Hassam, Leon Kroll, Gari Melchers, and others. From a contemporary perspective, perhaps the most fascinating activity related to the fund drive was the "Liberty Studio." Each day of the Liberty Loan Drive was dedicated to a single Allied nation (September 28 was Belgium Day; October 19 was U.S. Day, and so on). On each of those days a different artist (among the participants were William Glackens, Jonas Lie, and F. Luis Mora) would stand before an admiring crowd and paint a large picture—about 8 by 16 feet—representing the country of the day. The picture would then be moved to a Fifth Avenue shop window, designated the Liberty Theater.[13]

Of the many different artistic contributions to the war effort, Bellows's was among the most unusual and the most sustained. Beginning early in 1918, he set to work on what would become a group of dozens of drawings, sixteen lithographs, and five paintings, most of which depict "collateral damage"—the atrocities committed by the German army during the invasion of Belgium in August 1914.[14] The

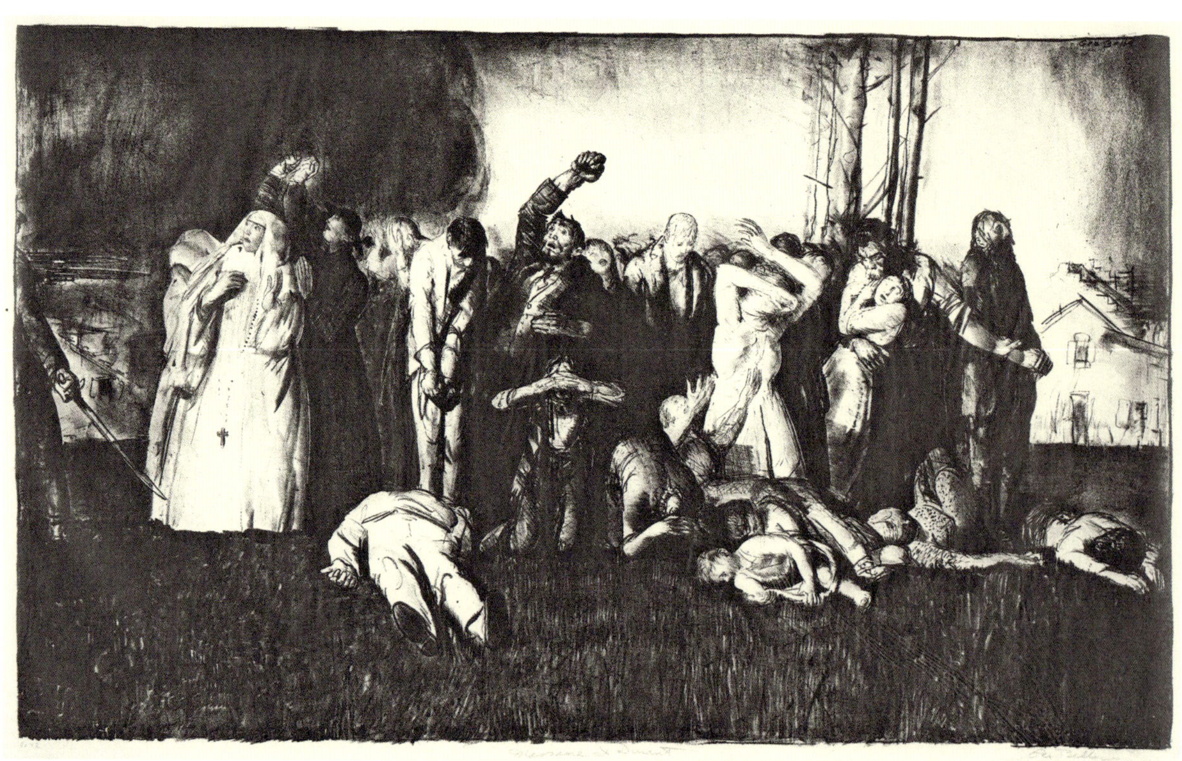

Fig. 114
George Bellows
Massacre at Dinant, 1918
Lithograph on paper
17 13/16 × 29 3/4 in. (45.2 × 75.6 cm)
Harvard Art Museums, Fogg Art Museum, Cambridge, Massachusetts; Purchase through the generosity of Diane and Michael Maher M25774

prints and paintings were put to various uses in service of the war effort. The lithographs *Massacre at Dinant* and *Murder of Edith Cavell* (Figs. 114, 115) were used to illustrate the article "The Hun" in the November 1918 issue of *Vanity Fair*. *Return of the Useless* (see Fig. 132) and *Edith Cavell* were reproduced in *Everybody's Magazine* in 1918 as illustrations for a series of articles about the German attack and occupation of Belgium. The painting *The Germans Arrive* (Fig. 112) was displayed in the window of Scott and Fowles Gallery on Fifth Avenue in the fall of 1918 to coincide with the Fourth Liberty Loan Drive. At the same time, the lithograph of the same subject (Fig. 124) was reproduced in *Collier's* as an ad for Liberty Bonds.

Shortly after the Armistice, one of Bellows's War Series paintings and several prints were chosen for the Allied War Salon organized by collectors Duncan Phillips and A. E. Gallatin and painter A.V. Tack.[15] That show, held at the American Art Galleries in New York, included more than 600 paintings, prints, sculptures, and posters by artists from the United States and five other Allied nations. Among the works shown were Hassam's *Early Morning on the Avenue in May* (1917; Addison Gallery of American Art, Phillips Academy, Andover, Massachusetts), another buoyant flag painting, and Luks's *Czecho-slovak Army* (1918; Los Angeles County Museum of Art), an imagined—and stirring—image of the Czech army entering Vladivostok, Siberia. Both the Hassam and the Luks are richly painted, with lively brushwork and clear, bright colors.

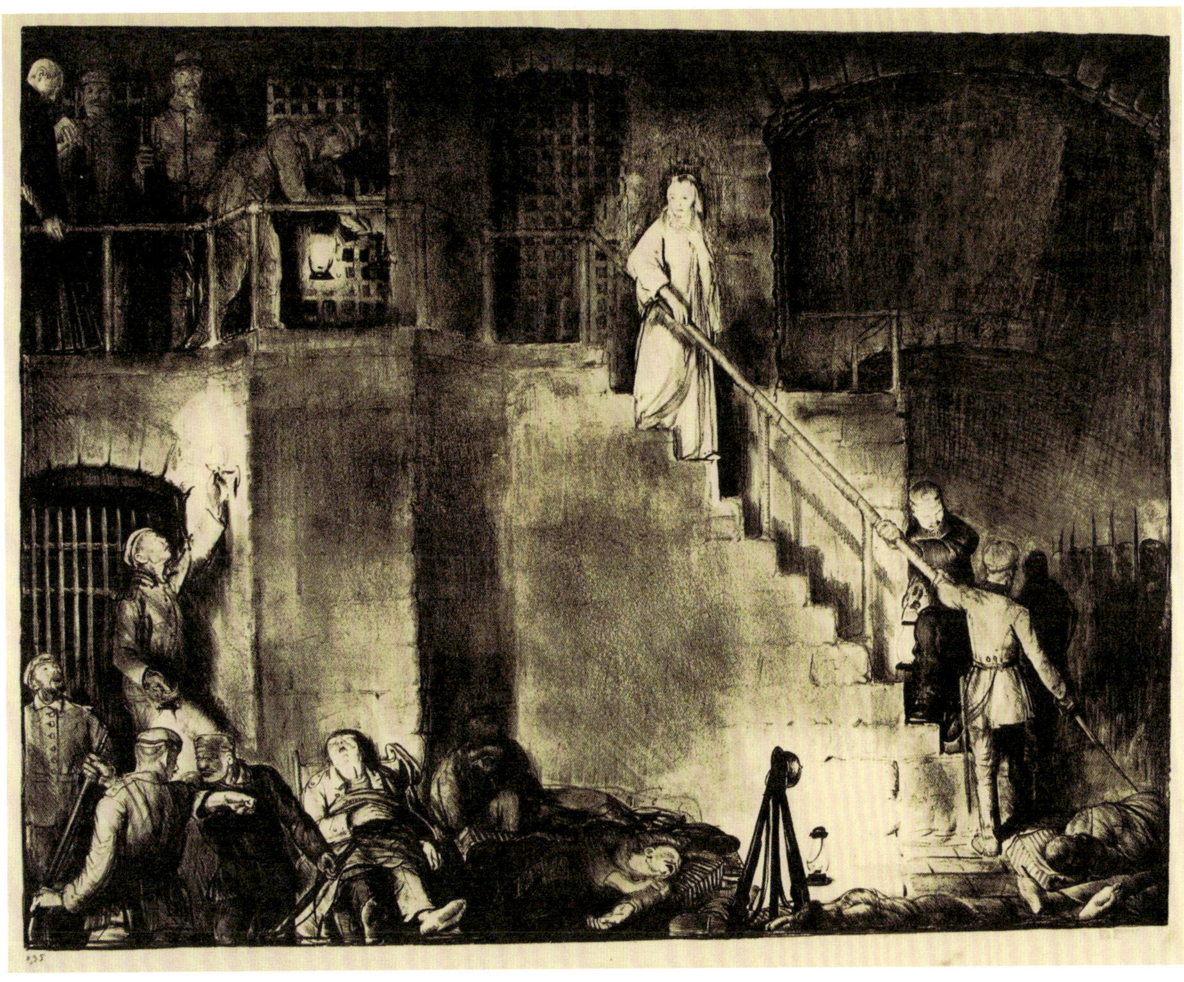

Fig. 115
George Bellows
Murder of Edith Cavell, 1918
Lithograph on paper
19 × 24 11/16 in. (48.3 × 62.7 cm)
Harvard Art Museums, Fogg Art Museum, Cambridge, Massachusetts; Purchase through the generosity of Diane and Michael Maher M25778

Bellows was represented by *Edith Cavell* (Fig. 116), a painting that is acid, murky, and anti-heroic, except for the main figure, dressed in white. Cavell (1865–1915), a British nurse, was the matron of the Brussels Surgical Institute, which would become a Red Cross hospital at the outset of the war. Shortly thereafter, she began sheltering Allied soldiers who had been trapped behind enemy lines. The hospital became a way station for these soldiers, and Cavell helped them escape to neutral Holland. Arrested and court-martialed for treason by the Germans in August 1915, she was executed by firing squad two months later, despite international protests. She subsequently was honored as a martyr to the Allied cause.[16] Bellows shows her on the way to her execution—her angelic demeanor in dramatic contrast to the bestial figures sprawled on the ground. While *Edith Cavell*, with its grim setting and hallucinatory lighting, is lurid enough, it is one of the less distressing of Bellows's war images. The events depicted in many of the other War Series pictures were even more disturbing.

The atrocities Bellows represented were first brought to the attention of the English-speaking world in gruesome detail in the Bryce Report. Published in England in May 1915, the report was prepared by Viscount James Bryce, head of a government-appointed committee charged with investigating events in Belgium. Bryce was a professional historian, a former British ambassador to the United States, and a delegate to the International Court in the Hague. He was highly respected and brought great credibility to the task. His report was based on the testimony of eyewitnesses and described looting and burning, random shootings, and beatings. It was especially graphic in its accounts of rape, mutilation, and the murder of children. Almost immediately after appearing in England, the Bryce Report was widely circulated, especially in the United States, where excerpts appeared in the *New York Times* in May 1915.[17] Some 41,000 copies of the report were shipped here almost immediately after publication in Europe as part of the British effort to involve the United States in the war.

It is not known whether Bellows paid particular attention to the Bryce Report at the time of its publication. But he did take notice a few years later, when, beginning in February 1918, *Everybody's Magazine* published a series of articles collectively titled "Belgium: The Crowning Crime" by fellow Ohioan Brand Whitlock, the American ambassador to Belgium. Whitlock too described in detail the atrocities committed against Belgian citizens and it is likely these articles inspired Bellows to seek out and read the Bryce Report. By early spring he was at work on the lithographs. As noted above, two of the prints were then reproduced as illustrations for later installments of Whitlock's series. Bellows began the paintings in July and turned them out at the rate of one per month—an astonishing achievement, since they are all very large, complicated, multi-figured compositions.

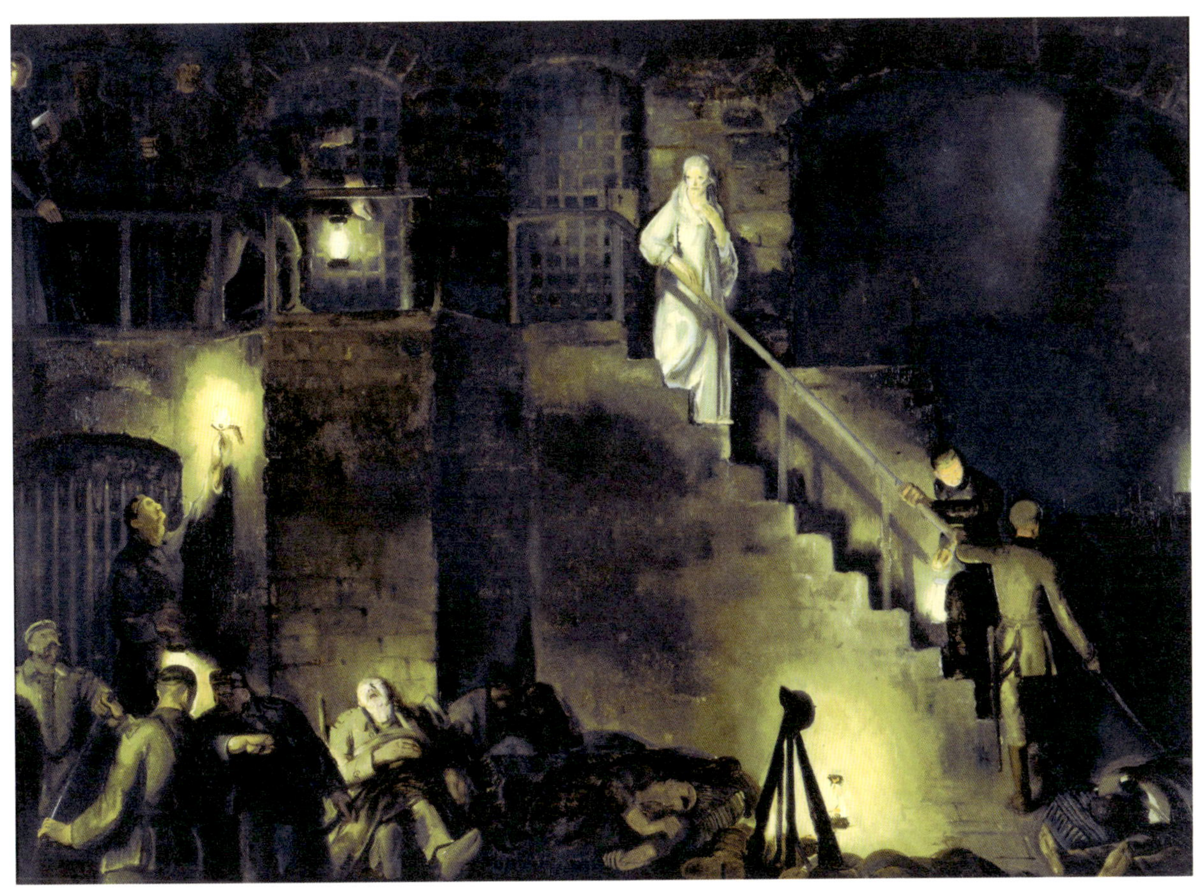

Fig. 116
George Bellows
Edith Cavell, 1918
Oil on canvas
45 × 63 in. (114.3 × 160 cm)
Michele and Donald D'Amour
Museum of Fine Arts, Springfield,
Massachusetts; The James Philip
Gray Collection

Two of the paintings, *The Barricade* (Fig. 121) and *Massacre at Dinant* (Fig. 127), illustrate the abuses of innocent townspeople at Liège and Dinant. When the Germans began their assault on Liège, they accused the Belgians of "perfidious conduct," which they used as an excuse to round up and shoot civilians—men, women, and children, even members of the clergy—from the surrounding hamlets. They then reportedly bayoneted the fallen to be sure none survived. Subsequently, as they entered the city, they used several hundred people, again, all civilians, as human shields. This was in mid-August 1914. A week later, the Germans massacred nearly 700 civilians at Dinant—10 percent of the population—and destroyed most of the buildings in the town.

Bellows apparently based a number of his War Series images directly on the Bryce Report[18]—among them *The Germans Arrive*, *Bacchanale*, and *The Cigarette* (Fig. 119). Whitlock's account provided stimulus for other images, including *Return of the Useless* (Fig. 132), which refers to the German army's practice of deporting Belgian citizens to Germany and occupied France to work in labor camps.[19] By the end of 1916 more than 100,000 had been deported. According to Whitlock:

> They went . . . penned in flat cars. They were exposed to all weathers, shivered from the cold, were wet to the skin. . . . "A cattle breeder, in taking care of his livestock," said a man [who witnessed the laborers' situation] "would not permit them to travel under such conditions."

And on their return, which Bellows chose to depict:

> [They had become] . . . pale, emaciated men whose physical condition made them useless as workers. . . . [They were] broken, maimed, helpless, hopeless; a few weeks in the slave compounds in Germany had so reduced [them] by sickness, exposure and starvation that they were hauled back to Belgium and flung down in their villages to die.[20]

Bellows was one of several artists to refer to events in Belgium. Ellsworth Young's poster *Remember Belgium* (Fig. 117), produced to encourage the purchase of Liberty Bonds, shows a terrified young woman being dragged along by a stereotypical German soldier—the hated Hun with spiked helmet and big moustache—while her city burns behind her. It became one of the best-known posters of the war. Equally well known were the drawings of the Dutch cartoonist Louis Raemaekers, which as early as 1916 were distributed in the United States, both as newspaper illustrations and in such anthologies as *Kultur in Cartoons*.[21] His images, such as *The Belgian Massacres* and *Shields of Rosselaere* (both 1916; see Fig. 118), represented some of the same atrocities Bellows would later depict. Raemaekers's work was seen as particularly credible because it came out of neutral Holland. Like the Bryce Report, these cartoons were part of the European Allies' efforts to draw the United States into the war.

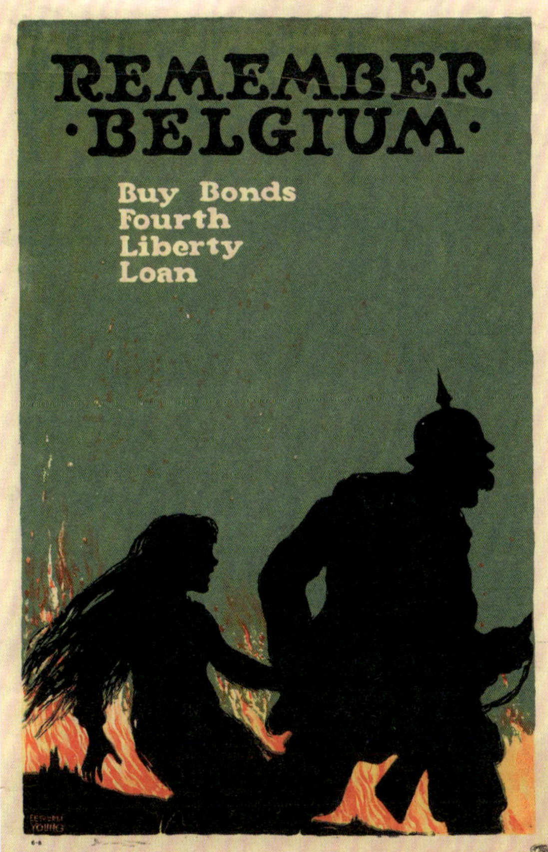

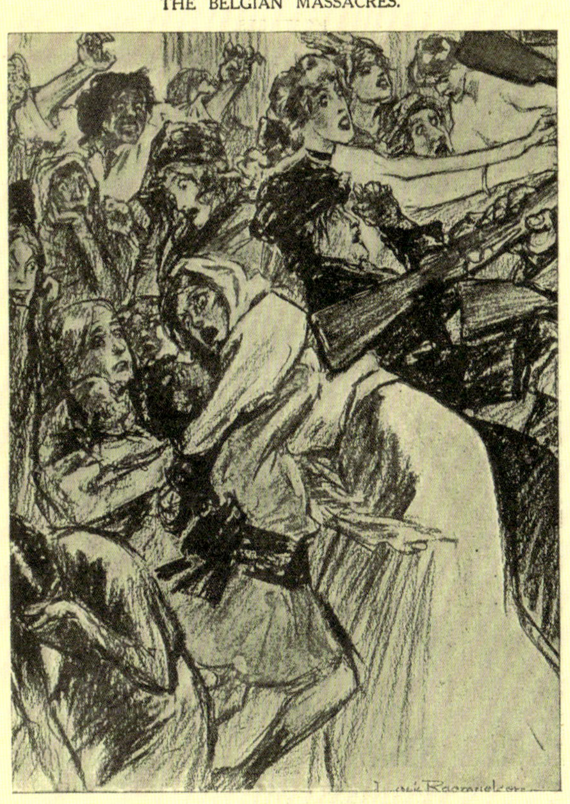

Fig. 117
Ellsworth Young
Remember Belgium, 1918
Lithographic poster
30 × 19¹³⁄₁₆ in. (76.2 × 50.3 cm)
Printed by U.S. Printing and Litho. Co., New York
The Museum of Modern Art, New York; Gift of Mrs. M.E. Wormser

Fig. 118
Louis Raemaekers
The Belgian Massacres
Pl. 4 in *Raemaekers Cartoons*
(London and New York: Hodder and Stoughton, 1916)

Such images met a sympathetic response here. They contributed to America's feelings of moral superiority to Europe, a sense of superiority that initially was used to justify detachment from international events. But as the war ground on, this belief allowed the United States to view its entry into the war as a campaign not merely to reestablish a rule of law and defend sovereignty, but to save civilization. For example, when *The Germans Arrive* (Fig. 124) was reproduced in *Collier's* magazine as an ad for Liberty Bonds, it was augmented with the caption "This is Kultur. There is no sharper contrast between German Kultur and the civilization that our forefathers died for, than the difference in the attitude of the two civilizations toward women and children."[22]

Responding to the display of Bellows's paintings in windows along the "Avenue of the Allies" and elsewhere, the press unabashedly sanctioned the inspirational, propagandistic quality of Bellows's images on both political and aesthetic grounds. As *American Art News* cheered, "The . . . [paintings] . . . stiffen the spines of the enlisted men who are here and make them realize what they face 'Over There.'"[23] A few weeks later, the critic for the *New York Times* wrote, "George Bellows has made use of every agency for the communication of horror in his picture 'The Germans Arrive.' . . . The treatment is characteristic and familiar to a public acquainted with the artist's pugilist subjects. Long practice in realistic illustration of scenes of physical violence has made possible a convincing report at second hand of what we have all heard."[24] In other words, Bellows's experience in representing the violence of the boxing ring gave his portrayals of the horrifying events in Belgium special credibility. His images were understood as a call to arms. If unflinching depictions of German brutality were motivators in the fight to save civilization, then Bellows was the man for the job.

Bellows himself said little about why he chose to respond to the war with images of such exceptional violence. Some years later he reportedly referred to the prints as "hallucinations,"[25] but offered no further explanation. However, it is reasonable to assume that he was particularly susceptible to the Bryce Report's emphasis on the bestiality of the enemy toward noncombatants. The report relied heavily on descriptions of rape and mutilation. In so doing, it appealed to the creed that no self-respecting man would allow women and children to suffer such abuse. Implicit in the report was a challenge to manhood, and Bellows was, after all, a husband and the father of daughters. Lithographs such as *The Cigarette* (Fig. 119) and *Belgian Farmyard*, which presumably depicts the aftermath of a rape, extended that challenge to Americans in a visual, visceral way.

Bellows had enjoyed his first successes as an artist during Theodore Roosevelt's administration, and no doubt identified more with Roosevelt, the man of action, than with the cerebral Woodrow Wilson. When Germany violated Belgium's neutrality in 1914, Roosevelt made little public comment, but reportedly lamented privately that, as nonparticipants, Americans would have "no opportunity for display of heroic qualities."[26]

Bellows's pictures would have been designed to prompt a heroic, manly response and to incite Americans to take on the role of saviors. But they may have served some private ambitions as well. Since 1916, Bellows had largely been involved with lithography. And while he continued to be quite prolific as a painter during this period, he produced fewer canvases of major consequence. His painting career had also been troubled by an unpleasant controversy over a portrait commissioned—and then rejected—by the Harvard Club of New York and by an unfortunate public quarrel with Forbes Watson, the well-regarded critic for the *New York Evening Post* (and later editor of *The Arts*).[27] For some time, Bellows had alternated between feeling optimistic and confident, and suffering discouragement and self-doubt. "I am so tired of depending on my past summer for present interest," he wrote to a friend during one of his periods of insecurity.[28] The summers of 1915 and 1916 had been particularly unsettling; he

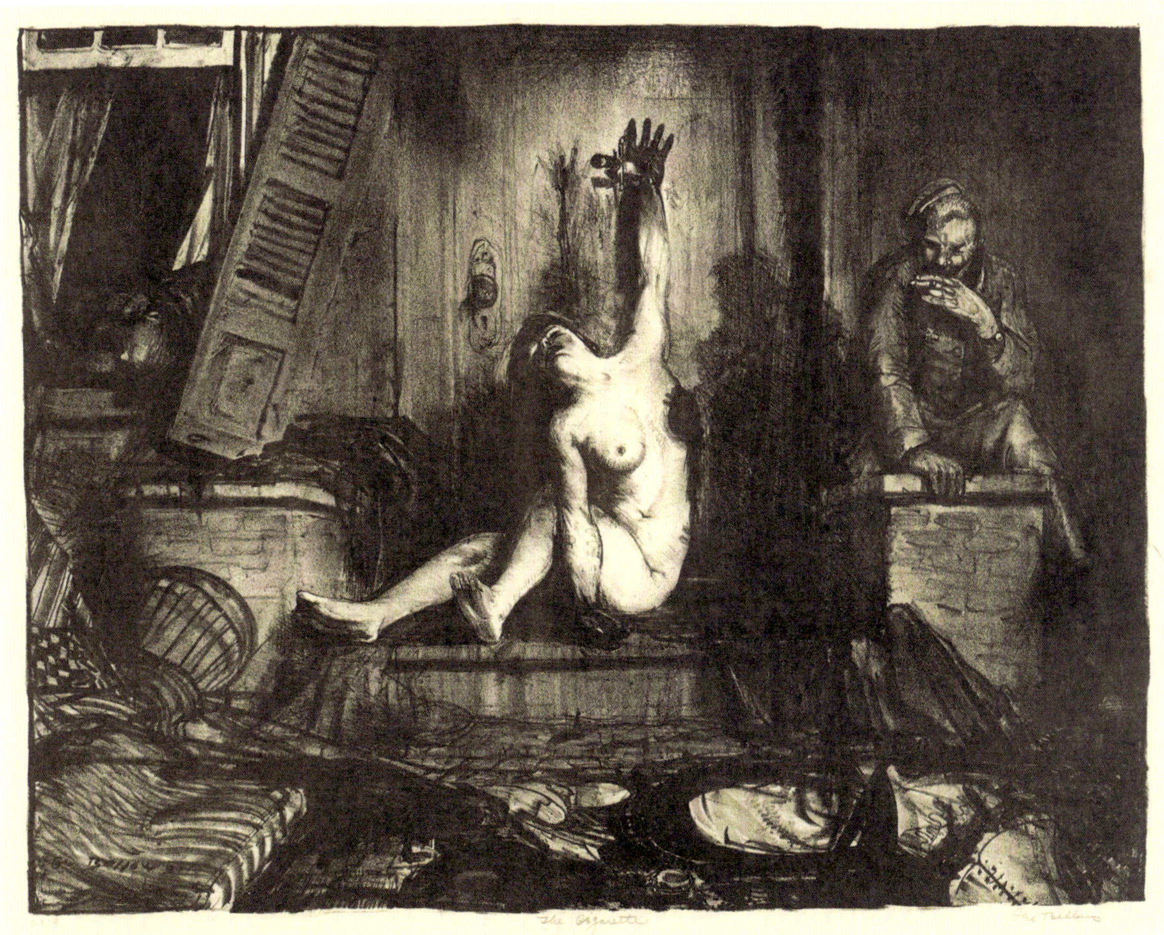

Fig. 119
George Bellows
The Cigarette, 1918
Lithograph on paper
14 13/16 × 19 5/16 in. (37.6 × 49.1 cm)
Harvard Art Museums, Fogg Art Museum, Cambridge, Massachusetts; Purchase through the generosity of Diane and Michael Maher M25773

had financial difficulties and seemed depressed. "He was in a rut," as his good friend Leon Kroll described it.[29]

Bellows's critical reputation was also floundering somewhat in that period. While his 1914 exhibition at the Montross Galleries received positive reviews,[30] his next solo show in New York, at Milch Galleries in March of 1917, was not especially well received. That show featured oils from Bellows's previous summers at Camden and Matinicus, in Maine, including pictures that were largely invented and not drawn specifically from his experience and observation, as had been his practice. He was self-conscious about these,[31] and undoubtedly was disappointed when critics did not applaud his new efforts. Henry McBride, for one, was disdainful of the new work: "The crowd will stop to see a Bellows in the window," he observed in his review for the *New York Sun*. "There is something about almost everything this artist does that arrests the idle glance. It is not everything he does, however, that holds it long. Success does not attend upon [all the works in the show]. Mr. Bellows's muse rides a recalcitrant steed."

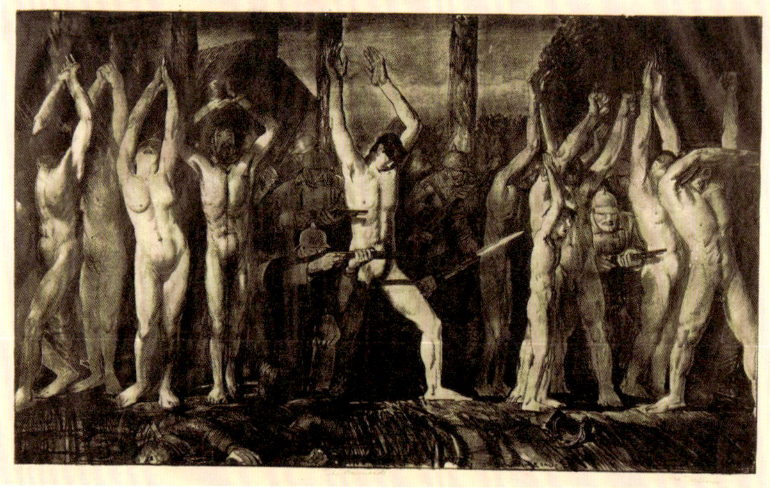

Fig. 120
George Bellows
The Barricade, No. 2, 1918
Lithograph on paper
17⅛ × 28¾ in. (43.5 × 73 cm)
Harvard Art Museums, Fogg Art Museum, Cambridge, Massachusetts; Purchase through the generosity of Diane and Michael Maher M25776

Of the lithographs in the show, McBride complained, "Mr. Bellows wields a lumbering stick where he should have employed the rapier." Of the landscapes "in which our artist attempts to poeticize, the less said the better." The only work McBride truly admired—he called it startling, disconcerting and "incomparably the best thing in the gallery"—was *Docks in Winter* (private collection), a rather tough, if gorgeously painted canvas dating from 1911.[32]

Bellows spent the summer and fall of 1917 in California and New Mexico, returning to New York in October. Once again he found himself depending on his summer experiences for pictures while searching for more significant subject matter. He would soon find it. By early spring he was at work on the War Series lithographs. In July 1918 Charles Dana Gibson called them "the finest things that have been done anywhere, anytime," and urged Bellows to do more to support the war effort.[33] Gibson's words bolstered Bellows's desire not only to take patriotic action but also to find subjects for his paintings that were outside his own experience and that were of real consequence. By the end of the month he had completed *Massacre at Dinant* (Fig. 127).

Bellows's process in producing the works in the War Series gives an indication of a new direction in his art. He began by making drawings in chalk, crayon, and graphite, which led to lithographs, some of which he then developed into monumental oils. The changes he made as he reworked the subject in each medium are subtle, but significant. With each iteration the image became less incidental and animated, and more solemn and universal. Bellows simplified the design as he worked. In *The Barricade*, for example, the details of the corpse and empty helmet in the lithograph are cleared away in the oil (Figs. 120, 121). He also successively minimized any sense of motion. In the drawing (Fig. 130), the figure at left seems to step forward, toward the viewer, as though prodded by a bayonet. The figure at the right

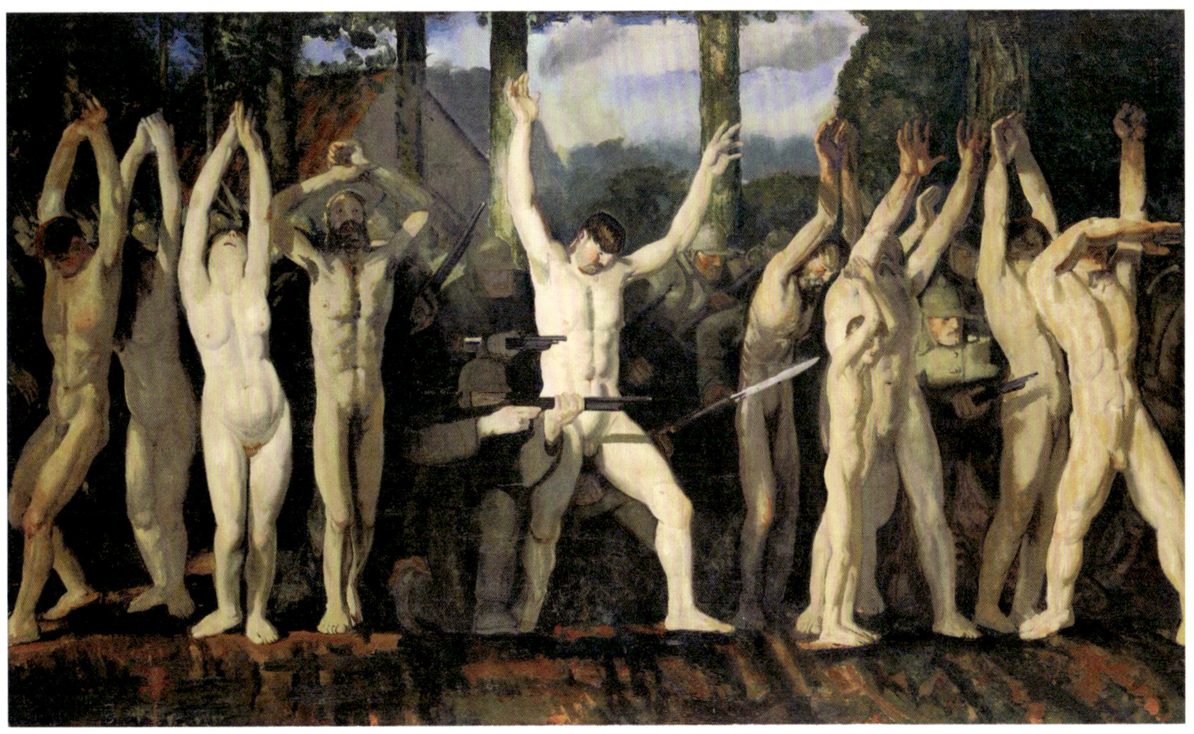

Fig. 121
George Bellows
The Barricade, 1918
Oil on canvas
48⅛ × 83½ in. (122.2 × 212.1 cm)
Birmingham Museum of Art, Alabama;
Museum purchase with funds provided
by the Harold and Regina Simon Fund,
the Friends of American Art, Margaret
Gresham Livingston, and Crawford Taylor

edge of the drawing crumples. In contrast, in the painting, the poses of the figures are more ritualized and their arrangement even more contained and frieze-like. Bodies become smoother and more sculptural; facial features are more generalized. So the face of the victim in *The Germans Arrive*, grotesque and contorted in pain in the lithograph (Fig. 124), becomes idealized into an almost handsome everyman in the painting (Fig. 112). Heroic agony replaces grimace. The face of Edith Cavell seems apprehensive in the drawing (Fig. 122) and lithograph (Fig. 115), but becomes serene, even bland, in the oil (Fig. 116). The relatively even lighting of the drawing becomes increasingly dramatic in the lithograph and then in the oil, where contrasts are further heightened. According to the *New York Times*, Cavell fainted before her execution and was shot while lying unconscious on the ground.[34] Nevertheless, Bellows chose to depict a heroic and theatrical moment when Cavell, dressed in virginal white, moves majestically and nobly to her fate, with her hand at her breast in the classic gesture of humility. Her dignity and grace are underscored by the contrast between the lanterns that illuminate the corners of the dank prison and the cool, ethereal light that emanates from her. Ultimately, the story is told not so much by expression or gesture as by Edith's angelic presence.

Bellows initially rendered his subjects in a direct and vigorous style to convey the chaos of the moment. But as he progressed, the particular incidents of brutality were transformed into epics of noble suffering. Passion became order. Bellows seemed to be striving to transcend the here and now, the reportorial, to arrive at a more formal, monumental, eternal statement.

This greater emphasis on structure in Bellows's paintings—not just in the War Series but in many of his works at this time—frequently is attributed to his interest in "Dynamic Symmetry."[35] This theory, like others he had adopted at various points in his career, appealed to Bellows as a means of elevating his own art and combating the rut in which he found himself. He first met Jay Hambidge and learned of his compositional system in a series of lectures in 1917 shortly before embarking on the War Series; these new ideas undoubtedly helped give him the confidence to undertake such paintings, which were more monumental in scale and momentous in theme than anything he had done before. Dynamic Symmetry, a system of proportions derived from classical antiquity and designed to provide pictorial compositions with a geometric foundation, enabled Bellows to impart a stately rhythm, a dramatic order, to chaotic, violent events. It was part of his quest to transcend immediate experiences and find a vocabulary for treating more consequential subjects.

He also sought such a vocabulary in the art of the past, which enabled him to suggest associations between his contemporary subjects and the great events of history. Bellows was an academically trained

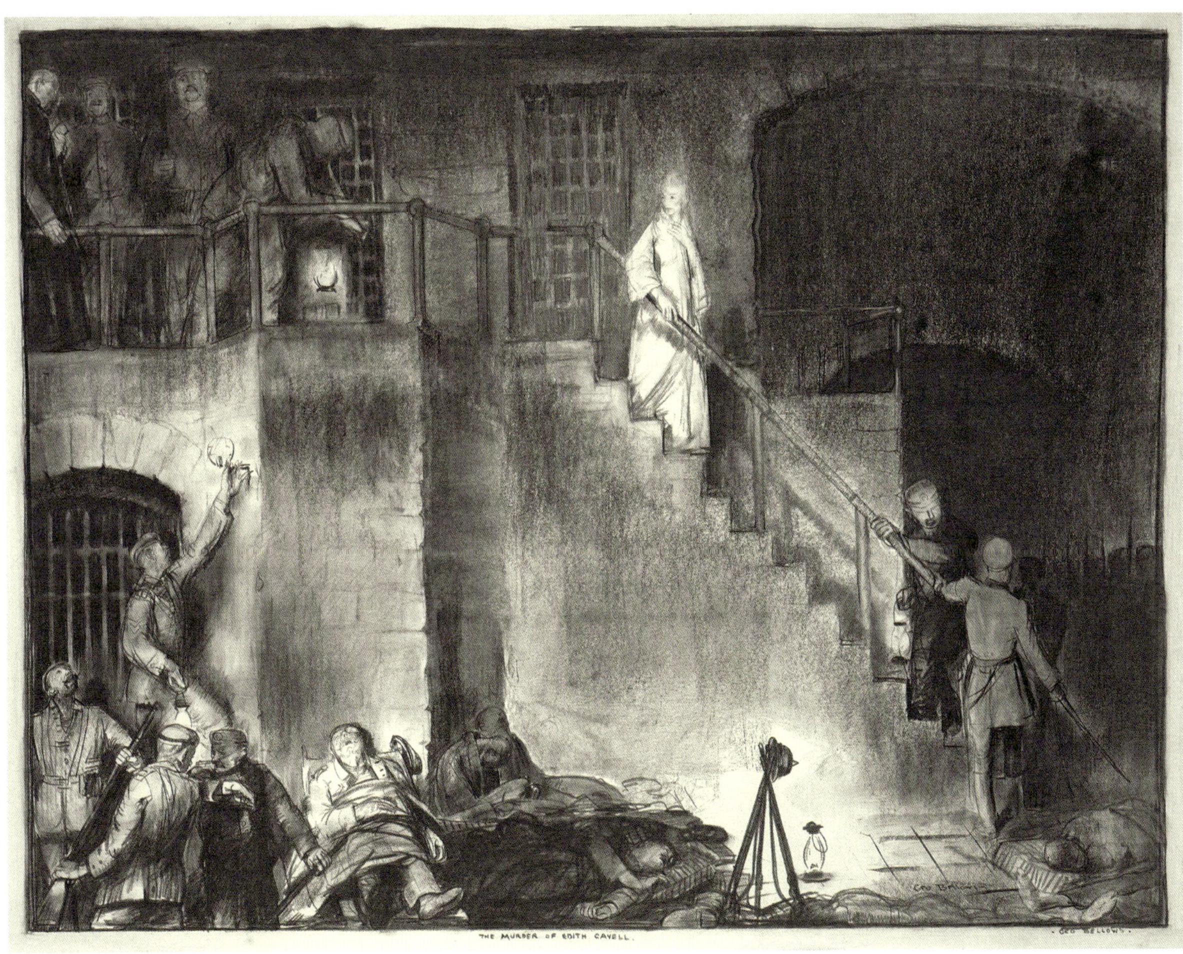

Fig. 122
George Bellows
The Murder of Edith Cavell, 1918
Black chalk and black crayon over charcoal on cream wove paper
$21\frac{1}{16} \times 26\frac{15}{16}$ in. (53.5×68.5 cm)
Princeton University Art Museum, New Jersey; Museum Purchase, Laura P. Hall Memorial Collection, 1958–61

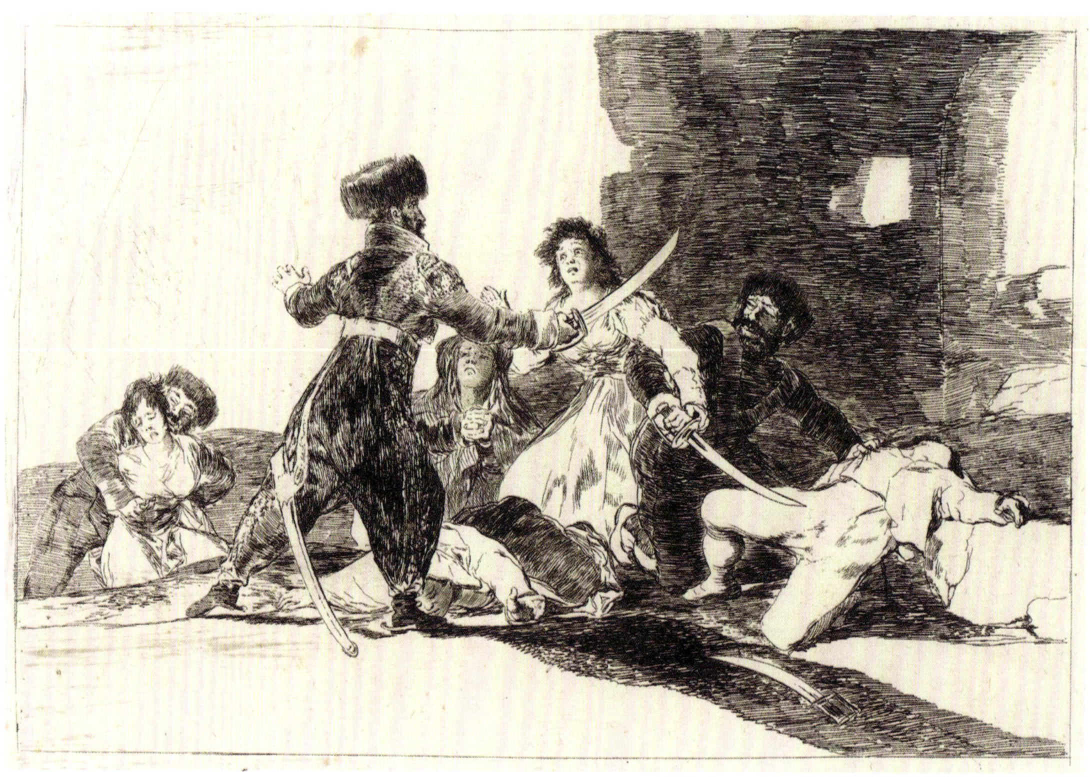

Fig. 123
Francisco de Goya y Lucientes
Ya no hay tiempo
(There Is No Longer Time)
Pl. 19 from *Disasters of War*,
1810–14, published 1863
Etching, drypoint, and burin
(working proof)
6 7/16 × 9 5/16 in. (16.3 × 23.7 cm)
Museum of Fine Arts,
Boston; 1951 Purchase Fund
51.1642

painter and the art of both the old and modern masters had always been part of his thinking. Now, however, with new subject matter that was more serious than anything he had previously attempted, these associations took on new weight.[36]

The most obvious antecedent for the War Series is the work of Francisco de Goya, particularly the series of etchings *Disasters of War*. Contemporary critics had noted the connection between the Spanish master's work and that of Bellows, both in his technique and in his taste for the unsettling and grotesque.[37] Bellows took up the medium of lithography, in fact, just as there was something of a Goya revival in New York. There were at least four major showings of Goya's work in the city between 1912 and 1917.[38] So when he began the War Series, Goya was on Bellows's mind and on the mind of his public. His own war lithographs would later be referred to as a "modern Disasters of War."[39] As Goya scholar Eleanor Tufts has noted, there are clear connections between Goya's disturbing images, such as *There Is No Longer Time* and *The Germans Arrive* (Figs. 123, 124), and other, equally terrible, scenes depicted by Bellows.[40]

Another Spanish master made perhaps an even greater contribution to the War Series. The always perceptive critic Henry McBride was the first to make the connection, observing a few years later that there was "more Greco than Goya" in Bellows's work.[41] Like Goya,

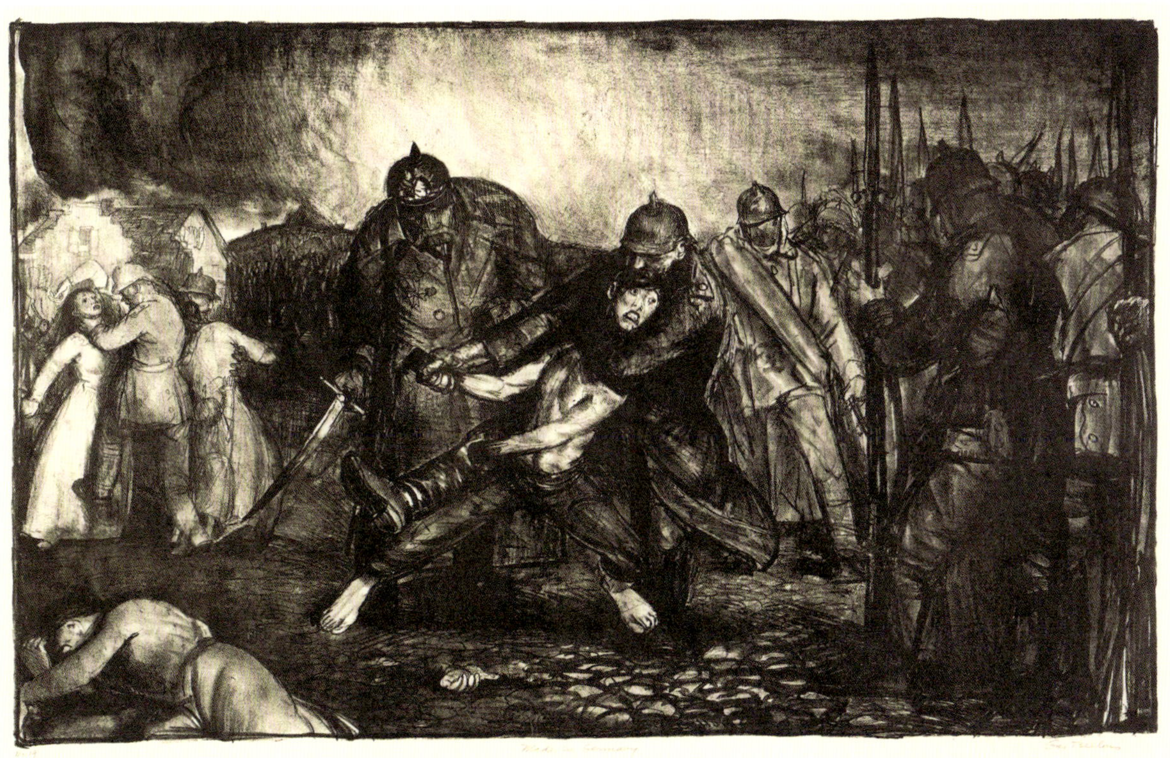

Fig. 124
George Bellows
The Germans Arrive (Made in Germany), 1918
Lithograph on chine appliqué
16 × 26 in. (40.6 × 66.1 cm)
Harvard Art Museums, Fogg Art Museum, Cambridge, Massachusetts; Purchase through the generosity of Diane and Michael Maher M25781

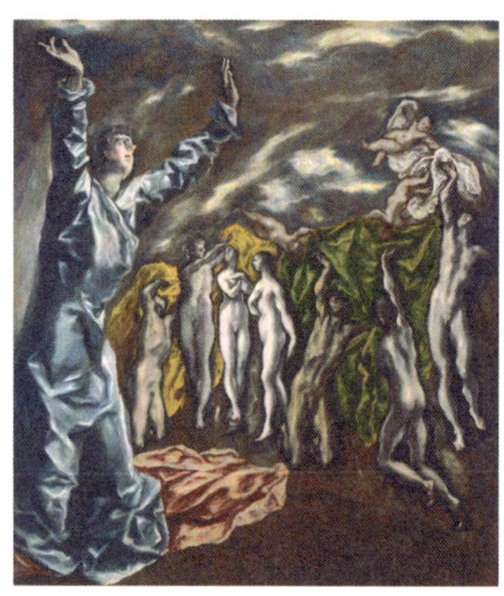

Fig. 125
El Greco [Domenikos Theotokopoulos]
The Vision of Saint John, 1608–14
Oil on canvas
87½ × 76 in. (222.3 × 199.4 cm)
The Metropolitan Museum of Art, New York; Rogers Fund, 1956

El Greco was quite visible in New York at this time. In fact, the two artists were shown together in 1912, 1913, and 1915. The 1912 and 1915 exhibitions were held at Knoedler's, where Bellows's work was also shown on occasion; the 1915 show was a benefit for the Belgian Relief Fund. By the end of the nineteenth century, El Greco's work was eagerly sought by such sophisticated collectors as Henry and Louisine Havemeyer, who also championed recent French painting. During Bellows's student days at the New York School of Art, he was one of the artists that famed instructor Robert Henri had especially recommended;[42] an enthusiasm for El Greco was increasingly associated with an appreciation of modern art.[43] In the teens, the press discussed his work in terms that would have provided a further recommendation to an artist like Bellows. The "undiluted energy and virility" seen in El Greco's paintings and his "passionate outlook on life"[44] were values with which Bellows identified. El Greco's work provided models for organizing many intertwined figures and several arenas of action into coherent compositions. The lurid color of the War Series paintings, their baroque theatricality and extravagantly gesturing figures (ecstatic in El Greco's work, such as *The Vision of St. John* [Fig. 125]; admittedly rather melodramatic in Bellows's [Fig. 127]) reflect Bellows's longstanding admiration for El Greco.[45]

The example of El Greco and others—the artists Bellows referred to in a 1917 interview as the "wise old guys of Italy and Spain"[46]—gave him a vocabulary with which to turn horrific incidents of war into universal events. These associations serve to heighten drama and pathos. So, for example, in *Edith Cavell*, the dank, eerily lit prison evokes the hallucinatory spaces of Piranesi (e.g., *The Arch with the Shell Ornament*, plate XI from the series *Carceri*, 1761), intensifying the nightmarish quality of the scene. In *Return of the Useless*, the pose of the sadistic German soldier brutalizing a Belgian worker is a pointed degradation of the characteristic pose of Neptune, one of the most bellicose of the gods, while inside the boxcar, in tender contrast, Bellows evokes a Pietà (Figs. 131, 132).

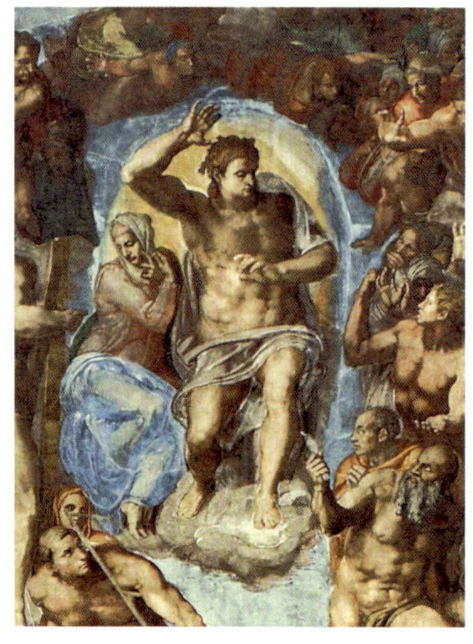

Fig. 126
Michelangelo Buonarroti
Retable of *The Last Judgment (Fall of the Damned)*, (detail) 1536–41
Fresco
Sistine Chapel, Vatican Palace, Rome

These associations also elevate the significance of what the viewer is asked to witness. So while the murder of nearly seven hundred civilians at Dinant was already understood as a horrible event, Bellows's *Massacre at Dinant* transforms it into a tragedy of an even more epic nature. The darkening skies bring to mind the biblical Golgotha, and the collapsing woman at right is reminiscent of the Virgin fainting at the foot of the cross. And the central figure, arm upraised and fist clenched, seems to be invoking the heavens and calling down judgment in a burgher's version of Michelangelo's God presiding over the Final Day (Figs. 126, 127).

Perhaps the clearest resonance with art of the past occurs in *The Barricade* (Fig 130), where any number of classical and Renaissance antecedents come to the viewer's mind, as they must have to Bellows.

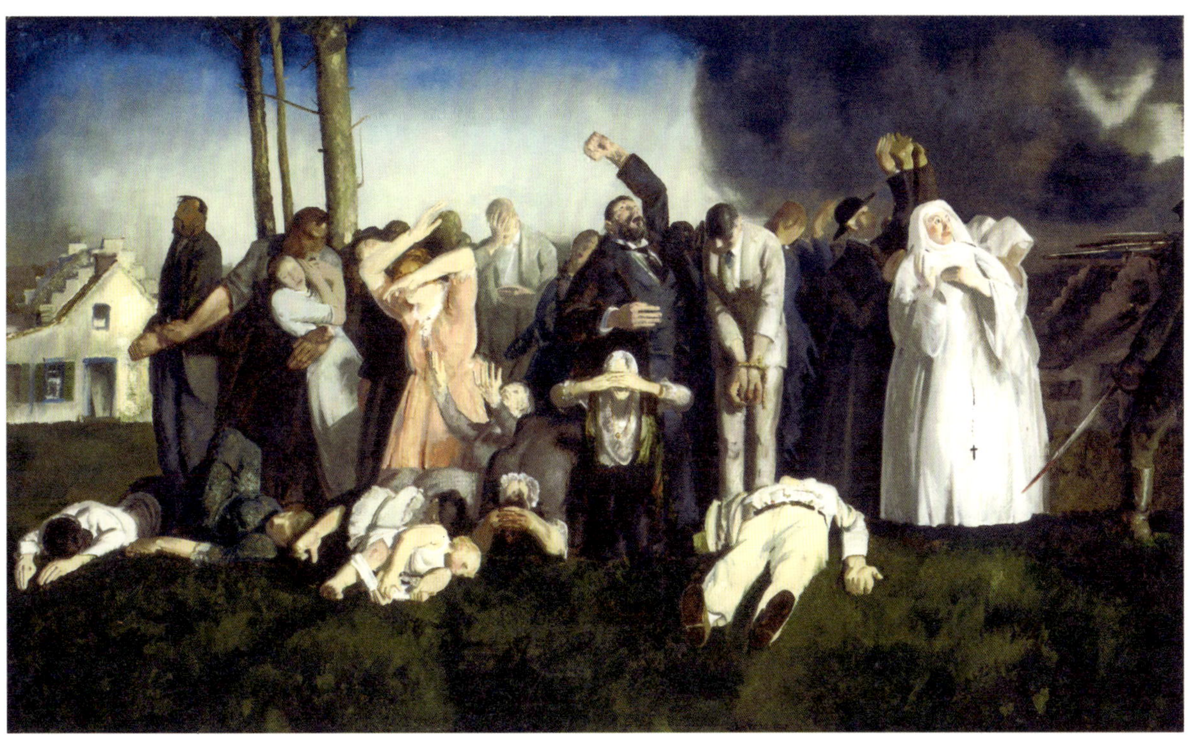

Fig. 127
George Bellows
Massacre at Dinant, 1918
Oil on canvas
49½ × 83 in. (125.7 × 210.8 cm)
Greenville County Museum of Art, Greenville, South Carolina; Gift of Minor M. Shaw, Buck A. Mickel, and Charles C. Mickel; and the Arthur and Holly Magill Fund

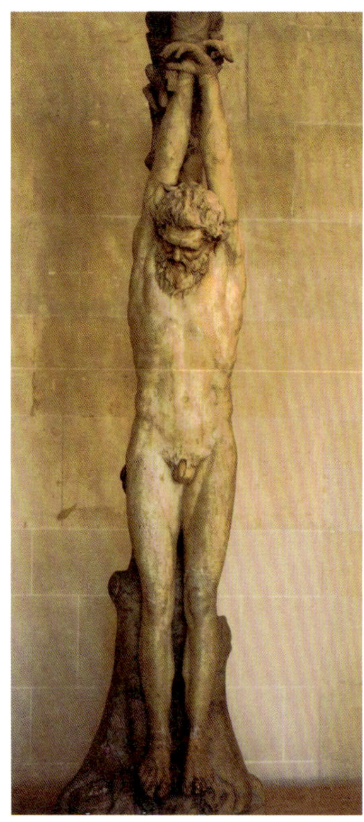

Fig. 128
The Torment of Marsyas,
1st–2nd century CE
Roman Imperial copy of a Hellenistic original
Marble
Height: 100⅞ in. (256 cm)
Musée du Louvre, Paris

The figures at left recall depictions of the flayed *Marsyas* (Fig. 128). The composition of the scene—a shallow, frieze-like space occupied by nude figures in conflict—reflects well-known images by Michelangelo and Pollaiuolo (Fig. 129). Antecedents for the stylized poses of several of the nudes are also found in these works and especially in Michelangelo's *Captives* (1527–28; Accademia, Florence), although Bellows would retain only the agony, and not the sensuousness of his Renaissance prototypes.

Though Bellows may not necessarily have copied specific poses and gestures from these works, he certainly knew them from museums, reproductions, and casts from art school. These venerable models were no doubt in his consciousness as he worked on these pictures and served as an expressive language with which to convey the profound meaning of his subject matter.[47]

Such references had a marked expressive effect. The figures in *The Barricade*, for example, not only appear more vulnerable for being shown in the nude, but also are ennobled by their generalized references to figures in classical and Renaissance art. By using hieratic compositional structures and stylized figures that echo art of the past, Bellows associates contemporary wartime incidents with the great tragedies of the ages. His dramatizations of the torture of the Belgians were meant to be timely and relevant. Yet these personal tragedies and individual degradations seem larger than life, imbued with the gravitas of history. They become more than just representations of collateral damage, more than just a means to generate sympathy for the suffering people of Belgium. In their evocation of momentous events, Bellows's subjects defined the necessary and sufficient justification for war.

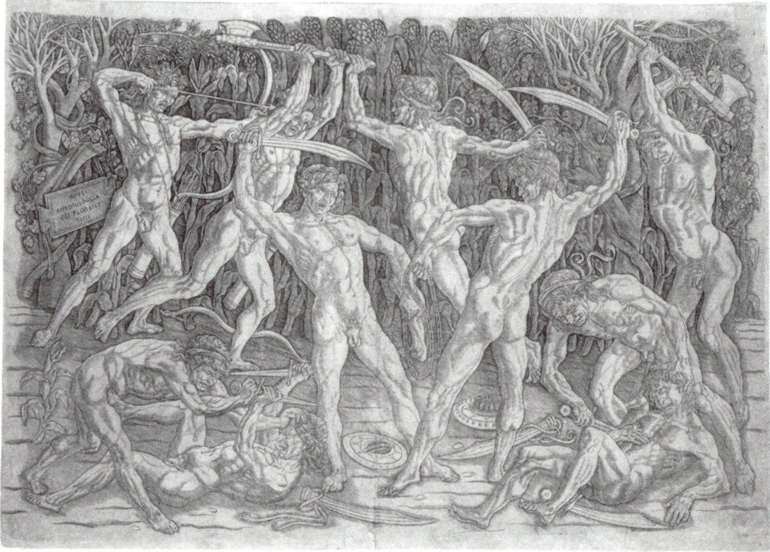

Fig. 129
Antonio del Pollaiuolo
Battle of the Nudes, c. 1470–75
Engraving on paper
Sheet: 16¹³⁄₁₆ × 24⁵⁄₁₆ in. (42.8 × 61.8 cm)
National Gallery of Art, Washington, D.C.; Gift of W. G. Russell Allen

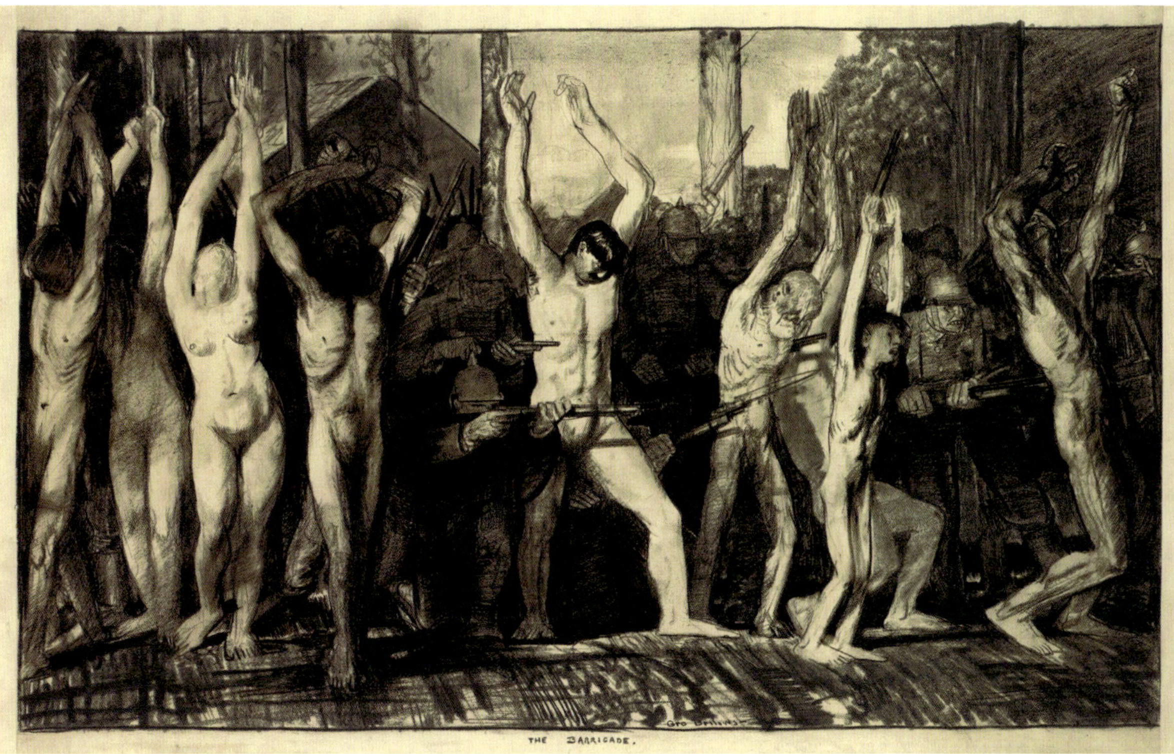

Fig. 130
George Bellows
The Barricade, 1918
Crayon on board
Sheet: 22⅞ × 28⅞ in. (58.2 × 73.5 cm);
image: $17^{13}/_{16}$ × 28⅞ in. (43.7 × 73.5 cm)
Boston Public Library; Print Department, Gift of Albert H. Wiggin 1943.1.3

However, it was not just patriotism—the wish to inspire his fellow Americans to heroism—that was behind Bellows's creation of the War Series. He was motivated both by what he called "profound reverence for the victims"[48] and by a desire to take on mortal themes. By asserting his relationship to artistic tradition, he was proclaiming the seriousness of his efforts. The War Series was part of Bellows's bid to make himself over into a history painter, a painter of grand universal themes; to transform himself from a painter of the here and now into one who still startles and disconcerts (to recall what McBride valued in his work), but who does so with deeply significant subject matter.

Over the next several years, this ambition played itself out with mixed results. For better or worse, Bellows continued to attempt hallowed themes, such as his El Greco-esque *Crucifixion* (1923; Lutheran Brotherhood, Fraternal Benefit Society, Minneapolis). In some of his illustrations, figures show heroic strivings in a classical style: In the case of *The Battle* (1922–23),[49] for example, Bellows's combatants echo the writhing forms of the *Laocoön* (1st century CE; Vatican Museums, Rome). His *Two Women* (1924; private collection) is an overt tipping of the hat to Titian's *Sacred and Profane Love* (c. 1514; Borghese Gallery, Rome).

Bellows's aspirations for his War Series played out with mixed results. Initially, the images were extremely well received. When *The Germans Arrive* was shown in the window of Scott and Fowles

Gallery in conjunction with the Liberty Loan Drive, it overshadowed all the other paintings on display on the street. Frank Crowninshield, editor of *Vanity Fair*, cabled Bellows, "Picture Scott and Fowles immense best thing on avenue."[50] Among a sea of rapturously inspirational pictures—Edwin Blashfield's *Carry On!* of 1917 (see Fig. 113) was perhaps the best-known—*The Germans Arrive* stood out as genuine and authentic. Tough times, the *Nation*'s critic admonished the fainthearted, called for tough pictures: "The message from art to-day, if we are to profit by it, must be delivered in strong, brutal language such as we get in . . . the . . . horrible canvas by George Bellows."[51] The critic for *Art News* went further: "The works are brutal, full of horror, but reeking with truth, which adds to their poignancy. After one has recovered from the shock of the subjects themselves . . . one sees that the pictures are full of strange beauty, conceived in bigness of vision that is rare and inspiring."[52]

But the effect of the War Series proved to be complicated. Unwittingly, the pictures fed an eager morbidity about the war that distorted the justifications for American involvement. Brand Whitlock reported a conversation at a dinner party in his hometown in Ohio in August 1917: "Now Brand," his dinner partner asked him, "did you ever see any German soldiers cutting off the hands of little children?" He wrote of his distress over the seductive effect of these sensational stories, "as though the justice of [the Allied] cause depended on whether Germans killed babies in Belgium, or not."[53] The operatic violence of Bellows's paintings, with their old-master underpinnings, both fueled and justified America's seemingly unflagging appetite for atrocity stories.

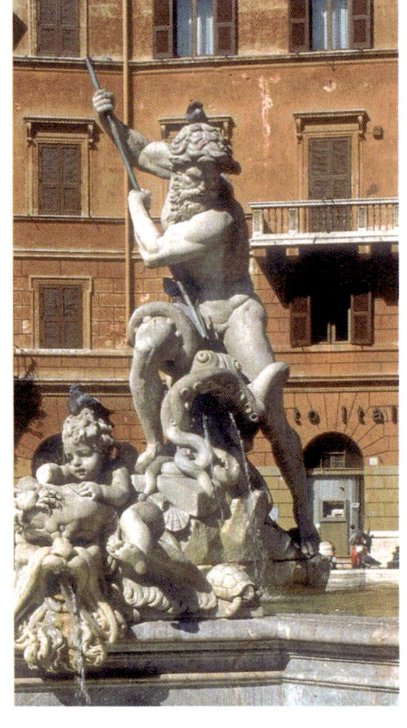

Fig. 131
Antonio della Bitta
Neptune, 1878
from *The Fountain of Neptune*
by Giacomo della Porta, 1574
Piazza Navona, Rome

Furthermore, the very qualities that elevate them from reportage to historical significance—their formality, their grand gestures, their baroque theatricality—undercut their affective power. In the oils, particularly, the lack of motion creates a kind of disjunction—each figure's suffering seems unrelated to that of his neighbor. The stagelike structure of the works sets up a chasm between action and viewer and so provides license for detachment and psychic escape. Bellows's paintings put the viewer in a morally ambiguous position. By presenting Germany's systematic, illegal terrorizing of Belgian citizens as a classical tragedy, by making it into theater, Bellows's paintings make the horrific and unthinkable more tolerable.

Bellows completed the last War Series painting, *Return of the Useless* (Fig. 132), just as the Armistice was declared in November 1918. During the next year, the war paintings were shown in New York—individually, never as a series—at the National Academy of Design, in the Allied Salon Exhibition, and at Knoedler's. They were also included in exhibitions in Buffalo, Cincinnati, Chicago, and Rochester. Over this period, the reputation of the pictures slowly began to erode. Critics protested Bellows's overreliance on theory,[54]

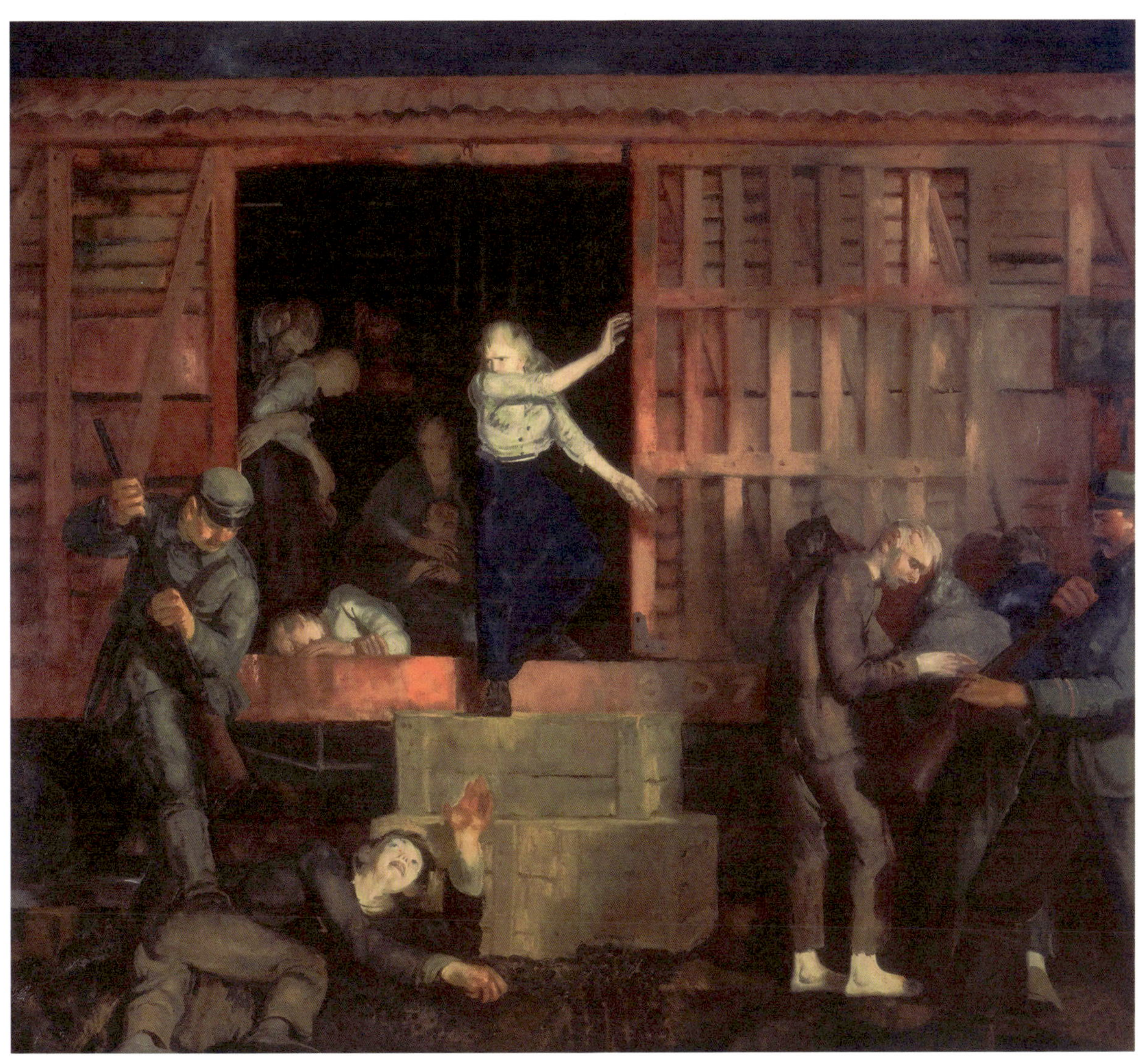

Fig. 132
George Bellows
Return of the Useless, 1918
Oil on canvas
59 × 66 in. (149.9 × 167.6 cm)
Crystal Bridges Museum of
American Art, Bentonville, Arkansas

and there were occasional complaints about flaws in his technique and the floridness of the lighting in some of the pictures. And the perception of stylistic weaknesses accompanied discomfort with the "extreme . . . intensity" of Bellows's subjects.[55] It wasn't just the intensity or the gruesomeness, however. Because so many abuses were shown at such a high theatrical pitch, critics began to question their credibility: "We have the horrors made familiar by printed reports with something subtracted from their frightfulness by the repetitions of emphasis that continually weaken the intended appeal in the work of Mr. Bellows."[56] Bellows was reminded that "Naturalness is always more intense than the most beautiful stage 'tirade'—even [those tirades] . . . studied from life as, of course, Mr. Bellows's massacres and other horrors cannot have been."[57]

In fact, the shift from perceiving Bellows's images as "reeking with truth" to comparing them to a "stage tirade" was linked as much to politics as to changes in artistic fashion, or the application of a more critical eye. Soon after the war, the methodology of Bellows's principal source, the Bryce Report, was discredited. Apparently, in the compilers' fervor to bring a case against the Germans that would bring the uncommitted into the war, they relied heavily on unnamed eyewitnesses as well as on second- and thirdhand accounts.[58] As a result, the stories of atrocities—the killing of babies, the cutting off of hands—that had been the focus of so much dinner party conversation began to be perceived as fictions.

Most of the horrors described in the Bryce Report had indeed occurred—the use of human shields, for example. But others could not be substantiated—German soldiers using bayonets with saw-like edges, stories of degradation of prisoners (especially what came to be known as the "myth of the Crucified Canadians," which was the subject of Bellows's lithograph *Gott Strafe England*; Fig. 133). Americans came to believe that claims of the unique bestiality and violence of the German army had been greatly exaggerated, devised to blacken the enemy. They felt that, as part of a manipulative propaganda campaign, they had been duped by overblown, even fictitious, accounts of assaults on Belgian citizens into unnecessarily entering the war.[59]

With their depictions of the atrocities inflicted by the Germans, Bellows's pictures came to be seen as part of the deception. Perhaps as a result, the works were mostly withdrawn from view after about 1920—the year of the Presidential campaign in which isolationist Warren Harding pledged a "return to normalcy." None of the paintings sold until 1949, when *Edith Cavell* was bought by the Museum of Fine Arts, Springfield, Massachusetts (now the D'Amour Museum of Fine Arts).

After Bellows's death in January 1925, the artist's widow and his close friends Glackens, Henri, Luks, Sloan, and Speicher organized a memorial exhibition at the Metropolitan Museum. To represent

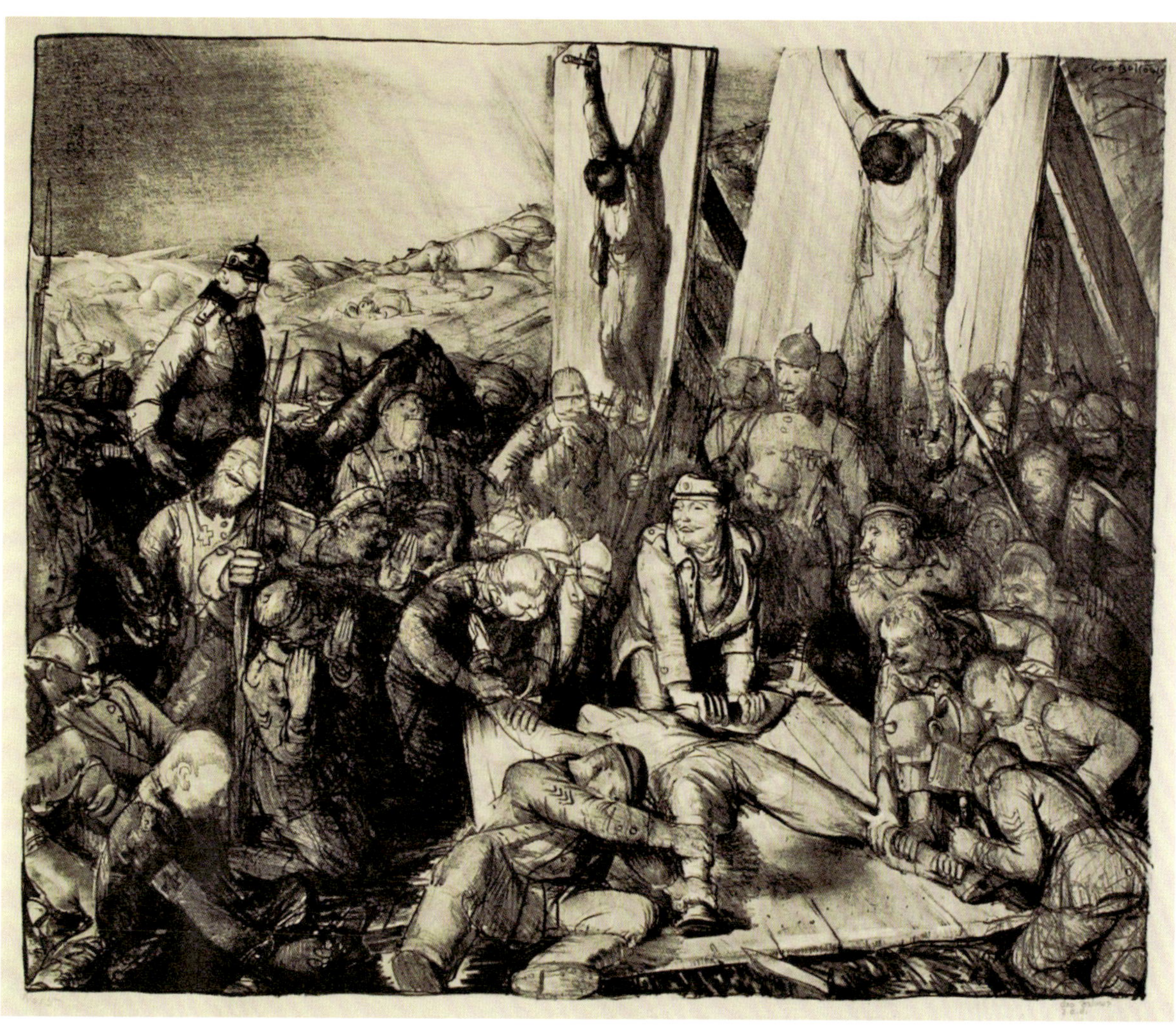

Fig. 133
George Bellows
Gott Strafe England, 1918
Lithograph on paper
15¼ × 18¾ in. (38.8 × 47.6 cm)
Harvard Art Museums, Fogg Art Museum, Cambridge, Massachusetts; Purchase through the generosity of Diane and Michael Maher M25777

the War Series, in which Bellows had invested a great deal of his ambition and nearly an entire year of his career, they selected the two least controversial paintings (*Edith Cavell* and *Return of the Useless*) and only one print (*Murder of Edith Cavell*). In his essay for the catalogue, Frank Crowninshield, a longtime admirer of Bellows, made no mention of those pictures, even in the section entitled "An Authentic Historian."[60] Commenting on the memorial exhibition of the prints held at the Keppel Gallery a few months before the show at the Metropolitan, critic and historian Virgil Barker was less restrained. While writing enthusiastically about the rest of Bellows's graphic output, he condemned the War Series as much for its politics as for its style. He found the prints as "ill-judged in their appeal to the passion of hatred as anything produced in America's most hysterical war years."[61]

NOTES

1. The most prominent exception was a group called the "vigilantes," led by Howard Chandler Christy, who opposed neutrality and pacifism well before the declaration of war. See Alan Axelrod, *Selling the Great War: The Making of American Propaganda* (New York: Palgrave Macmillan, 2009), p. 136.
2. "Authors' Club Sale for Belgian Relief," *New York Times*, May 13, 1915, p. 17.
3. Charles Hanson Towne, ed., *For France* (New York: Doubleday, Page and Company, 1917).
4. Peter Morse, *John Sloan's Prints: A Catalogue Raisonné of the Etchings, Lithographs, and Posters* (New Haven and London: Yale University Press, 1969), p. 215, no. 189.
5. For example, "German Facts" [Letter to the Editor], signed Childe Hassam, Gloucester, Mass., *New York Times,* July 22, 1918, p. 10.
6. For example, in September 1914, even as Germany moved brutally and destructively through Belgium, Stieglitz wrote to an equally pro-German Rockwell Kent, "as a people Germany undoubtedly stands at the head of civilization." Stieglitz to Kent, Sept. 14, 1914, Archives of American Art, Smithsonian Institution, quoted in Gail Levin, "Marsden Hartley's 'Amerika': Between Native American and German Folk Art," *American Art Review* 5 (Winter 1993), p. 122.
7. Hartley to Mabel Dodge, October 1914, Stieglitz Papers, Yale Collection of American Literature, Beinecke Rare Book and Manuscript Library, Yale University, New Haven, quoted in ibid.
8. Caption for Bellows's drawing, *Christ in Chains*, 1917, reproduced in *The Masses* 9 (July 1917), p. 4. For a summary of Bellows's prewar artistic activity, in particular his involvement with *The Masses*, see Charlene Engel, "The Man in the Middle: George Bellows, War, and 'Sergeant' Delaney," *American Art* 18 (Spring 2004), pp. 78–87; and also Rebecca Zurier, *Art for The Masses: A Radical Magazine and Its Graphics 1911–1917* (Philadelphia: Temple University Press, 1988), pp. 22–23, 58–59.
9. George Bellows, "The Big Idea: George Bellows Talks about Patriotism for Beauty," *Touchstone* 1 (July 1917), p. 269.
10. Among the few who did enlist, Stuart Davis volunteered and served as a cartographer in the U.S. Army Intelligence department. Ivan Albright made medical drawings in a hospital in Nantes, France, during his army service. Josephine Nivison, Edward Hopper's future wife, applied to go to Europe as part of the medical division of the American Expeditionary Forces and embarked for France the day before the Armistice was signed. And Edward Steichen's service in the Army Signal Corps' Photographic Section—one of a number of factors that probably contributed to his break with Stieglitz—resulted in his being awarded the Legion of Honor. For Steichen, see Barbara Haskell, *Edward Steichen* (New York: Whitney Museum of American Art, 2000), pp. 24–25; and Debra Bricker Balken, *Debating American Modernism: Stieglitz, Duchamp, and the New York Avant-Garde* (New York: American Federation of Arts, 2003), p. 47.
11. Ernest C. Peixotto, "The Use of Art in Warfare," *The American Magazine of Art* 8 (July 1917), pp. 370–71; "Art at Home and Abroad: Suggestions for Artists Desiring to Apply Their Knowledge to War Work," *New York Times,* September 22, 1918, p. 73; David M. Lubin, "Masks, Mutilation, and Modernity: Anna Coleman Ladd and the First World War," *Archives of American Art Journal* 47 (Fall 2008), pp. 5–15.
12. An extremely informative account of artists' contributions to the war effort is found in Ilene Susan Fort, *The Flag Paintings of Childe Hassam*, exh. cat. (Los Angeles: Los Angeles County Museum of Art, in association with Harry N. Abrams, 1988).

13. One of the most celebrated of these was Glackens's *Russia*, painted on October 16, 1918. On Glackens and the war effort, see William H. Gerdts, *William Glackens*, with essay by Jorge H. Santis (Fort Lauderdale, Fla.: Museum of Art, Fort Lauderdale, in association with Abbeville Press, 1996), pp. 133–34. Glackens's image probably does not survive, except in the stirring words of *New York Herald* critic Frederick James Gregg, who praised the artist's patriotism as much as his craftsmanship: "Mr. Glackens and the other artists who have worked from day to day in trying circumstances of time and place, to make the Fourth Liberty Loan a success, deserve all the credit that has been given to them. They have taught New York a lesson. They have shown that they are not apart from the life of the community and the nation. They brought into the great drive, into the great effort to raise money, an intellectual and imaginative quality of the greatest importance." Gregg, "William Glackens' Work Foremost in That Done for Liberty Loan," *New York Herald*, October 20, 1918, sec. 5, p. 7, quoted in Gerdts, p. 165, n. 23.
14. Although a few of the prints depict battlefield scenes and one—*Base Hospital*—shows a doctor's clinic, most deal with atrocities committed against civilians. The War Series was first shown in its entirety at Hirschl & Adler Galleries, New York, and the Museum of Fine Arts, Springfield, Mass., in 1983. See Glenn C. Peck and Gordon K. Allison, "Introduction," in *George Bellows and the War Series of 1918* (New York: Hirschl & Adler Galleries, 1983). Peck wrote another excellent essay on the War Series in the catalogue of a 2001 exhibition of the lithographs. See "George Bellows and the Conflicts of His Age," in *With My Profound Reverence for the Victims: George Bellows*, exh. cat. (New Paltz: Samuel Dorsky Museum of Art, State University of New York, 2001), pp. 6–8. For Bellows's print oeuvre, see Emma Bellows, *George W. Bellows: His Lithographs* (New York: Knopf, 1927); Lauris Mason, *The Lithographs of George Bellows: A Catalogue Raisonné* (Millwood, N.Y.: KTO Press, 1977; rev. ed., 1992); and Jane Myers and Linda Ayres, *George Bellows: The Artist and His Lithographs, 1916–1924*, exh. cat. (Fort Worth, Tex.: Amon Carter Museum, 1988).
15. Bellows was represented by the oil *Edith Cavell* and nine lithographs: *Murder of Edith Cavell, Sniped, Gott Strafe England, Massacre at Dinant, The Germans Arrive, Dressing Station, The Barricade, The Last Victim*, and *The Return of the Useless.*
16. See Brand Whitlock to Baron von der Lancken and German Military Governor Baron von Bissing, October 11, 1915. "Primary Documents: Brand Whitlock on the Execution of Edith Cavell, 11 October 1915." http://www.firstworldwar.com/source/cavell_whitlock.htm.
17. "Bryce Committee's Report on Deliberate Slaughter of Belgian Non-Combatants," *New York Times*, May 13, 1915, p. 6*ff.* See also http://www.firstworldwar.com/source/brycereport.htm.
18. Krystyna Wasserman, "George Wesley Bellows' War Lithographs and Paintings of 1918" (master's thesis, University of Maryland, 1981).
19. Larry Zuckerman, *The Rape of Belgium: The Untold Story of World War I* (New York and London: New York University Press, 2004), p. 164.
20. Brand Whitlock, *Belgium: A Personal Narrative,* 2 vols. (New York: D. Appleton and Company, 1919), vol. 2, pp. 609, 744.
21. Louis Raemaekers, *Kultur in Cartoons* (London, 1916; reis. New York: Century Co., 1917); also *Raemaekers' Cartoons* (Garden City, N.Y.: Doubleday, Page and Company, 1916) and similar volumes.
22. *Collier's: The National Weekly* 62 (September 28, 1918), p. 31.
23. G.D. Cotton, "Art News from Summer Colonies: Newport," *American Art News* 16 (September 14, 1918), p. 3. Three paintings were included in the exhibition

"Paintings and Lithographs of War Work by Vernon Howe Bailey and War Paintings and Lithographs by George Bellows" at the Art Association of Newport, Rhode Island. Bellows worked in Newport during the summer of 1918.

24. "'Avenue of the Allies' Is an Art Exhibit," *New York Times*, October 6, 1918, p. 44.
25. As noted in Mason, *The Lithographs of George Bellows*, p. 95.
26. Quoted in John Milton Cooper, Jr., *Pivotal Decades: The United States, 1900–1920* (New York: W. W. Norton and Company, 1990), p. 228.
27. See Jane Myers, "'The Most Searching Place in the World': Bellows and Portraiture," in Michael Quick et al., *The Paintings of George Bellows*, exh. cat. (Fort Worth, Tex.: Amon Carter Museum; Los Angeles: Los Angeles County Museum of Art, in association with Harry N. Abrams, 1992), p. 193.
28. Bellows to Joseph Taylor, January 15, 1914, Bellows Papers, Robert Frost Library, Amherst College, Amherst, Mass., Box I, folder 12.
29. Myers, "'The Most Searching Place in the World,'" p. 204 and n. 74
30. For example, responding to the landscapes Bellows produced on Monhegan Island the previous year, the critic for the *New York Post* wrote: "The romance of the place, the weight and power of the sea, the massive architecture of the ledges, the domination of the sky, and the relation of these elements to each other, have . . . appealed strongly to Bellows, and he conveys his feeling for them in a simple, large, and striking manner," *New York Post*, January 24, 1914, quoted in Franklin Kelly, "Bellows and the Sea," in Quick et al., *The Paintings of George Bellows*, p. 155.
31. Bellows to Robert Henri, September 8, 1916: "I have done a number of pictures this summer which have not arrived in my mind from direct impressions but are creations of fancy arising out of my knowledge and experience of the facts employed. The result while in continual danger of becoming illustration in a bad sense or melodrama has nevertheless evolved into very rare pictures." Quoted in Michael Quick, "Technique and Theory: The Evolution of George Bellows's Painting Style," in Quick et al., *The Paintings of George Bellows*, p. 57.
32. Henry McBride, "Unevenness of Bellows," *New York Sun*, March 18, 1917, reprinted in Daniel Catton Rich, ed., *The Flow of Art: Essays and Criticisms of Henry McBride* (New York: Atheneum Publishers, 1975), pp. 112–13.
33. Gibson to Bellows, July 12, 1918, Bellows Papers, Amherst College, Box II, folder 12.
34. "Miss Cavell Shot by German Officer. Englishwoman, Condemned to Death, Said to Have Fainted Before Firing Party," *New York Times*, October 18, 1915, p. 1.
35. The best discussion of Bellows's reliance on Dynamic Symmetry and other theories is found in Quick, "Technique and Theory," especially pp. 63–65.
36. The inspiration of painters of the Renaissance and Baroque, as well as the more recent masters of printmaking, had been an occasional part of Bellows's pictorial vocabulary since his student days under Robert Henri. He is known to have copied Daumier's great *Rue Transnonain* (1834) in 1908 (Charles W. Morgan, *George Bellows: Painter of America* [New York: Reynal and Company, 1965], p. 86). His African-American boxer in *Both Members of This Club* has been associated with the Borghese *Gladiator* (E. A. Carmean, Jr., "Bellows: The Boxing Paintings," in Carmean et al., *Bellows: The Boxing Pictures*, exh. cat. [Washington, D.C.: National Gallery of Art, 1982], p. 33.)
37. Edmund Wilson, "George Bellows," *The New Republic* 44 (October 28, 1925), p. 255.
38. "Loan Exhibition of Paintings by El Greco and Goya" (New York: M. Knoedler and Company, 1912); "Exhibition of a Few Spanish Paintings: El Greco, Francesco Goya and his Imitator Eugenio Lucas" (New York: Galleries of E. Gimpel

and Wildenstein, 1913); "Loan Exhibition of Paintings by El Greco and Goya for the Benefit of the American Women War Relief Fund and the Belgian Relief Fund" (New York: M. Knoedler and Company, 1915). An exhibition of etchings at the New York Public Library in 1917 also included prints by Goya.

39. See Morgan, *George Bellows*, p. 218.

40. See Eleanor M. Tufts, "Bellows and Goya," *Art Journal* 30 (Summer 1971), pp. 362–68, and Tufts, "Realism Revisited: Goya's Impact on George Bellows and Other American Responses to the Spanish Presence in Art," *Arts Magazine* 57 (February 1983), pp. 105–13. Tufts notes that Bellows undoubtedly knew the New York Public Library's collection of Goya prints, and owned a book on Goya, Aureliano de Beruete's *Goya, Pintor de Retratos* ("Realism Revisited," p. 106). Bellows himself acknowledged his debt to Goya for the War Series prints. When asked to paint more images of the German atrocities, he replied, "I'll Goya." *New York Sun*, April 27, 1919, quoted in Myers, "Lithographs of 1916–1918," in Myers and Ayres, *George Bellows: The Artist and His Lithographs*, p. 64.

41. Henry McBride, "Bellows's Crucifixion," *New York Herald*, January 6, 1924, in Rich, *The Flow of Art*, p. 184.

42. In *The Art Spirit*, Henri praised both the structure and the energy of El Greco's paintings: "His work is an illustration of what a composition should be, that is, he puts together forces and makes of these forces a great unit. Continuity is carried through the canvas with a positive control, a coordination. His work overlays and interplays like a brook. The rising movement in it is like a flame, and he makes much of the movement of light." Henri, *The Art Spirit,* comp. Margery Ryerson (Philadelphia and London, 1923; repr., Philadelphia and New York: J.B. Lippincott Company, 1930), p. 211.

43. "[El Greco's] work has been so closely associated with the modern school that it seems to belong more to the XIXth and XXth centuries than to the XVIth and XVIIth." "Havemeyer Collection at the Metropolitan Museum," *Art News* 28 (March 15, 1930), p. 43.

44. "Art at Home and Abroad: Paintings by El Greco and Goya Now on Exhibition," *New York Times*, April 12, 1912, p. 15.

45. An excellent discussion of the nature of Bellows's high regard for El Greco is found in Marianne Doezema, "The Real New York," in Quick et al., *The Paintings of George Bellows,* pp. 124–25.

46. Bellows, "The Big Idea," p. 270.

47. See Doezema, "The Real New York," p. 125.

48. Bellows, "Introduction," in *Catalogue of an Exhibition of Lithographs by George Bellows* (New York: Frederick Keppel and Co., 1918), p. 3.

49. The drawing, in black crayon with orange/red underdrawing (collection of the Boston Public Library), was reproduced as an illustration for the serialization of H.G. Wells's *Men Like Gods* in *Hearst's International Magazine*, March 1923.

50. Crowninshield to Bellows, telegram, October 1, 1918, Bellows Papers, Amherst College, Box II, folder 11.

51. N.N., "Art: A Great National War Pageant," *The Nation* 107 (October 26, 1918), p. 486. The current location of the Blashfield painting, purchased by the Metropolitan Museum of Art in 1918, is unknown. The painting was reproduced as a poster the same year; that version is illustrated here.

52. G.D. Cotton, "Art News from Summer Colonies," p. 3.

53. Brand Whitlock, *The Letters and Journal of Brand Whitlock*, ed. Allan Nevins (New York: Appleton-Century, 1936), pp. 234, 440; quoted in Zuckerman, *Rape of Belgium*, pp. 138, 195.

54. "Instead of cultivating the little instinct which he has got he strives to use in its place the theories of Hambidge and Marratta [*sic*], forgetting that the man who

depends too much upon his crutches will in time be quite unable to get along without them. Theories are props for the weak." "Comment on the Arts," *The Arts* 2 (November 1921), p. 114.

55. "Notes on Current Art: Paintings by George Bellows," *New York Times*, April 6, 1919, p. 40.
56. "George Bellows' Work on Exhibition," *New York Times*, November 10, 1918, p. 48.
57. "Notes on Current Art," *New York Times*, April 6, 1919, p. 40.
58. See Daniel M. Smith, *The Great Departure: The United States and World War I, 1914–1920* (New York: John Wiley, 1965), p. 5; and Zuckerman, *Rape of Belgium*, p. 132.
59. See John Horne and Alan Kramer, *German Atrocities, 1914: A History of Denial* (New Haven and London: Yale University Press, 2001), p. 3.
60. *Bellows Memorial Exhibition*, intro. Frank Crowninshield, exh. cat. (New York: The Metropolitan Museum of Art, 1925).
61. Virgil Barker, "New York Exhibitions. A Bellows Memorial," *The Arts* 7 (May 1925), p. 286.

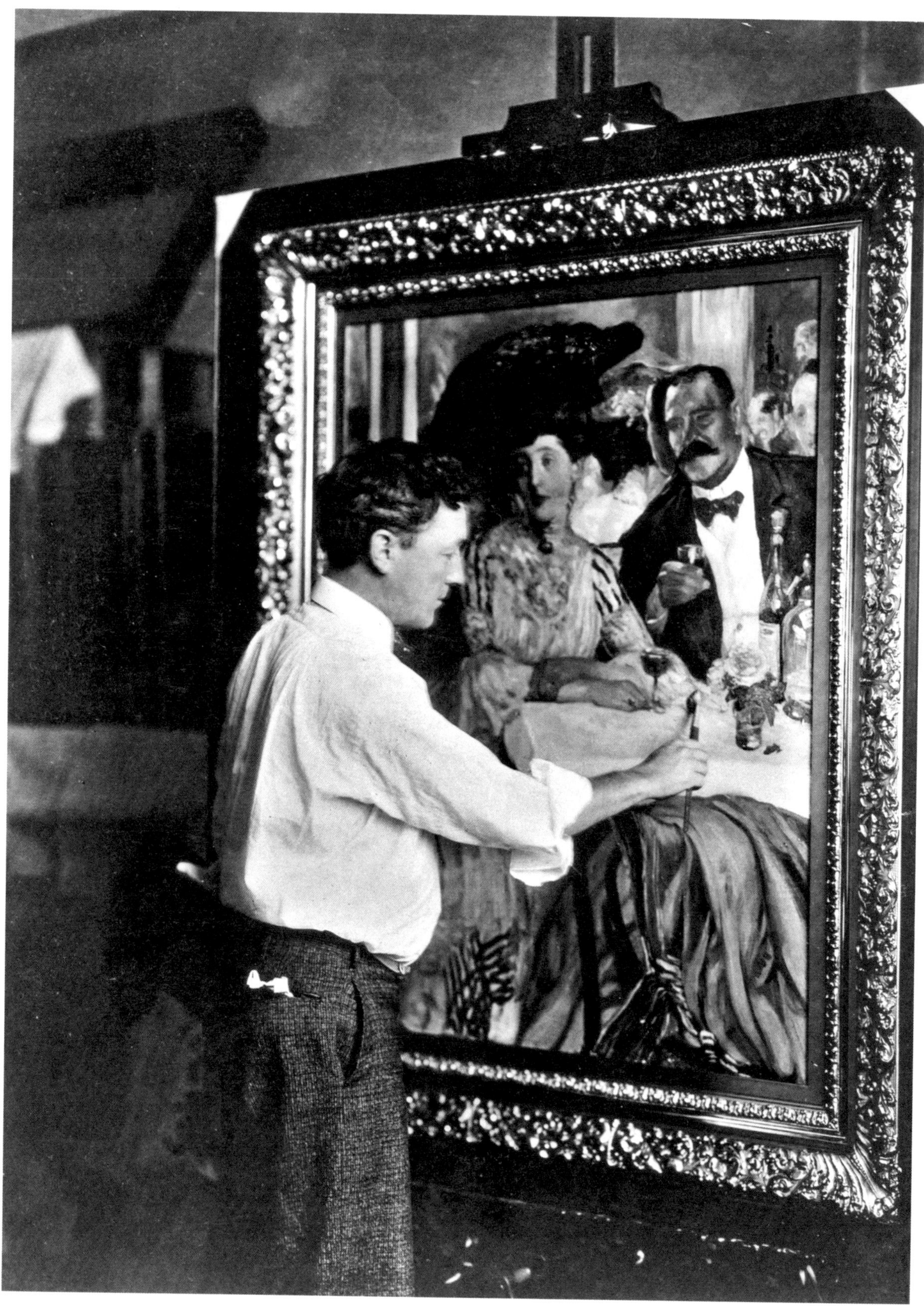

William Glackens touching up *Chez Mouquin*, 1905

A Brief Chronology: William Glackens 1870–1938

1870
March 13.
William James Glackens is born on Sansom Street in Philadelphia. He is the youngest of three children born to Samuel and Elizabeth Glackens.

1890
Graduates from Central High School, where his classmates include John Sloan and Albert C. Barnes.

1891–92
Begins to work as an artist-reporter on Philadelphia newspapers, including the *Philadelphia Record*. After a year, he moves to the staff of the *Philadelphia Press*. Attends night classes at the Pennsylvania Academy of the Fine Arts. Renews his friendship with John Sloan and meets Robert Henri, George Luks, Everett Shinn.

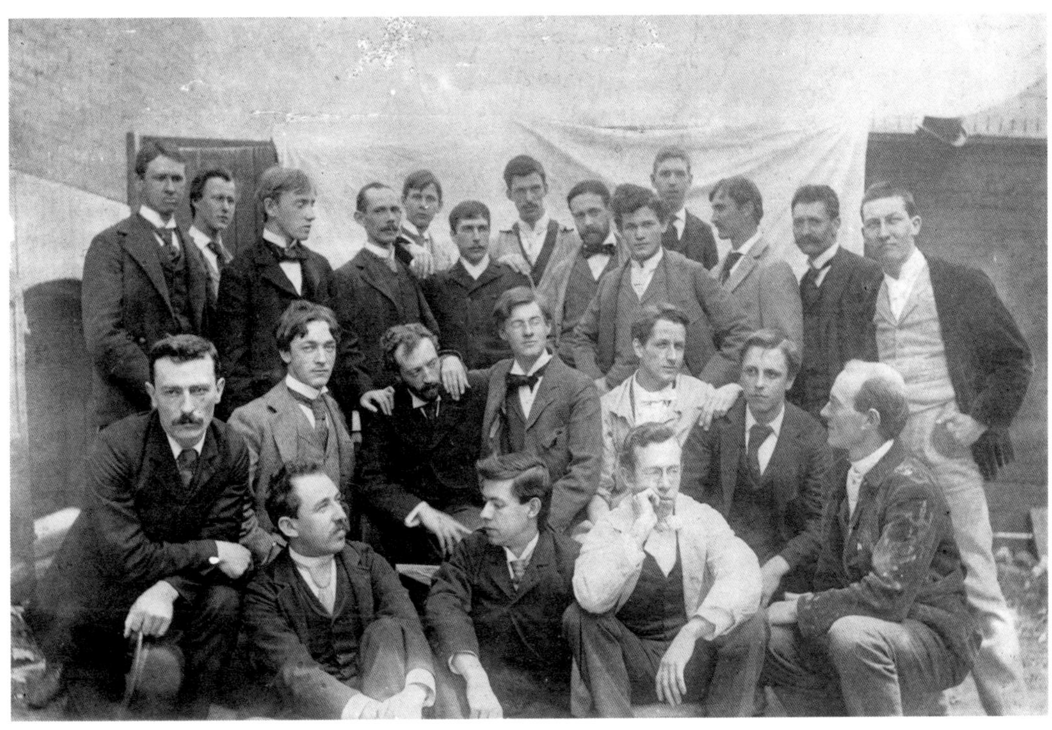

Students at the Pennsylvania Academy, c. 1894; Glackens is seated in the second row, second from the left.

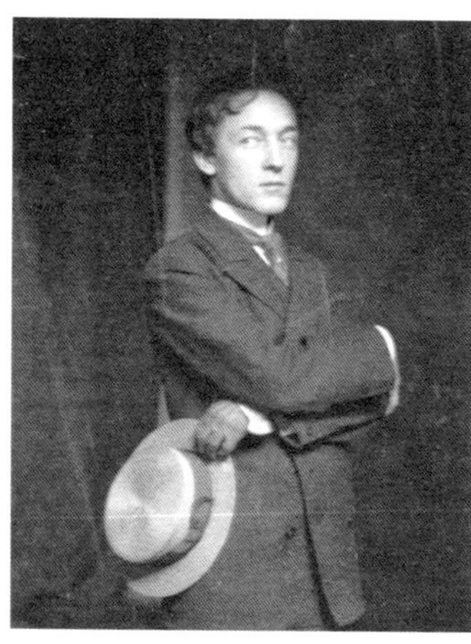

Portrait of William Glackens holding a straw hat in his hand, c. 1890s

1893
With Sloan and Henri, organizes The Charcoal Club, an informal group of artists who meet to critique and sketch from the model.

Paints *Philadelphia Landscape* (Fig.3), his earliest known oil.

1894
Shares a studio with Henri on Chestnut Street in Philadelphia.

Shows in the 64th Annual Exhibition at the Pennsylvania Academy of the Fine Arts.

1895
First of his many book illustrations appears in *Through the Great Campaign with Hastings and His Spellbinders* by George Nox McCain.

In June Glackens quits his job and sails to Europe on a cattle boat. Travels with Elmer Schofield and Henri through France, Belgium, and Holland. In the fall takes a studio in Montparnasse in Paris.

1896
Travels and paints for the first half of the year.

Exhibits at the Societé Nationale des Beaux-Arts. Returns to Philadelphia in the fall. Shortly thereafter is one of the first of the Philadelphia artist-reporters to move to New York.

Rents a studio on East Fifty-fifth Street and begins work at the *New York Sunday World* and the *New York Herald.*

1897
Works at the *New York Herald* as an artist-reporter and as a freelance illustrator for various magazines.

1898
Sent to Cuba to cover the Spanish-American War for *McClure's* magazine. His drawings are published in *McClure's* and *Munsey's.*

1899–1900
Works as a freelance illustrator for many of the popular magazines of the day, among them *Century, Collier's Weekly, Harper's Weekly, McClure's, Saturday Evening Post,* and *Scribner's.*

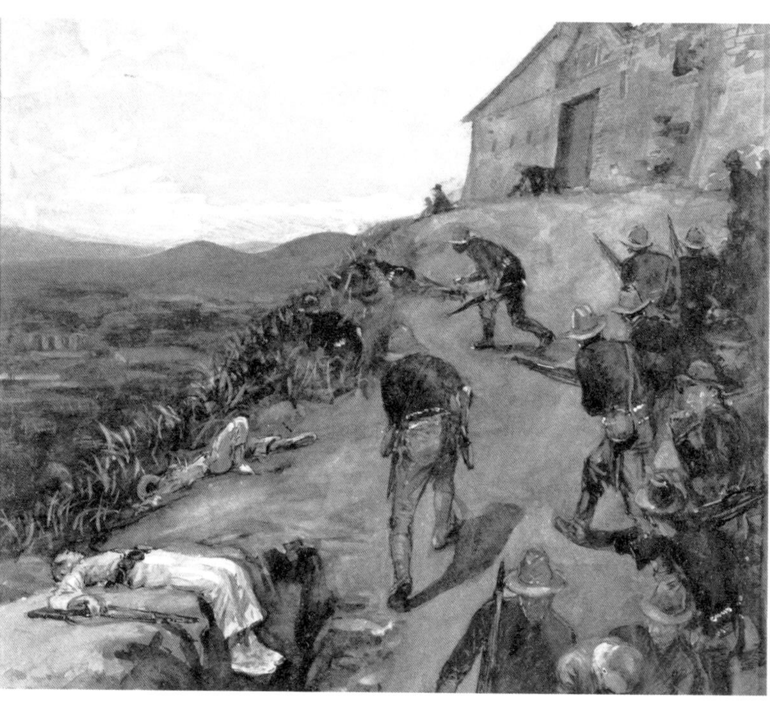

William Glackens
The Night after San Juan, 1898
Watercolor and pen on paper

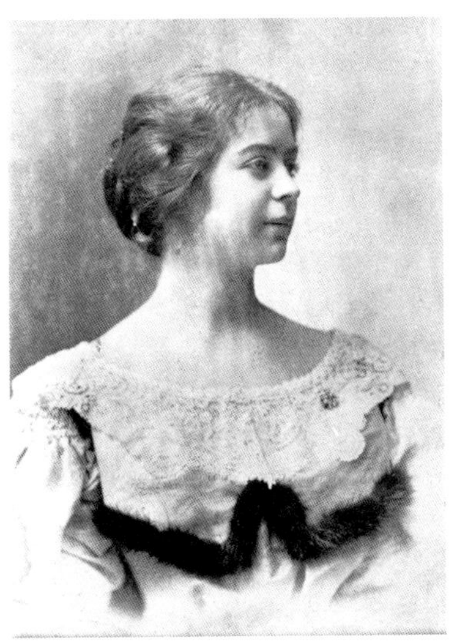

Portrait of Edith Dimock, c. 1902

1901
With Henri, Maurer, Sloan and others, exhibits work at the Allen Gallery in New York. Charles FitzGerald's review in the *New York Evening Sun* notes "... the work that he shows here reveals him as a painter ... of more than ordinary ability."

1904
In January, participates in a group show organized by Henri at the National Arts Club on Gramercy Park.

February 16.
Marries artist Edith Dimock of West Hartford, Connecticut, who studied with William Merritt Chase. The two move to 3 Washington Square North, and share a studio at 50 Washington Square South.

Receives the Silver Medal for Painting at the Louisiana Purchase Exposition in Saint Louis.

1905
Paints *Chez Mouquin* (*At Mouquin's*, The Art Institute of Chicago; see p. 192).

1906
With Edith, travels on an extended vacation to Europe.

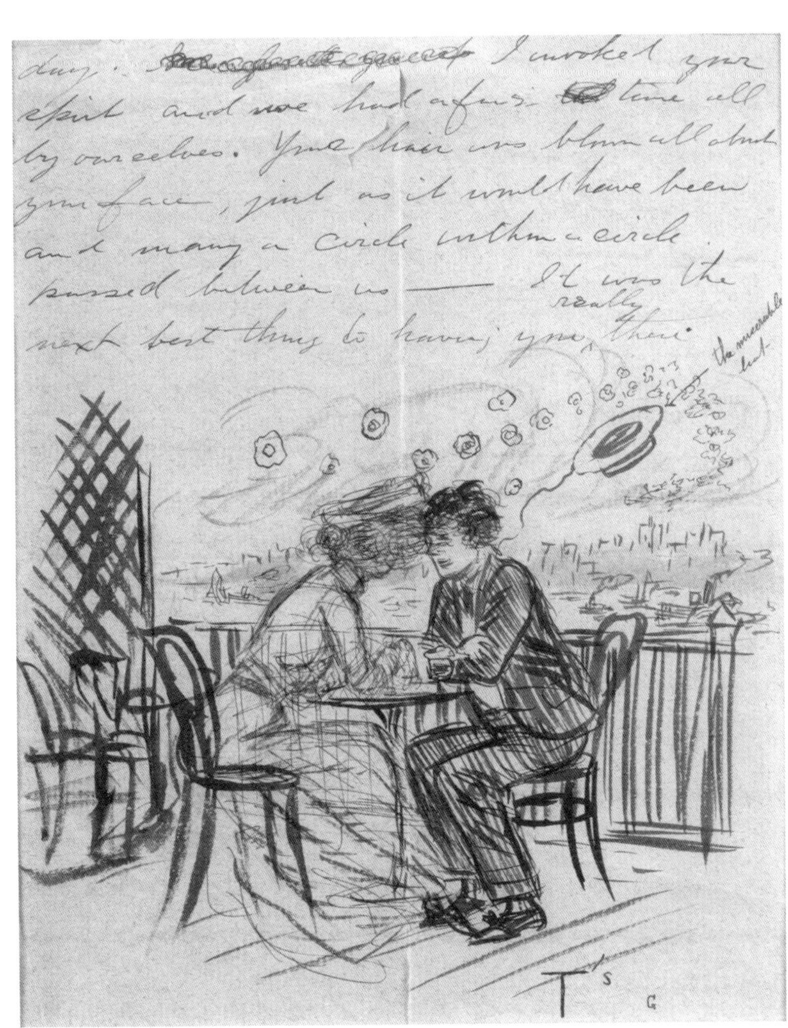

day. I invoked your spirit and we had a fine time all by ourselves. Your hair was blown all about your face, just as it would have been and many a circle within a circle passed between us — It was the really next best thing to having you there

Love Letter to Edith Dimock, His Future Bride, 1903
Ink and wash on paper

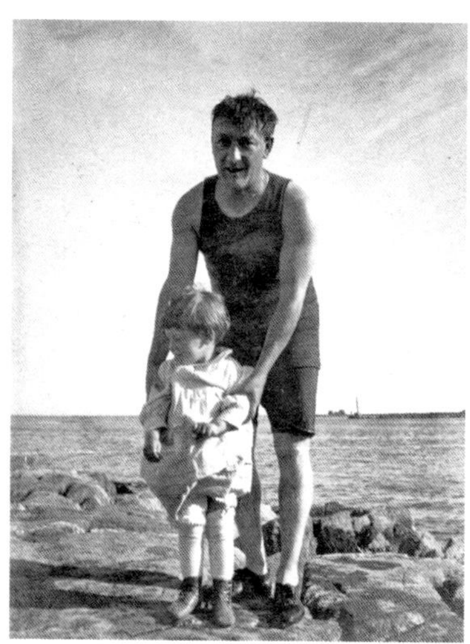

William Glackens with son, Ira, c. 1911

1907
July 4.
Son, Ira, is born.

1908
Participates in a landmark independent exhibition at William Macbeth's gallery in New York, with Arthur B. Davies, Robert Henri, Ernest Lawson, George Luks, Maurice Prendergast, Everett Shinn, and John Sloan, a group that would become known as "The Eight."

1909
Summer in Wickford, Rhode Island.

1910
April.
Shows *Nude with Apple* (Fig. 16) at the Exhibition of Independent Artists.

Summer in Nova Scotia.

1911
Becomes a charter member of the Association of American Painters and Sculptors, the group that will organize the Armory Show of 1913.

Rents a house in Bellport, Long Island, where he will spend the next five summers.

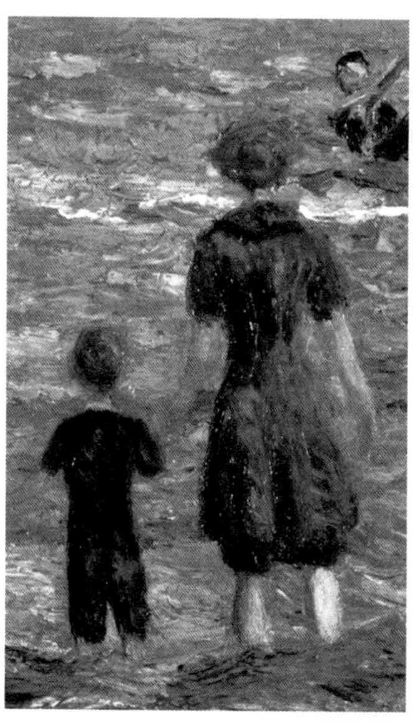

Bathing at Bellport, Long Island, detail. See Fig. 27.

1912
February.
Glackens's old friend Albert Barnes sends him to Paris with $20,000 to buy modern art for Barnes's collection.

March.
First one-artist show at the Madison Art Gallery in New York.

1913
The Armory Show opens in February. Glackens is chairman of the Committee on Domestic Exhibits. Glackens shows three oils and wife, Edith, shows eight watercolors.

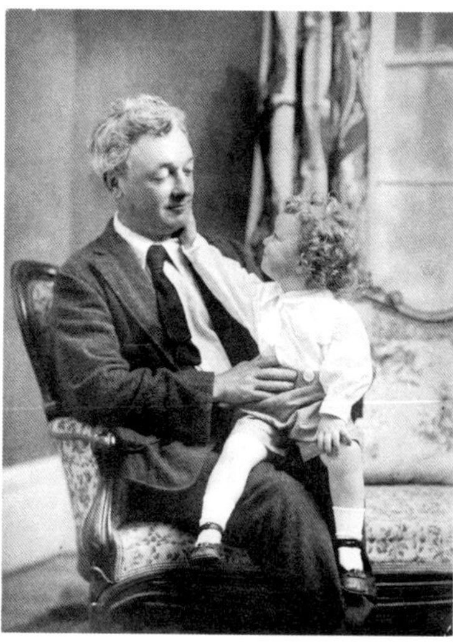

William Glackens with daughter, Lenna, c. 1915

1913
December 6.
Daughter, Lenna, is born.

1914
Though he continues to work as an illustrator from time to time, begins to devote himself primarily to painting.

1915
Bronze medal, Panama-Pacific Exposition, San Francisco.

1917
Elected first president of the Society of Independent Artists. Exhibits at several galleries in New York, and in the Exhibition of Independent Artists.

Edith's parents die, and the family spends much of the year in Hartford, Connecticut.

1918
Summer in Pequot, near New London, Connecticut.

1919
Illustrates his last story for *Collier's*. Buys a house on West Ninth Street in New York City.

Summer in Gloucester, Massachusetts.

1920
Vacations near Conway, New Hampshire, where he spends five summers.

1922
One-artist show at the Whitney Studio Club on West Eighth Street.

1924
Wins the Temple Gold Medal from the Pennsylvania Academy of the Fine Arts for a nude now known as the *Temple Gold Medal Nude.*

1925
First exhibition at Kraushaar Galleries, who will represent his work throughout his life.

1926
Travels in Italy and France. From 1926 through 1932, the Glackens family will spend a part of each year in France.

1932
Visits Ernest Lawson in Coral Gables, Florida.

1934
Summer in Vermont and Quebec.

1935
Paints *The Soda Fountain* (cover and fig. 41). The figure behind the counter is his son, Ira.

1936
Travels to England and France; summer in Rockport, Massachusetts.

1937
Receives the Grand Prix at the Paris Exposition for *Central Park, Winter* (Fig. 97). Paints *White Rose and Other Flowers*, his last canvas.

1938
May 22.
Glackens dies suddenly of a cerebral hemorrhage.

A memorial exhibition of his work is held at the Whitney Museum of American Art in New York.

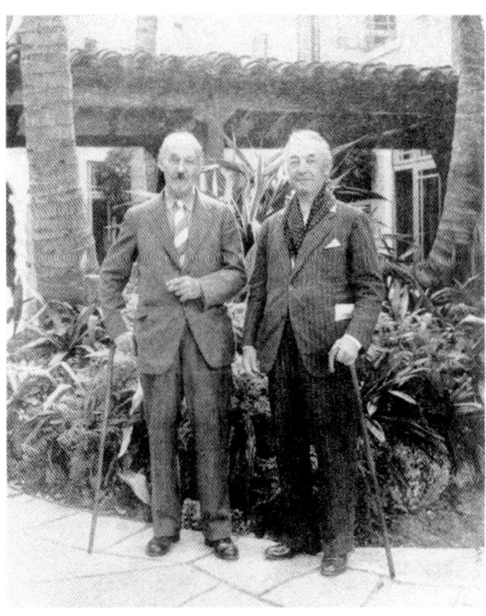

Ernest Lawson and William Glackens in Coral Gables, Florida, 1932

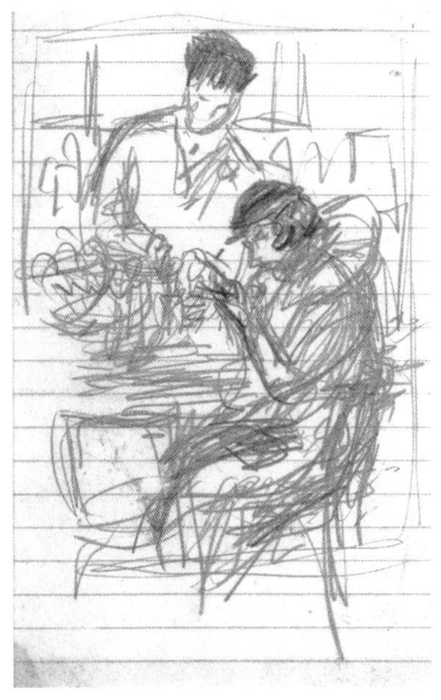

Early Sketch for
The Soda Fountain, 1935
Graphite on paper

The photographs for this chronology were graciously supplied by the Museum of Art/Fort Lauderdale, Nova Southeastern University, Florida, and reproduced with their permission. Photographs and *The Night after San Juan* (91.40.67) are courtesy of the Museum of Art/Fort Lauderdale, Nova Southeastern University; Bequest of Ira Glackens. Early Sketch for *The Soda Fountain*, 1935 (92.142), and *Love Letter to Edith Dimock, His Future Bride*, 1903 (92.133) are courtesy of the Museum of Art/Fort Lauderdale, Nova Southeastern University, Florida; Gift of the Sansom Foundation.

Selected Bibliography

Allyn, Nancy E. *William Glackens: Illustrator in New York, 1897–1919*. Exh. cat. Wilmington: Delaware Art Museum, 1985.

——, and Elizabeth H. Hawkes. *William Glackens: A Catalogue of His Book and Magazine Illustrations*. Wilmington: Delaware Art Museum, 1987.

The Art of John Sloan, 1871–1951. Exh. cat. Brunswick, Maine: Bowdoin College, 1962.

Axelrod, Alan. *Selling the Great War: The Making of American Propaganda*. New York: Palgrave Macmillan, 2009.

Barnes, Albert C. *The Art in Painting*. Merion, Pa.: The Barnes Foundation Press, 1925.

——. "How to Judge a Painting." *Arts and Decoration* 5 (April 1915), pp. 217–20, 246–50.

Berman, Avis. *Rebels on Eighth Street: Juliana Force and the Whitney Museum of American Art*. New York: Atheneum Publishers, 1990.

Blaugrund, Annette. *The Tenth Street Studio Building: Artist-Entrepreneurs from the Hudson River School to the American Impressionists*. Exh. cat. Southampton, N.Y.: Parrish Art Museum, 1997.

Brooks, Van Wyck. *John Sloan: A Painter's Life*. New York: E.P. Dutton, 1955.

Bryant, Keith L. *William Merritt Chase: A Genteel Bohemian*. Columbia: University of Missouri Press, 1991.

Burke, Doreen Bolger. *J. Alden Weir: An American Impressionist*. Newark: University of Delaware Press, 1983.

Cikovsky, Nicolai Jr., et al. *A Connecticut Place: Weir Farm, An American Painter's Rural Retreat*. Exh. cat. Wilton, Conn.: Weir Farm Trust, 2000.

Cuba, Stanley L., Nina Kasanof, and Judith H. O'Toole. *George Luks: An American Artist.* Exh. cat. Wilkes-Barre, Pa.: Sordoni Art Gallery, Wilkes College, 1987.

DeShazo, Edith. *Everett Shinn, 1876–1953: A Figure in His Time.* New York: Clarkson N. Potter, 1974.

Dewey, John, et al. *Art and Education.* Merion, Pa.: The Barnes Foundation Press, 1929.

Elzea, Rowland. *John Sloan's Oil Paintings: A Catalogue Raisonné.* 2 vols. Newark: University of Delaware Press, 1991.

Engel, Charlene. "The Man in the Middle: George Bellows, War, and 'Sergeant' Delaney." *American Art* 18, no. 1 (Spring 2004), pp. 78–87.

Epstein, Stacey B. *Alfred H. Maurer: Aestheticism to Modernism.* Exh. cat. New York: Hollis Taggart Galleries, 1999.

Flint, Janet A. *Drawings by William Glackens, 1870–1938.* Exh. cat. Washington, D.C.: National Collection of Fine Arts, Smithsonian Institution, 1972.

Fort, Ilene Susan. *The Flag Paintings of Childe Hassam.* Exh. cat. Los Angeles: Los Angeles County Museum of Art, in association with Harry N. Abrams, 1988.

Gallati, Barbara Dayer. *William Merritt Chase: Modern American Landscapes, 1886–1890.* Exh. cat. New York: Brooklyn Museum of Art, in association with Harry N. Abrams, 1999.

Gerdts, William H. *Masterworks of American Impressionism from the Pfeil Collection.* Exh. cat. Alexandria, Va.: Art Services International, 1992.

——. *William Glackens.* With essay by Jorge H. Santis. Fort Lauderdale, Fla.: Museum of Art, Fort Lauderdale, in association with Abbeville Press, 1996.

Glackens, Ira. *William Glackens and the Ashcan Group: The Emergence of Realism in American Art.* New York: Crown Publishers, 1957.

Gordon, Irene, ed. *Four Americans in Paris: The Collections of Gertrude Stein and Her Family.* New York: The Museum of Modern Art, 1970.

Henri, Robert. *The Art Spirit.* Compiled by Margery Ryerson. Philadelphia: J. B. Lippincott Company, 1923.

Hiesinger, Ulrich W. *Childe Hassam: American Impressionist.* New York and Munich: Prestel-Verlag, 1994.

Homer, William Innes, with the assistance of Violet Organ. *Robert Henri and His Circle.* Ithaca, N.Y., and London: Cornell University Press, 1969.

Hone, Joseph, ed. *J.B. Yeats: Letters to His Son W.B. Yeats and Others, 1869–1922*. New York: E.P. Dutton, 1946.

Horne, John, and Alan Kramer. *German Atrocities, 1914: A History of Denial.* New Haven and London: Yale University Press, 2001.

Johnston, Sona. *In Monet's Light: Theodore Robinson at Giverny*. Exh. cat. Baltimore: Baltimore Museum of Art, 2004.

Larkin, Susan G. *The Cos Cob Art Colony: Impressionists on the Connecticut Shore.* Exh. cat. New York: National Academy of Design, in association with Yale University Press, 2001.

Londraville, Janis, ed. *Prodigal Father Revisited: Artists and Writers in the World of John Butler Yeats.* West Cornwall, Conn.: Locust Hill Press, 2003.

Loughery, John. *John Sloan: Painter and Rebel.* New York: Henry Holt, 1995.

Mason, Lauris. *The Lithographs of George Bellows: A Catalogue Raisonné.* Millwood, N.Y.: KTO Press, 1977.

McCready, Sam. *A William Butler Yeats Encyclopedia.* Westport, Conn.: Greenwood Press, 1997.

Meier-Graefe, Julius. *Modern Art: Being a Contribution to a New System of Aesthetics.* Translated by Florence Simmonds and George William Chrystal. 2 vols. New York: G.P. Putnam's Sons, 1908.

Meyers, Mary Ann. *Art, Education, and African-American Culture: Albert Barnes and the Science of Philanthropy*. New Brunswick, N.J: Transaction Publishers, 2004.

Morse, Peter. *John Sloan's Prints: A Catalogue Raisonné of the Etchings, Lithographs, and Posters.* New Haven and London: Yale University Press, 1969.

Murphy, William M. *Family Secrets: William Butler Yeats and His Relatives.* Syracuse, N.Y.: Syracuse University Press, 1995.

——. *Prodigal Father: The Life of John Butler Yeats (1839–1922).* Ithaca, N.Y.: Cornell University Press, 1978.

Myers, Jane, and Linda Ayres. *George Bellows: The Artist and His Lithographs, 1916–1924.* Exh. cat. Fort Worth, Tex.: Amon Carter Museum, 1988.

Perlman, Bennard B. *Robert Henri: His Life and Art.* New York: Dover Publications, 1991.

——, ed. *Revolutionaries of Realism: The Letters of John Sloan and Robert Henri.* Princeton, N.J.: Princeton University Press, 1997.

Peters, Lisa N. *John Henry Twachtman: An American Impressionist.* Exh. cat. Atlanta: High Museum of Art, 1999.

Pisano, Ronald G. *A Leading Spirit in American Art: William Merritt Chase, 1849–1916.* Exh. cat. Seattle: Henry Art Gallery, University of Washington, 1983.

——. *William Merritt Chase: The Complete Catalogue of Known and Documented Work by William Merritt Chase (1849–1916).* 4 vols. New Haven and London: Yale University Press, 2006–2010.

Quick, Michael, et al. *The Paintings of George Bellows.* Exh. cat. Fort Worth, Tex.: Amon Carter Museum; Los Angeles: Los Angeles County Museum of Art, in association with Harry N. Abrams, 1992.

Reid, B.L. *The Man from New York: John Quinn and His Friends.* New York: Oxford University Press, 1968.

Rewald, John. *Cézanne and America: Dealers, Collectors, Artists and Critics, 1891–1921.* Princeton, N.J.: Princeton University Press, 1989.

Rich, Daniel Catton, ed. *The Flow of Art: Essays and Criticisms of Henry McBride.* New York: Atheneum Publishers, 1975.

Schack, William. *Art and Argyrol: The Life and Career of Dr. Albert C. Barnes.* New York: Thomas Yoseloff, 1960.

Sessions, Ralph, et al. *The Poetic Vision: American Tonalism.* Exh. cat. New York: Spanierman Gallery, 2005.

Shinn, Everett. "Everett Shinn on George Luks: An Unpublished Memoir." *Archives of American Art Journal* 6, no. 2 (April 1966), pp. 1–12.

——. "William Glackens as an Illustrator." *American Artist* 9, no. 9 (November 1945), pp. 22–27, 37.

Skalet, Linda Henefield. "The Market for American Painting in New York, 1870–1915." Ph.D. diss., Johns Hopkins University, 1980.

Sloan, John. *Gist of Art: Principles and Practise Expounded in the Classroom and Studio.* New York: American Artists Group, 1939.

St. John, Bruce, ed. *John Sloan's New York Scene: From the Diaries, Notes and Correspondence 1906–1913.* New York: Harper and Row, 1965.

Stein, Gertrude. *The Autobiography of Alice B. Toklas.* New York: Harcourt, Brace, 1933.

Stein, Leo. *Appreciation: Painting, Poetry and Prose.* New York: Crown Publishers, 1947.

——. *Journey Into the Self: Being the Letters, Papers, and Journals of*

Leo Stein. Edited by Edmund Fuller. New York: Crown Publishers, 1950.

Wasserman, Krystyna. "George Wesley Bellows' War Lithographs and Paintings of 1918." Master's thesis, University of Maryland, 1981.

Wattenmaker, Richard J. *American Paintings and Works on Paper in the Barnes Foundation.* Merion, Pa.: The Barnes Foundation, in association with Yale University Press, 2010.

——, et al. *Great French Paintings from the Barnes Foundation: Impressionist, Post-Impressionist, and Early Modern.* Exh. cat. Washington, D.C.: National Gallery of Art, 1993.

Weinberg, H. Barbara, Doreen Bolger, and David Park Curry. *American Impressionism and Realism: The Painting of Modern Life, 1885–1915.* Exh. cat. New York: The Metropolitan Museum of Art, 1994.

Weinberg, H. Barbara, et al. *Childe Hassam, American Impressionist.* Exh. cat. New York: The Metropolitan Museum of Art, 2004.

Wong, Janay. *Everett Shinn: The Spectacle of Life.* Exh. cat. New York: Berry-Hill Galleries, 2000.

Young, Dorothy Weir. *The Life and Letters of J. Alden Weir.* New Haven: Yale University Press, 1960.

Zuckerman, Larry. *The Rape of Belgium: The Untold Story of World War I.* New York and London: New York University Press, 2004.

Zurier, Rebecca. *Art for The Masses (1911–1917): A Radical Magazine and Its Graphics.* Exh. cat. New Haven: Yale University Art Gallery, 1985.

——. *Picturing the City: Urban Vision and the Ashcan School.* Berkeley: University of California Press, 2006.

——, Robert W. Snyder, and Virginia M. Mecklenburg. *Metropolitan Lives: The Ashcan Artists and Their New York.* Exh. cat. Washington, D.C.: National Museum of American Art, in association with W.W. Norton and Company, 1995.

Index

NOTE
Page numbers in *italics* refer to illustrations.

PHOTOGRAPH CREDITS

Most photographs were supplied by the owners or custodians of the works as indicated in the captions, and are reproduced by their permission; their courtesy is gratefully acknowledged. Additional credits are listed here.

Alinari/Art Resource, New York: fig. 131

©2011 Artists Rights Society (ARS), New York/SIAE, Rome: fig. 42

©2011 Artists Rights Society (ARS), New York/ADAGP, Paris/Succession Marcel Duchamp: fig. 43 (Marcel Duchamp, *Nude Descending a Staircase*)

©2010 reproduced with the permission of The Barnes Foundation: figs. 42, 48, 51, 52, 56, 59, 60, 61, 62, 105

Ricardo Barros. Reproduced with permission: fig. 25

Reis Birdwhistle: fig. 34

Courtesy of The Bridgeman Art Library; © 2011 Detroit Institute of Arts: fig. 38

Courtesy of The Bridgeman Art Library: fig. 88

Courtesy of Butler Library, Columbia University in the City of New York: fig. 118

©2010 Carnegie Museum of Art, Pittsburgh: fig. 84

Geoffrey Clements, fig. 71

Sheldan C. Collins: figs. 70, 100

©2002–2011 by Corbis Corporation. All visual media © by Corbis Corporation and/or its media providers. All rights reserved: fig. 113

Douglas Dalton: fig. 132

Courtesy Guy-Patrice Dauberville and Michel Dauberville, *Renoir : Catalogue raisonné des tableaux, pastels, dessins et aquarelles* (Paris : Éditions Bernheim-Jeune, 2007), vol. 1, p. 11: fig. 50

©2011 Delaware Art Museum/Artists Rights Society (ARS), New York: figs. 68, 70, 71, 74, 80, 96, 110, 111

©2011 Delaware Art Museum/Artists Rights Society (ARS), New York; Photograph from the John Sloan Manuscript Collection, Delaware Art Museum: fig. 81

Courtesy of the Huntington Art Collections, San Marino, California: figs. 4, 5

Imaging Department © President and Fellows of Harvard College: figs. 115, 120, 133

Katya Kallsen © President and Fellows of Harvard College: figs. 114, 119, 124

Erich Lessing/Art Resource, New York: fig. 126

Robert E. Mates: fig. 107

© 2011 Succession H. Matisse / Artists Rights Society (ARS), New York: fig. 60

Archive Timothy McCarthy/Art Resource, New York: fig. 128

© The Metropolitan Museum of Art/Art Resource, New York: figs. 49, 73, 85, 90, 94, 96, 97, 98, 101, 125

©2011 Museum of Fine Arts, Boston: figs. 104, 123

© The Museum of Modern Art/Licensed by Scala/Art Resource, New York: fig. 117

Courtesy National Gallery of Art, Washington, D.C.: fig. 112

©National Gallery of Canada: fig. 106

Courtesy of the National Gallery of Ireland: fig. 77

© National Portrait Gallery, Smithsonian Institution, Washington, D.C.: fig. 108

©2011 Estate of Pablo Picasso/Artists Rights Society (ARS), New York: figs. 49, 58

Tom Powel: fig. 83

© Greg Pyle Photography: fig. 92

Scala /Art Resource, New York: fig. 17

Martin Senn: fig. 122

©Sheldon Museum of Art: fig. 103

Lee Stalsworth: fig. 76

David Stansbury: fig. 116

Jerry L. Thompson: fig. 109

Wadsworth Atheneum Museum of Art/Art Resource, New York: fig. 15